Conversations with
Sam Shepard

Literary Conversations Series
Monika Gehlawat
General Editor

Conversations with Sam Shepard

Edited by Jackson R. Bryer,
Robert M. Dowling, and Mary C. Hartig

University Press of Mississippi / Jackson

The University Press of Mississippi is the scholarly publishing agency of the Mississippi Institutions of Higher Learning: Alcorn State University, Delta State University, Jackson State University, Mississippi State University, Mississippi University for Women, Mississippi Valley State University, University of Mississippi, and University of Southern Mississippi.

www.upress.state.ms.us

The University Press of Mississippi is a member of the Association of University Presses.

First printing 2021
∞

Library of Congress Control Number available
Hardback ISBN 978-1-4968-3660-1
Trade paperback ISBN 978-1-4968-3661-8
Epub single ISBN 978-1-4968-3711-0
Epub institutional ISBN 978-1-4968-3712-7
PDF single ISBN 978-1-4968-3713-4
PDF institutional ISBN 978-1-4968-3714-1

British Library Cataloging-in-Publication Data available

Works by Sam Shepard

Plays

Five Plays [*Chicago, Icarus's Mother, Red Cross, Fourteen Hundred Thousand, Melodrama Play*]. Indianapolis: Bobbs-Merrill, 1967.

La Turista. Introduction by Elizabeth Hardwick. Indianapolis: Bobbs-Merrill, 1968.

Operation Sidewinder: A Play in Two Acts. Indianapolis: Bobbs-Merrill, 1970.

Mad Dog Blues & Other Plays [*Mad Dog Blues, The Rock Garden, Cowboys #2, Cowboy Mouth*]. Introduction by Michael McClure. New York: Winter House, 1972.

The Unseen Hand and Other Plays [*The Unseen Hand, Forensic & the Navigators, The Holy Ghostly, Back Bog Beast Bait, Shaved Splits, 4-H Club*]. Indianapolis: Bobbs-Merrill, 1972.

The Tooth of Crime and Geography of a Horse Dreamer. New York: Grove Press, 1974.

Action and The Unseen Hand. London: Faber & Faber, 1975.

Angel City, Curse of the Starving Class, and Other Plays [*Angel City, Curse of the Starving Class, Killer's Head, Action, The Mad Dog Blues, Cowboy Mouth, The Rock Garden, Cowboys #2*]. Preface by Jack Gelber. New York: Urizen, 1976.

Buried Child and Seduced and Suicide in B♭. Introduction by Jack Richardson. Vancouver: Talon Books, 1979; New York: Urizen, 1979.

Four Two-Act Plays [*Operation Sidewinder, The Tooth of Crime, La Turista, Geography of a Horse Dreamer*]. Introduction by Elizabeth Hardwick. New York: Urizen, 1980.

True West. Garden City: Nelson Doubleday, 1981.

Seven Plays [*Buried Child, Curse of the Starving Class, The Tooth of Crime, La Turista, Tongues, Savage/Love, True West*]. Introduction by Richard Gilman. New York: Bantam, 1981.

Fool for Love. San Francisco: City Lights, 1983 [also contains the libretto and music for *The Sad Lament of Pecos Bill on the Eve of Killing His Wife*].

Fool for Love and Other Plays [*Fool for Love, Angel City, Geography of a Horse Dreamer, Action, Cowboy Mouth, Melodrama Play, Seduced, Suicide in B♭*]. Introduction by Ross Wetzsteon. New York: Bantam, 1984.

The Unseen Hand and Other Plays [*The Unseen Hand, The Rock Garden, Chicago, Icarus's Mother, 4-H Club, Fourteen Hundred Thousand, Red Cross, Cowboys #2,*

Forensic & the Navigators, The Holy Ghostly, Operation Sidewinder, The Mad Dog Blues, Back Bog Beast Bait, Killer's Head]. Introduction by Sam Shepard. New York: Bantam, 1986.

A Lie of the Mind. New York: New American Library, 1987 [also contains *The War in Heaven: (Angel's Monologue)*, co-written by Joseph Chaikin].

Simpatico. New York: Vintage, 1996.

Sam Shepard Plays: 3 [*A Lie of the Mind, States of Shock, Simpatico*]. London: Methuen, 1996.

The Late Henry Moss, Eyes for Consuela, When the World Was Green: Three Plays. New York: Vintage, 2002.

The God of Hell. New York: Vintage, 2005.

Tooth of Crime (Second Dance). New York: Vintage, 2006.

Kicking a Dead Horse. New York: Vintage, 2008.

Fifteen One-Act Plays [*Ages of the Moon; Evanescence, or Shakespeare in the Alley; Short Life of Trouble; The Unseen Hand; The Rock Garden; Chicago; Icarus's Mother; 4-H Club; Fourteen Hundred Thousand; Red Cross; Cowboys #2; Forensic & The Navigators; Holy Ghostly; Back Bog Beast Bait; Killer's Head]*. New York: Vintage, 2012.

Heartless. New York: Vintage, 2013.

A Particle of Dread: (Oedipus Variations). New York: Vintage, 2017.

Screenplays

Paris, Texas. New York: Ecco, 1984.

States of Shock, Far North, Silent Tongue: A Play and Two Screenplays. New York: Vintage, 1993.

Prose and Poetry

Hawk Moon: Short Stories, Poems, Monologues. Los Angeles: Black Sparrow, 1973.

Rolling Thunder Logbook. New York: Viking, 1977; Cambridge, MA: Da Capo, 2004 (Preface by Sam Shepard. Foreword by T-Bone Burnett).

Motel Chronicles. San Francisco: City Lights, 1982.

Cruising Paradise: Tales. New York: Alfred A. Knopf, 1996.

Great Dream of Heaven. New York: Alfred A. Knopf, 2002.

Day Out of Days: Stories. New York: Alfred A. Knopf, 2010.

The One Inside. New York: Alfred A. Knopf, 2017.

Spy of the First Person. New York: Alfred A. Knopf, 2017.

Sam Shepard: New Mexico (a collection of previously published prose and poetry about New Mexico). Photographs by Ed Ruscha. Preface by David Rakauer. Introduction by Taylor Sheridan. Afterword by Josh Brolin. Galisteo, NM: Lawless Media, 2020.

Letters

Joseph Chaikin & Sam Shepard: Letters and Texts, 1972–1984. Edited by Barry Daniels. New York: New American Library, 1989.

2 Prospectors: The Letters of Sam Shepard and Johnny Dark. Edited by Chad Hammett. Austin: University of Texas Press, 2013.

Contents

Introduction   xiii

Chronology   xxiii

Sam Shepard: Writer on the Way Up   3
  Mel Gussow / 1969

Sam Shepard: Metaphors, Mad Dogs, and Old Time Cowboys   5
  TQ *Editors and Kenneth Chubb / 1974*

Interview with *Newsweek*   27
  Newsweek / 1976

Sam Shepard: A Play for Every Life Style   37
  Sylvie Drake / 1979

Sam Shepard: Off-Broadway's Street Cowboy   43
  Robert Goldberg / 1980

Sam Shepard   52
  Stewart McBride / 1980

The *True West* Interviews   59
  John Dark / 1981

A Conversation with Sam Shepard   68
  Amy Lippman / 1983

The New American Hero 85
    Pete Hamill / 1983

Unknown Territory 98
    Ross Wetzsteon / 1985

Sam Shepard: Geography of a Horse Dreamer 105
    Kevin Sessums / 1988

"Silent Tongues": An Interview with Sam Shepard 126
    Carol Rosen / 1991

Sam Shepard, Tues., Dec. 14, 1993 150
    Mel Gussow / 1993

Slay 'em Again, Sam 166
    Brian Case / 1996

Sam Shepard 173
    Mona Simpson, Jeanne McCulloch, and Benjamin Howe / 1997

Shepard on Shepard: An Interview 185
    Matthew Roudané / 2000

Sam Shepard 201
    Mel Gussow / 2002

Rock-and-Roll Jesus with a Cowboy Mouth (Revisited) 225
    Don Shewey / 2004

Sam Shepard's Master Class in Playwriting 239
    Brian Bartels / 2006

A Nod from One Sam to Another 252
    Fintan O'Toole / 2007

Sam Shepard   257
   Michael Almereyda / 2011

Sam Shepard: "America Is on Its Way Out as a Culture"   270
   Laura Barton / 2014

An Urban Cowboy Returns to Broadway   276
   Alexis Soloski / 2016

Index   281

Introduction

In a career that spanned 53 years, Sam Shepard was a playwright, theater director, film and television actor, rock drummer, screenwriter, film director, fiction writer, and nonfiction writer. Often he pursued several of these disciplines simultaneously. His creative output and the honors he received are impressive: he wrote 56 produced plays, for which he won eight Obie Awards (for 11 plays), a Pulitzer Prize, and Drama Desk, Outer Critics Circle, and New York Drama Critics' Circle Awards; he won an Obie for directing and directed the premiere productions of 10 of his plays; he made more than 60 acting appearances in films and television and was nominated for an Academy Award for the role of Chuck Yeager in *The Right Stuff* (1983); he wrote or co-wrote six original screenplays and collaborated on many others, and he directed two films; he was a drummer for three rock groups; and he published eight books of prose and poetry. In 1980, Stewart McBride called him "arguably America's best practicing playwright"; in 1985, Ross Wetzsteon saw him as "one of the most gifted directors in the American theater"; in 1983, Shepard's fellow movie actor, Wilford Brimley, described him as "one hell of an actor" while Pete Hamill said he was "the male star of the 1980s." Despite his ubiquitous half-century presence on the international cultural scene, Shepard was known to be a very private person who shied away from publicity. As Hamill put it, "Shepard has a reputation for privacy that makes him sound like an amalgam of J. D. Salinger, Thomas Pynchon, and Howard Hughes." Many interviewers prefaced their published pieces with assurances that what followed would be a *rare* interview with the famously private playwright. Actually, Shepard gave many.

We located well over 100 interviews from which we selected the 23 included here. These conversations begin in 1969 when Shepard, already a multiple Obie winner and newly married, was 26 ("You get a certain spontaneous freaky thing if you write real fast" [Gussow]); they end in 2016, eighteen months before Shepard's death from complications of ALS at age 73 ("When you listen intensely to anything you see how it can be improved" [Soloski]). They reveal an artist evolving but also one who revisits numerous

subjects throughout his life. While we tried to choose interviews that focused on Shepard as a writer, he also spoke openly and often eloquently
about his acting, directing, and his thoughts on a wide range of topics. The
fact that Shepard did not participate in publicizing the films in which he
appeared—"I'm not into personal promotion," he told Goldberg in 1980—
coupled with an increasing reluctance, the more famous he became, to
speak of his private life, undoubtedly contributed to his reputation as someone who shunned the press. But those who respected his boundaries found
a man generous with his time, affable, open, modest, interesting, and prone
to laughter. Stewart McBride observed in 1980, "The time I spent with him
felt more like chewing the fat with a slightly older brother than interviewing one of the country's preeminent playwrights"; and Matthew Roudané in
2000 described him as "unpretentious and charismatic."

Among the subjects that Shepard was candid about was his youth in rural California: "My family was torn apart, torn to shreds from the inside
out," he told Sylvie Drake in 1979, "the sense of mother and father not really
able to make it or break it off." But, he acknowledged to Roudané, "there
is no escape from the family. . . . It's absolutely ridiculous to intellectually
think that you can sever yourself, I mean even if you didn't know who your
mother and father were, if you never met them, you are still intimately, inevitably, and entirely connected to who brought you into the world." He ad-
mitted to being especially baffled by and fascinated by his father—"There is
a mystery about him that still exasperates me, that still intrigues me. I don't
know who he was. I never really knew who he was. I think he was a mystery
to himself"—but also understood that writing plays "turned me toward my
life in a way that was quite unexpected. . . . It has given me an avenue to express certain areas that probably would have gone dormant if I hadn't found
a form" (Gussow 2002).

At age 19, Shepard escaped his troubled home life and joined a touring
repertory group, the Bishop's Company; after several months on the road,
he set himself down in New York in October 1963. There, while working as a
busboy at the Village Gate, he began writing one-act plays for Ralph Cook's
Off-Off-Broadway Theater Genesis; this suited him well because he "had
a place to go and put something on without having to go through a producer or go through the commercial network" (Hamill 1983). Looking back
on these first efforts, he was remarkably frank about them, describing them
to Hamill as "explosions that were coming out of some kind of inner turmoil
in me that I didn't understand at all. . . . a means of putting something outside rather than having it all inside," seeing himself as "kind of like a weird

stenographer . . . there were definitely things there, and I was just putting them down" (*Paris Review* 1997) and admitting that "I had this feeling . . . that nobody knew better than you what was good for your work. . . . I was a real pain in the ass, continuously uptight about the production, about what the actors were doing" (Drake 1979). His early work, he explained to Hamill, "was very hasty. . . . There wasn't much rewriting done. . . . It was like 'Take it or leave it—if you don't like this shit, tough luck,' and go on to the next one." Just about when he was "ready to pack it in and go back to California" (Chubb 1974), in October 1964 Michael Smith of the *Village Voice* gave a rave review to Shepard's *Cowboys* at Theater Genesis, and his career was launched. Over the next seven years, six of his plays were honored in the "Distinguished Plays" category at the Obie Awards; and in November 1969 he married actress O-Lan Johnson, who, in 1970, gave birth to their son Jesse.

In October 1971, Shepard, who "wanted to get out of the insanity"—including drug use and a love affair—of his life in New York (Roudané 2000), made what proved to be a professionally significant and life-changing choice when, with his wife and son, he left New York for London. The move affected his work as a writer in many different ways. "It wasn't until I came to England," he told Kenneth Chubb in 1974, "that I found out what it means to be an American. Nothing really makes sense when you're there, but the more distant you are from it, the more the implications of what you grew up with start to emerge." In London, he met English director Peter Brook. Brook "used to say we all work with the soil that we're born into. We're given a certain kind of soil. . . . That's where you plant your seeds. A little idea like that can liberate you, toward your own thing" (Gussow 1993). Brook, he explained to Pete Hamill in 1983, also "asked me this very simple question: 'What is character?'" and "it started a whole kind of thought in me. . . . We use terms like that all the time without really knowing exactly what we're talking about." As a result, character became "much more important to [him]" and he learned that "[a] playwright has to understand what an actor goes through" (McBride 1980). While in London, he wrote five plays: *The Tooth of Crime, Blue Bitch, Geography of a Horse Dreamer, Little Ocean,* and *Action.*

It was also in London that Shepard first directed a play. Directing the 1974 premiere of his *Geography of a Horse Dreamer* with Stephen Rea and Bob Hoskins—"for a first time directing job, you couldn't ask for better" (Gussow 1993)—taught him that a play "isn't a piece of paper, it's something that's really happening in real life. . . . the more you find out about it the more you can grow as a writer" (Chubb 1974). By the time he had directed half a dozen of his own plays, he understood well what he had first discovered while directing that London production, that a play is "a malleable thing, something that's in flux" which "has a lot to do with the actor" in that "you can say you have a vision of a character, but once the actor gets ahold of it, that thing necessarily changes" and "it *should* change because the actor is influencing it according to who he or she is. . . . I'm not trying to force the actor to *be* the character. I want to see what the meeting is between the actor and the character. That's the most interesting thing" (Lippman 1983). As a result of his directing experience, the published scripts of Shepard's plays were based on the first production rather than on the script he brought to the first rehearsal—"I leave it open until the production's complete and then go back to the whole thing and outline what we actually achieved in the production" (Wetzsteon 1985)—because he did much more rewriting based on the realization "that the actors are really what shape the production" (Gussow 1993).

In contrast to his early experience in New York, where he was frustrated "because the actors were in control of the material and I wasn't used to actors. . . . didn't know how to talk with them and I didn't want to learn" (*Paris Review* 1997), he told *Newsweek* in 1976, "What's really become interesting to me [is] how to work with an actor in such a way that he can put across something that you actually can't put on paper." "A really fine actor will influence your writing," he confided to Kevin Sessums in 1988. "Until you get up on stage and put yourself inside the character you'll never realize the dilemmas an actor faces." Shepard expressed an abiding admiration of English theater artists: "With English actors and directors, even in the alternative theater, there's a craftsman thing at work. In London I ran into a ton of people who were passionate and at the same time workmanlike" (Case 1996). The English actor, he felt, was "always relating the character to the story, to the whole spectrum and never losing himself entirely in the character at the expense of the story" (Gussow 1993).

Another major turning point in Shepard's life occurred in 1976, when film director Terrence Malik convinced him to play the role of The Farmer in *Days of Heaven.* Prior to that—other than some nonprofessional acting in California, his tour with the Bishop's Company in 1963, and some amateur theater in New York when he first arrived—his only other acting experience had been the opening night performance in *Cowboy Mouth,* the 1971 play he co-wrote and momentarily starred in with Patti Smith (for whom he had briefly left his wife). Following his well-received performance in *Days of Heaven*, he acted in more than 50 feature films; arguably, during the last four decades of his life, he was more widely known as a movie star than as a writer. Initially and for several years, he downplayed his film work; he told Lippman in 1983, "I think almost anyone can get away with being in a film"; and to Pete Hamill that same year: "The more I act the more resistance I have to it. . . . I don't like the kind of feeling of entrapment that you have to go through to make a film." He also contrasted acting in film with acting on stage: "You could always find many, many people off the street who could get away with a tight close-up, but they couldn't do a three-act play" (Wetzsteon 1985). But, as with other topics in these interviews, his views on films and on film-acting evolved; by 1991, he conceded to Carol Rosen that acting in movies was "starting to become more interesting, the whole process of being able to contact the character and to manipulate your concentration and your attention and move into areas that are more risky and that have real feeling"; and by 2002, he explained to Mel Gussow that "when I started out [as a film actor] I was full of armor. I was trying to not be revealed. As I've gone on, I found the opposite is true. You have to become more and more vulnerable. It's an interesting process because you don't really face that the same way as a writer." He also began to appreciate film as a medium, telling Rosen what was "great about film" was that "[y]ou can follow three or four stories in parallel time," while on stage "it's much more awkward to do that kind of instantaneous time shift." And, of course, movie-acting had a major impact on Shepard's personal life when, in 1981, while filming *Frances*, he met Jessica Lange; in 1983, he left his wife and their son for Lange. The couple would live together until 2010 and have two children.

A recurring theme in these interviews is Shepard's lifelong interest in music and how that affected his playwriting. It started early in his life; his father played drums with an amateur Dixieland band and Shepard was soon emulating him. When he arrived in New York in 1964, he reconnected with his high school friend Charles Mingus III (frequently referred to in these interviews as Charles Mingus Jr.), son of the great jazz musician and composer, and through the younger Mingus he got the job at the Village Gate where he saw performances by many of the jazz luminaries of the 1960s. During the mid- and late 1960s, he was a rock drummer, most famously with the Holy Modal Rounders, on two of whose albums he played. Despite the fact that he had more than 20 produced plays, when he came to London in 1971, as he told Kenneth Chubb in 1974, he went there "to get into music [because] London was notorious for its rock 'n' roll bands. . . . so I had this fantasy that I'd . . . somehow fall into a rock 'n' roll band," adding, "I much prefer playing music really to theater." But music also led him to writing, as he explained to Sylvie Drake in 1979: "I used to go and listen to Charlie Mingus and was stunned by his sense of polyrhythm—rhythm on top of rhythm on top of rhythm. I was fascinated by the idea of merging that with writing, seeing if there was a way of evoking the same kind of collage in the writing of plays." Music, he felt, "adds a whole different kind of perspective [to theater], it immediately brings the audience to terms with an emotional reality" because "nothing communicates emotions better than music" (Chubb 1974). Beyond using actual music in his plays, most notably in *The Tooth of Crime*, he saw "actors as musicians playing to each other, using their voices instead of instruments" (McBride 1980) and contended that "[w]riting is very rhythmic, there's a rhythmical flow to it—if it's working. I've always been fascinated by the rhythm of language, and language is musical, there's no way of getting around it" (Roudané 2000).

Despite his prolific career as a playwright and stage director, in several interviews Shepard made clear that only very infrequently did he go to the theater. He told Amy Lippman in 1983, "I don't go to the theater at all, I hate the theater. I really do, I can't stand it. I think it's totally disappointing for the most part," adding that only "every once in a while, something real is taking place." He did, however, admit to being influenced in different but complementary ways early in his life by two plays. He maintained that Samuel Beckett's *Waiting for Godot* "was like nothing I'd ever read before" (Chubb 1974); "I couldn't place it as a play, a poem, a novel, or anything else. It just seemed like a unique piece of writing. . . . it just struck me suddenly that with words you could do anything" (Hamill 1983). Beckett, he told the *Paris Review* interviewers in 1997, "made American theater look like it was on crutches." The second influential play was Eugene O'Neill's *Long Day's Journey Into Night*. Reading it and "seeing Sidney Lumet's [1962] black-and-white film adaptation" inspired him to start writing: "There was something wrong with the family. There was a demonic thing going on that nobody could put their finger on, but everybody knew the ship was sinking. Everybody was going down, and nobody knew why or how, and they were all taking desperate measures to stay afloat. So I thought that there was something about that that felt similar to my own background, and I felt I could maybe write some version of that" (Almereyda 2011). But he rebelled against the naturalistic style of O'Neill's drama, telling Carol Rosen in 1991, "Why should we be anchored to these notions of Eugene O'Neill and all this burden of having your character be believable from the outside in terms of the artist saying, well, he really is in a living room serving tea to his mother.

And he's really talking the way he would be talking in real life. What the hell is that? Where is that going to take us? Why doesn't he pour the tea on her head and start screaming and carrying on, climbing walls, and then come back and sit down." In 2016, near the end of his life, Shepard told Alexis Soloski, "[*Long Day's Journey Into Night* is] the greatest play ever written in America. But what I wanted to do was to destroy the idea of the American family drama. It's too psychological. Because this and that happened, you wet the bed? Who cares? Who cares when there's a dead baby in the backyard?" The latter, of course, is a reference to his own Pulitzer Prize–winning unconventional family drama *Buried Child*. Essentially, Shepard wedded Beckett's experimental style to O'Neill's domestic drama in his own family plays—*Curse of the Starving Class, Buried Child, True West, Fool for Love,* and *A Lie of the Mind*.

Among contemporary writers, Shepard often expressed admiration for playwright Peter Handke, who won the Nobel Prize for Literature two years after Shepard died: "He's exploring the truth in himself, and his plays open it up to everybody. There hasn't been a writer since Beckett that has been so adventurous" (McBride 1980); Shepard also praised Amiri Baraka (known early in his career as LeRoi Jones), telling Robert Goldberg in 1980, "LeRoi Jones, I think, is the greatest American playwright. I don't think there is a playwright in the country who speaks with that kind of conviction and intensity," and reiterating this to Michael Almereyda in 2011: Jones "wrote some brilliant plays like *The Toilet* [1964] and *Slave Ship* [1969]. I think he was the most brilliant playwright of his era. . . . I thought his plays were far and away above anything else that was going on, even though there were other people struggling to do that sort of experimental work." Among other writers Shepard admired were Bertolt Brecht ("my favorite playwright" [Chubb 1974]), Joan Didion ("She is ruthless with herself and doesn't allow self-indulgence" [McBride 1980]), Patti Smith ("She showed me what it's like to construct a line of language in a different way, putting ideas and images together" [Goldberg 1980]), César Vallejo ("a great, great writer" [Sessums 1988]), and Richard Ford ("an incredible writer" [Sessums 1988]).

Among theater practitioners, one of the greatest influences on Shepard was actor, playwright, and director Joseph Chaikin, with whom he had a working relationship and a personal friendship for decades. It began in the mid-1960s when Shepard "hung around the Open Theater" because his girlfriend at the time "was an actress in the company" (Lippman 1983) and lasted until Chaikin's death in 2003. In 1988, Shepard explained Chaikin's "tremendous influence" on him: "When I saw the way he was working with actors and what he was pursuing with them, it was a revelation to me. To see what he was searching for and the way in which he approached that search was an amazing lesson. He absolutely aggrandized people—they were held in this incredible spell. But . . . it was done from an absolute humility. He's a magical person. It was a miracle in my life ever to have met him" (Sessums). Shepard was particularly influenced by Chaikin's ideas about the audience: "I was pushed off into the world of writing a play and kind of disregarding the aspect of the audience. Which is a grave mistake, I think. What are we doing to an audience? What's an audience doing to us? What do we want to have done and how are we being influenced back and forth? So I think that was the first big idea that galvanized me to him as a theater person" (Rosen 1991). In 2006 when taking questions from an audience at New York's Cherry Lane Theatre, Shepard recalled one of Chaikin's acting exercises: "He'd do a Brecht play, a very simple, one-act Brecht play, like a clown piece; then he'd say, 'Do it as though the Queen of England was watching your show,' so it changed. 'Now do it as though Muhammad Ali is sitting there. Now do it as though the fascists are about to take over.' And it was amazing to see that and how it took over the actors" (Bartels).

It was Chaikin, too, who taught Shepard the importance of revision: "I used to be dead set against revisions because I couldn't stand rewriting. That changed when I started working with Chaikin. Joe was so persistent about finding the essence of something. He'd say, 'Does this mean what we're trying to make it mean? Can it be constructed some other way?' That fascinated me, because my tendency was to jam, like it was jazz or something. Thelonious Monk style" (*Paris Review* 1997). Over the years, Shepard's collaborations with Chaikin included stage plays—*Tongues* (1978), *Savage/Love* (1978), and *When the World Was Green* (1996)—and a radio-play, *The War in Heaven* (1984), as well as directing. In 1994, Theatre Communications Group published *Joseph Chaikin & Sam Shepard: Letters and Texts, 1972–1984*.

During these interviews, Shepard spoke frankly and articulately about the themes of his work, about specific productions of his plays, about the arts of writing and directing, about acting in film and on stage. Besides these subjects that one might expect a writer to discuss, Shepard, whose range of interests was as diverse as his talents, also talked about English dog racing, American "cutting" horses, agriculture versus agribusiness, the 1960s (he was not a fan), Hank Williams (he was a fan), and a great deal more.

One topic among many that Shepard discussed broadly was the American experience. In 1980, he suggested to Robert Goldberg that "one of the biggest tragedies" in American history "was moving from an agricultural to an urban-industrial society at the turn of the [nineteenth to the twentieth] century. It was a great undertow that demolished the family feelings that were well rooted in America. . . . It's a deeply painful experience, finding ourselves in these bodies that are essentially geared toward a rural civilization. It's as though we'd been transported to another planet and didn't know how we got there." In 2000, Shepard discussed "the myth of the American Dream": It's "always this fantasy that's promoted through advertising. We always prefer the fantasy over the reality" (Roudané). Lamenting Americans' disconnection from their own history, in his conversation with Irish critic Fintan O'Toole in 2007, Shepard observed that "in the States we've lost so much contact with our own past. You talk to kids about the Civil War, they don't know what you're talking about. This notion, this implication, that we're connected to something ancient—it's good for a writer to feel that there's some connection to something very, very old. And that there's a continuation." But he could also express appreciation for his native country, as he did to Mel Gussow in 2002: "America is an extraordinary thing, and much much more interesting than we make it out to be, particularly in this time of patriotism and flagwaving, the chauvinistic appeal. It's much more complex and much more interesting—the fabric of America. It's extraordinary what's happened in such a brief period of time, within 150 years. The amazing weave of American culture."

Carol Rosen began her 1991 interview by observing that, for Shepard, "every conversation is a discovery." Shepard was endlessly curious. As he commented to Rosen, "[O]ne of the thrills about writing is to remain open to all its possibilities, and not to try to put a bridle on it and squeeze it down into what your notion of it is. Not to say that you lose control, but I think you have to remain open." Shepard was not only open in his expression but also open to receiving new ideas and directions. That openness characterizes his work, his life, and these interviews.

In keeping with the conventions of the Literary Conversations Series, we have reprinted the interviews uncut and, wherever possible, arranged them chronologically by the date the interview was conducted rather than by its publication date. We have silently corrected typographical errors, regularized titles into italics, converted British spellings to American spellings, and have made other editing changes for consistency.

A word about our Chronology: the dates and venues of initial productions sometimes contradict those from common sources—even, at times, when a common source is the published play; through our examination of primary sources as well as biographer Robert M. Dowling's discussions with Shepard's contemporaries, we have done our best to discover and provide accurate information. Very occasionally, Shepard himself gives differing information from one interview to another; again, we have done our best in the Chronology to track down and provide accurate dates. Finally, our Chronology does not list all of the many films that Shepard appeared in as an actor since this volume is primarily concerned with him as a writer.

In addition to the interviewers and editors who gave us permission to reprint interviews, we wish to thank Mallory Haselberger, David A. Crespy, and, from the University Press of Mississippi, Mary Heath and Katie Keene.

JRB
RMD
MCH

Chronology

The dates and venues in this chronology are sometimes different from those found in common—and often erroneous—sources; we have made our best effort to provide accurate information.

1943	November 5: Born Samuel Shepard Rogers in Fort Sheridan, Illinois, first child of three to Samuel Shepard Rogers Jr. (to avoid confusion, the family refers to the future playwright as "Steve"), a bomber pilot for the Army Air Corps during World War II, and Jane Elaine Schook Rogers, a teacher.
1943–48	The Rogerses live the itinerant existence of a military family; Sam "Steve" Shepard Rogers and his mother, Jane Rogers, move from Fort Sheridan to join Sam Sr. at bases in South Dakota, Utah, Florida, and Guam. Sister Sandra Rogers is born in Guam in 1947. Eventually, the family lands in South Pasadena, outside of Los Angeles, with Jane's aunt, Grace Upton.
1948–61	Attends Lincoln Elementary School in South Pasadena (1948–1954), then South Pasadena Junior High School (1954–1957). Roxanne, the youngest of the three children, is born in 1955. In 1957, the family settles in nearby Bradbury, California, on an avocado farm. For the first few months, Shepard attends Monrovia-Arcadia-Duarte High School, during the final stages of construction for the new Duarte High School, from which he graduates in 1961. He also works on a horse ranch part-time while in high school.
1961–62	Spends three semesters after high school at Mt. San Antonio College ("Mt. SAC"), a local community college where he plans to major in agricultural science. He also acts in several college plays and writes *The Mildew*, his first known play, which is published in the college literary magazine, *MoSAiC*. (The world premiere of *The Mildew* will take place at Mt. Sac Studio Theater on February 13, 2018.)

1963   April: Cast in Thornton Wilder's Pulitzer Prize–winning *The Skin of Our Teeth* by the San Gabriel Civic Players Association. He then auditions for and joins the Bishop's Company, a traveling theater group, where he acts in repertory through Pennsylvania, New York, and New England. In October, he leaves the Bishop's Company in New York City.

1964   January: Contacts high school friend Charles Mingus III (the jazz great's son), who gets him a job as a busboy at the Village Gate jazz club, where he meets Ralph Cook, the artistic director of the fledgling Off-Off-Broadway repertory group Theater Genesis. March: Drops Rogers from his name and permanently becomes Sam Shepard. October 10: First two produced plays, *Cowboys* and *The Rock Garden*, appear on a double bill at Theater Genesis at St. Mark's Church-in-the-Bowery in New York. November 23: *Up to Thursday* is first produced by Edward Albee's Playwrights Unit Workshop at the Village South Theater in New York; the production moves to the Cherry Lane Theatre, opening on February 10, 1965.

1965   Writes *Three and Melons*, which is neither published nor produced. February 10: *Dog* and *Rocking Chair*, first produced on a double bill by La MaMa Experimental Theatre Club (ETC) in New York, opens. April 16: *Chicago* opens at Theater Genesis at St. Mark's Church-in-the-Bowery; it subsequently travels with the La MaMa Repertory Troupe's second European tour in 1966. The play wins an Obie in the category "Distinguished Plays"—the first of 10 Obies Shepard will win from 1966 to 1984 (including two for multiple plays, one for directing, and one for Sustained Achievement). September 9: *4-H Club*, first produced by Edward Albee's Playwrights Unit Workshop at the Village South Theatre in New York, opens there and then moves to the Cherry Lane Theatre. November 16: *Icarus's Mother*, first produced by Caffe Cino in New York, opens (Obie in the category "Distinguished Plays"). The play, under the title *Icarus*, will be recorded for Riverside Radio Theater on a double bill with *4-H* and broadcast on March 1, 1966.

1966   January 20: *Red Cross* opens at Judson Poets' Theater in New York (Obie in the category "Distinguished Plays"). March 11: *Fourteen Hundred Thousand* premieres at the Firehouse Theater in Minneapolis, Minnesota, on a double bill with Jean-Claude van Itallie's *Where's de Queen*. It is revived and filmed in the summer of

1966 for broadcast by National Educational Television (NET) for their series "NET Playhouse" and aired on January 20, 1967, with two other plays (*Pavane* by Jean-Claude van Itallie and *Recluse* by Paul Foster) under the title *La MaMa Playwrights*. Also in 1966: Writes *Replacement for Eight (A Four Act Play)*, his first full-length play, which is neither published nor produced. Becomes a drummer for three rock groups: the Heavy Metal Kid, the Moray Eels, and in the fall, the Holy Modal Rounders. He later drums on two Holy Modal Rounders albums: *Indian War Whoop* (1967) and *The Moral Eels Eat the Holy Modal Rounders* (1968).

1967   March 2: *La Turista: A Play in Two Acts*, Shepard's first produced full-length play, premieres at the American Place Theatre in St. Clement's Church in New York (Obie in the category "Distinguished Plays"). May 18: *Melodrama Play* opens at La MaMa ETC (Obie in the category "Distinguished Plays"), and then travels with the La MaMa Repertory Troupe's third European tour that summer. October 9: *Cowboys #2* opens for the Center Theatre Group's "New Theatre for Now" series in a 12 one-act final production titled *The Scene* at the Mark Taper Forum in Los Angeles. December 29: *Forensic & the Navigators* opens at Theater Genesis at St. Mark's Church-in-the-Bowery (Obie in the category "Distinguished Plays").

1968   January: Travels to Rome to work on the script of *Zabriskie Point* with Michelangelo Antonioni. While in Europe, he meets Rolling Stones guitarist Keith Richards and is invited to write a screenplay for the band, which becomes "Maxagasm: A Distorted Western for Soul and Psyche." The film is never produced. Summer–Fall: Tours California with the Holy Modal Rounders. September 1: *Me and My Brother*, a film written by Robert Frank, Allen Ginsberg, Peter Orlovsky, and Shepard from 1965 to 1968, premieres at the Venice Film Festival.

1969   June 17: *Oh, Calcutta!*—a theatrical revue—opens at the Eden Theatre Off-Broadway. Shepard is one among many contributors, including Samuel Beckett, Edna O'Brien, and John Lennon. Kenneth Tynan, its creator, chose to include from Shepard's work the third scene of *The Rock Garden*. November 9: Marries actress O-Lan Johnson (after her divorce from Shepard, she will change her name from O-Lan Shepard to O-Lan Jones), who is 19 and two and a half months pregnant with their child. December 26: *The Unseen Hand* opens at La MaMa ETC.

1970   February 9: Italian director Michelangelo Antonioni's *Zabriskie Point* is released. Shepard is one of several screenwriters on this film. March 8: *The Holy Ghostly* premieres at Princeton University's McCarter Theatre on a double bill with *Melodrama Play*, under the auspices of director Tom O'Horgan's short-lived The New Troupe (a break-away company from La MaMa); the 2 one-acts then go on to be played in the New Troupe's unsuccessful European tour that summer. March 12: *Operation Sidewinder*, Shepard's second full-length play to be staged after *La Turista* and his first uptown production, opens at the Repertory Theater at Lincoln Center's Vivian Beaumont Theater, New York, with musical accompaniment by the Holy Modal Rounders. May 25: First child Jesse Mojo Shepard is born. July: Buys a farm in West Advocate, Nova Scotia, where the family will spend most summers until 1982. July 27: *Shaved Splits* opens for four midnight performances at La MaMa ETC.

1971   March 4: *Mad Dog Blues* opens at Theater Genesis at St. Mark's Church-in-the-Bowery. April 2: *Cowboy Mouth* premieres, without contractual permission, at the Traverse Theatre in Edinburgh, Scotland, and runs for four late-night performances. April 29: *Back Bog Beast Bait* (with Shepard's wife, listed as O-Lan Johnson-Shepard, cast as Gris Gris) and *Cowboy Mouth* (written and performed with his then-lover Patti Smith) open as a double bill at the American Place Theatre. Shepard abandons the *Cowboy Mouth* production after opening night. Spends summer in Nova Scotia. October: Moves to London with O-Lan and Jesse.

1972   July 17: *The Tooth of Crime* opens at the Open Space Theatre in London. (The New York production will win an Obie in 1973 in the category of "Distinguished Plays.")

1973   January 19: *Blue Bitch*, a one-act prototype for his later full-length *Geography of a Horse Dreamer*, premieres at Theater Genesis, with Patti Smith playing the part of Dixie. January 31: *Hawk Moon*, a book of short stories, poems, and monologues, is published. June 7: *Nightwalk*, a collective theatrical work co-written with Megan Terry and Jean-Claude van Itallie, is first performed in workshop for a four-night run at London's Roundhouse, and then at Joseph Chaikin's Open Theater at New York's St. Clement's Church on September 8.

1974   February 21: *Geography of a Horse Dreamer* opens at the Royal Court Theatre in London, with Shepard for the first time directing his own work. March 31: *Geography of a Horse Dreamer*, filmed for television in England, airs on ITV. April 4: *Little Ocean* opens for a three-night run at Hampstead Theatre Club in London. September 15: *Action* opens at the Royal Court Theatre Upstairs in London. (The New York production will win an Obie in 1975, in the category of "Playwriting.") October: Returns to the US with O-Lan and Jesse, and settles in Marin County, California, with O-Lan's mother, Scarlett Johnson; her sister Kristy; and her stepfather, Johnny Dark.

1975   Completes his unpublished/unproduced two-act *Man Fly* (1974– 1975), an autobiographical treatment of Christopher Marlowe's *Doctor Faustus* (1604). April 15: *Killer's Head*, first produced at American Place Theatre in New York on a double bill with *Action*, opens. Begins his eight-year relationship with San Francisco's Magic Theatre, first on a Rockefeller Foundation writing grant, then as playwright-in-residence. *Killer's Head* (written specifically for the Magic) and *Action* open there on May 2. October 30– December 8: Joins and tours the Northeast with Bob Dylan's Rolling Thunder Revue, ostensibly as a screenwriter for a docudrama film idea Dylan has for the tour (this eventually becomes *Renaldo and Clara* [1978], which Shepard appears in, but for which he ultimately writes little dialogue).

1976   July 2: *Angel City* opens at the Magic Theatre in San Francisco, directed by Shepard. Late August: Filming of Terrence Malick's *Day of Heaven*, in which Malick has asked Shepard to act, begins in late August at Whiskey Gap in Alberta, Canada. October 15: *Suicide in Bb* (*A Mysterious Overture*) opens at Yale Repertory Theatre in New Haven. October 23: *The Sad Lament of Pecos Bill on the Eve of Killing His Wife* (*A Short Opera*) is first produced during the inaugural Bay Area Playwrights Festival, San Francisco.

1977   January 1: Completes a draft of his full-length play on artist Jackson Pollock titled *Jackson*, which he will return to in 1979 collaborating with lyricist Jacques Levy to create the retitled *Jackson's Dance* (*A Play in Three Acts with Music and Dance*). Because of complications with the copyright of Pollock's work, it remains unproduced as well as unpublished. March 2: *Curse of the Starving Class*, Shepard's first staged three-act play, having been commissioned by producer Joseph Papp for his New York Shakespeare Festival in 1975, premieres at Papp's Public Theater in New York.

(The production wins an Obie, in 1977, for "Best New American Play.") March 18: *Inacoma*, an improvisational work with accompaniment by the San Francisco Jazz Ensemble and based on the Karen Ann Quinlan euthanasia controversy, opens at the Magic Theatre, now established at Fort Mason in San Francisco; the production is directed by Shepard. July 4: *Rolling Thunder Logbook*, a chronicle of his experience touring in Bob Dylan's Rolling Thunder Revue, is published.

1978   April 21: *Seduced*, based on the life of Howard Hughes, premieres at the Trinity Repertory Company's Lederer Theater in Providence, Rhode Island. (Opens at the American Place Theatre in New York on January 19, 1979.) June 7: *Tongues*, a collaboration with Joseph Chaikin, opens at the Magic Theatre, San Francisco, Shepard directing. June 27: *Buried Child* opens at the Magic Theatre, San Francisco; the play will win the 1979 Pulitzer Prize for drama (and will also win an Obie in the category of "Playwriting"). July: Joins the faculty of the Padua Hills Playwrights' Workshop sponsored by La Verne University, led by his Off-Off Broadway colleagues Murray Mednick, Maria Irene Fornes, and Walter Hadler, where he writes the monologue *Red Woman*, which is performed on July 30. September 13: *Days of Heaven*, the film that launches Shepard's film-acting career, is released. Shepard will act in more than 60 films, including those made for television. Also in 1978, completes a screenplay titled "The Bodyguard," started in London in 1973, which is a contemporary adaptation of Thomas Middleton and William Rowley's Jacobean tragedy *The Changeling* (1622), and is never published or produced.

1979   June 7: *Jacaranda*, a 30-minute libretto for a dance choreographed and performed by Daniel Nagrin, opens at St. Clement's Church in New York City. September 6: *Savage/Love*—on a double bill with *Tongues*, both written in collaboration with Joseph Chaikin—is first produced by the Magic Theatre as the final production of the Eureka Theatre Summer Festival in California; the play is directed by Shepard.

1980   June 2: Wins an Obie for "Sustained Achievement." July 10: *True West* opens at the Magic Theatre, San Francisco. (Its 1982 Steppenwolf Theatre revival, starring Gary Sinese and John Malkovich, will move from Chicago to New York and subsequently, the play will become a finalist for the 1983 Pulitzer Prize.)

1981   July 3: *Superstitions,* a jazz/theater improvisational work using material from his forthcoming book *Motel Chronicles* (1982) along with some new dialogue and song lyrics, is performed by the Overtone Theatre at San Francisco's Intersection for the Arts Theater. Meets actress Jessica Lange that fall on the set of *Frances,* a film (released on December 3, 1982) based on the life of actress Frances Farmer starring Lange and Shepard.

1982   May 1: *Motel Chronicles,* an autobiographical collection of prose and poetry, is published. The book becomes the inspiration for the film *Paris, Texas* (1984).

1983   February 9: *Fool for Love* opens at the Magic Theatre, San Francisco, directed by Shepard. (When this Magic Theatre production is moved to New York, it will win Obies for "Best New American Play" and for "Direction" and the play will be a finalist for the Pulitzer Prize for 1984.) March: Shepard leaves his family in Marin County; he and Jessica Lange briefly move to Lange's home state of Minnesota, then settle in Santa Fe, New Mexico, with Lange's two-year-old daughter, Shura Baryshnikov.

1984   January 3: The Steppenwolf production of *True West,* starring Gary Sinese and John Malkovich, is adapted for television and airs on *American Playhouse.* February: Shepard is nominated for a Best Supporting Actor Oscar for his role as Chuck Yeager in the 1983 film *The Right Stuff.* March 24: Shepard's father, Samuel Shepard Rogers, who suffered from acute alcoholism for many years, dies in Bernalillo, New Mexico, at the age of 67 when he is hit by a car while drunk. May 19: *Paris, Texas,* a film for which Shepard wrote the majority of the screenplay (L. M. Kit Carson and the film's director Wim Wenders provided the ending) premieres at the Cannes Film Festival and on May 23 wins the top prize, the Palme D'Or, among other awards; it is released in the United States on November 3. September 28: The film *Country,* whose screenplay Shepard significantly helped revise, starring Shepard and Lange, is released. Late fall: Divorces O-Lan.

1985   January 8: *The War in Heaven (Angel's Monologue),* co-written by Shepard and Joseph Chaikin and performed as a radio play by Chaikin with musical accompaniment by Shepard, is broadcast for Free Speech Radio (WBAI) in New York City; it was prerecorded the previous October. Chaikin will perform it live for the first time at Sushi Gallery in San Diego, California, on

December 20. December 5: *A Lie of the Mind* opens at the Promenade Theatre in New York. Directed by Shepard and with musical accompaniment by the Red Clay Ramblers, the play wins Drama Desk, Outer Critics Circle, and New York Drama Critics' Circle awards (Outstanding Play, Outstanding New Off-Broadway Play, and Best Play, respectively, all presented in 1986). December 6: The film version of *Fool for Love*, directed by Robert Altman, with screenplay by Shepard and starring Shepard, Kim Bassinger, and Harry Dean Stanton, is released.

1986   January 13: Second child, Hannah Jane Shepard, is born. May 21: Shepard is inducted into the American Academy and Institute of Arts and Letters. July 14: "Brownsville Girl," a song co-written with Bob Dylan, is released on Dylan's *Knocked Out Loaded*. Summer: With Lange, buys Totier Creek Farm, a horse farm, in Scottsville, Virginia, where he breeds thoroughbreds.

1987   June 14: Third child, Samuel Walker Shepard, is born. July 1: *Esquire* magazine publishes *True Dylan: A One-Act Play as It Really Happened One Afternoon in California*, a dramatization of Shepard's interview with Bob Dylan the previous summer, later published—in September 2012—as *Short Life of Trouble* in his collection *Fifteen One-Act Plays*.

1988   September 10: The film *Far North*, written and directed by Shepard and starring Lange, is released.

1989   November: *Joseph Chaikin & Sam Shepard: Letters and Texts, 1972–1984*, edited by Barry Daniels, is published.

1991   May 16: *States of Shock* opens at the American Place Theatre in New York.

1993   January 28: The film *Silent Tongue*, written and directed by Shepard, premieres at the Sundance Film Festival.

1994   March 10: His mother, Jane Elaine Schook Rogers, dies at the age of 76. November 14: *Simpatico* opens at the Public Theater, New York, directed by Shepard.

1995   Summer: Moves with Lange and their children to Stillwater, Minnesota.

1996   Shepard becomes playwright-in-residence at the Signature Theatre in New York. April 30: *Cruising Paradise*, a collection of autobiographical short stories, is published. July 19: *When the World Was Green (A Chef's Fable)*, co-written with Joseph Chaikin, commissioned by Seven Stages, and first produced at the Olympics

	Arts Festival, 14th Street Playhouse Mainstage, Atlanta, Georgia, opens.
1998	February 10: *Eyes for Consuela* (from the story "The Blue Bouquet" by Octavio Paz) opens at New York's Manhattan Theatre Club.
2000	November 14: *The Late Henry Moss* opens with the all-star cast of Sean Penn, James Gammon, Nick Nolte, Woody Harrelson, and Cheech Marin, at the Magic Theatre, San Francisco, directed by Shepard. Michael Almereyda's documentary about the making of the production, *This So-Called Disaster*, premieres at the International Film Festival Rotterdam on January 24, 2003.
2002	October 22: *Great Dream of Heaven: Stories* is released.
2003	August 29: Buys a horse farm outside of Midway, Kentucky. For the sake of consistency in his horse-breeding business, he names it Totier Creek Farm and continues breeding thoroughbreds; it will remain his primary residence until his death.
2004	November 16: *The God of Hell*, produced by the Actors Studio Drama School Theatre, New York, opens.
2005	March 7: With Lange, buys an apartment in New York on Fifth Avenue. May 19: The film *Don't Come Knocking*, directed by Wim Wenders, screenplay by Shepard, and starring Shepard and Lange, premieres at the Cannes Film Festival.
2007	March 15: *Kicking a Dead Horse*, a one-act play written for Northern Irish actor Stephen Rea and directed by Shepard, opens at the Abbey Theatre, Dublin.
2009	March 3: *Ages of the Moon*, a one-act play also starring Stephen Rea with Sean McGinley, opens at the Abbey Theatre, Dublin.
2010	January 12: *Day Out of Days: Stories* is published. Separates from Lange early in the year after almost 30 years together; their breakup is not widely acknowledged until late 2011. Receives a Miller Distinguished Scholarship at the Santa Fe Institute, where he writes from December 2010 to December 2011. He will buy property in Santa Fe in November 2011 and continue to work at the Institute until 2015, mostly working on *Heartless* and *A Particle of Dread*, and dividing his time, not including film acting, between New Mexico and Kentucky.
2011	June 15: *Evanescence, or Shakespeare in the Alley* premieres in the three-part festival "10 x 25," a series of 10-minute plays by 25 playwrights, at the Atlantic Theater Company's Atlantic Stage 2 Theater in New York.

2012   August 7: *Heartless*, notably his first full-length play in which the majority of the cast are women, premieres at Signature Theatre in New York. December 7: Receives an Honorary Degree from Trinity College, Dublin.

2013   September 25: *Shepard and Dark*, a documentary about Shepard's long friendship with John Dark is released. October 13: *2 Prospectors: The Letters of Sam Shepard & Johnny Dark*, edited by Chad Hammett, is published. November 28: *A Particle of Dread*, Shepard's last new play produced in his lifetime, premieres at the Derry Playhouse, Derry, Northern Ireland; the production will move to New York's Signature Theatre the following fall, opening on November 23, 2014.

2017   February 7: *The One Inside*, Shepard's first novel, is published. June 18: *Never Here*, the final film in which Shepard acts, is released. July 27: Dies at home in Midway, Kentucky, age 73, from complications of ALS, also known as Lou Gehrig's disease. December 5: *Spy of the First Person*, a novelistic account of his physical and mental struggle with ALS, is published posthumously.

**Conversations with
Sam Shepard**

Sam Shepard: Writer on the Way Up

Mel Gussow / 1969

From *New York Times*, November 12, 1969, p. 42. © 1969 The New York Times Company. All rights reserved. Used under license. Mel Gussow was a theater critic for the *New York Times* for 35 years. He is the author of *Don't Say Yes Until I Finish Talking: A Biography of Darryl F. Zanuck* (1971), *Theater on the Edge: New Visions, New Voices* (1998), *Edward Albee: A Singular Journey* (1999), and *Gambon: A Life in Acting* (2005).

For five years, young Sam Shepard—he just turned 26, and got married—has been the most prolific and prominent playwright in the underground theater.

Only rarely has he surfaced even to Off-Broadway, but in the coming months he will be all over the place.

The Unseen Hand, directed by the author, opens the second week of December at Café La MaMa. Two of his one-acters, *Back Bog Beast Bait* and *Forensic & the Navigators*, are scheduled for Off-Broadway in mid-January. He is the co-author of Michelangelo Antonioni's *Zabriskie Point*, which opens in mid-December.

Most important of all, his full-length play *Operation Sidewinder* will mark the climax in March of the Lincoln Center season of American plays.

If up to now the commercial theater has been blissfully unaware of Mr. Shepard, he in turn has cherished his invisibility. "I prefer it that way," he said last week. "It's like the primitive feeling that if they take your photograph, your soul gets stolen. When someone's work becomes popular, you lose something."

At least once before he was in danger of success. Several seasons ago he barred critics from seeing his *La Turista*. But Elizabeth Hardwick, the critic, saw it, and proclaimed it "a work of superlative interest." "I didn't think it was a finished thing," says Mr. Shepard, and after a limited run, he coolly packed the play away.

Mr. Shepard, a lanky, loping figure, with the handsomeness and the style of a movie cowboy hero, was born in Fort Sheridan, Ill. In New York at 18, he looked for work as an actor, and took a job as a busboy at the Village Gate and began writing plays.

He never stopped writing, batting out more than 100 plays, some in less than a week. They were done throughout Off-Off-Broadway, many at Theater Genesis in St. Mark's in the Bowery, and by theater groups around the country. To support his non-commercial art, he has had to live on foundation fellowships and, this season, on income from his contribution (a slice of one [of] his plays) to *Oh! Calcutta!* For it, he is paid $68 a week.

Besides writing plays, his major interest is rock music. Recently he played drums and guitar with a group called the Holy Modal Rounders, whom he has written into *Operation Sidewinder*. "In music," he said, "what's commercial is what's really good"—such as the Beatles and the Rolling Stones. (He has written a movie for the Stones called "Maxagasm.")

In the theater, as he sees it, quite the opposite is true. He hardly ever visits Broadway, and in fact, has never seen a play at Lincoln Center. "I couldn't bring myself to go up there," he said. "It's a total bourgeois scene."

He is allowing his play to be done up there with many hesitations. "The main reason is because no one can really afford to do it any place else."

Sidewinder is a sprawling, highly plotted play that involves a snakelike computer, militant blacks, hawkish generals and flying saucers, all of which he believes in. "It's impossible to stage in a poverty situation," he said. "Forty actors! My idea was to write a movie for the stage."

As Mr. Shepard sees it, he is now writing a very different kind of play. For one thing, he is writing slower.

"You get a certain spontaneous freaky thing if you write real fast. You don't get anything heavy unless you spend real time." About his early fast plays, he said, "They're kind of facile. Now I'm dealing more with mythic characters, a combination of science fiction, Westerns and television."

In *Sidewinder* the snaky computer wanders all over the desert, and one of the strange wonders it performs is to strangle and rape a girl.

How will it be done on stage? "The computer does its thing," said Mr. Shepard calmly, "and the girl helps it."

On Sunday, Mr. Shepard married O-Lan Johnson, an actress, at St. Mark's in the Bowery (in a double ceremony with Walter Hadler and Georgia Lee Phillips).

"In a broken world and a polluted land," began the Rev. Michael Allen, "nothing could be more beautiful than a marriage."

After poetry and folk songs, Mr. Allen asked: "Who gives these people to be married to each other?" and the congregation, gayly dressed in antique finery, roared happily: "We do!"

Sam Shepard: Metaphors, Mad Dogs, and Old Time Cowboys

TQ Editors and Kenneth Chubb / 1974

From *Theatre Quarterly* 4 (August–October 1974): 3–16. Copyright © 1974 TQ Publications.
Reprinted with permission of the Licensor through PLSclear.

A one-time prodigy of Off-Broadway who lives in London and wrote his most distinctive American plays in Shepherd's Bush, Sam Shepard has absorbed, during a prolific playwriting career, the accumulative influences of early years in the rich but rootless society of southern California, a period of peak creativity on the Lower East Side—and such untrendy aspects of life in his adopted city as dog racing and draft Guinness. No less than six productions of his plays have been seen in London in the past year, one of the most recent being the first he has himself directed—*Geography of a Horse Dreamer* at the Royal Court. For this interview, the Editors of *TQ* were joined by Kenneth Chubb, director of the Wakefield Tricycle Company, who writes on the problems of directing Shepard's plays later in this issue. An intuitive craftsman, Sam Shepard talks more readily about the experiences that have shaped his work than of the work itself, though he is frank in discussing the lessons he has learned from his directing experience, and the problems of shaping a dramatic idiom that will retain the startling freshness of his best work while remaining accessible to actors. Full descriptive, critical and bibliographic analysis of Sam Shepard's work is available for the first time in the detailed checklist published in the current issue of *TQ*'s companion quarterly, *THEATREFACTS*.

Interviewer: Born 5 November 1943 at Fort Sheridan, Illinois, say my notes. . . .

Sam Shepard: They weren't kidding, it was a real fort, where army mothers had their babies. My father was in Italy then, I think, and we moved around, oh, to Rapid City, South Dakota, to Utah, to Florida—then to the Mariana Islands in the South Pacific, where we lived on Guam. There were three of us children.

Interviewer: Do you remember much about living on Guam?

Shepard: I remember the tin-roofed huts that we lived in, because it used to rain there a lot, and the rain would make this incredible sound on the tin roof. Also there were a lot of Japanese on the island, who had been forced back into living in the caves, and they would come down and steal clothes off the clothes-lines, and food and stuff. All the women were issued with army Lugers, and I remember my mother shooting at them. At that time everyone referred to oriental people or to Filipino people as gooks, and it wasn't until the Vietnam War that I realized that gook was a derogatory term—it had just been part of the army jargon, all the kids called them gooks too.

Interviewer: You were in Guam until your father left the army?

Shepard: Yeah, then we went to live with my aunt in South Pasadena, California—she somehow had some money through my mother's family, so we had a place to stay. But then we found a house of our own in South Pasadena, and I started going to high school.

Interviewer: What were your parents doing then?

Shepard: My dad was still trying to get his degree, after the interruptions of the army, and he had to work for his Bachelors by going to night school. But my mother already had this qualification for teaching kids, so they were working it out with jobs. He was very strict, my father, very aware of the need for discipline, so-called, very into studying and all that kind of stuff. I couldn't stand it—the whole thing of writing in notebooks, it was really like being jailed.

Interviewer: But you did share your father's liking for music?

Shepard: Yes, he used to listen to Dixieland music while he was studying, and he had this band—it wasn't really professional, more of a hobby, though they got paid for it. But he was a drummer, and that's how I learned to play, just banging on his set of drums. And then I started getting better than him.

Interviewer: What was the town like?

Shepard: Oh, one of these white, middle-class, insulated communities—not all that rich, but very proud of the municipal swimming plunge and the ice-skating rink, and all that small-town-America type stuff.

Interviewer: Did you have many friends?

Shepard: Yeah, I did. I had one good friend, Ernie Ernshaw—the first guy I started smoking cigarettes with. Later he joined the navy, and I went back to see him about ten years afterwards, and he'd turned into this Hollywood slick-guy with tight pants and a big fancy hair-do. It was fantastic.

Interviewer: But you left South Pasadena—when you were how old?

Shepard: About 11 or 12, something like that. We moved to this avocado ranch, it was a real nice place actually. It was like a little greenhouse that had been converted into a house, and it had livestock and horses and chickens and stuff like that. Plus about 65 avocado trees.

Interviewer: You worked on the farm?

Shepard: Yeah. You can't depend on the rain in California like you do here, so we had to rig up an irrigation system which had to be operated every day. And we had this little Wisconsin tractor with a spring-tooth harrow and a disc, and I made some money driving that for other people in the neighborhood—there were a lot of citrus groves.

Interviewer: Did you like the change from small-town life?

Shepard: I really liked being in contact with animals and the whole agricultural thing, but it was a bit of a shock leaving the friends I'd made. It was a funny community, divided into three very distinct social groups. There were the very wealthy people, who had ranches up in the mountains with white-faced Hereford cattle roaming around, and swimming pools and Cadillacs. And then you'd get these very straight middle-class communities, people who sold encyclopedias and stuff like that. It was the first place where I understood what it meant to be born on the wrong side of the tracks, because the railroad tracks cut right down through the middle of this place: and below the tracks were the blacks and Mexicans.

Interviewer: Did this create tensions in school?

Shepard: Oh yeah, there were a lot of anxieties. There were these Mexican guys who used to have tattoos and stuff, and I remember the incredible terror of looking into their eyes for even a flash of a second, because without knowing anything previously about the racial thing, just by looking at these guys you knew that you didn't have anything to do with them, and they didn't have anything to do with you. And that they wanted it to stay that way.

Interviewer: Were you a 97-pound weakling or a tough guy?

Shepard: I had a few fist-fights but I wouldn't say that I was a tough guy. I didn't grow until I was about 17 or 18, though, I was about five foot six.

Interviewer: Popular?

Shepard: I found that the friends I had were these sort of strange guys. There was one guy who was from British Columbia—the one I wrote about in *Tooth of Crime*. He'd just come down from Canada, and he looked exactly like Elvis Presley. He had this incredible black hair-do and flash clothes, which nobody wore in school except for a few Mexicans—the white kids all wore ivy league button-down numbers and loafers. So he was immediately ostracized, but he turned out to be a brilliant student—he didn't read any books, just got straight A grades. I got to be really good friends with him. And there were a couple of computer freaks, who were working at this aeronautics plant where they build computers for nose-cones. One guy used to bring in paper bags full of amphetamine and Benzedrine from Mexico. I swear to god, those pills—if you took two of them, you were just flying. And these guys would work in the plant on amphetamine, and steal all these parts and sell them. The pay was really good too, and they got something like triple the money if they worked overtime, so they'd buy these incredible cars and go out stealing and looting . . . all on Benzedrine and amphetamine.

Interviewer: Were they older than you, these guys?

Shepard: Yes, everybody was older than me, because I was born in November, so I was always one year younger than everybody in my class.

Interviewer: But you really just wanted to leave high school as soon as you could?

Shepard: Oh yeah, everybody did. I was thinking that I wanted to be a veterinarian. And I had a chance actually to manage a sheep ranch, but I didn't take it. I wanted to do something like that, working with animals. I even had the grand champion yearling ram at the Los Angeles County Fair one year. I did. It was a great ram.

Interviewer: Quite a break from this very pastoral sort of prospect, when you decided to go to New York?

Shepard: Yeah. At that time the whole beat generation was the big influence. It was just before the time of acid and the big dope freakout, which was then still very much under cover. We talked about Ferlinghetti and Corso and Kerouac and all those guys, and jazz. . . .

Interviewer: But you weren't writing yourself?

Shepard: No. I mean, I tried poetry and stuff, but it was pretty bad. But I went to New York with this guy Charles, who was a painter, and really just liked that whole idea of being independent, of being able to do something on your own. I tried to get into the acting scene in New York, though I really very soon dropped out of that. We were living on the Lower East Side, and there were these jazz musicians, Dannie Richmond who played drums, and

I got into this really exciting music scene. The world I was living in was the most interesting thing to me, and I thought the best thing I could do maybe would be to write about it, so I started writing plays.

Interviewer: Why plays, rather than novels or poetry?

Shepard: I always liked the idea that plays happened in three dimensions, that here was something that came to life in space rather than in a book. I never liked books or read very much.

Interviewer: Did you write anything before you started getting performed?

Shepard: Well, I'd written one very bad play in California—a sort of Tennessee Williams imitation, about some girl who got raped in a barn and her father getting mad at her or something . . . I forget. But the first play I wrote in New York was *Cowboys*.

Interviewer: Cowboys, why cowboys? Cowboys figure largely in lots of your plays. . . .

Shepard: Cowboys are really interesting to me—these guys, most of them really young, about 16 or 17, who decided they didn't want to have anything to do with the East Coast, with that way of life, and took on this immense country, and didn't have any real rules. Just moving cattle, from Texas to Kansas City, from the North to the South, or wherever it was.

Interviewer: Why *Cowboys No. 2*, not just another title?

Shepard: Well, I wrote the original *Cowboys*, and then I rewrote it and called it *No. 2*, that's all. The original is lost now—but, anyway, it got done at St. Mark's. And that just happened because Charles and me used to run around the streets playing cowboys in New York. We'd both had the experience of growing up in California, in that special kind of environment, and between the two of us there was a kind of camaraderie, in the midst of all these people who were into going to work and riding the buses. In about 1963, anyway—five years or so later it all suddenly broke down.

Interviewer: Had you had much to do with live theater?

Shepard: I hardly knew anything about the theater. I remember once in California I went to this guy's house who was called a beatnik by everybody in the school because he had a beard and he wore sandals. And we were listening to some jazz or something and he sort of shuffled over to me and threw this book on my lap and said, why don't you dig this, you know. I started reading this play he gave me, and it was like nothing I'd ever read before—it was *Waiting for Godot*. And I thought, what's this guy talking about, what is this? And I read it with a very keen interest, but I didn't know anything about what it *was*. I didn't really have any references for the theater, except for the few plays that I'd acted in. But in a way I think that was better for me, because I didn't have any idea about how to shape an action into what is seen—so the so-called originality of the early work just comes from ignorance. I just didn't know.

Interviewer: You were writing very prolifically around those early years.

Shepard: Yeah, there was nothing else to do.

Interviewer: So what were you doing for money?

Shepard: I was working at a place called the Village Gate, which is a big night club. Charles had a job there as a waiter, and he got me a job there too, and later I found out that all the waiters there were either actors or directors or painters or something like that who were out of work. It was a nice place to work because I got to see like the *cream* of American jazz, night after night for free. Plus I got paid for working there.

Interviewer: It was at night-time so you were free during the day?

Shepard: Right. I worked three nights a week, and got about 50 bucks a week for doing hardly anything, except cleaning up dishes and bringing Nina Simone ice, you know. It was fantastic.

Interviewer: All those early plays give the impression that once you'd got the habit you couldn't stop. . . .

Shepard: Yeah, I used to write very fast, I mean I wrote *Chicago* in one day. The stuff would just come out, and I wasn't really trying to shape it or make it into any big thing.

Interviewer: You wrote without any sort of planning?

Shepard: Yeah. I would have like a picture, and just start from there. A picture of a guy in a bathtub, or of two guys on stage with the sign blinking—you know, things like that.

Interviewer: How important was it to you when your plays started to get performed?

Shepard: It was frightening at first. I can remember defending myself against it mostly. I was really young for one thing, about 19, and I was very uptight about making a whole public thing out of something that you do privately. And I was strongly influenced by Charles—he was very into not selling out, and keeping himself within his own sphere of reference. I felt that by having the play become public, it was almost like giving it away or something. I was really hard to get along with in those days, actually. I would always bitch a lot during rehearsals and break things up. . . .

Interviewer: How did *Cowboys* first come to get on stage?

Shepard: The head waiter at the Village Gate was a guy named Ralph Cook, and he had been given this church, called St. Mark's in the Bowery, and he started a theater there called Theater Genesis. He said he was looking for new plays to do, and I said I had one. He came up and he read this play, and two of the waiters at the Village Gate were the actors in it. So it was sort of the Village Gate company. Well, Jerry Talmer from the *Post* came, and all these guys said it was a bunch of shit, imitated Beckett or something like that. I was ready to pack it in and go back to California. Then Michael Smith from *Village Voice* came up with this rave review, and people started coming to see it.

Interviewer: Did these early plays change much, between writing and the public performances?

Shepard: The writing didn't change, I never changed the words. That's even true now, but, depending on the people you have, the performance changes. I was very lucky to have arrived in New York at that time, though, because the whole Off-Off-Broadway theater was just starting—like Ellen Stewart with her little cafe, and Joe Cino, and the Judson Poets' Theater and all these places. It was just a lucky accident really that I arrived at the same time as that was all starting. This was before they had all become famous, of course—like Ellen just had this little loft, served hot chocolate and coffee, did these plays.

Interviewer: So how much money did you make from those early plays—not very much?

Shepard: No money. There wasn't any money at all, until the grants started coming in from Ford and Rockefeller and all these places that were supporting the theaters because of the publicity they started getting. Then they began paying the actors and playwrights—but it wasn't much, 100 dollars for five weeks' work or something.

Interviewer: How much did it matter to you that critics like Michael Smith started writing approvingly about your plays?

Shepard: Well, it changes everything you know, from being something that you do in quite a private way to something that you do publicly. Because no matter how much you don't like the critics, or you don't want them to pass judgment on what you're doing, the fact that they're there reflects the fact that a play's being done in public. It means that you steadily become aware of people going to see your plays—of audiences. Not just critics, but people.

Interviewer: Did you feel part of this developing Off-Off-Broadway "movement"?

Shepard: Not in anything to do with stagecraft so much as in the ingredients that go into a play. . . . On the Lower East Side there *was* a special sort of culture developing. You were so close to the people who were going to the plays, there was really no difference between you and them—your own experience was their experience, so that you began to develop that consciousness of what was happening. . . . I mean nobody knew what *was* happening. But there was a sense that something was going on. People were arriving from Texas and Arkansas in the middle of New York City, and a community was being established. It was a very exciting time.

Interviewer: Did you begin to think of playwriting as your real job?

Shepard: Well, I never thought of it as my job, because it was something that made me feel more relaxed, whereas I always thought of jobs as something that made you feel less alive—you know, the thing of working ten hours a day cleaning horseshit out of a stable.

Interviewer: Did the second play, *Rock Garden,* also emerge from your experience of New York?

Shepard: *Rock Garden* is about leaving my mom and dad. It happens in two scenes. In the first scene the mother is lying in bed ill while the son is sitting in a chair, and she's talking about this special sort of cookie that she makes, which is marshmallow on salt crackers melted under the oven. It's called angels on horseback, and she has a monologue about it. And then the father arrives in the second scene. The boy doesn't say anything, he's just sitting in this chair, and the father starts to talk about painting the fence around the house, and there's a monologue about that in the course of which the boy keeps dropping asleep and falling off his chair. Finally the boy has a monologue about orgasm that goes on for a couple of pages and ends in him coming all over the place, and then the father falls off the chair. The father also talks about this rock garden, which is his obsession, a garden where he collects all these rocks from different sojourns to the desert.

Interviewer: The orgasm scene was the one used in *Oh! Calcutta!* wasn't it?

Shepard: Yes—that production was pretty bad, and the play hasn't been done much in its entirety. Theater Genesis did the first production, but I don't think it's been seen in England.

Interviewer: Then came *Up to Thursday?*

Shepard: Yes. *Up to Thursday* was a bad exercise in absurdity, I guess. This kid is sleeping in an American flag, he's only wearing a jockstrap or something, and there's four people on stage who keep shifting their legs and talking. I can't remember it very well—it's only been done once. It was a terrible play, really. It was the first commercial production I'd done, and it was put on with a bunch of other plays, in this Off-Off-Broadway-moves-Off-Broadway kind of bill.

Interviewer: What about *Dog* and *Rocking Chair*?

Shepard: *Dog* was about a black guy—which later I found out it was un-cool for a white to write about in America. It was about a black guy on a park bench, a sort of *Zoo Story*–type play. I don't even remember *Rocking Chair*, except it was about somebody in a rocking chair.

Interviewer: How do you feel about those early plays now—a bit vague, it seems!

Shepard: Yeah, the thing is, I find it hard to remain with a certain attach-ment to things that I wrote. I've heard that a lot of writers make reams of notes before they even go into the thing, but with me I write plays before I go into something else. I may like write six one-act plays before I get to an-other kind of a play, and each play may be a sort of evolution to something else. I always feel like leaving those behind rather than hanging on to them.

Interviewer: You say the texts don't change much in rehearsal—do you revise much while you're writing?

Shepard: I hate to rewrite, but I can see the importance of it, mainly be-cause of what it means for an actor to actually meet the task of doing this thing on stage. Just from directing *Geography of a Horse Dreamer* myself, I've found I think I'm often too flippant about what I write—it's too easy to dash something off and say, okay, now act it: because when it comes down to the flesh-and-blood thing of making it work, it's a different world. I think that's where rewriting comes in—if it seems that the angle that the actor has to come at is too impossible or too difficult.

Interviewer: So it's revision of the mechanics rather than of the lan-guage . . . ?

Shepard: It may be that there's a hole somewhere that needs to be blocked. Something missing.

Interviewer: Are you concerned at all about how accessible your plays are going to be to an audience? I'm thinking of how you described earlier the common background of experience you shared in those early New York years. But now, obviously, you're going to be writing for wider audiences, who don't necessarily share any similarities of background. How far are you, or aren't you, concerned to give them a way in?

Shepard: It depends on whether you're writing in social terms, or whether the things that you're taking on can cut through that somehow. You always *start* with some sort of social terms, because of being white, or living in England, or whatever the conditions are, but hopefully it can then cut into something that everybody has some touch with—otherwise it just remains a kind of *cozy* accessibility.

Interviewer: Isn't there a change, too, between the exclusive emphasis on private worlds in the very early plays, and the almost political sense of an outside threat in *Icarus's Mother*?

Shepard: People talk about political consciousness as though it were a thing that you could decide in your head—that you can shift your ways of thinking and suddenly you have political consciousness. But I found that, especially in America, it came from the emotional context that you were moving in. I mean, people in New York are cutting themselves down every day of the week—from the inside, you know, but the conditions come from the outside. Junk, heroin and all that stuff is a social condition and it's also an emotional response to the society they're living in. . . . But I don't have any political theories, if that's what you mean.

Interviewer: Around the time we're talking of in the States, it was the peak of the anti-Bomb movement in England—were you caught up in anything like that?

Shepard: I was in a few Civil Rights marches and stuff like that—but it's different. When you see that on the news it's one thing, but when you're in it it's a different thing, it's a whole different thing.

Interviewer: Can you say something about how *Icarus's Mother* germinated?

Shepard: I was in Wisconsin, in Milwaukee, and for the Fourth of July we have this celebration—fireworks and all that kind of stuff—and I was in this sort of park with these people, with this display going on. You begin to have a feeling of this historical thing being played out in contemporary terms—I didn't even know what the Fourth of July meant, really, but here was this celebration taking place, with explosions. One of the weird things about being in America now, though I haven't been there much lately, is that you don't have any connection with the past, with what history means: so you can be there celebrating the Fourth of July, but all you know is that things are exploding in the sky. And then you've got this emotional thing that goes a long way back, which creates a certain kind of chaos, a kind of terror, you don't know what the fuck's going on. It's really hard to grab the whole of the experience.

Interviewer: And that's the circling airplane—Icarus's mother . . . ?

Shepard: There's a vague kind of terror going on, the people not really knowing what is happening. . . .

Interviewer: How "real" is the image in *4-H Club* of those four guys in a kitchen killing rats?

Shepard: Well, there's a big rat problem in New York, but maybe some of the people who talk about poverty and so on never had a rat in their house.

And it's different when you have a rat in your house—doesn't all come down to talk.

Interviewer: Had you experienced that kind of poverty?

Shepard: Yeah, in New York, sure—unless you have a million dollars lots of people experience that in New York. . . .

Interviewer: About your next play, *Fourteen Hundred Thousand*—I get the feeling that it changes direction two-thirds of the way through—there's this play about building a bookshelf, and this other play about a linear city. . . .

Shepard: Yeah, I had a long talk with an architect before I wrote that play, and stuck that into it. I was very interested in the idea of the linear city, because it struck me as being a strong visual conception as opposed to radial cities—the idea of having a whole country, especially like America, with these lines cutting across them. . . .

Interviewer: It makes a tremendous climax but it seems like the climax to another play somehow. . . .

Shepard: Yeah, right.

Interviewer: To go back to what you were saying earlier about your plays developing from images, from mental pictures—was this a case of the image, as it were, switching halfway through? And how should the switch work theatrically?

Shepard: When you talk about images, an image can be seen without looking at anything—you can see something in your head, or you can see something on stage, or you can see things that don't appear on stage, you know. The fantastic thing about theater is that it can make something be seen that's invisible, and that's where my interest in theater is—that you can be watching this thing happening with actors and costumes and light and set and language, and even plot, and something emerges from beyond that, and that's the image part that I'm looking for, that's the sort of added dimension.

Interviewer: Does *Fourteen Hundred Thousand* maybe represent a kind of watershed between these early plays, which were largely concerned with simple . . . well, not really simple, but single images, and the plays after this, which start to get very much more complex—and maybe the characters too start moving from the ordinary towards the extraordinary . . . ?

Shepard: They're the *same* people, but the situations are different. What I was interested in was, like, you see somebody, and you have an impression of that person from seeing them—the way they talk and behave—but underneath many, many different possibilities could be going on. And the possibilities that I brought out, like in *Icarus*, could have taken a completely different direction. It's not as though you started out with a character who suddenly developed into another character—it's the same character, who's enlivened by animals, or demons, or whatever is inside of him. Everybody's like that. . . .

Interviewer: But I still feel that the plays get more complex—perhaps that the early plays are images, the later plays are more like metaphors—creating not one segment of a society through a fairly direct image, but finding another way of representing it—say in *The Tooth of Crime.*

Shepard: To me, that's the only thing I can do, because . . . first of all, I don't know what this world is. I mean, look at it. Like when you look at Ted Heath and Harold Wilson giving their opinions and trying to sell people on their programs. If you showed those two guys on the stage it would be as boring as watching them on television—it wouldn't have any other dimension to it. Satire is another thing, but there's very few people can do it really well—Jules Feiffer, but even he has to create another world to show something about this one. . . .

Interviewer: Well, can we try another tack—clearly the early plays, from what you said about them, have their origins in your own childhood and adolescent world, and you're writing about that world. What are you harking back to, where do the images come from, for the later plays?

Shepard: Well, they come from all kinds of things, they come from the country, they come from that particular part of the country, they come from that particular sort of temporary society that you find in southern California, where nothing is permanent, where everything could be knocked down and it wouldn't be missed, and the feel of impermanence that comes from that—that you don't belong to any particular culture. I mean it wasn't until I came to England that I found out what it means to be an American. Nothing really makes sense when you're there, but the more distant you are from it, the more the implications of what you grew up with start to emerge.

Interviewer: Is there a point at which you stopped writing plays about southern California, say, and started writing plays about New York?

Shepard: Yeah, but it's very hard to talk about, because . . . obviously, if you were writing in Jamaica, you'd be writing under a different influence, or even if a man wanted to write about the Industrial Revolution in England but went to South Africa to do it, he'd be writing under those conditions. He'd have to take on the conditions of where he's writing, he can't escape that.

Interviewer: But all these things are accumulative, aren't they? You really haven't lost any of the early influences, you've simply put influences on. I mean, *Geography of a Horse Dreamer* is about dog racing in London, which is very much your immediate experience, and yet there's something very reminiscent in all your later work of the early plays. Is that the way the plays are building, complicating themselves as they go on, and maybe becoming more interesting the more complicated they get?

Shepard: Well, I don't know if they're more complicated, they're *different*, because, yes, you accumulate the experience of having written all those other plays, so they're all in you somewhere. But sometimes it gets in the way—you sit down and you find yourself writing the same play, which is a drag. Terrible feeling when you suddenly find yourself doing the same thing over and over again. . . .

Interviewer: How conscious are you of length when you write—do you write a short play consciously, or a long play, or does it just make its own length?

Shepard: Oh yeah, it makes its own length. The term full-length to me doesn't make any sense, because people call a two-act or a three-act play, or a play with a certain number of pages, a full-length play, but I think it's ridiculous, because . . . well, Beckett wrote *Come and Go* and it's five pages long but it's full-length, whereas some of O'Neill's. . . . No, people are always making distinctions about full-length plays, and I think it's really a shame that it's gotten into that kind of groove.

Interviewer: Well, I was going to ask, and perhaps I'll ask it anyway—it seems to me that quite apart from one being an early play and one being a later play, a great deal more conscious craftsmanship, or shaping, would have to go into writing say *Tooth of Crime* than say *Chicago*.

Shepard: No, I don't think so. Your craftsmanship always comes from some interior thing, it's not something you can stick onto the play to make it have a style or a form—it has to come out of what's making the play, what's motivating the play. It's not the size of it, it's the quality of it. I guess it's just a matter of terms really, but to me *Tooth of Crime* performs a different quality than *Chicago* does. Put another way, it's playing for different stakes. You can play for the high stakes or the low stakes, or you can play for a compromise in between: maybe *Geography* was playing for more modest stakes than *Tooth of Crime*. But what makes a play is how true it is to the stakes that you defined at the beginning.

Interviewer: But how do you define them—how did you know, say, that *Tooth of Crime* was going to play for high stakes?

Shepard: It's an interesting thing that happened with that play, because I wrote it in London—it's been called an American play, right, but it was written in the middle of Shepherd's Bush, and for about a month before that I was struggling to write this other play called *The Tooth of Crime*, which was a three-act epic number in a jail . . . and at the end it was a complete piece of shit, so I put it in the sink and burnt it, and then an hour later I started to write this one that's been performed. So, no, it's not so easy to say what it is when you sit down and write a play. You can sit down and say, now I know all the ingredients that are going to go into this and I'm shooting for something very big, and then you begin to write, and it may work out or it may not. The next time you may sit down, and say, I don't have an idea in my head, and yet something incredible may come out, you know. It has to do with the conditions at the time you sit down and write.

Interviewer: Fair enough. So say *Chicago* starts with the idea, the image, of a bloke in a bathtub—what does something like *Tooth of Crime* start with—what did it start with?

Shepard: It started with language—it started with hearing a certain sound which is coming from the voice of this character, Hoss. And also this sort of black figure appearing on stage with this throne, and the whole kind of world that he was involved in, came from this voice—I don't mean it was any weird psychological voice in the air thing, but that it was a very real kind of sound that I heard, and I started to write the play from there. It just accumulated force as I wrote it.

Interviewer: We've rather jumped to this very American play written in Shepherd's Bush: can you say something about your reasons for coming to London from New York?

Shepard: Well, when I first got to New York it was wide open, you were like a kid in a fun park, but then as it developed, as more and more elements came into it, things got more and more insane—you know, the difference between living in New York and working in New York became wider and wider, so that you were doing this thing called *theater* in these little places and you were bringing your so-called experience to it, and then going back and living in this kind of tight, insular, protective way, where you were defending yourself. And also I was into a lot of drugs then—it became very difficult you know, everything seemed to be sort of shattering. I didn't feel like going back to California, so I thought I'd come here—really to get into music, you know. I was in a band in New York, and I'd heard that this was the rock 'n' roll center of the world—so I came here with that kind of idea. London was notorious for its rock 'n' roll bands, and my favorite bands are The Who, groups like that, so I had this fantasy that I'd come over here and somehow fall into a rock 'n' roll band. It didn't work. . . .

Interviewer: In spite of the fact that people were already saying that you were the darling of Off-Broadway, you wanted to get into something else?

Shepard: I really wanted to find another kind of thing over here. I much prefer playing music really to theater, but it's hard to find the right situation.

Interviewer: Yet music doesn't seem to have played a large part in many of your plays, has it? People talk about there being a musical structure to your plays, which I'm sure is intuitive, and there have been a couple of plays which have had music connected with them—the one where it's most integral is *Mad Dog Blues*. But certainly in *The Tooth of Crime*, though it may have been the production I saw rather than anything else, the music seemed rather superficially connected. . . .

Shepard: It depends what you mean by music. I think music's really important, especially in plays and theater—it adds a whole different kind of perspective, it immediately brings the audience to terms with an emotional reality. Because nothing communicates emotions better than music, not even the greatest play in the world. But it's not a question of just putting music in plays. First of all there may be some plays that don't require music, like *Geography of a Horse Dreamer*—I've used music from records, but there wasn't any opportunity really for songs or anything like that.

Interviewer: But there was lots of room for it in *Tooth of Crime*, and yet it wasn't really used integrally?

Shepard: Yeah, I know what you're saying. I wanted the music in *Tooth of Crime* so that you could step out of the play for a minute, every time a song comes, and be brought to an emotional comment on what's been taking place in the play. When you go back to the play you go back to the spoken word, then when a song comes again, it takes you out of it just a little bit. I wanted the music to be used as a kind of sounding-board for the play, you know. At the Open Space, I worked with the band that did the music, Blunderpuss, and it was never right—they're a really good band, but *because* they're a band that already has an identity of its own, you're starting with the type of music that they can perform, that they've been used to performing, and the most you can get is a good compromise. The only way to do it really is to gather musicians together independently who can get along with each other and know how to play and create the music from scratch. That's what we'll do in the Royal Court production, so hopefully the music will be a little truer to the way it was written.

Interviewer: You say you think music can potentially affect an audience much more strongly than even the best playwright's words . . . ?

Shepard: Oh, yeah.

Interviewer: How do you feel about the vogue for so-called rock operas?

Shepard: I haven't ever seen a good rock opera. But I don't think that the music in theater necessarily has to take on a rock 'n' roll idiom—it could be any kind of music. What I think is that music, no matter what its structure, has a very powerful emotional influence, it can't help but have that—it's in the nature of music, it's when you can play a note and there's a response immediately—you don't have to build up to it through seven scenes.

Interviewer: Can you think of a play or a production which has achieved the impact you're talking about?

Shepard: With music? Brecht's plays. Plays like *Mahagonny*. He's my favorite playwright, Brecht. If you look at *Jungle of Cities*, it's a play—a bout, between these two characters, taken in a completely open-ended way, the bout is never defined as being anything but metaphysical.

Interviewer: Do you think the music works in Brecht in the way he wanted it to work, as a means of distancing?

Shepard: I never saw a production that he did, and I've seen very few good Brecht productions. It's very hard to do.

Interviewer: What effect would you like a play of yours—one that you really felt totally happy with, play and production—to have on an audience?

Shepard: Well, it depends on the play, but hopefully it would be something that would transform the emotions of the people watching. People come into the theater in very different circumstances, expecting something to happen, and then hopefully when they walk out of the theater the chemistry's changed. What specifically that is depends on the material of the play, because every play's different.

Interviewer: I find it rather surprising when you say things like that, that you haven't written a play that has required an environmental situation—some sort of a situation in which the audience comes into the play, or comes into a space that the play has taken over. . . .

Shepard: There's a whole myth about environmental theater as it's being practiced now in New York. The myth is that in order for the audience to be actively participating in the event that they're watching they have to be physically sloshed into something, which isn't true at all. An audience can sit in chairs and be watching something in front of them, and can be actively participating in the thing that's confronting them, you know. And it doesn't necessarily mean that if an audience walks into the building and people are swinging from the rafters and spaghetti's thrown all over them, or whatever the environment might be, that their participation in the play is going to be any closer. In fact it might very well be less so, because of the defenses that are put up as soon as that happens.

Interviewer: Can one relate that to Dick Schechner's production of *Tooth of Crime*?

Shepard: Well, I think he's lost. . . . I think he's lost in a certain area of experimentation which is valid for him. He feels that he wants to experiment with the environment of theater, which is okay, I've nothing against it. Except when you write a play it sets up certain assumptions about the context in which it's to be performed, and in that play they had nothing to do with what Schechner set up in the theater. You can take that or leave it. It can be okay—the playwright isn't a holy man, you know. Except I'd rather that the experimentation took place with something that left itself open to that—a play that from the start defines its context as undefinable, so that you can fuck around with it if you want to.

Interviewer: Do you visualize a particular type of performance space when you're writing—proscenium arch, open stage conditions, or whatever?

Shepard: Yes, sometimes I see a play in a particular theater, in a particular place—like I used to for Theater Genesis, because I was so familiar with that environment. . . .

Interviewer: Has it proved important that those plays should go on being done in that sort of theater?

Shepard: It's important in terms of the size of the play—in other words the number of characters. For one thing you feel that if you have too many people involved in a production it can only be done in very special financial circumstances—you can only have it done in Lincoln Center, for instance, which turns out to be a disaster, and from there on it can't really be performed in colleges or anything like that because it's too expensive. It's important to take into consideration the general environment the play's going to hit. It's more important to have a five-character play or less that can be done in a close, non-financial situation than it is to have a circus.

Interviewer: Have you seen many amateur and student productions of your plays? Do you think they work with amateurs and students?

Shepard: Yeah, sure. Again it depends on the play, some plays work very well with amateurs.

Interviewer: I was thinking, almost by analogy with Brecht, that maybe amateurs and students, not approaching your work with actorish preconceptions, might find a better style on occasions.

Shepard: Well, there's a certain excitement goes on with that kind of thing, because you know it's not being performed in this kind of blown-up way, it's not being performed for an anonymous audience—it's being done very specifically for people everybody knows.

Interviewer: How specifically do you conceive a play being staged when you're actually writing it?

Shepard: This experience with *Horse Dreamer* opened my eyes to all the possibilities of productions, because I've been very opinionated about productions before.

Interviewer: You've not found yourself getting on with your directors?

Shepard: Very rarely have I got on with them, except for a few instances.

Interviewer: You take an active part in rehearsals nonetheless? Where you can?

Shepard: Sometimes—it depends on the situation, it depends who you're working with. I like to take part in rehearsals, it's just very delicate, you have to watch out, it's easy to say the wrong things to the actors.

Interviewer: Was *Horse Dreamer* the first play of your own you've directed?

Shepard: Yeah, first time I ever did it. I much prefer working in England, though, because the actors I've found are much better equipped to do things. . . .

Interviewer: Technically?

Shepard: No, not only technically, but in other ways, like these guys I've gotten in *Horse Dreamer*, who are fantastic—the best actors I've ever worked with, they're really great. In New York you're lucky if you find anybody. Everybody's acting, and doing some lifestyle sort of thing at the same time, sort of mixing their lifestyles with their acting, so it's very hard to get the same dedication.

Interviewer: In terms of your future relationship with directors have you learned anything from directing *Horse Dreamer*?

Shepard: Well, I've learned that it's very important to have patience, and that things can't be rushed. I've learned that the rehearsal process is actually a process. The reason it takes three or four or five or six weeks is because it actually needs that amount of time to evolve. Whereas I used to think that a production was a miracle act, that actors very suddenly came to the play and it was realized in a matter of days. But that's not true, it takes a great deal of time, and in the production at the Court now, they're still finding things, still working on things and bringing new things to it.

Interviewer: Do you think you've found that a particular kind of rehearsal process suits your plays—from reading to blocking to working, or whatever?

Shepard: When I first went into this thing, because I didn't have any experience I called up several different directors that I knew and said, could you fill me in on the details? And some of them told me some very interesting things about the way they worked, the sort of process, but I found none of it held true for this particular experience. It's very like writing—you can't have any set kind of preconceptions about what it's going to be. You can *say* first week we're going to read it, second week we're going to block it, third week we're going to churn it out, but it doesn't make any difference, because when you get to the actual thing it makes its own rules.

Interviewer: So how did the rules work out?

Shepard: The rules came from the actors. Because they were so good and they've had so much experience, it wasn't me making absolute decisions, though I saw things that they were doing and pointed them out, and then try to mold a little bit from what they were doing.

Interviewer: There is a problem it seems to me, insofar as there are styles of playing on the one hand, and there are very clear literary things happening in the writing on the other, and sometimes the two don't quite go together. Did you find that at all with *Geography of a Horse Dreamer*?

Shepard: That play is different because it's more structured, it's more straightforward in its plot and that kind of thing. I think what you're talking about does come into a play like *Icarus's Mother*, though, which is really a bitch to produce. It's very difficult for actors to do—being physically there on stage and having monologues that run for a page and a half—to bridge that gap between the language and the physical acting of the play. Is that what you're talking about?

Interviewer: Yes—do you think you're getting closer to bridging that gap now?

Shepard: Yeah. One of the things I've found is that it's too much to expect an actor to do a vocal aria, standing there in the middle of the stage and have the thing work in space, without actually having him physically involved in what he's talking about. The speeches have been shaved quite considerably since the early plays, I don't go in for long speeches anymore.

Interviewer: Although there are some quite beautiful and very long speeches in *The Unseen Hand*.

Shepard: Yeah, right. But even so, even that is difficult, like I said.

Interviewer: But the first speech, for example, where Blue is on stage by himself. . . .

Shepard: He's got something to do, he's working with the car, and he's on the highway. . . . The imagery comes out of the situation. It also does in the earlier plays, except that there the characters are physically marooned by their speaking, which makes it hard.

Interviewer: What do you think about the criticism that's been made of *Geography of a Horse Dreamer*, that it doesn't contain the intensity of language of *Tooth of Crime* or *The Unseen Hand*?

Shepard: Well, I can see how people would be disappointed if they found that the language filled them out more, gave them more of a thing to spring from, but it's just not right for this play. It's not a play that's investigating a whole complicated language scheme. I was using language from Raymond Chandler, from Dashiell Hammett—from the thirties, which to me is a beautiful kind of language, and very idiomatic of a period in America which was really strong.

Interviewer: Is there something you can turn on without thinking—a particular idiom, whether it's of rock music or Dashiell Hammett—or do you have to think yourself into it?

Shepard: You have to make an adjustment, you have to sort of click into something: a trigger is set off, and then you're able to do it. . . .

Interviewer: Why the combination of the dog racing theme and the Raymond Chandler style? They're pretty disparate elements, aren't they?

Shepard: Not really, no, they both have to do with crime and the underworld. Raymond Chandler actually visited London a lot—he dug London. He never got involved in dog racing, but I think the kind of working-class people here who go to dog racing talk in the English version of what that American idiom is.

Interviewer: How did you get involved in the dog racing scene—what was the fascination?

Shepard: Well, I loved horseracing before, I really used to like the horse track, we lived right near one. But it's very expensive, as far as actually getting involved in it. Then when I came here I found dog racing is the second biggest spectator sport in England, you've got twelve tracks or something, and suddenly it was like all your romantic childhood dreams come true—only with dogs. So I thought, shit, this is great, and I got involved in it. It's really a sort of romantic impulse, you know. Being around the track, punters and all that kind of stuff—I like that world.

Interviewer: Do you consider yourself a romantic?

Shepard: What does that mean?

Interviewer: Well, you've been talking about things being romantic, in that they obviously have a primarily emotional pull. . . .

Shepard: Like for instance Wyoming . . . yes, just in that a thing pulls me in a certain way. In that sense I'm a romantic.

Interviewer: And in the sense that you don't pre-structure your plays?

Shepard: Yeah, but I wouldn't say that that was necessarily romantic. I like poetry a lot, I like the impulse that makes poetry happen, the feeling that language can occur out of an emotional context. I mean, it's not any specific poetry, it's just that I think that theater especially has a lot of room for that.

Interviewer: Is there maybe something romantic about your preoccupation with death, too?

Shepard: Death? The idea of dying and being reborn is really an interesting one, you know. It's always there at the back of my head.

Interviewer: In a religious, or metaphysical, or philosophical way, or what?

Shepard: In real terms, what it means to die and be born again. I mean, you can call it religious if you want. It's something I've wanted somehow to get into, but I've never really found how to make it work in the plays.

Interviewer: Were you raised in a religion?

Shepard: Yes, I was, but that's not necessarily where it's coming from—I was raised as an Episcopalian . . . but that was another kind of prison to get out of, you know. There's nothing worse than listening to a lot of people mumbling, and outside the sun is shining . . . but you have this personality, and somehow feel locked into it, jailed by all of your cultural influences and your psychological ones from your family, and all that. And somehow I feel that that isn't the whole of it, you know, that there's another possibility.

Interviewer: You still feel yourself escaping from those influences?

Shepard: You can't escape, that's the whole thing, you can't. You finally find yourself in a situation where, like, that's the way it is—you can't get out of it. But there is always that impulse towards another kind of world, something that doesn't necessarily confine you in that way. Like I've got a name, I speak English, I have gestures, wear a certain kind of clothes . . . but once upon a time I didn't have all that shit.

Interviewer: Do you have any ideas about the way you're going as a dramatist?

Shepard: I wish I did. I don't know. I'd like to try a whole different way of writing now, which is very stark and not so flashy and not full of a lot of mythic figures and everything, and try to scrape it down to the bone as much as possible.

Interviewer: But not realism?

Shepard: Well, it could be called realism, but not the kind of realism where husbands and wives squabble and that kind of stuff.

Interviewer: Are you keen to direct your own plays again, or to consider directing somebody else's?

Shepard: Yeah, without having a great deal of time to think about it first, though I wouldn't want to plunge right into another one. But that's a whole area of possibilities—where you begin to find out what it really means to write a play. That it isn't a piece of paper, it's something that's really happening in real life. And the more you find out about it the more you can grow as a writer. I'm very interested in the kind of chemistry that goes on with directing, finding the right language to use with the actors, finding the way an actor works. Every single actor in *Horse Dreamer* worked in a completely different way, and it took a couple of weeks to find that out. I was saying the same things to everybody, and then I began to find that you have to talk differently to each actor—something you say to one guy doesn't mean a thing to the next guy.

Interviewer: Is it important what people, professional critics or others, say about your plays?

Shepard: Well, it would be silly to say that I'm immune to it, because it affects you in one way or another. But with this particular play I'm not particularly concerned about the press criticism, because it's been such a strong experience. For three weeks you've been working with people, going through this very intricate process, and you arrive at this thing, and then it's judged by people who've never seen anything until that moment. So whatever they say about it, whether they like it or don't like it, whether it's constructive criticism or not, it doesn't have anything to do with that process that went on. I mean, that's what's important to me, and that's really the life of the play.

Interviewer: Anything else in England that has really turned you on, like dog racing?

Shepard: I like pubs and football a lot. There's nothing like pubs in America. And Guinness, I like Guinness.

Interviewer: Any of those going to be dramatically productive?

Shepard: Football . . . yeah, football very well might.

Interview with *Newsweek*

Newsweek / 1976

Transcript from the Magic Theatre Records, carton 4, folder 4.54 (BANC MSS 81/184), Bancroft Library, University of California, Berkeley. Unpublished interview conducted by *Newsweek* interviewer with Sam Shepard and John Lion, one of the founders of the Magic Theatre in San Francisco, on July 26, 1976. Published with the permission of The YGS Group.

Newsweek: I saw the play [*Angel City*] two and a half weeks ago and read some of the reviews that Patrick showed us, and I guess my first question would be in terms of style. In the reviews that I've seen you've been described as a playwright who seems to be somewhat successful with the populace of the world. Are you? Do you agree with that?

Sam Shepard: Not of the world. Of the mind.

N: Populace of the mind. Explain that.

SS: It seems like everything around in the outside world is a reflection of what goes on . . . and it sort of warrants going back to the source of it, rather than going out and looking for all the manifestations of it out there. It seems better to turn towards the source of it, because that's where it comes from.

N: If that's where it comes from, then explain, if you can, some of the background leading to *Angel City*. What was your source?

SS: The play is self-explanatory really. To talk about the actual experiences in Hollywood is kind of boring.

N: Tell me. . . .

SS: I had several experiences, all in Hollywood, under different situations. One was where I was very young. I was hired by Carlo Ponti to do this thing with Antonioni, and they swept me away to . . .

N: Which one was that? *Zabriskie Point*?

SS: Yeah. I was the first writer on that and I didn't know anything about the Hollywood machinery. I sort of got taken along for the ride.

N: How old were you then?

SS: Twenty-two, I think, twenty-one, something like that. And then from there you sort of pick up on the smell of money, which is what they all use anyway, and then I wrote a couple of screenplays in between there, one for the Rolling Stones, and some other people.

N: What did you write for the Rolling Stones?

SS: A script called "Maxagasm" that was a co-authorship thing and that fell through because Jagger decided he didn't want to do it. Then I just finished another screenplay about Appaloosa horseracing, that I took down there to see if I could sell outright, and *Angel City* is a direct outcrop of that.

N: Nobody wanted it?

SS: Plenty of people wanted to dicker around with it, but they didn't want to just take it as it was. Some people wanted to turn it into a TV show, but I just wanted it to be a movie. So *Angel City* is mainly from that, and the whole process of being naïve and stupid in the face of something that's very sophisticated on a certain level. . . .

N: And ingrained.

SS: Oh yeah. So that was mainly what *Angel City* comes from. It doesn't come from *Zabriskie Point* even though maybe . . .

N: *Zabriskie Point* started it, the catalyst was the last thing you did.

SS: Yeah.

N: How long ago was that, when you went down there?

SS: Only a couple of months ago, maybe longer, three months.

N: Now in the play, there's always this impending disaster coming. Is that basically what you felt when you were down in Los Angeles?

SS: Well, you see, it's a curious Hollywood phenomenon that they're dealing with . . . the story that I got everywhere I went down there was they were not interested in character drama, situations between two people, which is essentially what this script was about. It was just a small story. "We want disasters"; that was the thing I kept hearing all the time. This thing kept rebounding in my head over and over again to the point where it felt like the whole town was into that, which isn't so incredible. The place is sort of teetering on the verge of annihilation anyway. It just seemed curious how it paralleled that whole social thing that seems to be going on down there. It seemed like the town was just totally wasted, really wasted, in a bad way, in a really bad way. Like New York has a certain charm about its desolation, but Hollywood is just . . .

John Lion: No charm at all about it.

SS: Oh, God. . . .

N: Well, despite the fact that this play may have some difficulty playing in Los Angeles . . .

SS: There's no theater in L.A. There's no theater down there. I mean, there are theaters, but there's no real audience.

N: How would you describe the play, in terms of its attitude?

SS: What kind of play is it, do you mean?

N: No, in terms of the attitude that it kind of . . .

SS: I'm not so interested in that as going into it in terms of open questions. Like rather than saying that the play is trying to put across an attitude . . . to go into it more in terms of a mystery. We don't know really what's going on, even with the material, so we don't know exactly what's going on with the play. So we have to discover that in production, in the writing of it, and that's what's exciting to me about working in any kind of theater, is not knowing. If you know, then what's the point of doing it?

N: What questions does this play ask?

SS: What questions?

N: Yeah.

SS: Okay, for instance, where did all this stuff start? How could it come to pass that things are in that kind of condition? What was the seed of it? It didn't seem like that in the postcards in the twenties, with the orange groves and the promise of splendor that it sort of put to us. California in general had that kind of . . . the promised land, God's country, all that shit. So how did it get from that to this other thing, where it's encapsulated in a yellow film, and all that shit? Because I grew up down there. Not to say that I know it because I grew up down there, but my roots are down there. It's just a strange kind of thing.

N: Tell me about your growing up down there, how long . . .

SS: In five minutes?

N: Oh no, I've got time. Go ahead.

SS: Well, I grew up in this sort of semi-rural environment, about 50 miles east of L.A. A place called Duarte. It was basically rock quarries, and the only notorious. . . .

N: That's a bad word to use these days [a reference to the 1976 Chowchilla kidnapping, when 26 children and their school-bus driver were put into a truck that was buried in a quarry; they all eventually escaped].

SS: Rock quarries? Yeah, right. No kidnappings in mine. Lot of trailer camps, avocado orchards, basically the town was known for the City of Hope, which was a cancer research institute where I worked a couple of . . . a lot of horse ranches, and a varied environment. That's where I grew up.

N: And how old are you now?

SS: Now? Thirty-two.

N: When did you leave L.A.?

SS: When I was 19.

N: And you came right up here?

SS: Oh no. I went on tour with a repertory company that toured plays in churches and I wound up in New York.

N: That's where you started writing?

SS: Yeah.

N: Now *Angel City* is still playing at the Magic Theatre, but where is it going to go from here? Are there any plans to take it to New York?

SS: Well, we're going to do it in Seattle for a couple of performances and that's it, as far as the western thing goes.

N: Anything developing in the East?

SS: Well, it was sold to Princeton, and the National Theatre of London is going to do it at their new theater on the Thames.

N: Where do you think American playwriting is going?

SS: You see, all the people who are in charge of talking about where American theater is going don't understand that it's not a movement. It belongs to individuals. You can't talk about where American playwriting is going, because of the nature of writing. Playwrights don't have a mutual dialogue. They're not an army, so they don't have this thing of "collectively we're going somewhere." It doesn't work like that. It's on an individual basis, what is everybody doing, and I think that's how these so-called "movements" get started, is that individuals pick up on each other's work, through either hearsay or direct experience and begin to accumulate their own momentum. I think it's very dangerous to say that the new American playwrights are moving in a direction because I don't think it's true. Individuals maybe.

N: Well, what direction are you moving in?

SS: I'm moving in the direction of discovery, I hope. Where that discovery leads me is another thing. But right now it's opened up into the possibility of working directly in production, which I haven't been into in a long time.

N: You're directing this.

SS: And I directed the last one.

N: Which was?

JL: Which was *Action*.

SS: Now we have this possibility, with the Magic Theatre, to work an improvisational jazz workshop with musicians that have been working with us. I want to get into that.

N: When I sat and watched the play, my general reaction to the audience was that they liked the play very much, but it was an uncomfortable play for them to sit through.

SS: Because of the physical thing of the theater?

N: Well, no. Because of all the different things that were happening on the stage.

SS: Well, it's very different from night to night.

N: My question is, do you think it's a good idea that the audience is somewhat uncomfortable?

SS: I don't know what you mean by comfort. Physically comfortable? Psychically comfortable?

N: No. What I mean is that there's a lot of squirming around, not *Exorcist* squirming or *Omen* squirming, but the kind of squirming around that people were really saying, hey, they weren't sitting back and watching *The Pink Panther*. Do you know what I'm saying?

JL: Let me stick in two cents here, and Sam might even disagree, I don't know; but part of the structure and the way he writes, there's a lot of distancing techniques. Because, when you want to speak to an audience, it seems that plays go one of two ways. And one is they either [elicit] applause or they seduce you into involvement, so that you fall into the piece and you become totally identified with it and so on, sort of melodramatic. You care for the characters and what's going to happen to them. Sam, I think, in the respect of this uncomfortableness that you noticed, sort of looks to Bertolt Brecht a lot, in that he invents, when he writes, this sort of pendulum, where you are drawn into the action and then something happens where you are forced to get away from the action, so you can look at what is happening. I think he attempts to achieve some sort of objectivity for the audience, by constantly drawing them in and then pulling them back, so they can look and they can see. And I think that's where the uncomfortableness comes from, if you noticed that. It doesn't always happen. A lot of people just have no trouble with the style, so they can fall right into it. But I think that in order to say something in a complex way that you have to be able to rely on people not just identifying, but understanding. I think that maybe the understanding of his work is somewhere in that middle area.

N: Do you agree?

SS: Yeah, to a certain extent. The whole key to it, to me, is performance, which is based on the actor. You can write stage directions up the ass, but if you don't have that ignition happening with the actor it doesn't make any difference. So that's what's really become interesting to me; how to work with an actor in such a way that he can put across something that you actually can't put on paper. You can put the blueprint down, but when the actor steps into it, a new thing begins to happen.

N: I noticed in the play that you've got the saxophone player coming in and out. What was the idea for that?

SS: Ideas are based on some other intuitive kind of thing. They're not, like, so intellectual that you could say that jazz belongs to a certain era, Hollywood belongs to another era, so I'm going to mix them, even though that might be true. It seemed like that kind of music was right for that world of the play. It cut into it to a certain extent. And I'm interested in the whole form of jazz composition, because I think it relates to what the actor does directly. It's the same art, in a way, except that they are using different means.

JL: If everything goes well, we will be working on a Rockefeller Grant next year to create an ensemble that involves acting and jazz, and it's to find the . . . and again I hesitate to put words in Sam's mouth, but as I understand it, at least, it's to explore the emotional equivalent of jazz in terms of character and in terms of actors. The most surface thing you can recognize about it is the speech-rhythm trend. But jazz does have a personality. You hear Coltrane, you know it's Coltrane. So there really is a whole being that's coming at you. So why can't this work with character?

N: Now, I did not see *Action*, but did you have any music in that?

SS: No, well, about the third week through I put in a song at the beginning which is a really old gospel song that the actors sang at the beginning. But other than that we didn't. The production in London used the whale music, you know, the whale sounds; but I think the music in that play was just in terms of the language and things like that.

N: In terms of the distancing effect we were talking about before, pulling the audience in and kind of putting them back again, in this play, you have the movie mogul all of a sudden turning into the boxer, his partner coming in, turning green. Is that part of the same distancing effect of all of a sudden changing around characters, so that the audience, once they get into a character, all of a sudden has to get into another one?

SS: Somewhat. It's more based on the idea that each character, rather than the old style, where the character goes from birth to middle-age to death in the course of three acts, he can jump from different parts of himself. So why isn't it just as easy to accept a producer becoming a boxer as it is to see him go through this so-called "real-life" trip? Why not have him jump all over the place?

N: Exploring whatever fantasies he might have.

SS: Yeah.

N: Tell me a little bit about your lifestyle here in the valley, since we're not going up to the house.

SS: Why?

N: Why? Because it's important.

SS: No. I'd rather talk about the plays, or something else.

N: How long have you lived in Mill Valley?

SS: About a year.

N: In a house?

SS: On a ranch.

N: And I notice you have a tattoo on your left . . . what does that signify?

SS: Nothing really. I was drunk, and there was a girl called Volle from Italy. She was a gypsy, and she was in New York trying to raise money to support her dogs. She has about 50 dogs and she does tattoos, and so it's a first quarter moon.

N: Okay, that solves that problem. What next, before you get to the Rockefeller thing? Are you working on a play now?

SS: Well, I just finished a play for Yale that I've got to send off, and Joe Papp is doing a new thing.

N: What's it about?

SS: It's about my family in southern California. It's the first family play I've ever written.

N: Called "Angel Family"?

SS: No, it's got a very pretentious title, and it's called *Curse of the Starving Class*, which is the middle class.

N: And that's your family?

SS: Yeah. But it's a three-act play written in, more or less, the style of Eugene O'Neill, which I've never tried before.

N: What will it accomplish, in terms of that style? How will it differ?

SS: It just deals with a very real situation I went through as a kid. It's too complicated to get into.

N: Okay. When you look at something like Angel City, not the play, but the city, do you think things will get better, or are you really convinced it's satanic?

SS: I don't know what better is.

N: Well, everything being relative.

SS: I don't believe in social solutions or anything like that. It will probably take its natural course, whatever that is.

N: Like where it was necessary to destroy it in order to save it?

SS: I don't believe that at all.

N: Okay.

SS: Do you think that's true? Is it necessary to destroy it?

N: No, but if it takes its natural course, that will be destruction, right?

SS: I don't have any idea. I could easily see California being destroyed in the blink of an eye, but whether that will happen or not. . . . The whole earthquake thing is very exotic. It's an exotic idea because all these major earthquakes have happened in areas of the world that are, for the most part, poverty-stricken, and have been terrible kind of calamities. And if the same thing happened in California you can be sure that news-wise, the shit's going to hit the fan.

N: That's right. Not to mention the real estate salesmen committing suicide.

SS: It seems like natural disasters sort of correspond to social destruction at the same time. Plagues, holocausts, all that.

N: So what you're saying is that if you're living in Los Angeles, it might be a good time to get out, before the plagues?

SS: No. I'm not predicting anything.

N: No, you know what I'm saying.

SS: The last time they did that, everybody cut out and nothing happened.

JL: You know, I'm intrigued with this idea that the American theater is made up of individuals. It seems to me that there's entirely too much time spent on the so-called American movement, American regional theater movement, and so on. I don't think it happens that way at all. For instance, the Magic Theatre belongs to certain organizations and I go off to conferences once in a while, and deal with foundations in the East and such. The attempt here is really to set up things on an individual basis.

SS: What could be more American than that!

JL: Structurally, I look for lateral associations. When Sam came around, the thing I knew about him the most was that almost everything I had read that he had been talking about was his dissatisfaction with directors and what they have been doing with his work. Yet, ironically, here's a man who has had, what, fifty plays produced, and up until two years before he came to the west coast and he was in London, had never directed his own work, even though he railed and screamed and was dissatisfied. So it seemed utterly natural to me, when we got together, that he should be directing his own stuff, should be doing his own stuff, that's the direction that he wants to go. I think that in the future you're going to see more and more playwrights assuming a sort of auteur status, much like film directors. That is, I think the best kind of theater is moving away from that sort of a really strict specialization, where you have a writer and a director and a crew, and everyone is working in their little compartment. I really think that's the wave of the future. Even if you look, some of the younger playwrights want to be much more involved in their works these days, as the certain hegemony of large producers that I found, as a breed, are dying out. So it seemed natural to me. I'd rather have the Magic Theatre operate more like a wheel than like a pyramid, for what that's worth.

N: I just have one last question, and that is, talking about doing this next play about your family in the Eugene O'Neill style, how would you describe the Shepard style?

SS: I wouldn't. I wouldn't make any attempt to. I mean, I've heard that I have a style, but I have yet to find out what it is, because I think that's very deadly for a writer to embrace his own style, his own aesthetic, and all that kind of stuff, because right away it means that you're locked into a form that you've been trying to escape the whole time. The whole point is to try to explore new territory. What's the point of going over the old stuff all the time? If you find out you have a style, you're in trouble. You really are, because then you start just doing this thing. It's very easy to mimic yourself, really easy.

N: So what you're saying is that each play is totally different from the rest.

SS: I think so. To me they are. People talk about a style that I have, but if it's long speeches, okay, but other people write long speeches. I don't know.

N: I've got a couple of other questions that have just come to mind. You grew up in southern California, you left when you were 19, you went on the road. When you left when you were 19, were you in college?

SS: No, I went to Ag school for about three semesters.

N: In L.A.?

SS: Well, Mount San Antonio College in Walnut, California, really nice school, but I just couldn't handle it and I took off.

N: And you left after how long?

SS: Three semesters.

N: That's when you went on the road with the repertory group?

SS: Yeah, as an actor. Then I toured all through New England and the Midwest and such doing these church plays on the altars and staying in the clergies' houses.

N: Wasn't that a trip?

SS: Yeah, and then I left and just went to New York.

N: What age did you start writing?

SS: Around that time, twenty, something like that. But one of my best friends in high school was a painter and he sort of turned me on to the whole idea of being able to do something that wasn't dependent on another thing. Like an actor is always sort of enslaved to go around and peddle his thing, but if you're a painter or something like that you can do it on your own. So then I tried to think of how I could get into something that wouldn't be so dependent on other forces, and writing seemed very natural at the time.

N: With more than fifty plays produced, you seem to be a prolific writer, you write quickly. How long does it usually take you? Obviously you just finished a play, the one now about your family. How long did it take you actually from conception to taking it to the typist?

SS: Taking it to the typist? I *am* the typist. I took it to myself. The time is always dependent on the material. It's not like you just rip off something the same every time. With *Angel City* I rewrote it more than probably any other play. I went over and over it, very patchwork kind of approach. Another play, like *Action*, I wrote in about three sittings. It was really fast, but it was fluid. Everything felt right, and I didn't rewrite it at all.

N: *Angel City* was a harder thing to put together, right?

SS: *Angel City* was much more difficult. It didn't feel as organic, that's a corny word nowadays, but it didn't. *Tooth of Crime* I had to struggle with. I don't necessarily think that if you struggle hard with a play to write it, it's better than a play that just comes out. Both ways it's work, but one way it seems like everything's right, and the other way it just seems like everything's wrong, and you have to keep doing it. Plus, in that dimension, I don't know how many plays I've gotten fifty pages on and abandoned. There's just no way it's going to work. I wrote a play about Jackson Pollock. I wrote three acts on the thing, and it's terrible. It's just awful.

Sam Shepard: A Play for Every Life Style

Sylvie Drake / 1979

From *Los Angeles Times*, October 21, 1979, *Calendar*, pp. 1, 58, 62. Reprinted with the permission of the *Los Angeles Times*. Sylvie Drake was a theater critic for the *Los Angeles Times* for 32 years.

"It's like receiving the news that you have a terminal illness," Sam Shepard explained about winning the Pulitzer Prize for his play, *Buried Child.* "You have to get over it. In one way it's nice that there's a kind of recognition, but for the most part you have to get through it, accept it as well as you can and move on."

Shepard sat in the lunchtime penumbra of Trader Vic's, his slender frame leaning gracefully forward like a question mark in search of the right text. His jeans and leather jacket were in marked contrast to the Brooks Bros. rectitude of the environment. Reluctant to give interviews, he approached this one with an affability at once receptive and laconic.

Two West Coast productions of *Buried Child* are occurring simultaneously—one opened at the American Conservatory Theater here last week, the other is opening at the Los Angeles Actors' Theater Friday. The original edition of this play was staged by Robert Woodruff at San Francisco's Magic Theatre, with Shepard in attendance. But when Woodruff repeated his task Off-Broadway, Shepard declined to travel. He doesn't like to fly ("I get vertigo") and he deliberately stays away from most productions of his plays.

"Unless I have a personal relationship with someone in the production, someone I've worked with before or someone I'm interested in working with, I stay away. You can only exercise control if you have a common bond with someone, a real understanding. You can't exercise control by demanding it."

Some might call this willing abstention lack of curiosity. Shepard has not seen the *Buried Child* Off-Broadway that won the Pulitzer and has no plans to see it, nor did he see the Mark Taper Forum's 1973 *Tooth of Crime*, with Michael Cristofer playing the flamboyant rock superstar, Crow. He's never met Cristofer, who, like himself, has since become a Pulitzer Prize–winning actor-playwright. In fact, Shepard rarely goes to the theater at all. "For the most part," he says, "it's dull."

On the other hand, Shepard often has been actively involved with productions of his plays, directing some himself or working closely with directors he respects (Woodruff and Joseph Chaikin foremost among them) at the Magic Theatre, where he was playwright-in-residence, or the smaller Eureka Theatre. They're closest to home, physically and figuratively.

But then, Shepard is a total iconoclast. Opposing forces seem constantly at work in him and are reflected in the styles of his plays (from highly abstract to intricately structured) to the styles of his life. At 35, Shepard has been itinerant cowboy, percussionist, film actor, screenwriter and playwright, all these activities continuing side by side. He values his privacy and lives on the outskirts of San Francisco with his wife of ten years, O-Lan, herself an actress and writer, and their small son, Jesse.

"I live here because it's an intermediate kind of city," he said, "a good city. I live outside it and can come in easily. There's a contradiction in this and it's not as though I've resolved it. It's necessary, to a degree, to do what musicians call woodshed. You go into the woodshed and just chop. You do that privately, for a long time. And then it's necessary to come out and work with people, be public. You need both sides. Otherwise, a systematic thing happens. You've formed yourself too much. As soon as you take on this structure, it's time to break it."

Breakage is something Shepard knows about. He was born in Illinois (Ft. Sheridan), but his army-brat childhood was spent "all over the place. My mother was always chasing my father, trying to find out where he was stationed next, and I went along for the ride." These travels finally landed them in the San Gabriel Valley, where Shepard attended high school in Duarte. His interests at that time were rural, all veterinary medicine and animal husbandry.

"I was torn between staying in California in some agricultural job or just takin' off," he said. "I wound up takin' off because I had a traumatic breaking away from my family and decided to roam around."

Shepard is reluctant to discuss his breaking away ("Not important. I escaped."), but he admits elements of it are in *Curse of the Starving Class* (set in the San Gabriel Valley) and *Buried Child*, chilling plays both, about the disintegration of the nuclear family.

"I turned down a job herding sheep in Chino and did what a lot of other kids did," he continued. "I went to New York to become an actor."

This was curious. Shepard had been playing drums since he was 14 ("My dad was a drummer"), but he had no background in theater. In New York he roomed with Charles Mingus Jr., a high school buddy ("I'd no idea his father was a composer") who got him a job as busboy at the Village Gate.

Disenchantment set in rapidly, beginning with acting, which became "being at the mercy of other people." On and off, Shepard had "snuck around" and done some writing. Poetry and prose came first, but he wasn't comfortable with them. Then someone gave him a copy of *Waiting for Godot*.

"I'd never read a play before," he said, "and I thought, 'This is amazing. I don't understand it at all, but the words and the language amaze me.' I had no place to put it, no category, but once I started writing plays I felt the connection."

Shepard's first play was *Cowboys*, staged by Ralph Cook at Theater Genesis in 1964.

"It was about me and Charlie," he volunteered, "on the streets of New York, because that's what we used to do in Duarte, play cowboys in the street, and when we got to New York we just kept doing it. We were 19 or something. It seemed bizarre to me, this transplant, this sense of being from a desert region, then suddenly being surrounded by immigrants, pigeons and jazz musicians.

"I was extremely full of myself at that time. I had this feeling, fed by my friendship with Charlie, that nobody knew better than you what was good for your work, which in some ways is still true. But there was an arrogance in that. I was a real pain in the ass, continuously uptight about the production, about what the actors were doing. But Ralph was very good and the play somehow got a good production. So I decided I'd try again."

Thus it began. Shepard worked through "the tornado of the '60s, hanging in tooth and nail like everybody else, writing and playing music." A shy man, he never really identified with a theatrical movement ("The theater world as a social organism doesn't interest me at all.") nor came together much with his contemporaries—among them Lanford Wilson, John Guare, Leonard Melfi, Robert Patrick, Megan Terry and Jean-Claude van Itallie.

"Only in the sense that we were all there at the same time," he specified, "but I was still fishin' in the dark with no knowledge of theater, nothing to relate to. At one point, I only wanted to do music and travel with the Holy Modal Rounders."

Periodically, Shepard fled the urban jungle, coming up for air in the mountains of Chiapas, Mex. ("a real incredible place for me"). It was there that he wrote his first full-length play, *La Turista*, staged at the American Place.

"I was suffering from amoebic dysentery so the play has this very—hallucinogenic isn't really the right word. It was just very fractured. I threw out one act. It was in shambles. I was very surprised anyone could get a handle on it, but they did. Elizabeth Hardwick gave it a strong review in the *New York Review of Books*. Robert Lowell came. I thought, 'Jesus Christ. Serious.'"

Several one-acts later, Shepard took off for London. Chiapas was no longer adequate as a relief valve for New York. It was 1971 and Shepard was "having a very hard time coping with my life." In London he tried directing for the first time (his own *Geography of a Horse Dreamer* with a company of Northern Irish actors) and he wrote *Tooth of Crime*, first done at the Royal Court.

"It takes a tremendous amount of energy to direct," said Shepard. "I would do it once a year, at the most. But I love it."

Can he be objective about his own plays?

"Absolutely. Yes. It doesn't even seem like I wrote them."

After three years of rejuvenation in London, Shepard returned to California where he began to sink some roots. A lot has happened in the past 15 years. He married. He wrote the screenplay for Antonioni's *Zabriskie Point*, a less than thrilling experience that probably triggered his play, *Angel City*, which abstracts the corruptions of Hollywood. He made a name for himself as an actor in Terrence Malick's *Days of Heaven*. He recently completed the soon-to-be-released film, *Resurrection*, with Ellen Burstyn. And he won the Pulitzer.

Writing plays is about communication, not always verbal, not necessarily articulate, sometimes not immediately revealing. Shepard is seen by many as a giant in this field. Torrents of explanation accompany his plays, which is ironic, since, as an artist, he feels that "to thematically title things destroys the subject." Odder still is that Shepard came to this business of playwriting as unprepared as it is possible to be.

"There are so many influences you can't account for," he explained, "things that happen and throw you in a certain direction. One of those for me was jazz music. At one time it seemed like that was the most important art form for me, even though I wasn't an accomplished musician, just a drummer playing in rock bands.

"I used to go and listen to Charlie Mingus and was stunned by his sense of polyrhythm—rhythm on top of rhythm on top of rhythm. I was fascinated by the idea of merging that with writing, seeing if there was a way of evoking the same kind of collage in the writing of plays. Sometimes there was and sometimes there wasn't, but that was definitely a strong influence, more so than literature.

"Each piece of work is an independent, individual thing for me. It's influenced by everything in the past but presents itself as an entity of its own. I don't believe any artist is terribly aware of his artistic consciousness or the evolution of that consciousness, only as in a dream. . . ."

Do the plays write themselves then?

"No. There's this tendency sometimes to struggle for material, grab hold of it through a character or situation, and almost always it turns out that you go through this period of—of fighting with this thing, trying to shake it, and it collapses and something *else* starts and that something else is usually what you're looking for. There's a constriction, a tension. Then that drops away and the real thing begins.

"It's always a struggle between control and lack of control. I've been following two streams. One is the outside play, more improvisatory, the kind of writing that writes itself. I'm not ashamed to share those experiments. Beethoven and Mozart also improvised. The other is the inside play, the family play, much more structured."

Like *Curse of the Starving Class* and *Buried Child*?

"I think it's one of the tragedies of this country that the nuclear family has become so filled with distrust. My family was torn apart, torn to shreds from the inside out. I know I'm not alone in that. It's not my personal trauma, but it's characteristic of America, much more than Europe, the sense of mother and father not really able to make it or break it off.

"The fact of being born to parents, the fact that *they* were born to parents, is inescapable. There's a false ideology about being able to be independent of that. It's wrongheaded to blame the nuclear family for the turbulence in the country and there's a great schizophrenia about that, now that people feel a need to be related, attached to something in the past. There are still parts of this country that have this feeling of connection with the land. Wyoming. Montana. Texas. Whole towns in Texas are named for people who still live there."

Shepard recently completed another play called *True West*, which, he says, "is very structured." Joe Papp will produce it in New York with Robert Woodruff sought to direct it. Before that, on Nov. 6, Woodruff will "bodyguard" two short musical pieces originally developed in San Francisco with Joseph Chaikin called *Tongues* and *Savage/Love*. In the future is the development of an 18-part percussion piece and—who knows?—perhaps some stage acting?

"It's tempting," Shepard smiled, "but it's also terrifying because I don't have the training. But it's a great challenge—amazing what you have to put yourself through to find the character, form the channel to express the stuff."

It's a cinch that Shepard will continue to thrive on contradiction and listen only to the sound of his own impulse. Predictably unpredictable, he announced as he was leaving Trader Vic's that he'd be in Los Angeles for *Buried Child*. But first things first. There's jackpot roping this weekend in Santa Rosa and Shepard knows his priorities. "I'll be down after that," he said.

Sam Shepard: Off-Broadway's Street Cowboy

Robert Goldberg / 1980

From *Rolling Stone College Papers*, Winter 1980, pp. 43–45. Reprinted by permission.

Sam Shepard—playwright, musician, screenwriter and reticent actor—fidgets on the California set of *Resurrection* while a makeup artist provides last-minute ministrations. She pulls out a comb, parts his chaff-colored hair and applies a light pomade. Finally, Shepard says with an apologetic smile, "I guess this is sanctioned vanity."

Even sanctioned vanity is a large concession for the earthy, reclusive playwright to make. Despite his frenzied activity in the very public worlds of theater, film and rock & roll, he remains a very unpublic figure. His "oeuvre" includes more than 100 plays, ten of which earned him Obies (annual awards given by the *Village Voice* for Off-Broadway productions). He won a special Obie in 1980 for Sustained Achievement, and one play, *Buried Child*, won him a Pulitzer Prize. As a drummer, he's jammed with Ike and Tina Turner, Lou Reed's Velvet Underground and former lover-collaborator Patti Smith; he also traveled with Bob Dylan's Rolling Thunder Revue as unofficial chronicler. He has written several screenplays and worked with Michelangelo Antonioni on *Zabriskie Point*. Even his quiet, mannered acting debut in *Days of Heaven* earned him critical praise.

Shepard is currently co-starring with Ellen Burstyn in his second movie, *Resurrection*. Burstyn plays a woman who experiences near-death in an auto accident, then regains her health with new-found healing powers. Here, as in *Days of Heaven*, Shepard plays a character irrevocably tied to the American landscape—the Kansas-born, rabble-rousing son of an evangelist preacher.

Born November 5, 1943, Samuel Shepard Rogers VII spent the early years of his life following his father, an air-force man, to Idaho, South Dakota,

Florida and the South Pacific. The family eventually ended up in Duarte, a small town in California's San Gabriel Valley.

In his early teens, Shepard found solace in the outdoors—running tractors, grooming horses and riding his bike in the mountains. In high school, he would "cruise," celebrating "events of the body and his feelings," which included, not incidentally, booze and speed. After studying agriculture, he hit the road and wound up in New York.

The early sixties were his wired years, and Shepard turned out plays with an almost cathartic passion. In 1964, his first play, *Cowboys*, was produced on New York's Lower East Side, where experimental theater was spilling into churches and the streets. Before he was 30, the *New Yorker* had proclaimed him "one of the three or four most gifted playwrights alive." In 1971, he moved to London, where he found it "possible to function without having to go nuts all the time."

For the past five years, Shepard, 36, has lived on a ranch in northern California with his actress wife, O-Lan, and his son, Jesse Mojo. "This is the only family I've ever really known," he says. "It's miraculous. I dreamed about this family, and it's come true."

Later, in his dressing room, Shepard tells me, "I'm not into personal promotion." He is indeed loathe to make himself publicly available, and the following is his first extensive interview to appear in print.

Robert Goldberg: How did you first become interested in drama?

Sam Shepard: I was going to this agricultural school full of Four-H Club guys. There was this one guy who wore sandals, had long hair and a beard, and everybody called him a beatnik. He had a lot of jazz records, paintings, Kerouac, and all that. He handed me this play—it was *Waiting for Godot*. I had never read anything like it in my life. It was totally surprising.

So, in a way I was lucky, because I came to writing without a whole lot of background.

RG: You started out acting, right? With the Bishop's Company, a repertory group.

SS: I sort of used acting as a means to get out of my environment. In Duarte, nobody was doing anything except going to the Alpha Beta supermarket. Duarte was in the sticks—just one main road, a bank and a couple of motels. People stopped there on the way to other places.

All I wanted to do was travel. I couldn't see selling clothes or used cars, or working on ranches, which is what I'd done all through high school. The other alternative was staying in college, which I hated with a passion. Acting was a handy way of suddenly finding myself on the other side of the country, moving around, doing one-night stands, and having enough money to eat. But I wasn't a great actor by any means, just faking it.

RG: What got you into playwriting?

SS: At the time, I was living in Spanish Harlem. I saw in a gossip column that this guy I went to high school with, who happened to be Charles Mingus's son, was busing tables at the Village Gate. I went down there and he got me a job as a busboy. So, I was bringing ice to Nina Simone and hanging out with the waiters, who were mostly actors.

Finally I said, "This is terrible, this business of giving your picture to goons, trying to get into acting, which isn't really acting—it's personal promotion." So I started writing about my experiences with Charlie on the streets of New York, which was *Cowboys*. It didn't get any big notices until Michael Smith of the *Village Voice* saw it, then people started coming.

RG: You had moved to New York in your late teens?

SS: Yeah. New York was really an eye-lifter. I mean, I thought the big city was Pasadena. So when I got to New York, it was a mixture of being thrilled and awe-struck and scared all at the same time. But I finally got down to the Lower East Side, and there was an incredible feeling of community there in the early sixties, a community of artists and musicians. And everybody merged with the Puerto Rican trip. But that was completely blown apart when acid hit the streets.

RG: How did hallucinogens change things?

SS: Well, everybody suddenly felt liberated, and the restricted behavior that was a tradition in this country for years was blown apart.

When this influx of essentially white middle-class kids hit the streets, the indigenous people—the Puerto Ricans, the blacks, the street junkies and all the people who were really a part of the scene—felt this great animosity toward these flip-outs running around the Lower East Side in beads and hair down to their asses. There was this upsurge of violence and weirdness, and everybody started carrying guns and knives.

People will say the sixties was the greatest thing that ever hit America, that it was peace and love. Maybe in San Francisco, but in New York it got very scary.

RG: Did your plays change because of what was going on?

SS: My plays were influenced by everything happening to me. A lot of them came out of fear and anger, because that's what was going on. There was an extreme kind of street paranoia in those days—the Kennedy trip, Malcolm X and the Panthers. The shit was hitting the fan and everybody had the sense that there was a flood coming.

RG: Do you think the flood ever came?

SS: It's going on right now. We're just getting the first wave of it.

RG: That's a pretty grim vision.

SS: Depends on how you look at it, because afterward, something will be washed away. I've never known an elated time that didn't come immediately following almost getting drowned. I don't see it as being apocalyptic, because so far we haven't been wiped out.

RG: Did you see drugs playing a big role in what you were doing?

SS: Well, I was using a lot of drugs then—amphetamines, smack. Drugs were a big part of the whole experience of that time. It was part of a feeling that you wanted to experience different aspects of reality.

RG: What did drugs do for your writing?

SS: I didn't use drugs to write. I only used drugs to live [*laughs*]. But I was using heavy stuff, and I saw a lot of people go under from drugs, which was one of the main reasons I left the streets, because street life went hand in hand with that.

RG: It seems that the image of a battered American comes up a lot in your plays, which deal with both the myths and diseases of America. The shattering of the family, for instance.

SS: See, to me, one of the biggest tragedies was moving from an agricultural to an urban-industrial society at the turn of the century. It was a great undertow that demolished the family feelings that were well rooted in America. You know, the Ford Motor Company comes out with these little cars that suddenly allow kids who've been harvesting wheat all day to drive the fuck off the farm to the city.

It's a deeply painful experience, finding ourselves in these bodies that are essentially geared toward a rural civilization. It's as though we'd been transported to another planet and didn't know how we got there.

RG: Is that where you came up with all that imagery in *Buried Child*?

SS: You see, my grandfather had a pretty prosperous dairy farm, but then the dairy industry got all mechanized with electric milkers, and the individual farmer fell apart. Before he lost it, he used to grow corn. It's not agriculture anymore, it's agribusiness. It *was* a culture; it really *was* a culture. . . .

RG: You're living in a rural setting now. Do you see yourself getting back to working the land?

SS: Yeah. I grow vegetables, peaches and citrus, as well as apples. It's very small, but you can grow a lot of vegetables in a small space.

RG: Do you think living on a ranch has influenced your writing?

SS: Well, for me, language comes from the earth. If a man is raised on a mountain, he's going to talk according to that place. If a man is raised along a river, he's influenced by that river. And you can feel it in different areas of the country. The language grows like a crop from the place where it sprouted.

RG: The language in *The Tooth of Crime* is deadly, sharp. . . .

SS: There were guys on the Lower East Side in the sixties who spoke their own language. Steve Weber was one of them—the guitarist. He was called the fool-killer. He'd talk like a radio. Half of it was drug induced. And always, the people around him—this is the reason he was called the fool-killer—thought he meant something. But nobody could figure it out; he was just playing with his imagination.

RG: You also composed music for *The Tooth of Crime*. What sound were you aiming for?

SS: I wanted to bend Velvet Underground, mainly "Heroin."

RG: What comment were you making on the rock world in that play?

SS: I was amazed by the big turnaround in rock & roll. I felt that it committed suicide. Now rock & roll doesn't have any power. Music, of course, still has power—music without a name. Rock & roll's been co-opted.

RG: Into what?

SS: Into fads, into style and into filling the needs of self-destruction. Which is okay, but it started out in a different direction.

RG: You have other connections with the rock world, with Patti Smith, right?

SS: That was in 1969, 1970—turn of the century [*laughs*].

RG: You wrote the play *Cowboy Mouth* with her.

SS: Absolutely, and she's never really given credit for it in the productions. But she wrote at least half. It was a funny experience. I'd never written a play with somebody before, and we literally shoved the typewriter back and forth across the table. We wrote the whole thing like that, in two nights.

She was experimenting at that point in reading poetry with a guitar player. She would go down to St. Mark's Church and do poetry readings with Lenny [Kaye], who's now her lead guitar player.

RG: Did you have any influence on her?

SS: I'd say she had more influence on me at that time. For one thing, she introduced me to French poets I'd never even heard of. Villon and all those guys. And she showed me what it's like to construct a line of language in a different way, putting ideas and images together. A thing like Patti's—you learn it through the skin, you don't learn it through the head. She writes an animal poetry.

RG: Does it have something to do with rhythm?

SS: Yeah, a lot to do with rhythm. But it's not like a formula. You'd just look at her and it'd strike something in you. The way people are influenced isn't through imitation, it's through feeling.

RG: You appeared together in *Cowboy Mouth.*

SS: Yeah. But it didn't work out because the thing was too emotionally packed. I suddenly realized I didn't want to exhibit myself like that, playing my life on stage. It was like being in an aquarium.

RG: What do you think of Patti Smith's work now, the punk stuff?

SS: I've never heard it. Not because I don't want to, I just never got around to listening to it. But Patti is the real thing all the way down the line. She's a total street artist. Like Dylan. He is a street artist for sure, and people keep talking about him as if he went to Harvard. It's ridiculous.

RG: You met Dylan during the Rolling Thunder Revue, right?

SS: It was a real traveling art show, an adventure. Dylan's a gypsy, and he thrives on that kind of energy, when nobody knows exactly what's going on. I learned to respect the man through the tour. He knows how to play a part. He and Billy Graham are the two greatest actors in the world.

RG: I want to get back to the role of music in your plays. Your recent experiments are a step beyond your rock songs in *The Tooth of Crime* or the saxophone in *Angel City.*

SS: I'm trying to find a way to actually have the music become an actor, to make the music take part in the drama in the same way that language does.

RG: You've been doing experimental productions that overlap music and theater. *Tongues,* with Joe Chaikin, combined drumming and acting.

SS: I've known Joe a lot of years but never had a chance to work with him. Joe and I approached the thing without any definite structure; all we knew was that we wanted to construct a piece that had voices coming up, sort of visiting a person. The age-old idea is that a character evolves along a line, and any deviation from that has to be explained somehow. But I feel there are many voices in a person, many different people in one person, so why shouldn't they have a chance to come out?

RG: Do you think people are schizoid?

SS: Absolutely. I mean, everyone pretends a good game, but we're all equally crazy underneath, and occasionally it surfaces.

RG: So that's why Lanx in *Angel City* can have two personalities—that of a boxer and a big producer?

SS: Yeah. One character speaks for the other; they become each other.

RG: But isn't that jarring?

SS: Some people complain about it, and others find it stimulating. But it's all an experiment.

RG: You talk about writing as if it were jazz, like improvisation on a theme.

SS: Jazz was what got me started thinking about all this stuff—when I first listened to Mingus down at the Five Spot. That music calls you toward a certain approach. You don't feel obliged any longer to uphold the standards of Eugene O'Neill and Tennessee Williams.

RG: Are there any other writers you can point that out in?

SS: Well, LeRoi Jones, I think, is the greatest American playwright. I don't think there is a playwright in the country who speaks with that kind of conviction and intensity.

RG: How about European writers?

SS: Peter Handke is an inspiring writer. He may be the best in the world. Since Beckett, maybe. Handke can zero in on special moments of reality that most people pass over as mundane and make them incredibly important.

RG: In your plays, people have been jolted when a very realistic setting is undermined by flashes of the absurd. Take *Buried Child*, when that corn keeps sprouting up in a barren garden.

SS: Life doesn't strike me as a roller rink; it doesn't seem smooth. You know, there are a lot of shocks and mysterious things. And that's what I gravitate to. But it doesn't seem to be surrealistic either, it just seems to be the experience of finding your way.

RG: But are your monologues realistic?

SS: Well, I'm sure you've listened to yourself when you're not talking. For instance, before you fall asleep, there are dialogues, monologues going on that are monumental. But simply because these volcanoes aren't spoken, they don't seem to be out of the realm of language. So why not include them in a form like theater?

RG: A critic once described your writing as a search for lost innocence.

SS: I don't think you can regain the innocence you've lost, but you can maybe find a new innocence. Only in the moments, though, when suddenly everything seems miraculous. For instance, I drive this freeway that cuts through the geography of these valleys. As you're driving along, you're daydreaming, going through all kinds of inner monologues, inner dialogues, and you're not aware of what's happening around you. All of a sudden, you go into a pocket or a little valley, and the air radically changes—it becomes warm and smells different. When this happens, suddenly you feel as though it were a new moment, and it shocks you into the fact that you're alive. Those are the moments when the innocence presents itself.

RG: What are the moments like that in *Buried Child*?

SS: Well, when Tilden describes how he walked out in the rain and all of a sudden came across the corn, a moment like that—a moment that is delivered into the body and through the emotions.

RG: You've talked about writing in spurts. What goes on in the dry periods?

SS: Well, I wouldn't call it dry. Sometimes you feel the wish to write but there's nothing there, and I don't think you can force the issue. Some people say they get up at six in the morning, write for an hour and have breakfast, then they write for another hour; they're continually writing. But I can't just sit down and call it up. Writing is organic. There's a period of gestation, or periods where you let it go fallow, turn the ground over and let it sit for a while. Then the thing sprouts up. It comes real fast.

RG: How many plays have you written?

SS: A lot. I don't know what the numbers are, but probably too many.

RG: Too many?

SS: Yeah, many of those plays have embarrassed the hell out of me. When people look at your work, they're looking at you. Sometimes it's embarrassing, sometimes it's frightening.

RG: When is it good?

SS: Well, it's good to see actors working together and finding something lying dormant in the material, something that suddenly comes to life. It happens through the actor, always.

RG: What brought you back to acting? After all those years what made you decide to be in *Days of Heaven*?

SS: It was mainly Terry Malick, and this script that really struck me. Also, it's not good to do just one thing all the time. You get jaded, and it turns sour somehow.

RG: What drew you to *Resurrection*?

SS: It's an incredible script for one thing. Also, I wanted to work with Ellen Burstyn, because I think she's a genius. And I'm real interested in acting now.

RG: So do you see doing a lot more movies?

SS: No, not a lot more.

RG: You're getting pretty big parts.

SS: Well, yeah. 'Cause films are cast according to types, not how good an actor you are. If you fulfill certain types, you can get parts.

RG: How about acting in plays?

SS: No, I don't really have my chops as an actor. I think it's easier for a nonactor to work in movies than on stage. Film has to do with the surface of things; on stage, nonactors don't fool you for a second.

RG: What sort of theater have you been going to see?

SS: I don't go to the theater. For the most part, it's disappointing to me. A lot of people involved in theater don't attend it. Not because they don't feel actively involved in it—actually it's the opposite.

RG: What do you think of Off-Off-Broadway today?

SS: I don't know if it exists anymore. Alternative theater has to remain with the people, remain on a personal level. But the whole idea of an Off-Off-Broadway movement was a con job by the media.

RG: You've always made a point of avoiding Broadway.

SS: The closest I ever came to that territory was when *Operation Sidewinder* was produced at Lincoln Center, and that was a total disaster. The thing was mass produced. There was all this money involved in costumes and sets, and that took precedence over the work between actors. It also had too big an audience. I don't think theater can be received in a huge space with thousands of people. It becomes a spectacle.

RG: But wouldn't you like to have those mass audiences?

SS: I'm not interested in drawing wider audiences, because they aren't interested in my work [*laughs*]. I don't care. Moreover, I don't believe in plays running for thirteen years—it's ridiculous. A play has a life, a production has a life, and that life is almost tangible. Theater is ephemeral; it happens and it's gone. Like music. And there's a tendency in the scholastic world to try to make it permanent. I've run into a lot of friction because I don't see it as being for all time.

RG: Do you ever rewrite after getting several years' distance?

SS: No.

RG: You couldn't make it better?

SS: Sure you could, but why put energy into that when you can start something new? If a play is written in a certain period of your life, it has to include that period. When you see it later, that period is gone. So what's important is to write about where you are right now.

RG: Do you ever feel as if you don't quite know where a play will go?

SS: Always. When you start writing something, you're between the devil and the deep blue sea, you're between being lost and being found. But that's part of the thrill of writing. If you knew blow by blow what was going to happen, where's the adventure? It's not a thesis. It's a play. You're going on a journey. You don't know where—maybe. Or you have an idea, a clue. . . . I write because it's thrilling. And sometimes it goes down a blind alley. But that's the risk you take.

Sam Shepard

Stewart McBride / 1980

From *Christian Science Monitor*, December 26, 1980, B2–B3.

Opening night at the Magic Theatre. Drama critics, representing publications from the *Village Voice* to *Newsweek*, are jammed into the third-floor 99-seat theater on the San Francisco waterfront. Tonight they outnumber the paying customers for the world premiere of *True West*, the latest play by Sam Shepard, the winner of the Pulitzer Prize for drama.

The house lights dim, and in the green glow of the exit sign Shepard's harshest critic, a handsome rangy fellow in dark aviator glasses and tooled cowboy boots, slumps into the back row. He wears blue jeans, an orange T-shirt, a silver and turquoise belt buckle. He stares sternly at the stage set, the kitchen of a tract home 40 miles east of Los Angeles. In this suburban setting, *True West* uses a sibling rivalry to explore old myths and new realities of the American frontier. In one scene, Austin, who is writing a script for Hollywood—a western romance—is caught stuffing Wonder Bread into stolen chrome toasters while his brother Lee, a petty thief, axes Austin's typewriter with a 9 iron. The man with the cowboy boots in the back row begins to giggle. Now and then he cuts loose with a belly laugh. The other critics turn and glare.

To their surprise the gentleman making all the racket is the playwright. Normally his own toughest critic, tonight Shepard, twirling a single red rose, is thoroughly enjoying his newest creation.

"This is the first one of my plays I've been able to sit through night after night and not have my stomach ball up in knots of embarrassment," he later tells me in his easygoing western drawl. "I worked longer on this than any other play and rewrote it 13 times. *True West* is the first play I've truly felt hooked up to."

That is quite a confession coming from the man who is arguably America's best practicing playwright. After Tennessee Williams, Shepard is said to be the most produced American playwright in this country. Since 1964, when he was 20 years old and his first one-act showed in an Off-Off-Broadway theater more than 40 of his plays have been produced. Added to this mountainous achievement he has won seven Obie (Off-Broadway) awards, though ironically has never had one of his plays produced in a commercial Broadway theater. Among his counterculture credentials are collaborations with Bob Dylan, Michelangelo Antonioni, Mick Jagger, and New Wave poet-singer Patti Smith.

Shepard's plays are distinctly American in scope and subject: Old West cowboys, fading rock and roll stars, sci-fi monsters, Hollywood agents. Yet, like America's jazz men in the 1940s and '50s, he in many ways is better known on the other side of the Atlantic. In Europe Martin Esslin, former head of the BBC's drama division, says, "Sam Shepard is contemporary American theater."

True West, which opened this month in New York at the Public Theater, is thought by many critics to be the best play Shepard has ever written. It is the third in a trilogy of plays on the disintegration of the family and was preceded by *Curse of the Starving Class* in 1977 and in 1978 by *Buried Child*, for which he won the Pulitzer. *True West* is a sharp departure from his more experimental and often elliptical earlier plays.

This is his first true comedy and has the trademarks of great dramatic work: realism, well-crafted character, and economy of language. Shepard has edited out any heavy-handed metaphysical symbolism which invaded some of his earlier writing, thus making *True West* an intriguing play open to broad interpretation. The bucking bronco of the American theater has settled down, and the audience is the beneficiary.

As if maturation as a playwright were not enough, he has taken up, with startling success, a second career—acting. Two years ago he made his debut as the melancholy landowner in Terrence Malick's cinematic objet d'art, *Days of Heaven*. After rave reviews, Shepard was cast as the son of a Kansas preacher, alongside Ellen Burstyn in the current film *Resurrection*.

Just last month, Shepard returned from shooting in Texas yet a third film, *Raggedy Man*, co-starring Sissy Spacek. "If he [Shepard] wants it," *Newsweek* film critic David Ansen writes, "he stands on the brink of an extraordinary new career in the movies."

Becoming a movie star, however, appears to be the last thing Shepard has in mind. In the last year he has left Hollywood agents aghast by repeatedly turning his back on lucrative movie contracts. (He was offered the lead in *Urban Cowboy*, a role later accepted by John Travolta. The playwright also walked away from a recent offer to star in one of Warren Beatty's productions.)

At the moment, Shepard seems to want most to be left alone in his modest Marin County hacienda where he lives with his wife, O-Lan (a writer and director), their 11-year-old son, Jesse Mojo, O-Lan's mother and stepfather, and four dogs. More than ever, the friendly but reclusive playwright guards his privacy with the zeal of a J. D. Salinger, understandably shunning reporters and rarely granting interviews. Friends say Shepard is most himself roping calves in a small-time rodeo or playing drums with a local jazz group.

I met Sam Shepard at a playwright workshop he was giving at the Marin Community Playhouse in Kentfield, Calif., half an hour north of San Francisco. He was sitting cross-legged in a circle of drama students doing dialogue exercises near a row of redwoods.

On that particular day he had invited a musician friend, J. A. Deane ("Dino" to Sam), to "jam" with the young playwrights. Dino, one of the West Coast's most creative percussionists, traveled with the Ike and Tina Turner Revue and worked at the Overtones Theater in San Francisco on several of Shepard's music-word productions.

At the playwright workshop Dino had surrounded himself with the tools of his trade: bells, tambourine, cymbals, and rattles. As Dino improvised, Shepard instructed his students to use the sounds as "an environment for words" and write a scene. Roles were then flip-flopped and Dino translated the students' writing into music. When I arrived, he was crumbling an old milk carton to the line: "Romaine lettuce in the refrigerator crisper is two weeks old."

Shepard, an accomplished drummer and devotee of progressive jazz, often writes in a form that is more musical than dramatic. He uses Jack Kerouac's technique of "jazz sketching" or jamming with words. Like a musician jumping from key to key, improvising as he goes, Shepard treats dialogue like jazz riffs.

"I see actors as musicians, playing to each other, using their voices instead of instruments," he tells me during a workshop break. "I'm always surprised by the similarities between music and writing: the inner structure, tonality, rhythm, harmony. *True West* felt like a total improvisation spinning off itself. The writing of the play started when I heard the voice of Lee speaking very clearly, and then I heard Austin's response. The more I listened, the more the voices came.

"Listening is essential in writing and it takes a lot of practice. It's not just listening with the ear, but it's that inner sort of listening. It's like listening to yourself think when you're driving long distances through the night, or listening to yourself play an instrument. It's possible to play an instrument without listening and still hit all the right notes. But that's not music."

As his students read the simple dialogue they have written, Shepard constantly asks them, "Is that really what you heard when you listened?"

In the frenzy to create the well-made play, inexperienced writers "overwrite," he says. "Sometimes writing becomes so dense and impacted that there is no room to listen. Then you're not inviting the listener, you're pushing him away. Give the audience some breathing room. And leave some air around the actors. Let the lines nudge them into action. When dialogue is just words, it's like padding that cuts you off from the character instead of connecting you. Good dialogue comes from listening to your inner questioning and being vulnerable. Humility and questioning go hand in hand. Humility isn't something you make up. It's . . . coming up against the great unknown and admitting you just don't know." To his credit, *True West* embodies the humility and sparseness Shepard strives for.

Sam Shepard was born in 1943 at Fort Sheridan, Ill., an army basic training camp twenty-five miles north of Chicago. His father was a career officer, and during Shepard's youth the family shuttled from base to base, from South Dakota to Utah, from Florida to Guam and the Philippines before they finally settled on an avocado ranch in Duarte, east of Los Angeles. Sam belonged to the local 4-H Club, raised chickens and sheep, and one year a ram of his won grand prize at the Los Angeles County Fair. He was a casual student, played drums in the high school band, and spent a few semesters at a junior college before moving to New York.

There he dabbled in acting, worked in Greenwich Village, roomed with Charles Mingus Jr. (son of the great black jazz musician), and read Beckett and the Beat poets. In 1964 his first two one-act plays, *Cowboys* and *The Rock Garden*, were mounted by Theater Genesis at St. Mark's Church-in-the-Bowery. The *Village Voice* liked them, and Shepard's writing career was launched.

In the mid-1960s he played drums for a group called the Holy Modal Rounders and began writing the first of his rock and roll plays. In 1971 he gathered his wife and toddler son and moved to England, ostensibly looking for a new rock band. There he wrote *Geography of a Horse Dreamer* and *The Tooth of Crime*, which some critics still consider to be his best work. In 1975 Shepard toured with Bob Dylan's Rolling Thunder Revue through the Northeast and later wrote *The Rolling Thunder Logbook*.

How does Shepard look back on his earlier work?

"Mostly I try to forget it. Your work is a manifestation of who you are when you were at that place in time. I can't help but be a different person now doing different material. After *Buried Child* I wanted to simplify, to refine, and distill. That is the general direction I'm moving in.

"I used not to care about character. I would write these five-minute speeches, arias, and they were simply boring. Character has become much more important to me. I learned that from [British director] Peter Brook. A playwright has to understand what an actor goes through. I've seen Beckett made to look like Abbott and Costello. I don't see how a playwright can grow if he doesn't get involved in the production of his work."

One of the reasons Shepard doesn't see more of his own work produced is that he refuses to set foot on an airplane. He travels, when he has to, in his own pickup truck.

On the day of the playwright workshop, his truck was being repaired and he rode his green ten-speed bike to the community playhouse. After his class, Shepard lifted his bike into the back of my camper and we drove to have lunch at one of his favorite diners, Joe's, near a cloverleaf on Highway 101.

As we drive, we chat about raising Sundown sheep, his mother's trip to Alaska, and the time he encountered at Stanford an affectionate gorilla named Koko who spoke in sign language. "I stepped into the cage and she put her arm around me and kept giving me the sign: 'Tickle me. Chase me.'" While Shepard appears more comfortable speaking of animal husbandry than about his plays, he is capable of discussing his work without false modesty.

He focuses not on how far he has come, but on how far he must go, in a manner devoid of pretense. He is casual, good-humored. Once he is convinced that a reporter is not trying to play peek-a-boo with a movie star, Shepard is easy to talk to. The time I spent with him felt more like chewing the fat with a slightly older brother than interviewing one of the country's preeminent playwrights.

As we pull up in front of Joe's, I wonder aloud how the last two years of acting has influenced this playwright.

"It's the difference between training a horse on the ground and getting on his back," he says. "Until you get up on stage and put yourself inside the character you'll never realize the dilemmas an actor faces. A lot of playwrights think actors are automatons and can pick up wherever the writer leaves off. That doesn't happen.

"And another thing, the playwright's vision is not fixed. It has movement and life. A play is alive and continuously evolving, never dead or locked in certainty. What's all this superstition and stigma about the playwright getting involved in the production? The general impression is that play-wrights don't know anything about acting and sit in the background and whisper to the director."

Sometimes directors have exactly the opposite problem. Says Robert Woodruff, who has directed the premieres of six Shepard plays, including *True West*: "Some playwrights want to get up and direct because they have so much invested in their work. But Sam has got his chops down. His whole being isn't at stake and he can be objective. He knows when it's the writing or the acting that is bad. *True West* was a very different experience for him. Usually he paces around the lobby during a performance. For this one he's been sitting through the play and coming every night."

Joe's diner has green Naugahyde booths, all-weather carpet, and flag-stone walls hung with gold-framed pictures of river canyons at sunset. It is the sort of restaurant where waitresses are surly enough to presume they know better than your stomach what you would like for lunch. Shepard's stomach told him tomato and bacon sandwich, but our waitress bullied him: "No, darlin'. You don't want that. What you need is a good meat sandwich, like our beef or lamb."

Before Shepard's lamb sandwich arrived, I asked the man, attacked in his early days by critics for being an "obscurantist," whether he has an audience in mind when he's writing.

"When you're writing you don't worry about an audience. At that point the only audience is yourself. On the other hand, playwriting is about peo-ple. And if you exclude them, what have you got left? Playwriting is not a closet act. It is not an act of elitism. All I'm saying is that you can't treat the audience as some sort of ghost.

"I've written plays to which the audience has not been connected. *Horse Dreamer* was too much in the fable genre and created a distance between the audience. I want people to leave my plays with a sense of questioning, a sense of mystery, but not mystification. I don't want them puzzling over 'What does this mean?' I want my plays to open up whole new territories. We're at a transitional time in history. Old exteriors and values are crum-bling away and giving birth to new ones. People are turning toward ques-tioning their purpose, and the theater reflects that."

After lunch he saddled up his ten-speed to ride to the nearby car dealer where his truck was waiting. As we stood in the street in front of Joe's, Shepard took a final few minutes to explain what drives him as a writer:

"Playwriting is self-discovery. You are working out yourself. You're ask-ing questions and thinking about where your last play left off. And you don't always come up with the answers.

"Most writers are cooking up ideas that will make their next project, but the ideas aren't vital to them. The contemporary playwright I respect most is [Peter] Handke, his prose and his plays. He's exploring the truth in himself, and his plays open it up to everybody. There hasn't been a writer since Beckett that has been so adventurous. Joan Didion is that way, too. She is ruthless with herself and doesn't allow self-indulgence.

"Beckett surpasses everyone. He's like the Marlon Brando of writers. He persevered to keep the suffering of writing, but not in a masochistic way. For him it was the admission of not knowing but still keeping at it and refusing to settle for easy answers.

"I'm driven by a deep dissatisfaction. What you accomplish in your work always falls short of the possibilities you know are sneaking around. The work never gets easier. It gets harder and more provocative. And as it gets harder you are continually reminded there is more to accomplish. It's like digging for gold. And when you find the vein, you know there's a lot more where that came from."

The *True West* Interviews

John Dark / 1981

From *West Coast Plays* 9 (Summer 1981): 52–71. Included here are only the Sam Shepard sections of Dark's *True West* interviews; not included are the interviews with others involved in the production. Reprinted by permission of John Dark. Actor and comedian John Dark was Shepard's close friend and for a time his father-in-law. Their correspondence was published as *2 Prospectors: The Letters of Sam Shepard & Johnny Dark* (2013), edited by Chad Hammett.

On Seeing a Play

Once upon a time a man walked into a theater. He bought a ticket and he walked into the theater and he was expecting to see this play. And he sat down and he had his catalogue and he looked through the, you know, the . . . they don't call them catalogues in theater. They call them brochures? Programs—that's right, catalogues are for cattle auctions. So, anyway, he sits down and he reads the actors' biographies and where the author is from and what the director's last production was and then the play starts. And the play turns out to be nothing at all what he expected. And he finds himself entering another world. He just sort of walks into a totally unknown world and he can't quite figure out what the world's about but it looks real interesting to him and it's interesting because it reflects something about a part of his life that he feels and has partially experienced but he doesn't live in. But this play causes him to temporarily live in this world that he knows he carries around with him all the time. And he temporarily enters and lives inside this thing and then it's over. And everybody applauds and the actors bow and they leave. And he gets up and he walks out and for a while this thing sort of haunts him because it has brought him in contact with the unknown in himself. And he starts to wonder about it; just about that state. And then he forgets everything and he goes back to his regular life.
[. . . .]

On the San Francisco *True West*

I'm not really sure what the reasons are for doing *True West* again in San Francisco. I thought they were clear when we first initiated this but it's changed a lot for me. The vindication part of it has gone out the window as far as I'm concerned. It's just another production.

I did feel that it was a shame that New York didn't get to see the original. That's the one we sort of had our heart in. I did anyway. As opposed to the second one.

The original production of *True West* was a real thrill. It was the only production I kept feeling actively involved with all through the run. I just kept coming night after night. The play had a certain fascination about it—I don't know what it was, in the performance of it—that just never died for me.

On Seeing His Own Plays

Usually I'll stay for the first five minutes of one of my plays and then ditch out, go drinking and come back at the end. It's because I can't stand it. It's like watching yourself being operated on. Also I hate the fucking theater. Sometimes I like watching the thing come alive but for the most part it's pretty painful.

And the audience doesn't help either because they hardly ever like the same things I like. I mean like a lot of times I've been sitting in the middle of something of mine and people are gawfawing all around me and then something will strike me funny and I'll be the only person in the audience who will laugh. I don't know why that is. A lot of things people laughed at in *Buried Child* I never would have laughed at. Like the dead baby at the end. I keep picturing this review that starts off "The central character of the latest Pulitzer Prize–winning play is a DEAD BABY."

On New York and Regionalism

Right now I don't want to open anything in New York. I'd rather open everything here with no strings attached. I'm not saying I'd never do another show in New York.

This play was under Papp's umbrella to begin with and he condescended to let us do it first at the Magic. I don't want to be in that situation anymore—strung out between two poles. But there's no reason we couldn't do something here and take it to New York. We've got actors out here who are every bit as good as New York actors.

There isn't any national theater; there isn't any one theater in the country that absorbs it all. In Europe it's possible because it's so small. You can have a national theater in England but here you can't. So I see the regional thing becoming stronger as people become more and more aware of the place they're from. And it's not only the sense of geography, it's a sense of a community of artists. I think there really is a community of artists here in the Bay Area and still, there's a tendency to forfeit that in preference for some hypothetical home in New York. You continually hear people saying, "Well in New York they do this and that," and they're betraying their own home by doing that.

On Commercial Success

It will be fine if the play is successful once we get to a large commercial theater like the Marines' Memorial but I don't have personal hopes for it one way or the other. I would hope that it would attract an audience but it's not going to be the end of the line if it doesn't. Of course, if it does, the danger is that it encourages this attitude of "Whoopie, let's get this into a commercial production," which I don't think is where it's at either. One of the strong points about this area is that people are into doing small productions but there's this emblem that's usually held up of commercial theater being the proof of the pudding. I don't think it's true.

On What It Takes to Make a Production Work

The ingredients are everything. A lot of people fail to realize that. A play just doesn't exist unless the ingredients are there to cause it to come into being. You just can't throw any old group of people together and expect a play to have a life. I guess that's obvious. I felt like the relationship we had when we did it here [at the Magic Theatre in 1980] was real strong—you could feel a connection between everybody. And, of course, I was absent from the New York production. I can't complain too bitterly but the ingredients are everything. You can't even take brilliant actors and throw them together with different people and just expect something to happen—it has to be everybody.

On the Language of *True West*

With *True West* I tried to peel it back until I got the language exactly the way I wanted it to sound. I just tried to peel it down so that it didn't have any extra stuff to it and one of the results was that people were disappointed because it wasn't excessive—because it doesn't go off on tangents—but that's exactly what I wanted, to keep it away from this garrulousness. The words that are there are a mixture of something intended and something just coming out. A line comes out and then you start listening to it and the more you listen to it the more you hear how it's not sounding the way you intended for it to sound. So you ask yourself, what is throwing it off? And it may be just one word. So you take that word out and it brings you closer. It's a luxury because a musician who plays an improvisation and hits the wrong note can't go back.

On Rewrites

Of course, it's tedious, too, to go back and do rewrites on a play but I don't think it's analogous to running a play over and over. Rewrites are their own thing and the production of a play is something else because rewrites are appearing in the initial production. I used to avoid that process 1 think because I was basically lazy and I wanted to get on to the next thing and I was compulsive. And a lot of things just weren't worth rewriting.

On Working with Directors and Actors

Of course, it varies from piece to piece but it's hard to find the right balance between what's interfering with where the director's taking the piece and a determination to see it done the way you want to see it done. In some cases it's worth battling to see it done—I mean asserting your point of view or asserting your attitude about it—and other times it doesn't seem worth the emotional strain. With *True West* I've seen it done once real close to the way I wanted.

It's not like there's an original fixed vision—it's not set in granite. It's a moving thing. The characters, as I originally imagine them, are specific only within a range of movement. That's the difference between theater and making a piece of sculpture or a painting where you can fix it. So when you're working with an actor and characters, you're working with a movement. Now in case of Jim [Haynie, who plays Lee in *True West*] during the first production, he came real close to touching a scale from the bottom to the top, and that's incredible when that happens. He brought a whole lot to the character.

I mean for example seeing an actor evolve which is unbelievable—I mean if it's a good actor—to see him get closer and closer to this thing and then grab ahold of it. But then . . . a lot of times when an actor has to recreate a role or play a role for a long time, that disappears. It's gone. Often even in rehearsals it's gone. It's not there. But when an actor is first fishing for it, it's really great. And then when he suddenly discovers it's *in* him, he doesn't have to go outside to get it, that's exciting.

You can see actors who had that going for them and then they went off and did commercials for a year and they did jive plays in some regional theater and then they come back and they cut off, they need to work. You can see they really haven't "worked" in a while; they haven't had to stretch. They come back with a whole series of mannerisms that take the place of "work" and their emotional thing is cut off. They can only go so far and they get up to it and they just bang against it. They won't go through it. They're not opened up.

I saw the same thing in myself just in my limited experience in the movies. In *Raggedy Man* I'd be walking along and all of a sudden I'd see . . . "Well this is something I did before."

If you go into a production with one actor, wishing it was another actor, you're never going to be satisfied. But if you can accept the actor that's there in the role and start to work with who the actor is and go all the way, then no matter who he or she is the actor begins to contribute from themselves. Then the thing starts to have life.

What I get carried away with is *them* and the *character*. You sort of know something about the person and then you've got this character going and you're always fluctuating back and forth. It's emotional because there's all this stuff that's gone into it. That's when you're real wrapped up with a production.

I've walked into stuff that I've seen colleges doing . . . you don't know any of the actors and you couldn't care less. You say, "I don't know any of these people." I just don't have the feeling for the character without the person who's acting. *The actor is the character.* If I don't know the actor, I don't have the feeling. Like up at this college which recently did a play of mine . . . it was weird. I walked into this auditorium filled with people and this woman had designed this program where they did three scenes from *Curse* with a full audience and me sitting in the back and I didn't feel anything for the actors at all. I could see the play which was interesting but I didn't know the people.

I have no hopes for the play once it goes on the stage. I have a lot of hopes for the actors though. You see, what happens, I totally identify with the actors in the thing, not the play; I mean if I know the actors. And I start worrying about them, looking at their subjective state and getting worried about it. Both worried for the play's sake and personally worried about them. I start doing a lot of worrying.

On Going into Production

The approach is important—the way a play is approached from the very start. It's exciting to me when the actors have a lot of room in the beginning to explore their own intuitions . . . they're not given a lot of things . . . they're allowed to unravel so long as it's along the line. And then that unraveling starts to inform the director or the writer or whoever's there, and then things can be chosen from that so that it's all coming from the actor. That approach interests me a lot more than going in and trying to get the actors to do what you want them to do.

On Opening a Play

Now once the play opens it's both a death and a birth. It's both things. It's no longer in a room with just "us" . . . now suddenly it's being witnessed by all these strangers and it kills something right off. It also makes something else happen. It took me a long time to get used to that, especially when you direct it yourself. You suddenly realize that there's no way that the audience will ever be able to see what went into it. All they're seeing is the results. They'll never see all of the days and discussions and so on, the whole process . . . the whole movement toward "the play."

On Running a Play

Some plays shouldn't go more than six weeks, as good as they are. There's an initial thing when a play breaks the ice—that counts for something; and after that it becomes not so interesting. Long runs are tedious. Even for

JOHN DARK / 1981 **65**

actors. I mean if you're an actor, you don't want to be in a play for three years night after night after night. Who wants to do that? At a certain point the life goes out of it.

On Theatrical Specialists

I think all of the designated professions in the theater are really worthless . . . like costume designer, set designer, prop designer . . . are absolutely worthless. And the more they're defined, the more they tend to fragment the sense of the wholeness of the production. They're absolutely worthless. They're meaningless jobs that have become designated only because of a certain tradition. You don't have to have the aspects of the production designated by different people. Ideally, two people should do it all—the director and the writer. And it should be possible that between a director and a writer you can design lights, design a set, design the costumes, design the entire smell of the thing. Because the fewer people involved in those choices the better your results. You can only go wrong in two directions.

On Entertainment

There was entertainment and then there was serious art and the twain shall never meet. It was like, there's no way you can entertain and be serious. And people have tried to combine the two, like Brecht. He really wanted a cabaret theater where people came and drank and smoked and had a great time and listened to music and heard songs and saw showgirls, you know, and then inside he would insert these lessons—moral, philosophical and political lessons. I mean he was pretty incredible. But I don't think he was a playwright. He was a philosopher and a politician. (I hope that doesn't go down in history. "Shepard accuses Brecht of not being a playwright." You have to understand that these are all partial truths.)
[. . . .]

On Opening Night of *True West*

The lights were real good. I thought they were the best element of the technical side of it. What I liked about it was their hard edge . . . the intensity of it. When it was orange, it was really orange, you know. It wasn't pretending to be these in-between colors like amber and soft pink and all of those bullshit gels that are just "atmosphere" gels. 1 don't like atmosphere gels. Me and Woody [director Robert Woodruff] totally had a real clear idea about the lights. Initially, in the written script, the lights are pretty general, but then when we got down to the production, we defined it. That's one thing I think me and Woody see pretty much the same . . . the color of it, because we always come up with good colors together. Now the guy who did the lights really brought a whole lot to it technically and in other ways, too. But the great thing about him was that he was able to see actually what we were trying to describe to him and accomplish it which is as much a part of it as anything.

The actors, I felt, didn't really have a unity. There's some individual performances that are really fine but there isn't that unity. There's a lack of connection between them. Now I don't know whether that lack of connection comes from the way it was written or from the actors trying to work together. I think that a real unity between the actors and the director and the writer would mean that you're all agreed to open up to the unknown. I think Woody wants to go in that direction but it's real hard to develop it because you can't guarantee that everybody in a cast will want to go like that.

The production looks to me like a Cinerama version of the original. It looks like you took a home movie and then blew it up. And the audience relates to it like that because there's so many of them. They relate to it in this kind of "big" way . . . "This is a big thing now" and it's more "exterior" as a result. It's like an "exterior" vision. I feel like I'm looking at a kind of comedy play of the first play. The first production is inside of it and it's been eaten up by the second production . . . just like a big fish. Jonah and the whale.

The audiences seem to really like it a lot which surprises the hell out of me . . . really it does. I get surprised. There's a lot of laughing which is okay—I don't mind people laughing. People seem to be enjoying themselves. That's great. I always had this prejudice against entertainment which was something that was branded on everybody on the Lower East Side of New York in the sixties.

The costumes I felt lacked a certain kind of synthesis . . . like a relationship between all of them. Individually, they were pretty good but there wasn't a through line in the costumes that connected the brothers with the producer, with the mother. They were all broken.

The set I'd have to blame on my own description because my description of it and even my vision of it is not clear. It's too general. I've got a general idea of the set and it never seems to translate. For me, it would have been much more stark and not so much of an attempt made to make it a realistic set . . . just the barest elements; the sink, the refrigerator, and just exactly what you need and no trimmings. I could have gotten that, of course, but then I compensated. I felt somehow obliged to let the set designers have a couple of things that they wanted because they made a real effort to try to do exactly what I wanted and I thought they came pretty close. And then they started to add little bits and pieces which I felt intimidated to complain about; like the real colorful pan that sits on top of the counter, they got this pan that has a painted flower on it, and they got all these pots up above the stove and they put a chrome breather above the stove and stuff like that.

[. . . .]

I never intended the play to be a documentary of my personal life. It's always a mixture. But you can't get away from certain personal elements. I don't want to get away from certain personal elements that you use as hooks in a certain way. The further I get away from those personal things the more in the dark I am. *True West* is riddled with personal sketches like the tooth story for example.

A Conversation with Sam Shepard

Amy Lippman / 1983

From *The Harvard Advocate*, March 1983, pp. 2–6, 44–46. Reprinted by permission of *The Harvard Advocate*.

Sam Shepard is one of America's leading playwrights. His works include *Angel City, The Tooth of Crime, La Turista, Curse of the Starving Class*, and many one-acts. *Buried Child* became the first Off-Broadway play to be awarded the Pulitzer Prize in 1979. *True West* was performed at the ART in the spring of 1982, and is presently enjoying a successful run Off-Broadway at the Cherry Lane Theatre. Shepard is also an actor and has appeared in several major films since 1978: *Days of Heaven, Resurrection, Raggedy Man, Frances*, and *The Right Stuff*. He is the author of two collections of poetry and prose: *Hawk Moon* (1981) and the recently published *Motel Chronicles* (City Lights Press, 1982). His newest play, *Fool for Love*, opened in early February in San Francisco at the Magic Theatre, where many of Shepard's plays have debuted. This interview was conducted in San Francisco in January.

The Advocate: Can we begin by talking about the play you're working on now?

Shepard: It's called *Fool for Love*. But because I'm in the middle of it, I'd rather not talk about the nature of it.

The Advocate: In the past, you haven't always directed your own plays.

Shepard: I've directed, let's see, about five or six things of my own. I've never directed anybody else's.

The Advocate: While you are in the process of directing one of your own plays, does your original vision of the play significantly change?

Shepard: Well, yes, but I don't know about this whole idea of the "vision" of a play. I think there's a misunderstanding about that idea. In other words, I think a play has a vision that's in motion. I don't think it's a fixed vision. A lot of people speak of it as though it's a definitive vision. And it may be for some other writers, but it's never been like that for me. It's been a malleable thing, something that's in flux. It also has a lot to do with the actor. You can say you have a vision of a character, but once the actor gets ahold of it, that thing necessarily changes. It *should* change because the actor is influencing it according to who he or she is. And so you go with that. To me, that's exciting. I mean, I welcome that new thing that the actor brings with him, because it's who he is. I'm not trying to force the actor to *be* the character. I want to see what the meeting is between the actor and the character. That's the most interesting thing.

The Advocate: As you are writing a play, do you have a certain idea of what the play's ending will be?

Shepard: No. I think for me, every play has its own force, its own momentum, its own rhythm and tempo. That's the fascination of it. It's like people who hear music in their heads, or in the air, or whatever. They attract it in a certain way and it begins to speak to them. It has its own peculiar set of rules, and circumstances, and complicated structures that you can't necessarily dictate. I think a play is like that. What you're trying to do, in a way, is have a meeting. You're trying to have a meeting with this thing that's already taking place. So, I can't really say that I have a beginning, middle, and end every time I sit down to write a play. *Every moment* of the play is a beginning, a middle, and an end. It's like this Japanese thing. I don't know if you've ever heard of this Japanese acting thing . . .

The Advocate: Associated with Noh?

Shepard: Well, it's a technique inside of Noh. It's called *Jo ha kyu* and it means the beginning, middle, and end of every moment. So, if you look at it like that, then it's inevitable that every play I write has a beginning, middle, and end, but I don't know what it is because I'm trying to follow the presence of the whole thing. I'm trying to follow every moment, every action, every word, so that it becomes much more detailed than just a big, long, expanded piece.

The Advocate: So, it's a very ephemeral process?

Shepard: Yeah, it is. A play's like music. It's ephemeral. It's always elusive. It's appearing and disappearing all the time. You never reach a final point with it.

The Advocate: Even after the direction of the play has been formally completed and the performances begin?

Shepard: Sure. It's bound to change because it's a living performance. A performance is always changing. That's the beautiful thing about it. You're not trying to reach a certain point with it. No, what you're trying to find is a place where the actor can immediately understand. It's something intuitive. Then, you can take any actor who's worth his salt, and put him up against it, and he'll meet this place in the performance. It'll vary, because each time the actor's different. You perform it one time, someone else performs it another time. It will always have a certain kind of structural similarity, but it'll have all kinds of variations within that because of the nature of the people who perform it.

The Advocate: Many of your plays, as they appear in the published form, contain very specific prefaces. You're very explicit about how a set is to look, or how something is to sound. Aren't you then limiting interpretations by doing this?

Shepard: Yes. Sure. I want to limit the interpretations because, for the most part, the interpretations are lame. They're off the wall. I've had so many plays that have appeared like three-ring circuses, that I never intended to look like that at all. A lot of people think a play, particularly my plays, because they have this superficial quality of being pop art or something, give people the excuse to go bananas. And that's not true at all; that's not what I'm encouraging. I'm not encouraging people to go off the deep end with it. I *want* a limitation, but that limitation doesn't limit the actor in terms of what he can do. There are so many directors that go off the deep end because they figure they have the license to just take your stuff and go crazy with it. I'm not interested in that at all.

The Advocate: The prefaces seem more concerned with the appearance of the production than with any sort of characterizations.

Shepard: Yeah, because I trust the actors more than I do the directors.

The Advocate: Have you ever worked in conjunction with another director?

Shepard: Well, I had a relationship with a director recently—Woody, Robert Woodruff [at the Magic Theatre in San Francisco]. That was great for a while. But for the most part, I don't. I don't get involved with other directors. I either direct it myself, or I have somebody like Woody that I can work with as a partner. But every time a play is done, I don't rush off and collaborate with a director. I really don't care about it that much. I really only care about initial productions—the first ones. Once that first production happens, then I don't care what happens to it really. I'm not concerned in tracking it down, in following it around like an ex-lover or something.

The Advocate: Do you see productions of your own work?

Shepard: No. For the most part, it doesn't interest me, no. The initial production is very exciting because you're involved, you're engaged in it. After that point, though, I'd just as soon let it go and go on to the next play, because the next one's going to be even that much more exciting than the one before it. It's only that original thing, seeing it come into being. Then, I'm willing to let it go.

The Advocate: Critics of your plays such as *Curse of the Starving Class*, *Buried Child*, and *True West* have often referred to them as chronicling the break-up of the American family. To what extent is that a legitimate reading of those plays?

Shepard: I'm not interested in the American social scene at all. It totally bores me. I'm not interested in the social predicament. It's stupid. And the thing you bring up about the break-up of the family isn't particularly American; it's all over the world. Because I was born in America, it comes out as the American family. But I'm not interested in writing a treatise on the American family. That's ridiculous. I mean, that's not fair or unfair to read that into my plays. It just seems an incomplete, a partial way of looking at the play. People get off on tripping out on these social implications of the play and how that matches up to contemporary America. And that's okay. But that's not why I'm writing plays.

The Advocate: So, why are you writing plays?

Shepard: I have to. I have a mission [*laughs*]. No, I don't know why I do it. Why not?

The Advocate: You collaborated on the writing of two of your collected plays, *Tongues* and *Savage/Love*.

Shepard: Yeah, the ones with Joe [Joseph Chaikin]. Well, that was a very unique circumstance, working with someone that I'd known as a friend for a long time and never really had a chance to work intimately with, one on one. I was hanging around the Open Theater and I knew Joe. We had a lot of things in common. So we just sat down and collaborated on this thing, just cooked it up. The thing that was unique about them, I think, is that they were designed for one performer, for him in particular. That was the impulse behind the whole thing. It's very different than writing by yourself.

The Advocate: Is that something you're interested in doing again?

Shepard: Yes. We're going to do something else. But I don't know when because I'm involved in this other thing [*Fool for Love*].

The Advocate: Because of the financial restrictions of the contemporary theater, plays are being written more and more frequently with only a few characters. The logical consequence of this is a smaller kind of production. Do you see another possible consequence of this to be a falling back on mythic infrastructures? On the simple, direct themes of Greek tragedy, for example?

Shepard: Yeah, I'm real interested in simplification. The barest bones of the thing, so that it's not complicated by—

The Advocate: The barest bones of the *plot*?

Shepard: Of everything. Which is one of the main reasons why I like working with Joe. We started with nothing. We didn't start with fourteen actors in a big group and a lot of musicians and accoutrements. It was just him and me. It's very interesting then, because everything you come up with is distilled into just these bare bones, these necessities.

The Advocate: Is there a conscious connection between the way in which you craft a play and what you see as the craft of Greek theater?

Shepard: No. I'm not making any connection consciously. But, in crafting a play, I'm convinced more and more that it has to do with the inner nature of the thing itself. The inner rhythm of what you set off right at the very beginning. You don't come in and start crafting something if there's nothing there. It has to be a manifestation of what you set off. That's what craft is, being true to that. I don't feel connected to any theatrical traditions. I mean, maybe some of them have influenced me. The Greek plays have influenced me, but I can't say that I'm trying to write Greek plays.

The Advocate: How have they influenced you?

Shepard: In terms of what character means. That's the biggest influence they've had on me. I suddenly discovered that here were these characters that reached back and forth across time, and are still true today. These things, these emotional states, these forces that were set in motion. And they had names—Oedipus and all that. What interests me is where these emotions come from. They go so far back that they go right to the birth of man. And we're still living in the shadow of these things. But I'm not trying to set up a Greek tragedy.

The Advocate: Do you consider your work to revolve around myths?

Shepard: Well, so many people have different ideas of what the word means.

The Advocate: What does it mean to you?

Shepard: It means a lot of things to me. One thing it means is a lie. Another thing it means is an ancient formula that is expressed as a means of handing down a very specific knowledge. That's a true myth—an ancient myth like Osiris, an old Egyptian myth that comes down from antiquity. The thing that's powerful about a myth is that it's the communication of emotions, at the same time ancient and for all time. If, for instance, you look at *Romeo and Juliet* as a myth, the feelings that you are confronted with in a play like that are true for all time. They'll always be true.

The Advocate: What relationship does that have to your plays?

Shepard: Well, hopefully in writing a play, you can snare emotions that aren't just personal emotions, not just catharsis, not just psychological emotions that you're getting off your chest, but emotions and feelings that are connected with everybody. Hopefully. It's not true all the time; sometimes it's nothing but self-indulgence. But if you work hard enough toward being true to what you intuitively feel is going down in the play, you might be able to catch that kind of thing. So that you suddenly hook up with feelings that are on a very broad scale. But you start with something personal and see how it follows out and opens to something that's much bigger. That's what I'm interested in.

The Advocate: Should one then be able to project his own experience onto what has occurred on stage?

Shepard: Yeah, you can do that if you want to. But it doesn't have any real value. The only time it has value is when you hook up with something that you *don't* know. Something that you can't pin down. Something where you say, "I feel something here that's going on that's deeply mysterious. I know that it's true, but I can't put my finger on it." I'm not interested if it reminds you of your mother, or your sister, or your cousin, or anything like that. So what? Everybody has something like that. That's what I mean about this social thing, that similarities between social neuroses in American society really don't mean much in the long run because they're always going to change. But if emotions that come up during a play call up questions, or seem to remind you of something that you can't quite put your finger on, then it starts to get interesting. Then it starts to move in a direction we all know, regardless of where we come from or who we are. It starts to hook up in a certain way. Those, to me, are mythic emotions.

The Advocate: What ties do you feel to the American West?

Shepard: Well, it's all subjective. I just feel like the West is much more ancient than the East. Much more. It is. It was even founded before the East. I don't know if you've traveled out here at all but there are areas like Wyoming, Texas, Montana, and places like that, where you really feel this ancient thing about the land. Ancient. That it's primordial; that it goes way, way back. Of course, you can say that about New England. But it doesn't have the same power to me, because it's this thing about space. No wonder these mysterious cults in Indian religions sprung up, you know? It wasn't as though these people were just . . . just fell down from the sky. It has to do with the relationship between the land and the people. No wonder there were these religions that were so powerful, so awesome, and persisted for hundreds and hundreds of years. It's because of the land—the relationship between the human being and the ground. And I think that's typically Western and, I think, much more attractive than this tight, little, forest civilization that happened back East, on the East Coast. It's much more physical and emotional to me. New England and the East Coast have always been an intellectual community. Also, I was raised out here, so I guess it's just an outcome of my background. I just feel like I'll never get over the fact of being from here.

The Advocate: There's a very disorienting element in some of your plays. In certain places the dialogue is very realistic but the situation seems very surrealistic, and this dichotomy is never resolved.

Shepard: I think it's a cheap trick to resolve things. It's totally a complete lie to make resolutions. I've always felt that, particularly in theater when everything's tied up at the end with a neat little ribbon and you're delivered this package. You walk out of the theater feeling that everything's resolved and you know what the play's about. So what? It's almost as though why go through all that if you're just going to tie it all up at the end? It seems like a lie to me—the resolutions, the denouement, and all the rest of it. And it's been handed down as if that is the way to write plays.

The Advocate: What's the alternative?

Shepard: Well, there are many, many alternatives. But I think it's all dependent again on the elements that you start with and what your interest is in those elements. If you're only interested in taking a couple of characters, however many, and having them clash for a while, and then resolve their problems, then why not go to group therapy, or something?

The Advocate: What do *you* do?

Shepard: I think of it more like music. If you play an instrument and you meet somebody else who plays an instrument, and the two of you sit down and start to play music, it's really interesting to see where that music goes between two musicians. It might not go anywhere you thought it would go; it might go in directions that you never even thought of before. You see what I mean? So you take two characters and you set them in motion. It's very interesting to follow this thing that they're on. It's a great adventure—it's like getting on a wild horse.

The Advocate: But aren't you, the playwright, controlling everything? You're *creating* it, aren't you?

Shepard: I'm not creating that.

The Advocate: It doesn't happen by itself, does it?

Shepard: No, but in a way, it's already in the air. I really believe that's true. These things are in the air, all around us. And all I'm trying to do is latch onto them. I don't feel like it's a big creative act, like I'm inventing all of this. I mean, I'm not putting myself in the same category as Mozart at all, don't get me wrong, but the story with him was that he heard this music. It was going on, and he was just open to it somehow, latched onto it, and wrote it down. *True West* is like that. *True West* is following these two guys, blow by blow, just following them, trying to stick with them, and stick with the actual moment by moment thing of it. I mean, I wrote that thing . . . it took me a long time to write that play.

The Advocate: Why?

Shepard: Because I went down a lot of blind alleys. I tried to make them go in one direction, and they didn't want to go that way.

The Advocate: How did you know when it was right, then?

Shepard: I just *knew*. Just like you know it's right when you're with somebody. When you're with the wrong person, or when you're with the right person. You know it like that. You don't know it through the head—you have a feeling.

The Advocate: How did you know when to end it?

Shepard: Well, I've always had a problem with endings. I never know when to end a play. I'd just as soon not end anything. But you have to stop at some point, just to let people out of the theater. I don't like endings and I have a hard time with them. So *True West* doesn't really have an ending; it has a confrontation. A resolution isn't an ending; it's a strangulation.

The Advocate: Is the point then to leave the audience hanging?

Shepard: No, no. I'm not intentionally trying to leave people up in the air. But I also don't want to give people the impression that it's over [*laughs*].

The Advocate: Do you write for an audience?

Shepard: Well, you know, that's an interesting question because, here again, the question comes up, what is the audience? Who is the audience? In a way, you write for yourself as a certain kind of audience. In the midst of writing, it always feels as though I'm writing for the thing itself. I'm writing to have the thing itself be true. And then I feel like an audience would be able to relate to it. The theater's about a relationship.

The Advocate: Between the actors and the audience?

Shepard: If there's no relationship on stage, there's not going to be any in the theater. But that has to be answered first in the writing. If you and I sit down on stage as two actors, and we don't have a relationship, what's the point? . . . A relationship's both invisible and tangible at the same time, and you can see it between actors. You can also see the absence of it. If it's there, the audience is related immediately.

The Advocate: Do you have difficulty casting your plays for that reason?

Shepard: No, I have actors in this play here [*Fool for Love*] that are just exactly what I wanted. But for this play, I had certain actors in mind. But I don't always write like that; sometimes I write with no one in mind.

The Advocate: Can you achieve that "invisible and tangible" relationship only through the directing of a play?

Shepard: Yeah, I think so. And through the actors. The actors have to open to it. The director's responsible for opening the actors to that meeting, and every time they shy away from it, to open them more and more to it, to a point where it's always present. Like in that scene you saw today. You have two characters on the stage that don't want anything to do with each other. Superficially, they hate each other. They turn their backs to each other and there's *still* a relationship in that. They're related by turning away from each other. You see what I mean? So they don't need to be in communion with each other. They don't have to be in sympathy with each other—they're just flat-out related. Like a blind person and his dog, there's a relationship there.

The Advocate: How are you affected by criticism, both favorable and unfavorable, of your work?

Shepard: Well, I'm not immune to it. But you've got to follow this thing that you're on, no matter what. You've got to follow this thing that keeps telling you blow by blow what to do. It's very apparent [to you] what the next thing is. But critics can't tell you that. How could a critic know what your inner condition is as a writer? . . . I'm not saying [criticism] doesn't have a pull on me. It has a definite pull on me. But whether you believe it or not is what counts. It's like, I don't know, I've been in a few rodeos, and the first team roping that I won had more of a feeling of accomplishment and pride of achievement than I ever did getting the Pulitzer Prize. . . . At the same time, I'm not trying to throw anything up in anybody's face. I'm glad that the plays are successful and that they do something to people. But I'm not trying to win another Pulitzer Prize or anything.

The Advocate: Do you feel as if the media has certain expectations of you?

Shepard: Sure. It's hard to know what they're expecting. If they're expecting me to be myself, I can guarantee that will happen all the way down the line. If they're expecting me to be Eugene O'Neill, they may be disappointed [*laughs*].

The Advocate: What writers have influenced you? What playwrights?

Shepard: I don't know. What's the point?

The Advocate: Do you go to see plays?

Shepard: I don't go to the theater at all. I hate the theater. I really do, I can't stand it. I think it's totally disappointing for the most part. It's just always embarrassing, I find. But every once in a while, something real is taking place.

The Advocate: So, as for contemporary influences on your work—

Shepard: Have you ever been to a rodeo?

The Advocate: No.

Shepard: Well, there's more drama that goes down in a rodeo than one hundred plays you can go to see. It's a real confrontation, a real thing going on. With a real audience, an actively involved audience. You should go to a couple of rodeos after you go to the theater.

The Advocate: Well, do you see your plays fitting into any sort of dramatic context?

Shepard: Why? Why do I have to put them in any context? Why can't I look at it as a stream by itself? I'm not saying that it's totally unique. They're obviously things in it that are borrowed, or stolen . . . but I'd rather look at it as its own river. I really don't care if it reminds anybody of *Long Day's Journey Into Night* or if it reminds anybody of *Waiting for Godot*, you know? It doesn't matter. That's up to the people who want to categorize it, want to put it in its place [*laughs*].

The Advocate: Do you consider your plays "experimental"?

Shepard: I guess they are. I mean, it's all experimental. Experiment, by its very nature, has to do with risk. If there's no risk, there's no experiment. And every play's a risk. You take a huge risk with something like that.

The Advocate: In its appeal? Its success?

Shepard: No, a big risk in going into unknown territory. You don't know where you're going.

The Advocate: Are the risks in creating unusual situations, or a totally new way of presenting something? What risks do you mean?

Shepard: Well, I don't know if you feel this or not, but I feel like there are territories within us that are totally unknown. Huge territories. We think we know ourselves, when we really know only this little bitty part. We have this social person that we present to each other. We have all these galaxies inside of us. Huge, unknown territories. And if we don't enter those in art of one kind or another, whether it's playwriting, or painting, or music, or whatever, then I don't understand the point in doing anything. If you don't enter into these areas that are deeply mysterious and dangerous, then you're not doing anything as far as I can tell. You're just trying to make something so that people will like it.

The Advocate: How does that relate to your own work?

Shepard: It's the reason I write. I try to go into parts of myself that are unknown. And I think that those parts are related to everybody. They're not unique to me. They're not my personal domain.

The Advocate: Is there then something cathartic about the whole process of writing?

Shepard: No. Catharsis is getting rid of something. I'm not looking to get rid of it; I'm looking to find it. I'm not doing this in order to vent demons. I want to shake hands with them.

The Advocate: How long have you been writing plays?

Shepard: Seventeen, eighteen years.

The Advocate: How have your plays changed?

Shepard: Well, actually, they're the same. They're just closer to a verification of what these emotions are. In a way, that old cliché about somebody doing the same thing over, and over, and over again their whole lives is true. I feel like that's true. I'm doing the same thing over each time. I'm trying to get closer to the source.

The Advocate: Are you more adept at doing that now than you were eighteen years ago?

Shepard: I'm more . . . not adept, I'm more *determined* to do it. I'm less afraid. Because there's something absolutely terrifying about going into yourself. . . . It's something that I don't understand. If I understood it, I probably wouldn't write. That's why it's very difficult to talk about, and why a lot of this sounds like it's evasive.

The Advocate: Do you feel that you have discovered certain things, dealt with them in your plays, and then moved on to something else?

Shepard: Well, I haven't left anything behind. . . . That's not true. I've gotten rid of a lot of useless stuff. A lot of tricks.

The Advocate: Dramatic tricks?

Shepard: Yeah. Like allowing things to unravel in a direction that you know they're not going to go by themselves. Like this play [*Fool for Love*], for instance. I wrote about sixteen versions of it, and every time I came back to the first five pages. I'd write like seventy, eighty pages and then bring it all the way back to the first five pages and start again—throw out sixty, seventy pages. So, I've got literally at least a dozen different versions of the play, but the first five pages are the same in every one.

The Advocate: Is that because what you felt initially about it was the truest?

Shepard: Yes. The very first meeting there was something there. I knew there was something there, and I just had to keep trying. They weren't just drafts. Every time I think *this is the play*. I'm not writing a draft—I wrote twelve *plays*.

The Advocate: And in directing it, do you have the impulse to change anything?

Shepard: No, I know it's there now. I might internally change a few things, but the meat and potatoes are there. The emotional truth of it had to be met. Now it's just a matter of having the actors get it into their heads.

The Advocate: How do you do that?

Shepard: Well, through repetition. And through seeing the distance between the actors.

The Advocate: Before you begin work on stage, do you discuss the characters and their motivations with the actors?

Shepard: No, I think that's confusing. Because I'm not interested in actors acting from the head, acting from information they've cooked up. I try to avoid a lot of explanations. I'd rather the actor just discovered it through the body and the intuition. And that takes a particular kind of actor, too. You've got to know that you've got that actor to begin with.

The Advocate: As an actor, how do you approach a role?

Shepard: I don't really consider myself an actor. In film you can get away with a whole lot that you can't on stage. I think almost anyone can get away with being in a film.

The Advocate: Is that just the nature of the medium?

Shepard: Yeah. Because if you're in a tight close-up, you don't have to do much. You don't have to do anything; you just say the lines. You don't have to act. So, I mean, with film acting, for me, it's just a matter of corresponding certain parts of myself to the character, finding corresponding parts and just becoming those parts all the time. I'm not a method actor or anything. I don't have any complicated scheme behind it.

The Advocate: Could you act in your own plays?

Shepard: I could, but I don't want to.

The Advocate: Why?

Shepard: Well, because part of the reason for writing them is to see them. You can't see them if you're in them at the same time. I like having that distance.

The Advocate: Music plays a more significant role in some of your plays than in others.

Shepard: I think they're all musical. I like to look at the language and the inner rhythms of the play, and all that to me is related to music directly. In *True West* there are coyote sounds and crickets and things like that. And the dialogue is musical. It's a musical, *True West*. I think it's very related to music, the whole rhythmic structure of it. Rhythm is the delineation of time in space, but it only makes sense with silences on either side of it. You can't have a rhythm that doesn't have silence in it. I studied for a long time with a drummer from Ghana. He was totally amazing. And I found out that, particularly in African music, every rhythm is related. You can play 4/4, 5/8, and 6/8 all together at the same time and there's a convergence. At some point there's a convergence. Even though it sounds like these things are going off in totally crazy directions that are beating up against each other, they'll always come back. That was a big revelation to me, that rhythm on top of rhythm on top of rhythm always has a meaning. So the same is true on the stage. There are many possible rhythmic structures that an actor can hit, but there's only one true one. There's one moment that he has to meet.

The Advocate: How do you find that moment?

Shepard: Well, that's very complex. It has to do with an emotional relaxation, where suddenly the tension goes and it's just *there*. I was a drummer for a long time and I realized that a lot of the time you're straining to keep the time. And then there are times when all that drops away and everything just . . . it just all rides together. And those are the times it became simple. Absolutely simple.

The Advocate: Do you feel closer to certain plays because they contain more of a sense of that?

Shepard: Oh, yeah. Some of them have real dumb rhythms. It depends on each piece, though; every piece is different. Like there's only one little part of *Buried Child* that I like, that I could watch over and over and over again. One little tiny section. It's at the beginning of Act Two, I think. Just the little dialogue between the children and the old man on the couch by the television. That's the only part that interests me anymore.

The Advocate: Why?

Shepard: Because the rest of it just seems verbose and overblown. It seems unnecessarily complicated. But that little simple scene at the beginning of that act, it's great. It's perfect. I could watch that all day. It's just got a musical thing to it, you know? That kind of thing happened.

The Advocate: It's been said that nothing can shock anymore. Still, there's an element in some of your plays that seems determined to shock us.

Shepard: Yeah?

The Advocate: In *Curse of the Starving Class*, for example, you have a character pee on stage.

Shepard: Well, I wouldn't do that again if I had to do it over again. I was looking for a gesture, for something without words. It's funny how you look, you know? You look at all parts of yourself for it. Sometimes it comes out when someone pisses on stage. It's a little flashy, you know, and overblown, and maybe embarrassing, but that's the way it came out. It's just a gesture. Like the toasters in *True West*. There's an intention there that's intrinsic to itself. It only makes sense to itself. It doesn't *mean* anything. You can call it absurdist, or you can call it whatever you want to, I don't care what you call it, but it's true to itself. It takes the impulse that was behind it to its absolute extreme, further than you would expect. And that's what I wanted. Trying to figure it out is not the point. I think explanation destroys it and makes it less than it is.

The Advocate: How do you feel about working with a realistic set? Is that sometimes a hindrance to you?

Shepard: No, no, I love it. Because you can do anything. You do something in a weird space somewhere . . . you experiment with the space, you goof around with it, then it doesn't have the same impact. In the traditional theater situation, the impacts of things that come from it are made even more so because the physical situation is ordinary. But if you make that situation extraordinary to begin with, then everything is . . . nothing means anything. All of a sudden *everything* is off the wall.

The Advocate: What about your pieces that occur on an open, empty stage?

Shepard: I'm not against any kind of attempt. I'm not looking for one way to do something. I think you should try all kinds of ways. But it's not without its limitations; just having no set doesn't mean that you are unlimited. You're immediately limited by all kinds of things—all kinds of notions about what a play means because it has no set. And all the kinds of prejudices that have been built in about no-set theater. Audiences are very tricky these days; they've got all kinds of ideas.

The Advocate: Is that a consideration? Are you concerned with that?

Shepard: You have to deal with people's attitudes, sure. You have to take them into consideration.

The Advocate: People thinking that no-set theater is "artsy"? That it has "meaning"?

Shepard: Yes. I like to stay away from that if possible. In other words, I like to approach the play to begin with in the most ordinary way. I like to set it up at the beginning so that everybody's happy, so that nobody's trying to figure anything out. Everything's okay to begin with. To begin with something that is immediately unrecognizable to immediately mysterious is confusing, because no one knows where to go. But if everybody starts out thinking they know where they're going, *then* you can go in a different direction. *Then* you can go off into territory unknown. If you want to have a meeting with people, you have to pick the place. You can't just say, "Oh, we'll meet somewhere." You have to know where you're going to meet. Then you can go on a voyage. But that's really important to people.

The Advocate: Are the two pieces that you did with Joseph Chaikin [*Tongues* and *Savage/Love*] exceptions to that?

Shepard: No. It's very obvious where the meeting is. It's a direct confrontation between one actor and an audience. He has more of a meeting than maybe a lot of stuff I've written.

The Advocate: Where in *Buried Child*, for example, do you make that shift from the immediately recognizable to the mysterious?

Shepard: When he [the character Tilden] brings in the corn.

The Advocate: Well, in that instance, a character is sitting there husking corn and another character [Bradley] walks in and says something like "What the hell is happening here?" He acknowledges the strangeness of the situation. Doesn't that form of acknowledgment within the play itself negate the surreal quality of the action?

Shepard: No, I think the opposite. It brings attention to it. . . . Those gestures have a law unto themselves.

The Advocate: Peeling vegetables, you mean?

Shepard: Yeah. Here again, they have an absolute intrinsic meaning that's true to itself. Whether it means something socially, politically, religiously, all of that, I'm not interested. That's not what it's about. It's there because the guy had to do that. And I don't know *why*—I really don't. I did decide on corn because it was Illinois. The choice of vegetable was very conscious.

The Advocate: That conjures up a very strange image of you sitting at a typewriter writing.

Shepard: Yeah [*laughs*].

The Advocate: How do you write?

Shepard: You mean the technical thing? I write by hand first. I write everything in notebooks. Then, after I get everything where I want it pretty much, I start typing it. And as I'm typing it, I'm rewriting it. I'm copying from the notebook and I'm rewriting on the typewriter. I mean, that's just the way I found it best to work.

The Advocate: You do no preliminary work? No outlines, scenarios?

Shepard: No. Writing is writing, so why write a scenario when you can write a play? It's much more exciting. If it were a screenplay or something, I'd write a sketch or an outline.

The Advocate: You just finished work on a screenplay.

Shepard: Yeah, I just wrote a screenplay with Wim Wenders that we're going to shoot in March. And that was great. It was really incredible. It was a great collaboration. I've done screenplays before, mostly disappointing events.

The Advocate: Why?

Shepard: Well, I wrote two original screenplays that I sold innocently, thinking that they'd be made into movies. They ended up in the archives of Hollywood someplace; they'll never be made. Then I wrote a film with Robert Frank and Antonioni [*Zabriskie Point*, 1970]. Those are the only other two collaborators.

The Advocate: What is the nature of the screenplay you did with Wenders?

Shepard: Well, it's not really a screenplay. It's more a description of a film, an involved outline. I'll write the dialogue on the set scene by scene as we do it, because that's the way he's used to working. It was an uncanny kind of meeting. We had met about a year and a half ago because he wanted me to do this film *Hammett* that he was working on. I was being considered for that part, and I got along with him really great. And then it turned out that Frederick Forrest did it instead, and he said he wanted to do something with me. I just had this new book that came out by City Lights called *Motel Chronicles* and he got ahold of it and wanted to make a film based on the book. So we sat down and started talking about it and soon discovered that it wasn't the kind of thing you could adapt. We took characters from the stories, states of mind or whatever you want to call it from the stories, and developed characters and made a whole new screenplay out of it. It has a lot of similarities [to the book], but it's not a strict adaptation.

The Advocate: Will you act in it?

Shepard: No, I doubt it. I'm going to be writing and working on the outside of it.

The Advocate: Do you consider yourself a poet?

Shepard: That's a very high thing to be, a poet. César Vallejo is a poet. I'm not a poet yet; I'm working on it. I think a poet is a musician. Poetry is music. So it doesn't matter what form it's in, whether a line extends across the page or goes vertically. That has nothing to do with it. It's the musical nature of the language and everything that's going on in it. Vallejo, Neruda,

Hank Williams. He was one of the original country-western singers. Have you ever heard any of his stuff? Great American poet. "I'm So Lonesome I Could Cry"? You never heard this? Jimmie Rodgers? You've got to look into this.

The Advocate: Do you see more poetry in music than in the more traditional written form?

Shepard: Well, traditionally poetry and music were connected. They had to do with religion, prayer, and celebration—all that stuff. There was no separation between the poet and the musician, they were the same thing. . . . I don't know what broke that all up. Now poets are . . . what are poets? They're alcoholics and neurotics. They used to be seers. They used to be people who could deliver things from another world. A poem isn't something that's easy to come by. You've got to earn it.

The Advocate: Could you have written this play, *Fool for Love*, say, ten years ago?

Shepard: No. That would have been impossible just in terms of the experience of it. Not the experience of writing it, the experience in life. I couldn't have written it ten years ago. A play has to be tied to a part of you. It's all coming out of your experience in one way or another.

The Advocate: Do you see your work as evolving to a certain point?

Shepard: No, I don't see it like that at all. Maybe it's just going in a circle. I don't know; I really can't tell you whether it's evolving or not. I mean, it's definitely different than it was. There's more at stake now; there's a bigger risk.

The New American Hero

Pete Hamill / 1983

From *New York*, December 5, 1983, pp. 74–102. Copyright © 1983 by Pete Hamill. Reprinted by permission of ICM Partners. Pete Hamill was a columnist and editor for the *New York Post* and the *New York Daily News*. He is the author of ten novels, two collections of short stories, and *A Drinking Life: A Memoir* (1995), *Why Sinatra Matters* (1999), and *Downtown: My Manhattan* (2004).

I remember trying to imitate Burt Lancaster's smile after I saw him and Gary Cooper in *Vera Cruz*. For days I practiced in the backyard. Weaving through the tomato plants. Sneering. Grinning that grin. Sliding my upper lip over my teeth. After a few days of practice I tried it out on the girls at school. They didn't seem to notice.

—Sam Shepard, *Motel Chronicles*

The blond woman is standing beside a mailbox, holding a baby. At a right angle to the two-lane blacktop, a dirt road leads to a barn the color of dried blood, a few spare trees, a small white frame house. On the other side of the paved road is farmland, so rich and black it looks like tar, wet from the night's rain. The woman has a letter in her hand. The Iowa sky presses low on the land. A dank wind blows from the north. Then a 1982 Ford pickup truck moves slowly down the paved road, past trailers, vans, parked cars, knots of lumpy people in winter clothes, their breath pluming in the cold, past a table bearing a coffee pot and paper cups, past a still photographer clicking away with a motor-driven Nikon. The man driving the truck wears the empty look of failure. Beside him is a bearded man with a hand-held movie camera, shooting past him at the blond woman as the truck draws closer. Then the man stops the truck. He talks with the blond woman, the words torn away by the wind.

"That was fine," says the balding man in the heavy coat. His name is Dick Pearce. He is a movie director. The blond woman, who is the actress Jessica

Lange, nods. The man in the truck smiles crookedly. "You sure?" he says. The director says, "It was fine, Sam." Behind the wheel of the truck, Sam Shepard glances off at the horizon, as if wishing he could put the truck in gear, tell everyone to leave him alone, and drive off into the blankness.

Then he runs a hand through Jessica Lange's hair and kisses her on the brow and smiles his crooked smile. It is true: he doesn't look at all like Burt Lancaster.

"You see that Sam Shepard?" still man Dean Williams says. "My father was a farmer. And my father lost his farm, just like the farmer in this movie. And when I see Sam coming down the road in that truck, or I see him walking around the fields, or just eating lunch, I swear, I feel like crying. 'Cause this guy is a *farmer*. I mean, I know he's a great writer, I know he's a movie star and all that. But when I look at him, he's a farmer. And he makes me want to die."

The movie they are making here in the farmland near Waterloo, Iowa, is called *Country*. It's about a modern farm family that is being wiped out by recession and debt and faceless bureaucracies; the Walt Disney people are financing it; the screenplay is by William D. Wittliff, a Texas book publisher (Encino Press), whose screenplays include *Raggedy Man*.

There have been some problems. Wittliff, who is co-producing the movie with Jessica Lange, was the original director; after two weeks, everyone agreed his directing debut wasn't working out. He agreed to step aside for Dick Pearce, who was a top documentary-maker for years before making the feature films *Heartland* and *Threshold*.

"I think it's gonna be a hell of a movie," says actor Wilford Brimley one lunch hour on location. "Jessica's great, and Sam, hey, he's one hell of an actor." Brimley shakes his head, standing beside a heater in the tent where the crew eats lunch. "It's funny in this business," he says. "I guess now it's Sam's time."

He may be right. After one of the previews of *The Right Stuff*, in which Sam Shepard plays test pilot Chuck Yeager, someone turned to me and said, "John Glenn? To hell with John Glenn. Sam Shepard for president." Women I know who saw the film talked about none of the other actors; they all wanted to know about Sam Shepard. When I told a few friends that I was going to Iowa to interview Shepard, I received calls from three women photographers who wanted the assignment. A decade ago, it was this way with Robert Redford. At age 40, Sam Shepard seems to be emerging as the male star of the 1980s.

"It's not just the way he looks," a woman friend said. "It's everything else."

Everything else is pretty remarkable. Sam Shepard is not primarily an actor; he's a writer. More than 40 of his plays have been produced in New York in the past twenty years; he won the 1979 Pulitzer Prize for drama for

Buried Child; two of his plays, *True West* and *Fool for Love*, are currently having successful runs Off-Broadway. His books of prose and poetry, *Hawk Moon* and *Motel Chronicles*, are in the bookstores, along with a Bantam edition of seven of his plays. Critics as varied as Michael Smith, Stanley Kauffmann, and Ross Wetzsteon have praised him as the finest playwright of his generation, and there is a sense that his best work has not yet been written. He is an accomplished musician, a former drummer with a rock 'n' roll band called the Holy Modal Rounders. His screenplay, *Paris, Texas*, is now being directed by Wim Wenders. And after acting in only six movies, he turns away far more offers than he accepts, and his price has climbed to the million-dollar range. If such weren't enough, he now lives in Santa Fe with . . . Jessica Lange. To some people, the combination hardly seems fair.

> EDDIE: I never repeat myself.
> MAY: You do nothing but repeat yourself. That's all you do. You just go in a big circle.
> —Sam Shepard, *Fool for Love*

On this gray afternoon, Sam Shepard is sitting in his trailer behind the old red barn. A copy of *Western Horseman* lies open on the couch. A new Remington 870 pump-action shotgun, propped against a wall, gleams dully. There is a bag of Red Man chewing tobacco on the table. He talks about the new albums by Bob Dylan and the Rolling Stones, about the Duran-Hagler fight, about the late Keith Moon ("That was the greatest rock 'n' roll drummer I ever saw; he got so carried away one night that he fell over backwards, right out of the kit"). Shepard has a reputation for privacy that makes him sound like an amalgam of J. D. Salinger, Thomas Pynchon, and Howard Hughes (who was transformed into "Henry Hackamore" in Shepard's play *Seduced*). Here in this trailer, between takes of this movie, he isn't like that at all; privacy seems more a strategy for a writer who works hard than some slickly calculated device to build up a personal mystique.

"It isn't calculated," he says, nibbling on the tobacco. "I always had the feeling that there was something about when you *do* something—let's say you invent a spoon. Then someone comes along and starts interrogating you about this invention. I mean, I know this is a stupid example, but still, the interrogation, or the fascination about you as the inventor, is a wholly different thing from the invention. The two things are so separated, in a way, that if you start mixing them the invention becomes confused. You start to mix it up with images of yourself as an inventor, or it becomes distorted, it gets clouded." He lights a cigarette. "Plus, I prefer a life that isn't being eaten off of. It's very easy to be *fed* off of, in a certain way that distorts and actually diminishes you completely, destroys you to the point where you don't have a life anymore."

The man who played test pilot Chuck Yeager does not fly, so he doesn't come to the openings of his play in New York; he does little promotion, gave no post-production interviews for *The Right Stuff.*

"I never felt any compulsion to sell the stuff," he says. "And I feel like a lot of the time what's being asked of you is to sell it. I've already *done* it. Making a movie is hard enough. And then somebody comes around and wants you to advertise it in order for it to sell. I don't give a shit if it sells. Why should I care? I'm not on the promotional end of it; this thing of going out and doing promotional campaigns is just a totally separate deal from what I do."

What Shepard does is reveal through his writing (and to some extent his acting) a vision of America that is cutting, comic, and, most important, tragic. His world is populated by gangsters and farmers, rock stars and cowboys, gamblers and movie stars and people of myth. In one play (*The Mad Dog Blues*), we meet Mae West, Captain Kidd, Paul Bunyan, Jesse James; in another, we live with Pecos Bill. Shepard has lacerated Hollywood in *Angel City*, examines the disturbed core of the American family in three major plays (*Curse of the Starving Class, Buried Child, True West*).

His form is often anarchic, always surprising, yet there is a moral sense brooding behind the dazzling surface of action and language. In some ways, Shepard is as American as Huckleberry Finn; he often looks back to a lost innocence, sometimes symbolized by the emptiness of the western desert, sometimes by the people of masculine myths, and his characters often long to join Huck by lightin' out for the territories.

Play after play revolves around disappearance: A woman wants to live like author B. Traven; a man wants to vanish into the air itself; others choose car and truck and the romance of the road. In the later plays, the symbol of the circle recurs. The characters are imprisoned within the circles of their lives, or seem to be making a wide circle home. As does Shepard himself.

"It's like you gotta go a long way away to come back," he says on this afternoon in Iowa. "Something like that."

> SHELLEY: Can't we just drive on to New Mexico? This is terrible, Vince! I don't want to stay here. In this house. I thought it was going to be turkey dinners and apple pie and all that kinda stuff.
> VINCE: Well I hate to disappoint you!
> —Sam Shepard, *Buried Child*

He grew up with another name, Samuel Shepard Rogers, and was known to everyone as Steve. He was born November 5, 1943, at Fort Sheridan, in Illinois, an army base about 25 miles from Chicago. His father, Sam, was in the Army Air Corps in Italy. The father came home soon after, damaged by the war. The family began to travel—wounded father, mother, the boy, and two sisters—going from base to base, this month in Rapid City, South Dakota, next month in Utah, this year in Florida, and then across the country and across the Pacific to Guam. Pieces of those years continue to seed Shepard's work. On Guam:

[*See* lines 1–7 from "12/26/81 Homestead Valley, Ca." in *Motel Chronicles.*]

At last, the army behind them, the family landed on the shores of California. They stayed a while with an aunt in Pasadena, and then the father bought an avocado ranch in Duarte, sixteen miles east of Los Angeles. Memories of that place and time were fresh decades later when Shepard wrote in *Hawk Moon*, "The red awning. The garage door. The strip of lawn down the center of the driveway. The Pyracantha berries. The Robins that ate them. Close-ups of the Robin's beak guzzling red berries." He can still walk in memory "past the snarling Tiger painted on silk, brought back by my Dad from the Philippines; past the portrait of a train conductor painted by my Grandfather; past the pink Hibiscus flowers growing in the light from the bathroom."

The father was an amateur musician who played drums with a local Dixieland band. Soon, young Steve Rogers was learning to play drums, too, and doing better than his father. "He had a great record collection, all old swing music, Dixieland, that kind of thing," Sam Shepard says now. "I hated it all at the time, but now I know I was getting an education in American music without even knowing it."

At Duarte High School, he was an indifferent student, but he liked the farm, was a member of 4-H, once raised a prize ram, thought about becoming a veterinarian. At the same time, life in Duarte began to feel like a prison, and he dreamed of escape. "There was no way I was gonna stay in Duarte," he says. "What would have happened if I'd stayed? God knows."

He had visions of escape; some were provided by the movies.

"There was this powerful impression when I was a kid going to those films and absolutely believing that this was a way to *be*," he says. "It wasn't just an actor acting; this was a *life form.* One you could suddenly assume and step into. There were times—and this isn't special with me, it happens to other people—where you'd go into a film and come out feeling like John Wayne. That whole swagger, or whatever it was, you'd walk out of the theater with it. Even now, after seeing a great film, I feel that little twinge of assuming the character. I come out of the theater walking with it."

And he began to be interested in literature, most of it by Jack Kerouac, Lawrence Ferlinghetti, and Gregory Corso. Shepard was still in high school when someone mentioned to him that "there were these guys called the beatniks. One of these local guys was a painter. He wore sandals and had a beard—you know, all that stuff. One time I went over to his place, and he had all these books, and he threw this play at me. It was *Waiting for Godot*. I never had seen anything like it. I didn't understand it, I didn't know what the hell was going on, I didn't know what it *was*, I couldn't place it as a play, a poem, a novel, or anything else. It just seemed like a unique piece of writing. It didn't stick with me as a model or anything. But it just struck me suddenly that with words you could do *anything*."

At graduation from Duarte High School, Shepard was forced to make a choice: take a job managing a sheep ranch in Chino or leave.

"And just accidentally I went and auditioned for this acting company," he says. "I saw an advertisement in the paper. They were auditioning actors for something called the Bishop's Company; they did plays on church altars, one-night stands, adaptations of novels and stuff. I went in there and they hired me. And the next day I was sent to Pennsylvania on a bus, and I toured with the company for about six months. That was how I first saw New York. Just came in on the bus and got off and stayed."

In his work, Shepard talks about the way he assumed various masks during his high-school years: movie stars, musicians, the recurring figure of the cowboy.

"I had a feeling of vulnerability at that time that I didn't understand," he says. "And there was this constant attempt to deal with it. I wasn't knocked over the head all the time; I mean, that's something everybody goes through, but I really wanted to get *out* of there. Like a lot of people who grow up in a little hick town, you just want out altogether. And at the same time, being out meant you were even *more* vulnerable. And I wound up in New York, where you couldn't be *more* vulnerable."

Nineteen, adrift in the city, Shepard wandered for days. Then he read in a gossip column that Charles Mingus Jr. was working as a busboy at the Village Gate. The son of the great jazz musician had grown up in Duarte and gone to school with Shepard.

"I went down there and looked him up," Shepard remembers, "and he's the one who got me a job there."

By now, Steve Rogers had transformed himself into Sam Shepard. He changed his name while on the road.

"I always thought Rogers was a corny name," he says, "because of Roy Rogers and all the associations with that. But Samuel Shepard Rogers was kind of a long handle. So I just dropped the Rogers part of it. That had gone on for generations, that name, seven generations of it. It kind of shocked my grandparents more than anybody, I think, 'cause they kind of hoped I would carry it on. Then I called my kid Jesse, so that blew it entirely. Now in a way I kind of regret it. But it was, you know, one of those reactions to your background." He laughs. "Years later, I found out that Steve Rogers was the original name of Captain America in the comics."

He arrived in New York in 1963, and nobody was happier to say good-bye to the fifties. Later he would write:

[*See* lines 1–7 from "And So Does Your Mother."]

Sam Shepard wrote his first play *Cowboys* in true pioneer style . . . on the back of used Tootsie Roll wrappers.

> There were ice caps on the waters. He laid waiting for the year to end and the white buffalo to come raging from the ocean.
> —Patti Smith, "9 Random Years (7 + 2)"

In New York, he moved into an apartment on Avenue C with Mingus junior and the drummer Dannie Richmond, and worked three nights a week at the Village Gate. "Art D'Lugoff [the owner of the Village Gate] was great," Shepard remembers. "I liked Art, and what's her name? The blond woman who was there [Edith Gordon]. Mingus and I were busboys, and we heard some great shit down there. Nina Simone, in a crazy wig, Monk, the Adderley Brothers, Mingus. Incredible. Woody Allen was doing stand-up comedy with Flip Wilson; they'd get up there and open the show. But jazz . . . that changed me. And I wasn't there long before I started writing."

The headwaiter at the Gate was a man named Ralph Cook, who had just started Theater Genesis, at St. Mark's in the Bowery, on Second Avenue and 10th Street. He was looking for material, and when Shepard wrote his first play, Cook came to Avenue C to read it. He agreed to put it on, and the following week they went into rehearsals. The play was called *Cowboys*.

"The early work was very hasty," Shepard says. "There wasn't much rewriting done. I had this whole attitude toward that work that it was somehow violating it to go back and rework it. It was like 'Take it or leave it—if you don't like this shit, tough luck,' and go on to the next one. Why spend the time rewriting when there was another one to do?"

With one play in production and a good review from Michael Smith of the *Village Voice*, Shepard began to write in a kind of frenzy. The Off-Off-Broadway scene was exploding, there was a sense of ferment and excitement in the air, and Shepard plunged into it.

"It was just all astounding," he says. "You know, coming from a little hick town and all of a sudden living on the streets. It was like joining the carnival. We just went wild." There are stories of Shepard and Mingus junior playing cowboys and Indians on the streets, staying up three days straight, playing drums and loud music, all of it infused with a notion that everything was possible. Shepard saw a few plays: Edward Albee's *Zoo Story*; *Dutchman* and *The Slave*, by LeRoi Jones. ("This guy was a beautiful writer and a great playwright.") But he spent more time writing than seeing plays, and even more time absorbing everything around him.

"When I arrived in New York there was this environment of *art* going on," he says. "I mean, it was really tangible. And you were right *in* the thing, especially on the Lower East Side. La MaMa, Theater Genesis, Caffe Cino, all those theaters were just starting. So that was a great coincidence. I had a place to just go and put something on without having to go through a producer or go through the commercial network. All of that was in response to the tightness of Broadway and Off-Broadway, where you couldn't get a play done.

"Off-Off-Broadway was just to see new work done; it wasn't done as a showcase to move it somewhere else. That came later. It was all in cahoots with poetry and jazz and all that. And the actors. Actors wanted something new, too. People went to it from that community, with no thought about the future of it. It was kind of a phenomenon, 'cause it all happened right there, in that time, and took off like a shot."

Much of Shepard's style and his experiments with form were inspired by jazz musicians.

"Jazz could move in surprising territories, without qualifying itself," he says. "You could follow a traditional melody and then break away, and then come back, or drop into polyrhythms. You could have three, four things going on simultaneously. But, more important, it was an emotional thing. You could move in all these *emotional* territories, and you could do it with *passion*. You could throw yourself into a passage, and then you could calm down, then you could ride this thing, then you could throw yourself *in* again. There was form in a formless sense. Music communicates emotion better than anything else I know, just *anything*! Just bam! And there it is. And you can't explain exactly how the process is taking place, but you know for sure that you're hooked. Who can say why D minor affects you differently than C? But those chords definitely have emotional content that affects everybody, I think, in similar ways. Maybe not identically, but a violent piece of music is violent for most everybody, a peaceful piece is peaceful. Who can tell why that is?"

But while Shepard explored jazz more deeply, another part of him began to rise in reaction. This would become a pattern, part of the circle.

"At first I was reacting against this notion that I wasn't sophisticated," he remembers. "You know, I didn't have this vast experience, this knowledge of what was going down. And I felt this urban thing was what was really happening. Jazz was what I wanted to dive into; it represented a kind of sophistication. Then after a while I started reacting against *that*, this whole jazz influence. You know: 'This is beatnik horseshit,' I'd say, 'sitting around and snapping your fingers—what's *this* all about?' So I began to think rock 'n' roll represented another kind of back-to-a-raw-gut kind of American shitkicker thing. Then that came to a dead end. Now I'm back to country music, all the way full circle back to the simplest C-F-G changes. Hank Williams, he's more beautiful, more pure poet, than anyone else. Merle Haggard comes close. And George Jones, now there's a guy who can sing his ass off."

The job at the Village Gate ended abruptly after three years. "I was stoned one night at the Gate and dumped a candle on this businessman," he says. "They had these candles on all the tables, and I think I cleared some whiskey-sour glasses off, and I knocked the candle over and just coated this guy with wax, and the maître d' fired me. They brought me into the kitchen and said, 'We can't handle this.' I think Gerry Mulligan was playing at the time." But by now Shepard had become a writer. He wasn't making much money as a writer, but he was a writer.

The East Village changed after 1966. Drugs arrived in a heavy way; Shepard was not immune. He tried most things. He also married the actress O-Lan Johnson in 1969, fathered a child (Jesse Mojo), then left his wife for an interlude with Patti Smith in the Chelsea Hotel. "Everything seemed to be shattering," he would say later. He was writing frantically, using a lot of drugs, playing drums in the Holy Modal Rounders, trying to mount his play *Operation Sidewinder* at Lincoln Center.

He and Patti Smith, legend has it, wrote *Cowboy Mouth* together. It's about a woman named Cavale who wants to turn a character named Slim into "a rock-and-roll Jesus with a cowboy mouth." The play is riddled with

Slim's remorse at leaving his wife; the last word of dialogue in the play is "escape." After Shepard and Smith appeared in the play, at the American Place Theatre in the spring of 1971, and *Operation Sidewinder* had been a terrible failure, and after the Holy Modal Rounders broke up, that's what Shepard did. He escaped. With his wife and child. And moved to England. He would be gone three years.

> "My vision. I see. Even in the dark, I still see. Do you want to know what I see, Raul? It's the same thing I saw in Texas when I was a boy. The same thing I've always seen. I saw myself. Alone. Standing in open country. Flat, barren. Wasted. As far as the eyes could take in. Enormous country. Primitive. Screaming with hostility toward men. Toward us. Toward me. As though men didn't belong there. As though men were a joke in the face of it. I heard rattlesnakes laughing. Coyotes. Cactus stabbing the blue air. Miles of heat and wind and red rock where nothing grew but the sand. And far off, invisible little men were huddled against it in cities. In tiny towns. In organizations. Protected. I saw the whole world of men as pathetic. Sad, demented little morons moving in circles. Always in the same circles. Always away from the truth."
>
> —Sam Shepard, *Seduced*

England probably saved Shepard's life; it certainly matured and deepened his art. For more than three years, he, O-Lan, and Jesse lived in Shepherd's Bush and Hampstead while Sam raced a pair of greyhounds at tracks in Walthamstow and Birmingham, and wrote *Tooth of Crime* and *Geography of a Horse Dreamer*. His first contact in England was with director Charles Marowitz.

"I forget why I contacted him, because I hadn't known him before," Shepard says. "But when I got there I didn't know a soul. I knew The Who and The Stones—the music. But nobody else. I guess Marowitz's theater was the theater in London at the time that was doing new stuff. So I thought he'd be open to doing something new. And he was. But when we got into production, we had a big falling-out. He mounted the first production of *Tooth of Crime*, but he wanted to twist it in his direction, and we had a big falling-out. We did it later at the Royal Court."

A more profound influence was the director Peter Brook.

"I don't know him that well, and I've had only a few brief meetings with him, but he's had a real influence on me over the years," Shepard says. "He's phenomenal. He just fills you with more information than you can possibly take in in one sitting. And it all has this tremendous perspective, because he's digested the whole history of theater, and at the same time he's coming at it from the absolute grass roots. He's presented things to me that I still think about *now*, that were presented to me back in the early seventies."

Brook forced Shepard to think about certain essentials of his craft.

"For one thing, he asked me this very simple question: 'What is character?' He just asked me that directly. And it started a whole kind of thought in me about it that is still going on. The simplicity of it, and the mystery of it. What exactly is character? We use terms like that all the time without really knowing exactly what we're talking about. When I started writing, I wasn't interested in character at all. In fact, I thought it was useless, old-fashioned, stuck in a certain way.

"In fact, I preferred a character that was constantly unidentifiable, shifting through the actor, so that the actor could almost play anything, and the audience was never expected to identify with the character. There's something to be said for that too. But I had broken away from the idea of character without understanding it. Do you see what I mean?"

From the perspective of London, Shepard began to think, as many expatriates had done before him, about America, about New York, about the West, about his reactions to his own country through his work. He became more conscious of craft, of working hard at writing, and he developed some distance from his own early work.

"I think of them now as survival kits, in a way," he says of the first plays. "They were explosions that were coming out of some kind of inner turmoil in me that I didn't understand at all. There are areas in some of them that are still mysterious to me. I don't want to make them sound cathartic, because they weren't. They were just these things that came out of the situation inside me that needed a kind of expression. They were just survival techniques, a means of putting something outside rather than having it all inside."

When at last it was time to come home, Shepard didn't return to the Lower East Side. He and the family circled home to California, where they took a house in Marin County. Shepard was soon working with the Magic Theatre, in San Francisco. His father-in-law, Johnny Dark, moved in; other relatives came around; it sounds like a household out of Chekhov, a playwright Shepard doesn't care for (he likes Sophocles, Brecht, Peter Handke, Strindberg).

In 1975, he took a break and went on the road for six weeks with Bob Dylan and the Rolling Thunder Revue, ostensibly to help write the script for a movie that Dylan and the others would make while touring small towns in the Northeast. It became impossible to make the movie in the turbulent atmosphere of the road, but some of the footage became part of *Renaldo and Clara,* Dylan's home movie. It marked Shepard's debut as a movie actor.

"It got real crazy out there," Shepard says now. "But it was . . . fun? Is that the word?"

At one point on the road, he wandered into the Combat Zone, in Boston, with writer Larry Sloman and found himself among punk rockers and their fans, who chose to watch a group called the Tubes while Dylan and Joan Baez and Joni Mitchell and Roger McGuinn were a few blocks away. For the first time, Shepard began to feel old. In his book about the tour, he mused,

> What are all those kids doing watching this shit when they could be hearing good music? What do they care about good music? What do they care about a bunch of West Village folk singers from the Sixties? They wanna see some action. They wanna see brains dripping from the ceiling. Is this that generation stuff that you hear about all the time? What's going on anyway? Am I part of the old folks now? Is Dylan? Is Dylan unheard of in certain circles? Like Frank Sinatra? Bing Crosby? Is this time flying? Is this time flying right past us on all sides? Can anybody see what's really going on?

He came back off the road, started writing hard, and then in 1976 his life changed. Director Terrence Malick asked him to act with Brooke Adams and Richard Gere in *Days of Heaven.* Shepard's experience with the movies had been grim; he had done a script for Michelangelo Antonioni's *Zabriskie Point* that was thrown away; a script for Mick Jagger called "Maxagasm" was never made, and neither was "The Bodyguard," for Tony Richardson. He had written and completed a Robert Frank movie called *Me and My Brother,* but his vision of the movie world was probably best expressed at the end of *Angel City,* when a Hollywood producer begins to cover the stage with oozing green slime. But he liked Malick's work, and agreed to do the part. Shepard discovered that he had some talent, a strong presence onscreen, and a little fear too.

"There's a definite fear about being diminished through film," he says. "It's very easy to do too much of it, to a point where you're lost. Image-making is really what film acting is about. It's image-making, as opposed to character-making, and in some cases it's not true. The real fine actors can go in there and do it. But there is so much imagery involved that you do feel that something has definitely been taken away."

Shepard often laughs at himself when he talks about his acting. "There's something about acting in film that's a dubious achievement. I mean, I've only done six films, so I really don't think I'm any kind of an authority on acting. There are some fine actors working in movies. But the tradition that I grew up in—in the New York theater—was dead set against this style of acting, which is basically behaviorism."

In spite of his doubts, Shepard clearly can become a major star—if he wants it. His lean, laconic performance in *The Right Stuff* moved him solidly into the moviegoing public's imagination and seems certain to bring him an Academy Award nomination. But he was also very good in *Frances*, which starred Jessica Lange. When the film was being made, in 1981, Miss Lange was living with Mikhail Baryshnikov, with whom she'd had a child. Her fierce, heartbreaking performance in *Frances* (along with her quite different part in *Tootsie*) had vaulted her to stardom a year before it happened to Shepard. Last winter, Shepard left his wife and son in California and moved to Santa Fe, New Mexico, where he now lives with Lange and her son, not far from the desert home of Shepard's father. In some New York places, this raised the inevitable question, Can a former Village Gate busboy find true love in the arms of a former Lion's Head waitress? Everybody south of 14th Street certainly hopes so.

"Ah, hell, who knows what's gonna happen?" he says. "Nobody ever knows."

After *The Right Stuff*, and the reviews, and the pictures and the big magazines, does Shepard think of himself now as a writer who acts or an actor who writes?

"I'm a writer," he says. "The more I act, the more resistance I have to it. Now it seems to me that being an actor in films is like being sentenced to a trailer for twelve weeks. With people walking around with walkie-talkies, banging on your door. I don't like the kind of feeling of entrapment that you have to go through to make a film. It's just an imbalance between the few moments of satisfaction that you get playing the part. I don't know if I'll do it much longer." Pause. "But then, it's also insidious. There's this whole temptation of . . . here's another project, here's another project.

"It's all very tempting. I think you have to find a way to refuse much, much more than you accept, just in order to keep going with your own work."

After *Country* finishes shooting, Shepard plans to work again with Joseph Chaikin, the only man he has ever felt comfortable with as a collaborator.

"And after that," he says, "I want to write a comedy. Something funny. Like Laurel and Hardy."

Unknown Territory

Ross Wetzsteon / 1985

From *The Village Voice*, December 10, 1985, pp. 55–56. Ross Wetzsteon was a theater critic and theater editor of *The Village Voice* for 33 years. He is the author of *Republic of Dreams: Greenwich Village: The American Bohemia, 1910–1960* (2002).

"Aw right, we're gonna begin now." Standing in the aisle between the orchestra and the mezzanine, he plants his feet, swings his hips and arms back and forth in a sweeping arc to shake out the tension, halts abruptly, extends his right arm straight forward, and points at the stage with his forefinger. "A-one, a-two, *go*."

It's the first run-through of the first act of his new play, *A Lie of the Mind* (which opens at the Promenade Theatre on December 5, a day before the film version of *Fool for Love* opens at the Plaza). He lights a cigarette, tiptoes along the aisle, taps rhythmically on the cigarette with his forefinger. Music from the five-piece Red Clay Ramblers comes in under the dialogue—he stops pacing, raises both hands, palms outward, to lower the volume, then forms a circle with his thumb and forefinger. He walks up the stairs to the back row, sits down, lights another cigarette, breaks into a giggle when one of the actresses muffs her lines. After a few minutes, he walks back down the stairs, hoists himself up on the railing between the orchestra and the mezzanine, boots dangling, and lights another cigarette.

He's restless, but doesn't let the actors see it. "We're gonna need somethin' for the switch here," he says with soft-spoken authority when one of the actors looks up at him for guidance. "Try somethin' in that territory where you just were. . . . Yeah, that's it, that's it."

The run-through resumes, one of his trademark scenes—the second before the explosion, the second held, held, held, its imminence nearly unendurable. "Yeah, yeah," he says quietly almost to himself. "Now here's where you come on real strong," he calls down to the stage, lifting his right foot, cocking his right elbow, forming a fist with his right hand. Beat, beat, "*here*."

He abruptly stomps his foot and drives his fist toward the floor like a piston. "Oh *yeah*," he says with a grin. "That's the place. Real strong. *Yeah*."

Those who think it's unfair that the preeminent playwright of his generation should also be one of the most virile screen icons of the '80s aren't going to like this one bit, but in addition to his other two talents, he's also one of the most gifted directors in the American theater. His 1983 staging of *Fool for Love*, in fact, won as many accolades as his script. It's a violently claustrophobic play: shrieks bounce off the walls, bodies slam against them—a single flaccid moment in the direction would have been fatal. And, as so often in his plays, the images are even more resonant than the language: in *Fool for Love*, Eddie, so cooped up he could kill, fiercely lassoing the bedpost; in *A Lie of the Mind*, Jake, gently blowing at the box containing his father's ashes, the ashes softly swirling in a shaft of light. He has a particular gift for staging such scenes with visceral exactitude, neither diminishing their rawness in a mechanical precision nor dissipating their clarity in a sloppy emotionalism.

Same clothes as in the old days at Genesis, Judson, La MaMa, the Cino—cowboy hat, denim jacket, silver-buckled belt, jeans, boots. But like a lot of gangly, bony-faced men, he's become far more handsome in his forties, the eyes less nervous, wary, the smile less edgy, suspicious. He's more relaxed these days, more open, not a trace of the protective cynicism he once used to keep people at a distance, no more of that sullen-cowpoke pose he often pulled when he was uneasy. One of the countermyths of our success-oriented culture is that success corrupts character, turning people graciously condescending or aloofly self-satisfied, but in his case it seems to have released an instinctive, good-humored warmth. And, most striking, though he still turns down nearly all requests for interviews, he no longer leaves the impression that he hates to discuss his work, that to talk seriously about his craft will turn him into some kinda fuckin' intellectual.

So why did he start directing his own plays? He lounges back in an easy chair, his hands crossed behind his head. "Well, I got sick of this indirect relationship of having to speak continually through a director to actors because the situation is so fragile to begin with. I wanted a more direct contact with the actors. And the more I worked with directors the more I was disappointed. Not so much in their direction, but in the relationship of having to always be indirect, you know. And, whenever I talked directly to actors with the director present, they would always be uptight and it would create this odd tension which I couldn't really understand. But then at a certain point I thought why not just try to do it myself—make all my own mistakes?

"It's very exciting working with actors," he goes on, leaning forward with his hands gripped between his knees, "because suddenly from working in a solitary, isolated way in the writing of the play, you're now in a community with actors. It's kind of a completion, this cycle of going through absolute isolation to a community." He picks at his chin with his thumb and forefinger. "It's like having a mechanic work on your car as opposed to you changing the oil yourself and getting in there and seeing what the engine's made of."

Like a lot of playwrights, he once had a reputation as difficult to work with. Has the experience made him more tolerant of other directors? "Well, it's not directors so much as that the appreciation of the actor grows and grows and grows each time you set out. Because you start to realize what an incredible undertaking it is for an actor. Acting's an amazing . . . it's probably the most mysterious art form I can think of. Because the actor's using nothing but himself, you know. And discovering territories that are virtually invisible. I don't see directing as some specific blow-by-blow event. Directing, for me, is a process of seeing the actor, and trying to see what the actor has to find. Helping the actor find somebody.

"It doesn't have much to do with your familiarity with them from the past," he continues. "It has to do with an attitude toward acting. What they want to find in acting. Many actors feel they know the whole story. And they don't want to be told what to do, they don't want to listen, they don't want to have any kind of new ideas—they want to just be reaffirmed that they're doing the right thing. And you can't go very far with those kind of actors because they're—there's a psychological arrogance inherent to their thing and a lot of the time it comes out of their notoriety. The more notoriety they get as an actor, very often the more closed they become. They're not going to open up to let you in.

"Another kind of actor, like Ed Harris, absolutely open—a wide-open actor. Good on the screen but incredible on the stage, because he's continually opening, opening, opening, waiting for any kind of adventure. And Kathy Baker was the same way. In *Fool for Love* we were continually thrown into new stuff. They were just courageous. Other actors you come to a brick wall."

Has directing had any influence on his writing? Having to actually stage a text instead of seeing this idealized production in his head? "It depends on how attached you are to that original fantasy of the play. If you're very attached to it, of course you're always going to be disappointed. Sometimes I had this kind of imagined event in my head, and then when I saw this pragmatic thing with the actors and everything, it was a big disappointment. But now I've gone on to find something else that's much more exciting than when you were working with the page. And oftentimes, if the actor's adventurous, you can go into territory that's much more exciting than what you originally conceived. Because it's basically intellectual when you're working with the page. It's an abstraction. But then when the actor makes it concrete, it starts to become very thrilling because you're going with this flesh-and-blood event and you have to, as a director, you have to go with what the actor is. You can't try to shape this actor into something he's not. You have to find out who he is and then start to go on this adventure with him.

"Writing's a weird thing because you go continually back and forth between getting lost in your mind and trying to come back to the actual sensation of what it might be like to see this thing in a space with real people and real people watching. You're continually going back and forth, so you can't say, you know, absolutely, I'm more in touch with the fact of the actor's participation now, because it's not true. Sometimes that's true. Other times you go off into never-never land and you make the same mistakes you always make. The more practical experiences you have with production, the more you're hooked to this knowledge of what the actor has to accomplish."

Does he make more changes in the text now that he's directing? "Staging is always wide-open. I don't have any cut-and-dried—you know, actor move stage left, stage right, just for the sake of it. The actor is going to move in the direction he's organically moving in. I'm not going to say, 'It says on the page you've got to go upstage and you're going downstage.' That's ridiculous. It's just like, you know, driving cattle upstream. You can't do that.

"In fact, now I didn't even write the costumes or anything like that into it because I want the actors to develop the costumes in the course of production. Many, many of the things that I would have put in the script before—now, knowing that I'm going to direct it, I leave open until the production's complete and then go back to the whole thing and outline what we actually achieved in the production. And that becomes the public's version."

But what about changes in the language? "Not scenes so much as the impetus behind a speech, maybe. Or the direction behind something. Like an actor gets ahold of it and he'll start working with it in a certain direction and all of a sudden it'll turn a little bit and you'll want to go with that turn rather than force it in that first direction because the actor's actually begging for something over here. So you fulfill that. Or can you abbreviate it, or something. I mean it can all change.

"It's not so much that I want the actors to feel this gesture just because it's written on the page. I want the actor to embody the whole attitude behind the gesture. In other words, that gesture is a manifestation of an attitude that has to be completely embodied, and the more you take the actor into that gesture the more that attitude starts to swim in his body. At other times there's an avoidance, the actor doesn't want to go into certain territory because he's afraid, he's resisting it out of some mental ideas that it's wrong or something like that. So you have to always maintain this balance between the actors. Many actors get abstract. Many even great actors tend to get up into the head and start asking theoretical questions that their body doesn't know anything about. Their body is much more intelligent than their mind in some ways."

One thing that's changed in his writing over the years, he uses far fewer monologues. Is that a reaction to his experience as a director? That those famous "arias" read beautifully but are hell on actors? "The way I started to look at it was that many of those things were mental abstractions. That an actor needs things that have to do with his body. And if it gets too mentally abstract he's marooned in his body and he's still in there having to use all this language, and trip off of minds, and it's asking a lot of an actor to simply become a poetry recital person. We experimented a lot with that in the '60s and '70s and stuff. But then it became less and less interesting. Became more like this pretentious kind of language masturbation that just didn't really get to the meat and potatoes of what I was looking for. But now I find that the way to go with it is really through the actor. And to really stay rooted with the actor's body. Anything that deviates from that into the mind somewhere you've got to be very careful with. Because something's lost, something's hidden."

But that's an abstraction itself, isn't it? How does it work concretely, in rehearsal? "Well, I like to start from zero. From absolutely nothing. Every actor has a different method of approach, depending on his school, depending on his experience, all that stuff. So you have to, right from the beginning, accept the fact that everybody's going to be working subjectively in a different way. So the task of the director seems to me how to pull everybody into one territory of equality and also allow them to go ahead and work individually. And the equality seems to be the body because everybody knows, more or less, the functions that are involved in the sensory experiences. So if you take that as a first base, everybody's connected on that level and starts to work just strictly from the physical body and how it has to find its way into the character. Then everybody begins to work on similar levels. And you allow all the rest of it to go on. I mean, if somebody wants to work by Lee Strasberg's method or Stanislavski or something else, you allow all that. So long as everybody's connected with this idea that the sensory experience is the essential. In other words, how does a character smell, taste, see, hear, and feel? And then from there you have a ground for it."

But not a ground for psychologizing, right? The way most directors work on plays these days? "No, because to me that background stuff is the homework of the actor. I can help in certain areas but I sure don't want to get in there and start to say 'Well, you're doing this because of this and that or the other thing.' In other words, to give motivations for activity. I'd much rather work in the moment with the actor. And there's one curious thing that happens—a lot of times actors feel that they have to only play one thing. It has to be just this one attitude that makes everything manifest. And it's not. It can be two, it can be three things, an actor can have three or four things going on simultaneously in the moment, and when they begin to discover that it's possible, they'll start to go in directions they never even dreamed of, and it's very exciting when that starts to happen. Many actors will just get on fire."

And the play itself has three or four things going on simultaneously, not like the director is saying, "This is what the playwright means"? "Yeah, you don't write a play out of a sense of wanting to interpret an idea. You don't have a thesis that a play is an explanation of. The play is an adventure in the same sense that acting is an adventure. You're going into unknown territory. And you find pieces and bits here and there of what you're searching for."

What about his own experiences as an actor? Has that had any effect on his work as a director? He gives a half-amused, half-contemptuous snort. "Film acting is a different animal altogether. As much as—I don't like to make broad statements about it but—I mean obviously excellent stage actors can act in film, but the reverse isn't necessarily true. People who can't act a lick on stage can be in front of a camera and get away with it. Those same people, if they step on stage, can fall apart. They don't have any sense of the wholeness of playing a character. Me? Film? I feel like I'm getting away with it all. You know what I mean? Because to do a tight close-up or something like that isn't that big a deal. You could always find many, many people off the street who could get away with a tight close-up, but they couldn't do a three-act play."

What about *A Lie of the Mind*? Anything he wants to say about his new play before it opens? He shifts uneasily in the chair. "To try to be succinct about it is kind of excruciating. A love ballad, I guess you'd call it. A little legend about love."

The legend culminates in a breathtaking image—a fire in the snow. In fact, the concluding images of plays like *Red Cross, Melodrama Play, La Turista*, and a half-dozen others are among the most stunning in the American theater—yet he's been quoted as saying he has trouble with endings. Come on. "Well, when I said trouble with endings, I didn't mean so much what I came up with as the struggle to find it. The struggle to find this conclusion and the thing actually never is concluded, do you know what I mean? There's always something false about an ending to me. There's an obligation involved and yet at the same time it feels false. It continues—there isn't any ending." He spreads his hands in frustration, then breaks into that big-skyed grin. "'The End.' I wonder who came up with 'The End'?"

Sam Shepard: Geography of a Horse Dreamer

Kevin Sessums / 1988

From *Interview* 18 (September 1988): 70–79. Kevin Sessums is the author of *I Left It on the Mountain: A Memoir* (2015).

A few hours before I was going to meet Sam Shepard out by a pond filled with a week's worth of rain and damn too many geese, I read in the *Washington Post* that Beckett's latest published work was scheduled to come out that very same day. A guy named Lipson had unearthed a 1,200-word sentence that Sam—the one over in Paris—had written 30 years earlier and was bringing it out as Beckett's sparest volume yet. *L'Image*, which the ten pages had been titled, concerns a man's involvement with a woman, their walk in the countryside, some sandwiches, a dog washing its genitals. Mud is Beckett's central motif in *L'Image*, as it was in Shepard's Pulitzer Prize–winning play, *Buried Child*. Along with Federico García Lorca, Beckett has been the seminal literary influence in Shepard's life—after reading *Waiting for Godot* as a teenager, he realized the dramatic power, if not yet the meaning, of the written word.

I tore the article out of the *Post* and gave it to him later that afternoon. He quickly skimmed the story, laughing when he got to one particular line. Shepard laughs a lot—not much of a chuckle, but what's there lassoed on about the third try.

"'I have to speak while having nothing to say,'" he quoted Beckett back at me. "That's it, isn't it? That's absolutely it."

Shepard's own image is anything but spare. A cultural hybrid claimed by what's left of the Hollywood and literary establishments, he's been compared to Gary Cooper and Eugene O'Neill. He has written such diverse and critically debated plays as *Curse of the Starving Class*, *Icarus's Mother*, *True*

West, Fool for Love, Geography of a Horse Dreamer, Angel City, A Lie of the Mind, Suicide in B♭*, The Tooth of Crime,* and *La Turista.* Moviegoers have paid good money to see his quiet attempts at acting in *Days of Heaven, Resurrection, Raggedy Man, Frances, Country, Fool for Love, Crimes of the Heart,* and *Baby Boom;* he was nominated for an Academy Award for his portrayal of Chuck Yeager in *The Right Stuff.* Next he'll be Dolly Parton's husband in the film version of *Steel Magnolias.*

An avid horseman, instinctive musician, and amateur landscape architect, Shepard continually combines disciplines in a way that projects a rather undisciplined, shit-kickin' demeanor. He has no patience for those who heap too much praise on his many endeavors. As a follower of the master teacher G. I. Gurdjieff, his life is all about the work itself. To use one of his own favorite terms, he's just a guy who accomplishes all this stuff.

Samuel Shepard Rogers III was born on November 5, 1943—though he was, in fact, the seventh-generation male to be burdened with the three names. Everybody called him Steve. Steve Rogers's father was in the service, and the family followed him from their initial army base in Illinois to others in South Dakota, Utah, Florida, and Guam. After the war, they settled on an avocado ranch in Duarte, California, where Steve spent his teenage years. Most teenagers have self-dramatized problems with their parents, but Steve's were deeply rooted. His father, a believer in education and a lover of poetry, was also an alcoholic with a propensity for violence. At 19, increasingly unhappy with his surroundings, Steve found a literal means of escape as a member of an itinerant theater troupe known as the Bishop's Company Repertory Players. It got him to New York.

Soon after he arrived in the city he dropped the Rogers from his name—"I always thought it was corny because of Roy Rogers"—and moved into an apartment on Avenue C with Charlie Mingus Jr., son of the jazz great and a high school friend who had also migrated east. Through Mingus, and now named Sam Shepard, he got a job busing tables at the Village Gate, the legendary jazz club, where he would wash a few dishes, bring Nina Simone her ice cubes, and listen to the late-night rhythms that would later fuel his work.

Headwaiter Ralph Cook announced one day that he had been given the use of St. Mark's Church to house Theater Genesis, a company he was founding in order to produce new plays. He asked the members of the staff if they knew of any plays in need of production. The skinny busboy from California, who up to that point had spent his time cultivating a drug-taking renegade reputation with his buddy Mingus, surprised Cook by telling him that he himself had written a couple of one-acts. Cook produced both *The*

Rock Garden and the appropriately titled *Cowboys*. Sam Shepard's career as a playwright had begun.

It is a career that has been able to sustain an array of theatrical impulses—from the humble spirituality of Joe Chaikin's Open Theater to the preening machismo of those early days at Theater Genesis, where he met the actress O-Lan, who later became his wife and the mother of their son, Jesse, now 17. The energy of his work's irreverence can be traced to the lust he felt at one point for rock-and-roll—whether he was drumming with the Holy Modal Rounders, the group he helped found in the '60s, or performing with Patti Smith during their public love affair in the early '70s.

That affair helped push Shepard over the edge. Finally burned out on New York and its sexual intrigues, theatrical politics, and, most of all, the drugs he had been ingesting for years, he packed up O-Lan and Jesse and escaped to London. There, he found a respect for his work that he had never experienced in quite the same way in America. (A brief excerpt from his first play, *The Rock Garden*, appears in *Oh! Calcutta!* and is the only work Shepard has had produced on Broadway.)

"Look it—they have a tremendous theatrical culture over there in England," he told me as he rubbed the cusp of the hawk-moon tattoo on the back of his left hand. "It's not just for the upper classes—it's widespread. And they have great actors. I worked with Bobby Hoskins, who's now a big movie star. I worked with great guys—cockneys, Irishmen, Scotsmen, some Londoners. They were all willing to explore anything you wanted to go into. I started directing my own stuff over there upstairs at the Royal Court Theatre. They gave me the room and told me to do whatever I wanted. And then I was into greyhound dog racing—so I had that going."

But he missed the American West. He again packed up O-Lan and Jesse and this time rented a ranch outside San Francisco. There he became involved with a Theater Genesis-like company called the Magic Theatre, where he was a playwright-in-residence. But surrounded by O-Lan's extended family and having to keep up the ranch, Shepard found himself in need of money. Luckily, director Terrence Malick visited him and offered him a role in his upcoming film, *Days of Heaven*.

Film would change Shepard's life in more than a monetary way, for it was later, on the set of *Frances*, that he met Jessica Lange. He left O-Lan, and he and Lange began to live together. They have now moved from New Mexico to a farm down South, where they live with Aleksandra, Lange's daughter by Mikhail Baryshnikov, as well as their own two children, a daughter named Hannah and a son whom Shepard lovingly refers to as "The Boy."

It is a moniker that no longer applies to Shepard himself. *Far North*, his latest work, is an artistic and personal step forward. The first film he has ever directed, it is also the first time he has so concentrated on the woman's point of view. For years critics have accused him of being overtly macho instead of seeing him for what he is—an artist who has consistently found the poetry in machismo. But with *Far North* he finally admits that it is the female of the species that seems to find the genetic and spiritual will to survive.

The two events that form *Far North*'s story are a grandmother's 100th birthday and a father's injuries sustained after his horse has broken loose from his wagon and dragged him along the roadside. Charles Durning is the father and Jessica Lange the daughter he summons home to his Minnesota hospital bed. He unhappily finds himself down the hall from his brother-in-law, played by Donald Moffat, who is there to dry out. Durning wants Lange to avenge his wounded pride by killing old Mel, the horse that has been in the family for years. The three other women in the family, however, refuse to let her carry out the act. They are her sister, who still lives on the farm, played by Tess Harper; Harper's hell-raising daughter, played by Patricia Arquette; and Ann Wedgeworth, who portrays the poetically unhinged mother of Harper and Lange.

When our conversation turned to filmmaking, the boyish quality that has shadowed Shepard all his life began to surface. His face relaxed. He became more animated. Even his voice took on the inflections of a kid telling his first hunting tale.

"The curious thing was, with all the exterior stuff I knew exactly what to do. I know exactly where to put the camera, how to move it, all that stuff," he grinned, the stub of a Camel in his mouth. "But once I got inside, it was like a nightmare. I couldn't believe it. All this over-the-shoulder shit! I just couldn't stand that stuff. I wanted to shoot in more complete takes."

He lassoed a chuckle. Lit another Camel.

"I learned a lot, yet there was a whole lot I didn't even get next to. I was just feeling like I was gettin' it when we shut down. But it was an exhilarating experience. I'm real good at clubbing people up, you know, gettin' 'em into a tribe. And a lot of that has to do with making a movie. When you get that feeling that everyone is together in a thing . . . well, that's just fun."

He pulled on the Camel—the smoke whiter than his teeth—and rested his chin on his hand. A deep and nasty puncture wound stared back at me from the middle of his palm. Patti Smith as Cavale in their two-character theater vérité, *Cowboy Mouth*, had gotten it right after all. There it was, the image made flesh. "You're a performer, man," she accused Shepard's character, Slim. "You gotta be like a rock-and-roll Jesus with a cowboy mouth."

Slim's next line was "You fucking cunt!"

This was Shepard's: "I was exploring the female side of life in *Far North*—that's a whole 'nother reason it was kinda fun. I'm absolutely fascinated by this female stuff right now, 'cause I'm beginning to realize that the female side knows so much more than the male side. About childbirth. About death. About where it's at."

He shifted his chin on the palm of his hand. The whiskers avoided the wound.

KEVIN SESSUMS: Now that you're becoming a Southerner, do you ever miss the West, especially Santa Fe?

SAM SHEPARD: Well, the town just got inundated with Texas oil people. And the face of it changed into this shopping-mall thing with adobe siding. It was getting weird. You couldn't even get across the downtown plaza, it was so full of tourists. But it's amazing country. The town itself used to be great back in the '50s and '60s.

KS: Do you miss the light out West? Now that you're a movie director you can talk like that.

SS: Yeah [*laughs*]. "The light."

KS: Before I saw *Far North* I thought, "I know this is Sam Shepard, but he's still never directed a movie before."

SS: [*Laughs*] During what part of the movie did you start to worry?

KS: This was before. Once it started I knew that things were under control.

SS: Did you like the music?

KS: A lot. It's the Red Clay Ramblers—the same guys who did the music for *A Lie of the Mind.*

SS: Right. We worked real hard on the music.

KS: Their being a part of the film is an example of how . . . well, comfortable the whole thing feels. You've gone home to all these motifs that run through your theater work.

SS: [*Laughs*] A repetition of events, huh?

KS: Yeah. There is, of course, the symbol of the horse. There's the tribal instinct. The violent impulse. The need for family and the sensuality of food. The love of land. The way we bolt into consciousness from a deep sleep. Even a man robed in a blanket. There are many "Shepardesque" theatrical details. Did you write the script specifically for film, or was it originally a play?

SS: This was a screenplay from the beginning. I wrote it about a year ago. I finished it out in California when I went out there to play polo and got injured pretty bad. I cracked two vertebrae and couldn't play, so I was forced to write. I sat down and finished this thing—it took me about two weeks, but I'd already had most of it done.

KS: One of the things you've done with *Far North* is lay to rest the argument that you don't write good women's roles. You began to do that with your cycle of family plays [*Curse of the Starving Class, Buried Child, A Lie of the Mind*]. But this particular script is truly about women.

SS: Or the female . . .

KS: . . . force . . .

SS: Yeah.

KS: Was this a conscious choice?

SS: Well, you know, with all stuff that you write it's an exchange of intent and accident. I can't say that it was all absolutely intentional, because you start with certain impulses, and then other things start coming in and start to influence it. And you, of course, want to go with things that start to arise out of the material. I did mean for it to be about those women, but it's also about those two men. They're *there*. They're present in the film.

KS: But they're . . .

SS: . . . a little more pathetic [*laughs*].

KS: The women are much stronger. There is an element of pussy-whipped men.

SS: They aren't meant to come off like that exactly; they're more estranged. There's a sense of the men losing their place. And as a result of those men losing their place, the women find theirs. It's odd.

KS: For women to find their place, do men have to be replaced?

SS: That's something for sociological people to figure out. I don't have any answers to that.

KS: Can a man fall in love with a woman without being pussy-whipped?

SS: Oh, yeah. You're really talking about power there. Everybody talks about power as if they know what it means. You have to examine what all these things mean. What is power?

KS: Maybe the ones who have power are the ones who give us our definitions.

SS: Maybe. I dunno. But I don't think love has anything to do with power. Love has nothing to do with an individual's willfulness. Love is a power of its own. If you don't fall under it, you don't fall in love.

KS: Fall under it like you'd fall under starlight or the front wheels of a truck?

SS: It's like a spell. You don't have any choice in the matter either. You can set up to fall in love with somebody, but that's no guarantee. You can set up *not* to fall in love with somebody, and that's still no guarantee. It has nothing to do with your willfulness, which a lot of people think is power.

KS: Did you have a sense of power as a movie director?

SS: There's a difference between power and influence. Being able to influence people in the right direction is something that takes a lot of time to understand. And that doesn't necessarily mean you wield power over people. The most influential people artistically are those who others feel they can entrust something to. Not that they are bending to their will—you can't whip people. That means once that trust is cultivated you can begin to influence them in a certain direction. You can't just go in there and say, "Do this. Do that." Nobody's gonna fall for it. Especially nowadays, when everybody thinks they're individuals with power [*laughs*]. It's a delicate thing, especially with actors.

KS: In your writing, particularly in the early plays, there is a heightened element of trust. There isn't this system in your plays of action-motivation-action. You must trust the material itself. You must walk to the precipice, step off, and catch the wind current.

SS: But not foolhardily. You wouldn't ever expect an actor to walk off a cliff unless he was going to get caught. And I assume you wouldn't ever want to lead actors in that direction. That's where they begin to mistrust you—if you're asking them for something that's gonna make 'em crash. They have to know that they're not gonna crash. Then they'll take the leap. Grotowski once said a great thing about directing. He said you have to *seduce* the actor; you actually have to invite actors into a world where they feel they've never been before, but which they're willing to try out. That's the kind of thing I'm after. You make an invitation. There's a demand, too, but the demand has to do with something that's gonna pay off. It's not for nothing; it's not for its own sake. The payoff is that the actor discovers a *life*. And you hope that it's a life that they haven't really found before. Or maybe they've found a little part of it, and you'll help them to find more. More than anything you have to encourage actors to be courageous. Most of them want to be, but there's a tremendous fear. Almost every really good actor I've come across in some part of himself is terrified. And you have to make that terror less prevalent by inviting him to explore something that may be dangerous but in the end is going to pay off.

KS: When you write do you have to experience the same sort of trust?

SS: Oh, yeah.

KS: So who or what is the force that seduces you into that last?

SS: [*Laughs*] Oh, well, that's a whole 'nother thing. You're talking about ghosts and things that have to do with stuff in the air.

KS: There is that conjuring aspect to your work. Is that something you believe in—the act of conjuring?

SS: Oh, yeah. But not in a superstitious way. There's nothing superstitious about it.

KS: Not at all. I mean it in a friendly way. But even your life at times seems conjured. It seems magically normal.

SS: [*Laughs*] Well, it may *seem* like that.

KS: With *Far North*, do you have a different sense of the audience since it's a movie and not a play?

SS: Yeah. You use a different mechanism to gauge the point of view. In other words, with theater you're gauging the point of view based on a room in which everybody is aware of everybody else. In film, that's not true; everybody is unaware of everybody else. They go into a dream individually—even people who come with a date. They lose touch with each other. They go into the film in a mental way. So the whole point of view, the whole stance of an audience is psychologically completely different from film to theater. In that regard, you construct the thing according to the law that governs each one. There's absolutely no question that a film audience is distinct from a theater audience—even though the same people may go to both. The activity of the audience and the expectation of the audience and the role that the audience plays are completely different. So you can't design a play with the same perspective that you design a film. It's impossible. The film takes place in the mind. A play takes place in the flesh and blood.

KS: Now that you've directed a film, is the theater going to lose you?

SS: Oh, no. I'm not through writing plays. But I've also just begun making films. I want to make a lot of them. This particular film, *Far North*, was just so much fun to work on. There are so many aspects to it. There's this phenomenal amount of things that have to be attended to and each one is fascinating. You can see that you can spend the rest of your life and not get to the bottom of it. It took me twenty years to learn how to write a play [*laughs*]. I don't know how long it's gonna take me to learn how to make a movie.

KS: Are there directors from whom you've learned simply by watching their work?

SS: Sure. I love Jacques Tati. He did *Traffic* and *Mr. Hulot's Holiday* and *My Uncle*, these classics of physical comedy. They're almost devoid of language. And the language he does use is a mixture of French, English, Spanish, German—and they're all like little vignette things. And Buñuel I love. Kurosawa.

Buñuel is one of the all-time wonders of film-making. Most films you see, you get the sense either they're completely or, at least, partially contrived. There's something not whole about them; they don't exist as a whole animal. With Buñuel's films I've always felt they existed as if they lived somewhere else before, and he just found them and delivered them to the world. There's a wonderful completeness about them. And not only that; he's also got all these levels. You think you're in one world and suddenly discover you're someplace completely different—inside the character's mind, or somebody opens a pocketbook, and there's a dead chicken in there. Just phenomenal things. And yet he never loses the sense of storytelling.

KS: You're describing your own plays.

SS: You do like to gravitate toward people who remind you not only of your own work but also your own life and what you're trying to work toward. I mean, I'd never compare myself to Buñuel. He's a master of contemporary films. Have you ever seen *That Obscure Object of Desire*? What an incredible movie. And that came about by using those two women. One of them flipped out, and he had to hire somebody else. But then he used both women in the film. Now that's a poet for you. If that had happened in Hollywood they'd have thrown the whole thing out and started shooting it over again.

KS: And hired John Landis.

SS: [*Laughs*] Exactly.

KS: Was the horse, the central image in *Far North*, a male or a female? I never got a good look under it.

SS: We used three different horses. They're all geldings. Mares are just too hard to handle. They're way, way too . . . well, feisty.

KS: What sort of metaphor were you going after with that horse?

SS: I never deal with it that way. I'm not trying to set up metaphors, because as soon as you do that it becomes an intellectual game. I wasn't at all looking for anything metaphorical. I was just looking for a handle—if you want to call it that—a premise from which things can reverberate. It seemed like an interesting premise. Trite maybe to begin with [*laughs*], but it opens up. ✓

KS: There's a line in the film that keeps being repeated: "Where are all the men?" Halie asked the same thing in *Buried Child*. Where are they, Sam? All sitting behind the camera?

SS: No, no, no—look it . . . part of this had to do with the specific locale where *Far North* takes place, which is upper Minnesota, a very far northern atmosphere in which the roles of men and women seem very distinct to me. I mean, they do in other parts of the country, too—say, in Texas, where they are the reverse of Minnesota. But up there, there's a sense that men have lost their place, they've kind of evaporated. And women seem very strong and clannish and family oriented to the extent that even if they have not exactly turned away from the men, they sure don't need them anymore. And they will continue to exist whether men are there or not. The men seem to be adrift. I don't know why that is, whether it's because of the country or the Scandinavian thing or the cold winters. . . .

KS: Maybe the cold winters just make their cocks shrivel.

SS: [*Laughs*] It's more than just a sexual thing. It's way more than that. That's probably the least of it. It's something *other* than that.

KS: Is it the fault of the men, or the women, or simply the fault of the society in which they find themselves?

SS: It's nobody's fault. I don't think there's any blame involved at all. It's just a condition that's come about through the years. I have no idea why it's come about.

KS: So yet again in your work you're raising the questions but refusing to give any answers.

SS: Right. It's pretentious to give answers. Who has the answers? It's a ridiculous proposition to give answers. Only fools and politicians give answers.

KS: Your work really isn't political.

SS: Well, you could maybe look at it politically.

KS: But you don't write from any political point of view.

SS: I'm not interested in politics *at all*. I don't think politics has ever solved any of the profound questions we're confronted with. If anything, it's made everything worse. Everybody's getting into an uproar over these candidates who are all in bed with each other. Who gives a shit? They're all equally as lame as the other one. I just don't see any hope in that as a solution to the stuff that we're facing.

KS: Do you think that there are political issues that one really can't write about—that even an attempt would not only cheapen the work but also cheapen the issue itself?

SS: The whole thing about issues is that they're ephemeral. If you start writing about them, then tomorrow they'll change. Hell, in five minutes they'll change. Issues are not the important questions. There's something deeper than issues—there's things to do with . . . ancient stuff. And that stuff hasn't changed. It'll always be the same. It's the same thing we're always confronted with. And that is what cuts through issues. And that's what has to be addressed. I don't mean to be evasive about it. But it *is* mysterious. At the same time it is something you can address. And the only way to address it is by a poetic stance—in the truest sense. You go after it through feelings in the same way a musician does. A musician doesn't address issues; he addresses something deeper.

KS: Does it embarrass you when people refer to you as a poet?

SS: No. Because that's the highest thing you can possibly aspire to. I'm talking about being a poet in the real sense—not just making rhymes. I mean, it's an old game. It's a real old, ancient thing—and it all started out in the same place: the theater. Music, literature, all that shit—they all came together at one time in the theater.

KS: Tolstoy—or one of those Russians—once wrote that happy families are all alike, but every unhappy family is unhappy in its own way. Family is a subject that you write a lot about. You seem as horrified by the concept as you do in need of it. But whatever your shifting response, the reality of family seems to fuel your work. Your own father was a strange and important presence in your life. Has your relationship with him changed—deepened perhaps—since the old man's death?

SS: My relationship with him is the same. Exactly the same. It's a relationship of absolute unknowing. I never knew him, although he was around all the time. There's no point in dwelling on it. I mean, my relationship with him now is exactly the same as when he was alive. It's just as mysterious.

KS: Did you resent him because you loved him, in spite of everything?

SS: Whew—all of that stuff is mixed up together. It's not one or the other. Resentment is the other side of love. It's something to write about, but I can't talk about it.

KS: He really didn't succeed in life—he sort of gave in to the bottle. Do you have any guilt about becoming such a success and leaving him behind?

SS: Naw . . . well, there was some guilt at one time. But not anymore. All that does is stop you. You can't get wrapped up in that. And besides, my dad was a poet himself in a certain way . . . [*laughs*] in a certain weird way. Because of circumstances he never really had the chance to prove himself. Who knows if my work is better than his? That has nothing to do with it. One thing that I'll always be eternally grateful to him for was that he introduced me to García Lorca when I was a kid—in Spanish, no less. He spoke fluent Spanish. That's kind of unusual. He told me all about García Lorca's life with the gypsies and all that. That got me fascinated about poetry at an early age. He also loved New Orleans jazz. So I grew up reading García Lorca and listening to jazz.

KS: [*Laughs*] And that explains it all.

SS: [*Laughs*] Yeah. That's your basic plot right there.

KS: Do you think fate has set up a different set of problems for your own children? They don't have to cope with a father's feelings but live up to his success. Do you ever think about that?

SS: Not really. I've got a seventeen-year-old. He likes to shoot guns and ride horses. But he's also getting into sculpting—doing some work with bronze—which is great. We get along really good. There's no competitive edge at all.

KS: When there's competition in your plays—in *The Tooth of Crime*, for instance—there's a tendency for it to spill over into some form of violence. Violence and its repellingly seductive nature is a theme that surfaces in your writing—especially early on. Do you find violence redemptive?

SS: No. I think violence is absolutely hopeless. It's the main source of tragedy. It's an incredibly hopeless pit that we can't seem to escape from.

KS: Do you think there's a difference between violence that takes place between a man and a woman and violence that takes place solely between men?

SS: Violence is violence. Anybody that tells you anything different is crazy.

KS: But there is that edge of violence to so many of your plays. At least at one point you were drawn to it in some way.

SS: I was raised with it; I was raised violently. So it's been a part of my life. But it's gotten less violent as I've gotten older. My fascination with it has ebbed.

KS: You were of draft age during the Vietnam War, but you managed to escape the service. I would think that back then you would have wanted to go over there and experience some of that "manly" violence. It would have been a cowboylike thing to do.

SS: Are you kidding?

KS: [*Laughs*] Yeah. I am. I'm trying to prick you.

SS: [*Laughs*] They didn't have any horses over there in Nam. There's no cowboy without a horse.

KS: What is your fascination with horses? Is it because there's a sense of majesty when you sit up there? Is it a pedestal? Do you just like the feel of flesh between your legs?

SS: [*Laughs*] You orient everything sexually, don't you?

KS: [*Laughs*] Yep.

SS: Look it . . . from the very origins of the horse culture in this country—which was ancient, it went back to the Spanish stuff—there's been a big distinction between men on horseback and men on foot. A huge distinction.

One culture was the farming culture, which was the hole people—they chop the earth—and they were looked down on by men on horseback. There's a reason for that. If you get up on a horse and see what kind of ground you can cover and all the rest of it, you'll see that there is a completely different feeling from being earthbound. There's just an amazing *sense*—not so much of power, but you're just in a different relationship to the earth.

KS: Do you feel that the horse is a part of you or that you're a part of the horse?

SS: Both. It depends on what horse you're on, too [*laughs*]. Sometimes you're not with each other at all.

KS: You're passionate about playing polo. It's sort of incongruous with your good-ole-boy image.

SS: That's because people associate polo with royalty and rich people. It's true that there are a lot of people who have a lot of money who are involved with it. But the fact of the sport itself is that it is the toughest sport I've ever played—physically and every other way, just an incredibly tough, hard sport.

KS: Is there a sense of getting out of yourself when you're playing?

SS: No. There's a feeling of getting *into* yourself.

KS: Is it the same sort of getting into yourself that you feel from writing?

SS: Yeah. It's very similar. But you have to be much more aware on the polo field . . . [*laughs*] . . . because you can get killed. You can't dream on the polo field.

KS: When you do write, do you write from image to image or from sound to sound?

SS: They're the same. Sounds are images; images are sounds. The two things are very connected. I don't know. I'm probably oriented more to sound that I am to image. But I think they're intimately connected. Hopefully, whatever you're writing is whole enough so that the sounds and images are one piece. They're not divided into this over here and that over there. Mainly when I write it has to do with movement. Something is *moving.*

KS: You write in notebooks, right? You have to have that physical sensation of putting it down.

SS: I also type. I learned how.

KS: You ever use a word processor?

SS: Naw. I don't like anything where it can disappear on you.

KS: [*Laughs*] Into the air with all those other ghosts.

SS: [*Laughs*] Right.

KS: Your writing is different from your acting. There's a laconic quality to your acting, whereas your writing seems more muscular, visceral. When you're in front of the camera it's almost like Zen and the Art of Method Acting Maintenance. There's a spareness to your work on screen. A comfort.

SS: Oh, no, it's the opposite.

KS: You're a good actor then.

SS: It's very uncomfortable. You know, the difference for me is that with acting—especially in front of the camera—it's very easy to hide. But with writing, you can't hide anything, not a thing. Now the very best actors are the ones that don't hide. I'm not by any stretch of the imagination a great film actor, so I do my best to hide. I say that truthfully—what I'm doing is trying to hide certain aspects of myself. I don't want certain aspects to be public. They're not for public consumption. They're private, they belong to me, they don't belong to everybody, and I refuse to let them out there. In the same way that certain people refuse to have their photograph taken—because it's nobody's business. And the parts I agree to have photographed are the parts that are visible. But the other parts nobody's gonna see. The exception is the writing. 'Cause in the writing I have a free channel to these personal things, and it's my prerogative as an artist to use it. I don't feel that as an actor I want to be De Niro. It's like certain saxophone players will never be John Coltrane, so they play tunes they can play. But if they try to swap octaves or something like Charlie Parker they're gonna fall on their face. I'm not kidding myself.

KS: You got this "macho dude" image, Sam.

SS: [*Laughs*] Shit.

KS: You do. Deal with it. But in directing this new film you seem to be getting in touch with some part of yourself that you haven't dealt with before . . . a more sensitive side. Vulnerable. Even feminine. Is this a conscious choice?

SS: Well, I mean, you're conscious of it to the degree that you're able to pursue it. Look it—you start out as an artist, I started out when I was 19, and you're full of defenses. You have all of this stuff to prove. You have all of these shields in front of you. All your weapons are out. It's like you're going into battle. You can accomplish a certain amount that way. But then you get to a point where you say, "But there's this whole other territory I'm leaving out." And that territory becomes more important as you grow older. You begin to see that you leave out so much when you go to battle with the shield and all the rest of it. You have to start including that other side or die a horrible death as an artist with your shield stuck on the front of your face forever. You can't grow that way. And I don't think you can grow as a person that way, either. There just comes a point when you have to relinquish some of that and risk becoming more open to the vulnerable side, which I think is the female side.

KS: Are you in awe of that side of life?

SS: Sure. It's much more courageous than the male side.

KS: There are levels of awe in all your writing. There is not only the awe the reader or audience member feels at witnessing the work but also the awe that the writer seems to feel at being able to write this stuff to begin with.

SS: Right.

KS: Then there's the awe that the characters themselves feel at the absurd power of life going on around them.

SS: I think it is the difference between being touched by something and being assaulted by it. There's so much that tries to pass itself off as art, and there's so little that actually touches us, that invites us to experience feelings we don't normally open ourselves to. To be touched in that way is a much more difficult process artistically—and every other way—than to be battered over the head with something.

KS: Did your work with Chaikin influence your thinking in that direction? Your work with him seemed to be the first steps you took toward this more feminine side in your character.

SS: Right. Joe was a tremendous influence on that particular aspect of opening. Although he suffered a stroke a few years ago, he still has that aspect about him. But before, when he was articulate, there was something magical about his fine-tuning—particularly in his relationships to other people.

KS: Before your work with Chaikin, your plays concentrated on the male-warrior quality you alluded to earlier. But meeting Chaikin not only seemed to open you up because of the process he introduced to you, but also because he was a sensitive man you could respect without feeling your own masculinity was threatened.

SS: Absolutely. He was a tremendous influence on me in that way. When I saw the way he was working with actors and what he was pursuing with them, it was a revelation to me. To see what he was searching for and the way in which he approached that search was an amazing lesson. He absolutely aggrandized people—they were held in this incredible spell. But not out of some kind of bullshit. Not out of some impresarial kind of thing. He didn't play at being the Grand Theater Man. It was a completely different thing. It was done from an absolute humility. He's a magical person. It was a miracle in my life ever to have met him.

KS: Do you think you'll ever let anyone else direct your plays or screen-plays—or are you at the point where you want that initial control for yourself?

SS: I want to direct my own stuff, because if there are going to be mistakes made I want to make them myself. At least with the plays, I want to direct the premieres before I turn them over to other people.

KS: You don't think they need a director who has a little more distance?

SS: No, because I don't think anybody can have the same sort of distance that I have—and the same closeness. So why not do it myself? Plus, I love working with actors, especially good ones. There's so much you can learn, not only about that aspect of it but also about writing. A really fine actor will influence your writing.

KS: What do you do when an actor says to you: "I can't say this line, Sam. It's not truthful"?

SS: It depends absolutely on his sense of the truth—whether he's bullshit-ting himself or bullshitting me or whether he is, in fact, saying something that's real. And you can tell that right away. There are some actors that'll say that to you, and what they're really saying is that they're *afraid* to say the line because it's *too* true. But then you come across actors who can abso-lutely nail all the false moments in the play. Totally nail 'em. And you have to honor that—or be an idiot.

KS: What was it like working as an actor in your own work? The last ex-ample of that would be the film version of *Fool for Love*. You didn't look like you were having much fun in that.

SS: You're right, I wasn't. I felt very uncomfortable. I was *not* having a good time. I didn't get off on that [*laughs*]. First of all, this was a situation I tried to avoid for a long, long time—acting in my own stuff—because I al-ways felt it was silly and pretentious. You know: acted and written by and all that crap. Appearing in! Jesus . . . I didn't feel comfortable with that at all. And I don't think I'll ever do it again if I can help it.

KS: Why did you do it that time?

SS: I liked Altman's stuff up to a certain point. [Robert Altman directed the film version of *Fool for Love.—ed.*] And I was fooled into believing that he was going to have integrity in this thing. Later on, I just felt he kind of shined me on. That surprised me. I just felt like he blasted through the thing and didn't give it everything he told me he was going to give it. But that's all water under the bridge.

KS: Let's say you write a screenplay, but you can only get it done if some-one else directs it. Would you give in?

SS: Naw . . . I'll never put myself in that situation. I'm never going to get into a situation where I have somebody else breathing down my neck. It's just not worth it—no matter how much money they say they're going to give you. I was very lucky on *Far North* to get final cut and full artistic freedom. Now that I've got it, I don't see any reason to give it up. I'm just not going to go into that studio situation where you have executives telling you how to cut your film.

KS: Let me play executive. There was one element in the film that bothered me a bit. It's the visual explanation during Charles Durning's monologue of how tribal women can be. When you cut into that monologue and show us the women with tribal make-up on and then later go further and show them riding at him in full savage regalia, I just thought it was well . . . heavy-handed. But then I thought, "It's just Sam feeling comfortable and going back to these theatrical motifs." It was like you were back in the East Village. It was this—

SS: [*Laughs*]—hippie shit.

KS: [*Laughs*] Right.

SS: Naw . . . I didn't want that overtone. It's a difficult thing to get those inserts. I discovered late the fault was in the lighting of the faces. We should have shot them exterior instead of interior. But you only discover that in the cutting room. But the lighting on those faces is too commercial. It's superficial lighting. But I was looking for a rhythmic thing in there, too. You know, where those things came as punctuations.

KS: It is like music, the way the segment has been edited. It's like percussion.

SS: Did you like the percussion in the film?

KS: Yeah.

SS: That's a guy I worked with for years in San Francisco. We did a thing called *Inacoma* at Magic Theatre. His name is J. A. Deane. He's just brilliant.

[A percussive commotion erupts next to the pond: two geese have clamped their bills on each other's throats and the rest of the gaggle circles them.]

[*Squawks*]

Look at those things. They're just like people. They all stand around and cheer.

[A hawk lowers the sky.]

[The geese stop and swim away.]

KS: The person who was in New York years ago—that crazy, angry, drug person—would you know him if he swam over here past those geese and stood in front of us?

SS: [*Laughs*] Now which person was that?

KS: [*Laughs*] You, asshole.

SS: Oh, him.

KS: Would you recognize him?

SS: Yeah. I would. I mean, all those aspects somehow stay with you. You can't just shed 'em. You can't get rid of 'em that easily. That person you're talking about was the product of the times, though.

KS: Are you happy down here in the South? Do you think you'll stay put for a while?

SS: Yeah. I like it down here.

KS: You said earlier that your father taught you about the gypsies when he was reading you García Lorca. There is that gypsy part of your soul. You seem to put down roots somewhere, then move on. It's been a pattern in your life since childhood.

SS: I feel more like staying in one place than I have in a long time. I mean, it always makes me sick to pack a bag [*laughs*], although I do very well on the road. It's very unsettling, this thing that you really don't have a home. Even though home is really always an illusion.

KS: Is your mother still alive?

SS: Yeah. She was living with us for a while, but she just went back to the West Coast. She's got stuff to do back there.

KS: A sense of family really does fuel your work, doesn't it?

SS: It's a thing that everybody can relate to. You can't escape this thing of being related by blood. And everybody somehow or other knows what those relationships are. Even though people are very different, those relationships are so similar they form a field for people to relate in. It's interesting to me that it is those ties that you never really get away from—as much as you might want to try.

KS: Since you've created your own family, how does that change your relationship with the one you were born into? Being a father, can you cease being a son?

SS: I don't know. I'm confused about it. Having never really had a father in the sense that he was a "father" to me, I'm still experimenting with trying to find what that role is. I just don't know. I don't have any answers to that one.

KS: Part of the legend that surrounds you is your refusal to board an airplane. Do you think your aversion to flying is simply an aversion to your own father, since he was very proud of being a flyer in World War II?

SS: [*Laughs*] It's probably *deeply* psychological.

KS: Do you think you'll ever fly again? Maybe you should pilot the fucking plane.

SS: I was just thinking about that a few weeks back—learning how to fly. I think maybe I'll get around to that about ten years from now. I have to get off horses first.

KS: Pegasus might be the answer.

SS: There you go—wings!

KS: Your plays are sort of like Pegasus: they're sweaty animals with nostrils and flanks, yet they seem to be able to sprout wings and take off. They contain a hooved spirituality. Is that something you're in touch with—the spiritual side of life?

SS: Hopefully that's what you're after, but it's so elusive. But that's what you're always after—the invisible part of things. I wouldn't say I was in *touch* with it, but I'm really *hunting* for it.

KS: You write a lot about the double nature of things. You yourself are a man of contradictions. You have an image of being a loner, and yet you are a family man. You love working with the land, and along with that you're a cerebral artist. You also have the love of the cowboy myth within you, yet within your plays you often employ elements of Indian ritual. That seems in opposition because of what the cowboys did to the Indians.

SS: Wait a minute. The cowboys didn't do anything to the Indians. It was the U. S. government.

KS: Then your love of cowboys and your love of Indians come from the same impulse?

SS: Yeah. Absolutely. They're both from the horse culture. It wasn't the cowboys who exterminated the American Indians. Ever. [*Laughs*] They may have shot a couple of 'em.

KS: What I'm getting at is, do you have trouble in your own life being a man of these contradictions or do you revel in them?

SS: Look it—life is made up of contradictions. The tricky part is to stay in the middle and not take sides, not walk over to one side in preference to the other. If you can stay right in the middle of a contradiction, that's where life is. *Exactly* where it is. Right in the middle. It's when you're torn that things start to fall apart. You know, when you go over to one side, and then you leap over to the other. But to be right in the middle of a conflict—right exactly in the middle—and let it play itself out where you can see . . . well, that's where things begin to get exciting. You can't avoid contradictions. You can't avoid paradoxes.

KS: Do you think it's easier as you get older to ride that middle ground, or is it more difficult?

SS: It's more difficult, but given the things you've seen and the experiences you've had, if you know how to take them in the right way, it becomes more possible. Unless you're absolutely stupid, then you become an alcoholic or a drug addict or suicidal or a domestic idiot. But contradiction is rich territory—the two things, not just the one.

KS: I know Beckett was an early influence on you. Were there others? I mean, like it or not, you are now an influence for a younger generation of playwrights.

SS: [*Laughs*] A bad influence.

KS: But were there others besides Beckett?

SS: Yeah. I began to read some people after I began writing plays. Brecht. Eugene O'Neill.

KS: How about any of your contemporaries? Do you go to the theater? Do you read new plays?

SS: No. Not really.

KS: How about other sorts of writers? Who do you read?

SS: There's tons of writers, but most of 'em are poets. César Vallejo is one of my favorite writers, but he's a poet, not a playwright. He's a great, great writer.

KS: Any American fiction writers you respond to?

SS: Richard Ford is an incredible writer. There's Charlie Portis. He wrote *True Grit, Norwood, The Dog of the South*. He's a great writer. From Arkansas.

KS: Do you think you'll ever write a novel?

SS: I don't think so. I've tried it. It's just a whole different discipline. It's so incredibly austere.

KS: And lonely.

SS: [*Laughs*] Oh, man, I've tried it and tried it. The only serious attempt I really made, I guess, was with *Motel Chronicles*, but it just broke into a million pieces. A novel just seems beyond me. A different person writes a novel. A very dedicated breed. I just can't spend that much time at it.

KS: Is it a question of discipline?

SS: It's not only that. It's being able to prolong the impulse and carry on about it that much. The thing that's so great about plays and screenplays is that they're to the bone. They have to be absolutely economical. You can't rattle on. I like writing them for that reason. It has to be very sparse—for the most part.

KS: Where do you get your titles? You come up with great titles. Are they in the air with the ghosts?

SS: [*Laughs*] At one time I was writing plays based on titles, but I gave that up.

KS: Are you after the same stakes that you've always been after, or do the stakes change for you as an artist?

SS: The great thing about writing is that in the course of going after it, it teaches you something. You start out thinking you know something about it, but then you discover you hardly know anything. And the more you do it, the more things begin to inform you about where you're going. Now I've come to a point where I'm not interested in anything that doesn't have a kind of wholeness to it. I'm not interested anymore in little fragmented bits and pieces of stuff that might be interesting for five minutes. I need something that has more of a definite wholeness to it. That has a sense of being a story that's already been told . . . and that you're just coming to it.

KS: Is writing a form of immortality for you? Is it a way of saying, I will not—

SS: Die? [*Laughs*]

KS: Well, not so much die as *give in*.

SS: No. Death doesn't scare me so much. My terrors now have more to do with being alienated from life. What's most frightening to me right now is this estrangement from life. People and things are becoming more and more removed from the actual. We are becoming more and more removed from the Earth to the point that people just don't know themselves or each other or anything. We're this incredible global race of strangers—millions of people who don't know each other [*laughs*]. That's terrifying. Things are so dispensable now. People live together for a while—a year, a few years, months—then they split, and they never see each other again. Then they get together with somebody else—split. Have kids—split. Then the kids never see each other. It's absolutely frightening—this incessant estrangement that's going on. People are being amputated from each other and from themselves.

KS: Does your fame feed that sense of estrangement in your own life? Can you trust people as easily now as you once could?

SS: Well, I'm not hunting for friends. You maybe have a handful of friends in your whole life, if you're lucky. That's not what I mean exactly. It's not that I'm looking for friends. What I'm talking about is this sense . . . this sense that—I don't know . . . you could just . . . drift away. . . .

[A goose walks by.]

[*Silence*]

"Silent Tongues": An Interview with Sam Shepard

Carol Rosen / 1991

From *Sam Shepard: A "Poetic Rodeo"* by Carol Rosen (New York: Palgrave Macmillan, 2004), 212–45. Reprinted by permission of Carol Rosen. Carol Rosen was a professor of English at Stony Brook University. She is also the author of *Plays of Impasse: Contemporary Drama Set in Confining Institutions* (1983).

[This interview took place in Virginia in August 1991. It was first published in the *Village Voice*, August 4, 1992, with a front-page banner headline reading "Sam Shepard Speaks: A Rare Interview with the Cowboy Playwright." A shorter version appeared as "'Emotional Territory': An Interview with Sam Shepard" in *Modern Drama* 36 (March 1993). The abbreviated version included excerpts pertaining to Shepard's theatrical style, use of stage imagery, concepts of rhythm, myth, voice, and transformations, and his continuing sense of character as fluid.]

Sam Shepard feels incredibly lucky. He often says so, and he often laughs. His gift for writing is one he accepts; he never expects to run dry and will easily discard work that strikes him as gone awry; his gift has delivered him from his demons. His demons—"actual demons" he used to feel in the air and in his life—have mercifully left him in peace. He has escaped. Shepard makes a good living as an actor now, and is more and more comfortable in that skin, but still, this family man, gentleman farmer, and rodeo and racing aficionado shies away from public recognition. He has absolutely no interest in self-promotion. Throughout our lengthy interview, he never even mentioned the most recent films in which he had been featured: Volker Schlondorff's *Voyager*, a film adaptation of Max Frisch's *Homo Faber*, in which he played the engineer; *Bright Angel*, a film of Richard Ford's *Rock Springs* stories; or *Thunderheart*, in which he co-starred with Val Kilmer. He guffawed at a stranger's mention of *Defenseless*, a romantic thriller in release at the time of our visit and in which he played a taciturn and persistent police detective.

On film Shepard cultivates the brooding, somber, firm-jawed presence that has been his forte since *Days of Heaven* and *The Right Stuff*. But in the flesh, he exudes mischief and a relaxation of spirit. In frayed denims, with his signature widow's peak obscured by a new "Lazy Riding" cap, Shepard sank incognito into a chair.

"Drowning in coffee" and chain-smoking, Shepard has a gritty, twangy voice that is a dead ringer for Richard Farnsworth's. He looks brittle and almost frail, ready to play the remembered father in *Fool for Love*. But even in his raggedy man getup, his hawk face and lanky frame are easy to spot. "Aren't you Sam Shepard?" asked more than one hesitant admirer. "Naw," he said, moving fast out the door to a dusty pickup truck that rambles down the blacktop to the sounds of Bonnie Raitt's blues.

Trying to maintain some degree of privacy, Shepard consistently turns down requests for interviews. Even his polite refusals have become fodder for quotes. Once, when asked to be interviewed for a *Vanity Fair* profile of Jessica Lange, he declined. "I've decided not to talk," *Vanity Fair* recounted him saying. "I've taken too many risks in that area and been burned too many times. I'm not going to put myself out like that anymore, particularly when it has to do with something private."

But in our interview for this book on his work, Shepard graciously talked at length about myth, character, music, food, and women in his plays; his influences in the theater and his method of writing and revising; his work as a film director and prose writer; the Gulf War; broken pacts and emotional territory. When I told him that I had packed several blank tapes, Shepard joked, "That's in case we really get rolling, right?" Right. "You're going to regret this when you play it all back," he warned, and roared with laughter. No regrets.

Apologetic whenever he hears himself sounding "esoteric" or "intellectual," he is, of course, both despite his poker face and laconic manner. With Shepard, famous for "burning bridges" and "escaping" to "new territory," every conversation is a discovery. He is, after all, the most original and vital playwright of our age.

Shepard's first major American interview appeared in the *Village Voice* in 1975, under the headline "The Most Promising Playwright in America Today is Sam Shepard." He has made good on that promise. The following 1991 interview, appropriately enough, also first appeared in the *Village Voice*.

CAROL ROSEN: Starting with some of your most recent stage work, I thought the piece you did for Joseph Chaikin, *War in Heaven*, was very beautiful.

SAM SHEPARD: You know the history of that thing? We started in Boston before his stroke and did a lot of work up there and then that fell through. Then after the stroke, we just started back up again and completely redid it. I think it was the second or third week of his rehabilitation, right after that, when he still could hardly speak at all.

ROSEN: There was something so beautiful about watching him speak, because this is one of the purest voices in the theater.

SHEPARD: Oh yes, he had a great, great voice. . . . He still has enormous ability to put meaning in his voice.

ROSEN: Given Chaikin's highly specific way of working with actors, and given his importance to your work, have you as a director developed your own particular way to communicate with actors? Is there a Shepardesque actor?

SHEPARD: When I started, with the first play I ever directed in London, I was terrified of the situation because I'd never done it before. So I immediately conferred with two people who I thought were the best directors in the world. One was Peter Brook and the other was Joe [Chaikin]. When I went in, I found myself sort of trying to imitate certain things from their points of view, but discovered that it was futile, that you have to deal with the actors you've got right in front of you and find out what the experience is like: directing. You can't use a formula to approach it.

ROSEN: What kind of actor are you drawn to?

SHEPARD: I like actors who are incredibly courageous and enthusiastic. I don't like sulking actors. I don't like actors who I have to pamper or who I have to go through a big song and dance with to come at a very simple thing. I like actors who are pretty much their own person and don't need a lot of care. It's a waste of time. I'd sooner start out with somebody who already is his own person, and not only that, has a combination of enthusiasm and courage. And intelligence. I don't want to work with dumb actors. Because I found the essence of comedy, great comedians, is intelligence. Maybe sometimes they come off very stupid, but they're the smartest actors.

ROSEN: Like Chaplin?

SHEPARD: Or like Buster Keaton.

ROSEN: Yes, but are there "Shepard" actors? With a look on their faces like anything can happen?

SHEPARD: I think John Malkovich is a good example: extremely intelligent, fearless, and enthusiastic. Just does not give a shit about how this fits into somebody else's idea of what it should be, just goes for ideas that are completely off the wall. They may be wrong but he'll go for them.

ROSEN: Marlon Brando is just such an actor. In *Far North* [Shepard's debut as director of a film he had scripted], I felt you needed Marlon Brando as the father.

SHEPARD: I asked him. And he considered it but he was in bad health then.

ROSEN: I'd like to hear about your film directing.

SHEPARD: I haven't done the second one yet. It was all set to go in October but now we're delayed. I've just done one.

ROSEN: There are certain things you can do on film you can't do on stage or in a novel. There are several images in *Far North*—the loon, the shot of an eagle flying with a horse, the shot of the horse's profile turning into Katie's profile—certain images that are filmic, certain visual techniques that can't be achieved on stage or in a novel.

SHEPARD: One thing that's great about film, I think, if you actually are lucky enough to get to make one, is the thing of parallel time, which is very difficult on stage. I tried it in *A Lie of the Mind* to a certain extent, but it's very cumbersome. It works, but with film it's immediate. You can follow three or four stories in parallel time. It's like music—you just move into time. Or you can go to the past or the future or wherever you want. Whereas on stage, it's much more awkward to do that kind of instantaneous time shift.

ROSEN: On stage, flashbacks have to emerge from language.

SHEPARD: Or from some sort of standard shadow of the character in the background. Backlighting, whatever.

ROSEN: You know all the tricks, right?

SHEPARD: Well, I've been doing it for 25 years.

ROSEN: When you structure a play in an unusual way, then, you have made a conscious choice. It's not that you aren't familiar with conventional techniques. Are you aiming for particular effects?

SHEPARD: Not effects so much, it's territory, emotional territory. I am interested in effects only to the extent that they serve some purpose of emotional terrain. Developing a new style of theater is not something I'm interested in.

ROSEN: You've used that term "emotional territory" in the past to suggest the destination of your plays. Which of your plays do you think go there? To emotional territory.

SHEPARD: Oh, they all do.

ROSEN: All of them?

SHEPARD: Yes, but some of them do it better than the others. When you begin, your great hope is that it moves into something that is true. Sometimes that happens, sometimes it doesn't happen. Like with *Fool for Love*, it began to move into a certain kind of territory. I don't think it eventually succeeded. It became too formal toward the end. But it attempted to move into a certain kind of emotional terrain that was true to itself. It depicted itself. That's what I'm looking for—something that is its own feature.

ROSEN: It's not imitating something else.

SHEPARD: Right. Or it's not trying to represent something else. It becomes its own animal.

ROSEN: Reality is just the jumping-off point.

SHEPARD: Well, we could talk about reality forever.

ROSEN: But you are making an important distinction between art and biography.

SHEPARD: It's all real. I don't mean to be difficult, but I don't see where these distinctions lie, really, between so-called realism and super-realism and naturalism and surrealism and absurdism and—you know what I mean?

ROSEN: Pigeonholing.

SHEPARD: All of these things that have so conveniently been delineated over the years don't really seem to make any sense. And in fact, in some ways, they do nothing but curtail something from happening, which is the reason, I think, a big reason why *States of Shock* wasn't received by the critics. They couldn't find a place to put it. . . . Some of them called it absurdism or . . . they couldn't fit it into anything. It was so radically different from *A Lie of the Mind*, and I guess their expectations were in that vein.

ROSEN: I think you have a really nice definition of realism in *Fool for Love*. The old man turns to this picture of Barbara Mandrell on the wall and says, "I'm married to her in my mind. That's realism." Or is realism just a "lie of the mind"?

SHEPARD: No, what I'm saying is I think those definitions are fruitless, they don't get anywhere, they don't make anything new possible. All they do, really, is put a fence around something. And why is a play like *A Lie of the Mind* more realistic than a play like *States of Shock*? It doesn't make any sense. *A Lie of the Mind* isn't realistic. You've got two parallel situations going on. One guy's running around the stage in his underwear with an

American flag. And somebody else is rubbing somebody's feet. Why is that considered realism? Or why should it be considered absurd? It's just . . . it is what it is.

ROSEN: Which is?

SHEPARD: I don't know. I don't have a name for it. Why should I put a name on it?

ROSEN: You called *A Lie of the Mind* a love ballad.

SHEPARD: Okay, yeah.

ROSEN: And it felt like a very old story.

SHEPARD: I guess when you start something, you always kind of have a half-baked notion about what you hope it to be. But it may not go in that direction at all. It may go somewhere completely different, which isn't to say that you failed, it's just that it turns and becomes something. . . . But I think one of the thrills about writing is to remain open to all its possibilities, and not to try to put a bridle on it and squeeze it down into what your notion of it is. Not to say that you lose control, but I think you have to remain open.

ROSEN: Did *Lie of the Mind* start out one way and end up another?

SHEPARD: I wrote about 11, 12 drafts of that thing. It changed, it shifted directions a lot of times. But then I discovered something in rewriting that was interesting. I would trace back to the moment where I thought it started to go wrong and then I would throw everything away up to that—past that point and start again at that moment. Sometimes it would go back 25, 30 pages. And I'd just take that and throw it away and start over.

ROSEN: *A Lie of the Mind* opened really well, with the two levels and that phone call from nowhere. I think Jake was calling his brother from nowhere. He didn't know where, somewhere on a highway, from one nowhere to another. But you never used that level of the stage again.

SHEPARD: No, we did. See, originally the play was much longer. I cut a lot out of it in production. We had a lot of scenes come out. There was one scene where he's walking up there on the highway and a couple other scenes that we cut out.

ROSEN: Of your stage plays, the only one you've adapted for film is *Fool for Love. A Lie of the Mind* would be a good candidate for film.

SHEPARD: Yes, because of that parallel time thing. Actually, Milos Forman wanted to make it into a movie. But I said no.

ROSEN: Much has been made about that eagle and tomcat story in the monologue that ends *Curse of the Starving Class.*

SHEPARD: I didn't intend it as a metaphor. It was just an image, which actually happened. I remember that happening, not exactly as it was written, but I remember that was the case. When you castrated ram lambs, there would always be a hawk or something around. And then I think later I came across a story similar to that in an old Western magazine, about an eagle. But I think it was with calf testes. I just kind of adapted it. But I didn't mean it as a metaphor. It can be taken that way, if you want. It's not about masculinity or anything like that. Unless you want it to be.

ROSEN: I'd like to ask you about all your imagery of food.

SHEPARD: [*Laughs*]

ROSEN: I can't think of a single play of yours where characters haven't been having breakfast, or boiling artichokes, or burning toast, or spilling cream of broccoli soup all over the bed, or . . .

SHEPARD: Well, it was an interesting thing, because I don't think I really discovered the meaning of it, if you want to put it that way, until I worked with Joe [Chaikin] on *Tongues*. In *Tongues* we have a little monologue about hunger, where he gets into: do you want to eat, why do you want to eat now? You know, I have a hunger. And it builds into this momentum. When we got into that, Joe started to talk about it in a way that suddenly revealed what it really was to me, I think. Because I don't think I'd really understood it before. But his sense of it was that a person's profound emptiness, the profound sense of emptiness in a person's life is answered by eating in many ways. Somehow, when you eat, food fills some kind of void that's not only physical but emotional. And I think that there's something to that. People who have the hunger for anything—the hunger for drugs, the hunger for sex—this hunger is a direct response to a profound sense of emptiness and aloneness, maybe, or disconnectedness. And I think that there's some truth to that.

ROSEN: With *States of Shock* I thought you finally decided, "I'm going to give you a food fight to end all food fights."

SHEPARD: Yes. There were a couple of things in production which I thought were great, but then after the first night Wynn Handman [artistic director of the American Place Theatre] hit the roof because we started getting all the cleaning bills from the front row. "We can't have these cleaning bills."

ROSEN: I saw it a few times and every time it was different, depending on how long it took for the banana split to melt.

SHEPARD: But John [Malkovich] would really aim it to that front row. I love slapstick comedy. I just think that if theater loses the ability to enjoy slapstick because the audience has become too cool, then we have really cut ourselves off, we've shot ourselves in the foot.

ROSEN: There's lots of slapstick in *True West*. When Malkovich played Lee, he seemed just crazy. It was as if he was going to destroy the stage.

SHEPARD: Yes, with the golf club.

ROSEN: And then there was slapstick when the toast was hurled everywhere. Do you aim for that kind of anarchy in production?

SHEPARD: It's a controlled anarchy. It's not "everybody go crazy and have fun." It's really controlled. Like, for instance, when Malkovich hit his partner, Gary Sinise [who played Austin in the Steppenwolf production of *True West*], Sinise had glasses on, and Malkovich tapped his glasses with the golf club. That's controlled, that's absolute control. The character is freaking out, and the actor has the ability to be able to draw that stroke with the golf club so that he can tap his glasses like that and not hurt somebody. That's what we're looking for.

ROSEN: This is a point that was often made by Lee Strasberg at the Actors Studio.

SHEPARD: I think Strasberg ruined more actors than he helped. He set American acting back about 100 years.

ROSEN: Why do you think that?

SHEPARD: Well, because now you have this whole generation of young actors who think James Dean was where it was at. James Dean was brilliant at what he did. But he was kind of a phenomenon. He wasn't somebody you'd want to imitate. That wasn't the penultimate American actor. There is this whole kind of self-indulgent, neurotic belief that somehow the purpose for doing a play for these actors is to work out their private problems. They don't have the sense of serving the script. It's serving their own . . . unraveling their emotional problems. Which is a disaster.

ROSEN: I want to ask you about myth.

SHEPARD: You've never seen that word in my plays. It comes up after the fact.

ROSEN: In an interview you once said a myth is a lie of the mind.

SHEPARD: Yes, but our language has been so laundered that we don't . . . we can say the same word to each other and not know what we mean.

ROSEN: That's why I ask what you mean.

SHEPARD: There's myth in the sense of a lie. There's myth in the sense of fantasy. There's myth in all those senses. But the traditional meaning of myth, the ancient meaning of myth, is that it served a purpose in our life. The purpose had to do with being able to trace ourselves back through time and follow our emotional self. Myth served as a story in which people could connect themselves in time to the past. And thereby connect themselves to the present and the future. Because they were hooked up with the lineage of myth. It was so powerful and so strong that it acted as a thread in culture.

And that's been destroyed. Myth in its truest form has been demolished. It doesn't exist anymore. All we have is fantasies about it. Or ideas that don't speak to our inner self at all, they just speak to some lame notions about the past. But they don't connect with anything. We've lost touch with the essence of myth.

ROSEN: Many of your characters try to connect with that essence, don't they?

SHEPARD: Fruitlessly, yes.

ROSEN: In *Buried Child,* Vince has that speech about the face reflected in the windshield. And in *Far North,* Katie has a very similar speech, tracing her lineage.

SHEPARD: Well, those instances are more in terms of just immediate hereditary things, having to do with family. But see, myth not only connects you and me to our personal families, it connects us to the family of generations and generations of races of people, tribes, the mythology of the ancient people. The same with the American Indians—they were connected to their ancestors, people they never knew but are connected to through myth, through prayer, through ritual, through dance, music, all of those forms that lead people into a river of myth. And there was a connecting river, not a fragmented river.

ROSEN: And that's gone.

SHEPARD: It's gone, yes.

ROSEN: Does Wesley attempt to create a ritual that will lead into a river of myth in *Curse of the Starving Class*? He fails.

SHEPARD: Yes, but all contemporary efforts will fail. They have to be connected to ancient stuff. They can't be just contemporary or else it will come apart. It will become a fashion show, like rap music.

ROSEN: Do you think you might write a "musical"?

SHEPARD: What is a musical? *Guys and Gals*?

ROSEN: *Tooth of Crime* is a musical.

SHEPARD: Yes, well so is *States of Shock. Lie of the Mind* is a musical. It's got a lot of music in it. You don't have to have actors standing around singing to each other for it to be a musical. I think the traditional American musical is pretty hard to pull off these days. I mean, how are you going to do *that*? I haven't found a good . . . you need a good story to write a musical.

ROSEN: What was the process involved in writing the music for *States of Shock*?

SHEPARD: I worked with a composer I've worked with for a long, long time, J. A. Deane. He did some of the music for *Far North* and we worked a lot in San Francisco with the improvisational group. They did *Angel City* and all kinds of stuff. So I kind of composed it with him. He's just an incredible guy to work with. And I've worked with one of those drummers who's backstage, Joe [Joseph Sabella].

ROSEN: In terms of musical structure, do your plays end the way music ends?

SHEPARD: I hate endings. You have to end it somehow. I like beginnings. Middles are tough, but endings are just a pain in the ass. It's very hard to end stuff.

ROSEN: *Lie of the Mind* ended perfectly.

SHEPARD: Yeah, I found a good ending for that. I liked the ending of *True West.*

ROSEN: Yes, but *True West* doesn't end.

SHEPARD: No, but that's why I like it.

ROSEN: *A Lie of the Mind* ends with a silhouette, one of those images that Peter Brook talks about in *The Empty Space.*

SHEPARD: Yes, I finally discovered an ending for that. Endings are so hard. Because the temptation always is a sense that you're supposed to wrap it up somehow. You're supposed to culminate it in something fruitful. And it always feels so phony when you try to wrap it all up.

ROSEN: That's why it seems more like music, because music is not supposed to wrap it up, it's supposed to keep going in your mind.

SHEPARD: Yes, I think that's the right kind of ending. That it leaves you on the next note. See, what interested me is the seven-note scale. That the first and the seventh are the same note, just an octave higher, so things are cycled. So you go through something you are really returning to—the place you began. But then you get into scales from other countries, like China or Japan, and they go on . . . what are they, 13-note scales or 21 sometimes?

ROSEN: Do you ever think about *Far North* or *A Lie of the Mind* as feminist pieces?

SHEPARD: What does that mean? What is a feminist piece? Following the feminist cause or something?

ROSEN: That they perceive the world from the point of view of women as opposed to superimposing a male view on history.

SHEPARD: To a certain extent, yes. But what became curious for me was . . . there was that certain period of time, and now I think it's actually over, or it's changed into something else, but there was a period of time when there was a kind of awareness happening about the female side of things. Not necessarily women but just the female force in nature becoming interesting to people. And it became more and more interesting to me because of how that female thing relates to being a man. You know, in yourself, that the female part of one's self as a man is, for the most part, battered and beaten up and kicked to shit just like some women in relationships. That men themselves batter their own female part to their own detriment. And it became interesting from that angle—as a man, what is it like to embrace the female part of yourself that you historically damaged for one reason or another? So from that point of view, it was interesting to me. But not from the cultural feminist point of view because I don't really understand that. I would never try to be a spokesman for it.

ROSEN: Starting with Emma in *Curse of the Starving Class*, you create some really vibrant women characters. And in *A Lie of the Mind* and in *Far North*, you explore the female side of character, even in the men.

SHEPARD: I felt that too. That was one of the big changes for me in those few pieces, that the women suddenly took on a different light than they had before. Because before it felt so sort of overwhelmed by the confusion about masculinity, about the confusion about how these men identify themselves. That sort of overwhelmed the female. There wasn't even any room to consider the female, because the men were so fucked up. You spent the whole play trying to figure out what these men were about, who had no idea themselves. But then, when the women characters began to emerge, then something began to make more sense for the men, too.

ROSEN: To explore the "female side of things," did you ever think of doing *True West* with women? Two sisters?

SHEPARD: No. People get funny ideas about writers, like, for instance, Beckett stopped a production of *Endgame* that was a black production. He didn't stop it because he's a racist, he stopped it because he wrote it with a certain inclination. And to cast it black, regardless of how good the actors are, is going to completely throw something else into it. He's just protecting his play. I wouldn't want to see *True West* done by women because it's a scam on the play, it's not the play. I don't have anything against women. I'm just telling you it would distort the play.

ROSEN: Your plays have a lot of broken pacts. In *Fool for Love*, May has to break the pact in order to escape. *A Lie of the Mind* has a pact that can't be broken. The premise of *Paris, Texas* is a broken pact. And in *Far North*, there's a pact between the daughter and the father, which is really a one-way pact. I ask you, as you once asked Bob Dylan, do you believe in a pact?

SHEPARD: I think we don't really know anymore what a pact is. That's another thing that's been lost, along with myths. If you make a pact, you're suddenly cut off from the whole territory of so-called independence. Which is the reason a lot of people don't want to get married, or when they do get married, they make a contract. They don't make a pact, they make a contract, so that one can't sue the other. Well, a contract isn't a pact. A pact is something that has to do with something *felt*. In order to have a pact, you have to know that both of you feel the same thing. It's very difficult because hardly anybody knows it.

ROSEN: In your plays there are a lot of presumed pacts.

SHEPARD: Broken, yes. But there are even pacts of friendship. They don't have to be between men and women necessarily. It has to do with honor, and exchange of honor in the real sense. You don't betray each other in any way. Not just sexually, but any way.

ROSEN: Who breaks the pact in *States of Shock*?

SHEPARD: Well, I'm not sure there ever was an actual pact made between the two of them, but the betrayal is definitely on the side of the father. There's no such thing as a one-sided pact, so you would both have to know about it or it ain't a pact.

ROSEN: In some of your plays there are one-sided pacts. In *Far North* the father demands that Katie keep her end of a pact she never agreed to.

SHEPARD: Kind of a deal, yes.

ROSEN: Yes. In *Paris, Texas* there's a one-sided pact the wife rejected. Characters presume they have a pact when they don't.

SHEPARD: "Everything Is Broken"—Dylan. It's a great tune.

ROSEN: How does your work with Chaikin feed your other work?

SHEPARD: It's a long story. For years I hung around with Joe in the Open Theater, but for a long time I never actually worked with him. I just listened and sat in on sessions and was greatly influenced by what he had to say, particularly about the relationship between the audience and the stage. These were notions that I hadn't really considered strongly before, because I was so wrapped up in my writing that, for some reason, I was pushed off into the world of writing a play and kind of disregarding the aspect of the audience. Which is a grave mistake, I think. What are we doing to an audience? What's an audience doing to us? What do we want to have done and how are we being influenced back and forth? So I think that was the first big idea that galvanized me to him as a theater person. Then much later, I got lucky enough to work with him, and to write and direct—and the music and all the rest of it. Then we just kind of moved into a kind of agreement about how to work.

ROSEN: Does it affect the way you create characters? Or think about character?

SHEPARD: To some extent, yes. But it also affected the way I thought about play, the plays, the whole . . . I mean, one of the great things he said to me when we'd just started to do *Tongues*, the first time we'd worked directly together, was, he says, "You know, it doesn't have to be a play."

ROSEN: What would you call it?

SHEPARD: A bunch of monologues. It can be a presentation. It can be something not pretending to be a play. It's just something between an audience and a performer. And we don't even have to call it a performance piece. You don't have to call it anything.

ROSEN: In *Angel City* and in other plays, you sometimes leave characters, as you've put it, "marooned with language," isolated with long reveries of transformation.

SHEPARD: Yes, that whole severe break with so-called naturalism happened back there. And I think it was a healthy thing. Why should we be anchored to these notions of Eugene O'Neill and all this burden of having your character be believable from the outside in terms of the artist saying, well, he really is in a living room serving tea to his mother. And he's really talking the way he would be talking in real life. What the hell is that? Where is that going to take us? Why doesn't he pour the tea on her head and start screaming and carrying on, climbing walls, and then come back and sit down and. . . . You know what I mean?

ROSEN: Why not just jump through the wall?

SHEPARD: Yes, or whatever. And I think that a lot of those breaks back then had to do with incredible frustration, the straitjacket of that kind of theater that we had been told was great theater.

ROSEN: Dead theater.

SHEPARD: Dead theater, yes. Living room theater.

ROSEN: Is character larger than personality?

SHEPARD: Well see, I don't think character really has anything to do with personality. I think character and personality are two entirely different animals. Really. When you get right down to it. See, I think character is something that can't be helped, it can't be . . . it's like destiny. And maybe it includes personality, but personality is something so frivolous compared to character, they're not even in the same ballpark. Personality is putting on a different hat.

ROSEN: But character is permanent?

SHEPARD: Character is an essential tendency. It can be covered up, it can be messed with, it can be screwed around with, but it can't be ultimately changed. It's like the structure of our bones, the blood that runs through our veins.

ROSEN: Is character the same for a whole family?

SHEPARD: There is a character, characteristics, if you want to call them that, that run through families that are undeniable. So many people get screwed up because they try to deny them, try to say, "I'm not like my father, I'm not like my mother, I'm not going to be this way, I'm not going to be that way." When, in fact, there's nothing you can do about it [*laughs*].

ROSEN: So many of your plays revolve around the hopelessness of getting out of that bind. Unless a character embraces that family character, or accepts it, he is doomed.

SHEPARD: Yes, I think so. I think that there is no escape, that the wholehearted acceptance of it leads to another possibility. But the possibility of somehow miraculously making myself into a different person is a hoax, a futile game. And it leads to insanity, actually [*laughs*].

ROSEN: In the plays?

SHEPARD: No, in people. People go insane trying to deny what they really are.

ROSEN: I want to know about angels.

SHEPARD: What do you want to know about angels?

ROSEN: Sometimes you write about angels, and you often allude to them. You wrote an angel's monologue for Chaikin.

SHEPARD: Well, you know there is a hierarchy of angels. It's been around a long, long time. And there are all kinds of angels. Just like there are all kinds of demons.

ROSEN: It's not a facetious question.

SHEPARD: No, I'm not answering flippantly, it's just that I'm not an authority on the subject, but I do know that there's considerable historical evidence that there are these creatures, or this world exists, the world of angels and demons.

ROSEN: Where would this world be in your plays? How would it affect the plays?

SHEPARD: Well, just that it's a part of the world of the character's notions about good and evil, his notions about fate and chance and this, that, and the other. Or his lack of that. Certain characters might be surrounded by certain things. I don't mean to sound esoteric [*laughs*] but . . . influences. It's just influences, we're influenced.

ROSEN: The characters are influenced?

SHEPARD: Um-hum. Just like we are.

ROSEN: By angels and demons. Which are real forces.

SHEPARD: Well, I think so, yes. I think forces exist that—

ROSEN: In many of your plays, such as *A Lie of the Mind*, characters fight with these internalized angels and demons. And now you've written a character in *The War in Heaven* who is an angel.

SHEPARD: Yes. To me, it [the angel] is a great character for Joe [Chaikin], because, particularly nowadays, it's very difficult to write a hero or to write a good person or a person pure of heart or a person with spiritual integrity or whatever you want to call it. It's very difficult to write that and not have it be the corniest thing on earth. So the only way to take it was to this absolute extreme—the world of angels. And I thought it would be very risky to try the premise of an angel crashing to earth. So that's where . . . I thought if any actor could play it, it would be Joe, because he has that amazing innocence about him.

ROSEN: Do you think about heroes the way you did when you wrote all those plays about the hero corrupted by his society and facing danger?

SHEPARD: Did I write those? [*Laughs*]

ROSEN: In *Geography of a Horse Dreamer* the hero's got to do what he's got to do because he gets kidnapped and forced to serve. And in *Angel City*—

SHEPARD: Yeah. The exploited artist.

ROSEN: Do you still have that feeling about the exploited artist as hero?

SHEPARD: Not to the extent that I want to defend it anymore. I've grown out of that phase of being outraged that the artist isn't treated with real respect anymore. It doesn't matter to me now. It did then.

ROSEN: Many plays recall *Angel City*, plays about the artist devoured by movies.

SHEPARD: Yes, but they've been singing that song forever. What was the great . . . *Day of the Locust*? It was such a brilliant book. There's no reason . . . I mean, that book says the whole thing about Hollywood and dealing with Hollywood and dealing with the machinery of it. And the thing of it is, Hollywood is impervious to criticism. You cannot puncture the skin of that mechanism. Even more so today. It's like steel armor. You can't even get next to it, because it's so completely locked up, guarded by the mechanism.

ROSEN: I thought you got around that with *Paris, Texas* by working with Wim Wenders, a German filmmaker who sees America the way you do. You don't see America the way an American does. You step away from it and look at it from a distance.

SHEPARD: [*Laughs*] Right. It's true Europeans, particularly Germans, have a very critical eye—not a critical eye but an eye that *embraces* a certain thing about America that I don't think Americans have. For the most part, I think Americans have lost compassion for their own country.

ROSEN: I'd like to know about this movie you're working on. What is the title?

SHEPARD: *Silent Tongue.*

ROSEN: Which of course I would recognize as one of your titles.

SHEPARD: Yeah, I'm running out of titles.

ROSEN: Is it true that you used to make up titles first and plays later?

SHEPARD: I did that a couple of times. *Unseen Hand.* I just liked the title so much I wrote a play to fit the title.

ROSEN: And *Tooth of Crime*? Is that from Mallarmé?

SHEPARD: Yeah. Actually, I may have had that title before the play, I'm not sure. *The Unseen Hand*—I know for sure I had the title first.

ROSEN: What is *Silent Tongue* about?

SHEPARD: It's about a woman who had her tongue cut out for lying. It takes place in 1876, and there's a medicine show. And a half-breed woman who has her tongue cut out. I don't want to say too much about it. Suffice it to say it's a period piece.

ROSEN: A great deal has been written about medicine shows as popular entertainment.

SHEPARD: I've researched a lot of it. It's a pretty amazing era. It lasted up into the '50s, which is incredible, before it disappeared. The mid-1800s to the 1950s.

ROSEN: Touring America.

SHEPARD: Wagons and all that stuff. It says something about Americans. There's a cure somewhere and the cure resides in some kind of magic potion, a miracle. The gullibility of it is incredible.

ROSEN: Yes, the magic solution. What did you think of Jack Gelber calling you "the playwright as shaman"?

SHEPARD: It's very flattering, but the problem I find with that kind of stuff is that in a way it's embarrassing, because having come across some of this stuff for real, you realize how far you personally are, say, from real shamanism or real magic or real wisdom, that kind of stuff.

ROSEN: In many of your plays, characters try to come up with "potions." In *Fool for Love*, Eddie's coming up with something that's going to fix everything.

SHEPARD: Yeah, it fails.

ROSEN: But in *Silent Tongue* are you dealing with characters who are real shamans? Concocting real potions?

SHEPARD: Oh, no, those guys were all bogus. None of those medicine show guys were for real. They sold snake oil and actually the mixture was

70 percent alcohol. So people got drunk and felt great, and the next day woke up and discovered they'd been duped and the medicine show was out of town. But no, none of those guys were shamans in any sense of the word. They were just charlatans. Those were side shows.

ROSEN: But your title character—is she genuine, but involved with this fake world?

SHEPARD: She was and then got out of it.

ROSEN: And can she really cure people?

SHEPARD: No. It's not about . . . she's not a holy person.

ROSEN: What brought about *States of Shock*? Where did that come from?

SHEPARD: When that war started [in Iraq]—I was in Kentucky when the war opened. I was in a bar that I go to a lot down there because it's a horsemen's bar. Normally that bar is just a din of conversation and people having a great time and talking about horses and this, that, and the other. And I walked in the bar and it was stone silence. The TV was on, and these planes were coming in, and suddenly . . . it just seemed like doomsday to me. I could not believe the systematic kind of insensitivity of it. That there was this punitive attitude—we're going to just knock these people off the face of the earth. And then it's devastating. Not only that, but they've convinced the American public that this was a good deed, that this was in fact a heroic fucking war, and welcome the heroes back. What fucking heroes, man? I mean, they bombed the shit out of these people. They knocked the stew out of them over there with bombing and bombing and bombing. The notion of this being a heroic event is just outrageous. I couldn't believe it. I still can't believe it. I can't believe that, having come out of the '60s and the incredible reaction to Vietnam, that voice has all but disappeared. Vanished. There's no voice anymore. This is supposed to be what America's about? This fucking military . . . I had just spent eight weeks on the Pine Ridge Indian Reservation in South Dakota, the most devastated culture in America—80 percent alcoholism and the poverty rate is just . . . you can't even believe the poverty [Shepard was there on location filming *Thunderheart*]. And watching these F-104s and F-15s, these fighter jets flying across every day to Ellsworth air base. I don't know. You really start to wonder.

ROSEN: So that's how the play started?

SHEPARD: *States of Shock*, yes. I just got so outraged by the whole hoax of it, and the way everything is choked down and censored in the media. Frightening situation.

ROSEN: But *States of Shock* doesn't only respond to the Gulf War.

SHEPARD: No. I wanted to create a character of such outrageous, repulsive, military, fascist demonism that the audience would recognize it, and say, "Oh, this is the essence of this thing." I thought Malkovich came pretty close to it. Just creating this monster fascist.

ROSEN: What was the purpose of all that stage business about balancing?

SHEPARD: Just a way to get the waitress across the stage.

ROSEN: He [the Colonel played by Malkovich] also had a lot of bits about rhythm and timing and . . .

SHEPARD: Oh yes, manipulating is a better word. Manipulating things. He knew how to manipulate—manipulate the public, manipulate machinery, whatever.

ROSEN: But the play didn't do that. Do you think the play succeeded in getting audiences galvanized against the war?

SHEPARD: No, not at all. I don't know what happened. It only succeeded in pissing off the critics, it seems like [*laughs*]. That was part of its purpose. I don't know.

ROSEN: Do you think you'll ever offer another playwrights' workshop like the ones you led in Mill Valley?

SHEPARD: Yes, actually, I do want to do something like that again. I'm not sure when or where, you know, but I wouldn't mind working with writers.

ROSEN: Why have you created this wall around yourself and made yourself so inaccessible?

SHEPARD: Well, you have to protect a certain territory. Otherwise, it becomes exploited and taken away from you.

ROSEN: But I don't mean the private self, I mean the public self—the artist, the writer, the director.

SHEPARD: Same thing, same thing. I mean, particularly with your work, you have to protect the air around it. Otherwise, it gets co-opted and taken over. It's not a paranoid statement. Writers are isolated individuals, for good reason.

ROSEN: How do your plays take shape?

SHEPARD: Every single one of them comes about in a different way. I don't systematically sit down every morning and write three hours and then have a sandwich and then write for another two hours. I never have been able to work like that. If I have a piece of work that begins to have momentum and force, then I'll pay attention to it and I'll work very systematically. But I don't just sit down and arbitrarily punch keys on the typewriter, hoping for the best. I think that's a lost cause, for me anyway. I've never had any luck with that.

ROSEN: So you wait for the work to announce itself?

SHEPARD: To a certain extent, yes. And then it happens differently each time. Sometimes it turns in a different way or another idea comes out and you begin something else and abandon that one and go off to this one. So right now I'm working on a book, two books.

ROSEN: Fiction?

SHEPARD: Yes. I've got one up to 200 pages and the other more than 30 pages.

ROSEN: Somebody said he started out being a novelist, but then he noticed that when you type a play, it takes a lot of space on the page for the name of the character.

SHEPARD: Who was *that* person? [*laughs*].

ROSEN: Right, *you* said that.

SHEPARD: You fill up the pages faster. Yeah, it's true, dialogue flies [*laughs*].

ROSEN: But now you're writing novels.

SHEPARD: Well, I wouldn't call them novels. They're books, you know, just books. I don't know if they're novels.

ROSEN: You mean like *Motel Chronicles*?

SHEPARD: No. One of them is an actual long story. It's about 150 pages. Might be a novel. And the other one is a kind of chronicle, but it's mixed with fiction and fact. I don't know what you would call them.

ROSEN: Where do you stand on the question of an artist's privacy in regard to notebooks and first drafts being made available?

SHEPARD: It depends on what people are interested in. Are they interested in the life of the artist or the artist's work?

ROSEN: Sometimes one is interested in the artist's process.

SHEPARD: I doubt that very seriously. I think most people are just interested in gossip. The process has nothing to do with it. In fact, I don't think anybody has ever been able to objectively explain process. How can you explain process? Did you ever read those interviews—*Paris Review* did a whole great series of interviews—the one with Céline in it? The Céline one just knocks me out. The end of it is they're sitting on some park bench somewhere. The interviewer says something to him about, "Well, how are you going to go on from here?" Céline turns to him and says, "I just want to be left alone." [*Laughs uproariously*] I just want to be left alone.

ROSEN: Are there playwrights working today whom you admire?

SHEPARD: I don't know any playwrights.

ROSEN: You don't pay attention to anybody else's work?

SHEPARD: I don't know playwright one. I don't hang out with play-wrights. I can't say I dislike them, but for the most part theater doesn't inter-est me. I like writing plays because they have so much movement, there's so much possibility of movement, and language moves. But I'm not a theater buff. Most theater bores the hell out of me. But I do like the possibilities. I think of all the forms that we've got now, probably theater has more possi-bilities than anything else. Really. Of real experimentation and real surprise and real emotional contact with an audience. More than movies. Movies have just become a kind of hallucination. An excuse to go hallucinate, like drugs. Movies are a dreamworld. Eat popcorn and dream. But theater still has that very exciting possibility because you can put all the elements in there. You've got music and actors and so many possibilities. And language: language can do so many things.

ROSEN: Are movies anti-language?

SHEPARD: Yes. They don't want to know about language. Nobody lis-tens anymore. Listening is not a part of the program.

ROSEN: When you direct a film, what is your attitude toward language?

SHEPARD: Oh, well, I intend . . . I mean, I wrote *Silent Tongue* as a screenplay. It's intended to be filmed. It's not an adaptation of anything. So a good screenplay is intentionally a visual event. That's what the medium is about. So you do tend to shy away from dialogue. Whereas in plays, entirely composed of dialogue, that's the meat and potatoes of it.

ROSEN: Language is one of the strongest elements of your plays. When you write a movie, you're really working without a net.

SHEPARD: Yes, although I think there's a lot of exciting possibilities with film. I'm not saying it's without possibilities. One great thing about theater, too, is the nuts and bolts aspect of it. You're just working at a very physical level. Like when we were doing *States of Shock*, we were trying to figure out a good whipping sound for the drummers in the back. And every-body was checking out everybody's belts. People would go, "Try this one." Whap! "That's pretty good. Let's try that one over there." And that's what it's about, you know—okay, let's try everybody's belt. The light technician, "Do you have a good belt?" Till we get the right sound. That kind of thing. You never in a million years see that in a movie. You go to the prop person who's got 20 different varieties of belts hanging there. But you wouldn't be going around asking the caterer to take his belt off.

ROSEN: You never go to the theater at all?

SHEPARD: Oh no. But I've been to a lot of rodeo lately [*laughs*].

ROSEN: Do you romanticize the rodeo?

SHEPARD: Romanticize it? Well, I suppose, to a certain extent. But on the other side, you can't romanticize it if you *do* it.

ROSEN: The rodeo is not a representation of anything. It's real.

SHEPARD: Yes. If you rope an 800-pound steer and dally off your saddle on him and pull all that steer, and the rope comes across your leg, it's real.

ROSEN: Should theater be real, and dangerous, in the same way?

SHEPARD: Well, to a certain extent. You don't want to hurt anybody. I don't think that's what Artaud meant by "the theater of cruelty." But on the emotional level, there can be a comparable experience without hurting anyone.

ROSEN: On the emotional level, are you aiming toward Artaud's idea of theater exteriorizing latent cruelty? Your plays do put audiences in touch with things they don't think about when they think about themselves as civilized.

SHEPARD: Yes, hopefully, although it sounds highfalutin' when you couch it with Artaud, because Artaud has become so misused over the years. He's become an excuse for a whole kind of theater that he probably wouldn't endorse if he was alive today. He'd laugh at it. Or maybe he wouldn't; I don't know because I never met the man.

ROSEN: Are you aware of all the playwrights who have been influenced by you?

SHEPARD: No. Well, I mean, I heard tell of it. But see, I don't follow theater so I don't know.

ROSEN: You've had a tremendous impact on the way people shape plays, and the kind of language and energy that they think is possible on stage.

SHEPARD: It's an interesting thing, though, that question of energy. Because I think there is a certain capacity, and if you try to push past that capacity you shoot yourself in the foot. I think there's only a certain *amount* of energy that can be contained on stage. I think it's finite. I don't think that it just goes on forever. A lot of the time, the mistake I see is that there is an effusiveness that doesn't have a focus. So it becomes just chaotic. It needs to have a leash on it to a certain extent so that it can do something. Otherwise, it's just like a force with no handle.

ROSEN: In *Fool for Love*, when Ed Harris was lassoing bedposts, he was very focused, very contained.

SHEPARD: Yes, but full of energy. Right to the brim. Malkovich is the same way.

ROSEN: Why do you act? Is it just a way to raise money?

SHEPARD: Actually, it's become more interesting over the years, I must say. At first, I was really disappointed in film acting. Not only by its possibilities, but by mine. I felt very limited. I felt very intimidated, and unable to take many risks. Now I feel like more and more I can . . . I'm actually beginning to find a way to make an expression of character and to follow something that wasn't possible when I started out. I don't know how that's happened, but it's evolved over the years of doing it, I guess, just from practice. It's become more interesting. But still, the difficult part of film acting is not the acting, but the hanging around and the waiting and all the time that's burned up.

ROSEN: Becoming an actor made you famous in a way that you could not have anticipated. Could becoming a movie star have been a bad move on your part as an artist?

SHEPARD: Yeah, it may have been, yeah. But life has a lot of surprises.

ROSEN: Ironically, Eddie in *Fool for Love* is really the best role you've ever had.

SHEPARD: I suppose. Yes.

ROSEN: If you were playing him now, would you do it differently?

SHEPARD: I don't know. I was so confused during that time about what exactly I was doing. See, originally, Jessie [Jessica Lange] and I were supposed to do it, with Robert Altman. And then she decided, because she was pregnant at the time, that it would probably be better not to. And I just said, well, I'd go ahead with it even though I was sort of halfhearted since she wasn't going to do it. I would never want to redo it. But on the other hand, it wasn't bad. It was just kind of ill thought-out. Like, for instance, Altman wanting all the flashbacks to be random and disconnected and deliberately confusing.

ROSEN: Do you get some kind of pleasure out of acting?

SHEPARD: Well, I'm not saying pleasure, but it's starting to become more interesting, the whole process of being able to contact the character and to manipulate your concentration and your attention and move into areas that are more risky and that have real feeling and stuff like that. I couldn't do that when I first started. All I could do was sit and hang onto the saddle horn and go.

ROSEN: Do you think you might ever act on stage again?

SHEPARD: No, I doubt it. Unless it was a very, very particular situation and it lasted a very short time. I did a play with Patti Smith, *Cowboy Mouth*. I think we did it one night. A one-night stand.

ROSEN: Are you still fond of any of your early plays?

SHEPARD: Yes, I like *Action*. And I like *Rock Garden*, all right. The funny thing about *Rock Garden* is, if you look at that play, it's surprising even to me because when I look at it, I see the germ right in that little play of a whole lot of different things. The germ is in that play of many, many to come, much more so than *Cowboys*, for instance, or a lot of those other plays. *Rock Garden* was sort of the beginning of something that reverberated from there, which I didn't realize at the time.

ROSEN: And why are you fond of *Action*?

SHEPARD: Because it was such a complete breakaway from anything I'd done before. It's completely in another domain. The play itself surprised me, the way it moved and the idiosyncrasy of it and the way it shifted. I thought it was a satisfying combination of slapstick and something more serious. I don't know what you call it, realism or something like that.

ROSEN: *Action* has that haunting speech about the moths.

SHEPARD: The moths and the breaking of the chair and the clothes on the clothesline and things like that. And I think it's an interesting play. And, in fact, *States of Shock* is probably an outcome of that play, in form, in structure, in its quirkiness, its instant changes. Things like that.

ROSEN: And do you have any fondness for *Tooth of Crime*?

SHEPARD: To some extent. But I think it's dated now. A lot of that early stuff I couldn't really say was dated. But *Tooth of Crime* seems too topical. The combat thing is interesting, the clash of forces, but then the whole thing about pop culture kind of turns me off. There's this pretense of being a commentary on pop culture.

ROSEN: There's a scene in *Tooth of Crime* where Hoss is talking to his father, and it connects . . . I suppose everything connects.

SHEPARD: Yes, whether you've connected it or not is another story, but I think it all *is* connected by itself.

ROSEN: What are you reading lately?

SHEPARD: Oh, I read *The Thoroughbred Times* [*laughs*]. I was reading a lot of short fiction and some history, about the Plains country, the grassland country.

ROSEN: What are you doing next?

SHEPARD: I'm working on these two books. It's a huge amount of work because one of them is totally handwritten and I've got to retype the whole thing. And the other one . . . they both basically have got to be reworked with the machines.

ROSEN: So you revise it as you type?

SHEPARD: Yes, as I go. And then also, when I start typing, there's new writing that goes into that, that isn't necessarily in the handwritten version.

ROSEN: Is it a very lonely process?

SHEPARD: Oh, I don't feel it as being that. I've heard writers complain about that, but I don't think they're writers. That's what writing is, an act of isolation. You either accept it or you don't. I don't think there's any complaining about it.

ROSEN: I've read that you've wished you would never have to write another play.

SHEPARD: That was a little period I was going through.

ROSEN: But not anymore? You no longer feel it's some kind of curse: you have to write and you would like to be free of it?

SHEPARD: No, not necessarily. Because see, the thing that's interesting about writing is if it really is something that you get in your blood, it keeps opening and opening and opening. It doesn't shut down. I think to a certain extent the play thing has narrowed. But then there's other kinds of writing that have opened up as a result of that narrowing down. And you get involved in that and then maybe, who knows, the playwriting all comes back up again. You can't really predict that stuff.

ROSEN: You can't turn your back on a gift like that.

SHEPARD: It's not only a gift, it's a kind of way of life. I feel lucky that I have something like that where experience can be shuffled back into another form, as opposed to not having a form or structure to put an expression into. I suppose you do that with anything, but with writing. . . . It's really lucky to be a writer, I think.

Sam Shepard, Tues., Dec. 14, 1993

Mel Gussow / 1993

Transcript of interview conducted on December 14, 1993. Container 139.1, Mel Gussow Collection, Harry Ransom Center, University of Texas. Published by permission of Harry Ransom Center, The University of Texas at Austin.

Sam Shepard is having a cappuccino at the Time Café, and two women at a nearby table are talking to him. Later he smokes Camels. He is dressed informally, with open collar workshirt and dungarees, still the essential cowboy. He has just come from working on his piece with Joseph Chaikin at the Public Theater, but he looks more as if he has just come from roping a steer. Has he been roping another play?

Mel Gussow: What happened with *Simpatico*?
Sam Shepard: It fell apart, you know.
MG: Your second Spanish play after *La Turista*.
SS: By title, yeah. Completely [fell apart]. Kind of a mysterious evolution. Back in August when I first contacted Lewis [Allen], the money apparently was all there. Signed, sealed and delivered. Then piece by piece it began to fall apart. Every day the scenario changed. There was new money coming in. Then it would fall out. Ultimately there just wasn't enough time to get it going. The shame of it is losing the cast. It was an extraordinary cast: Ed Harris, Fred Forrest, Jennifer Jason Leigh, Beverly D'Angelo and Jim Gammon. To corral that many really fine actors together again is tough. Now it's late in the game, the end of the year. I'm going to try to regroup and do it at the Public next year. I had just good luck with Lewis with *Lie of the Mind*. I thought I'd go with him again. To be fair, it wasn't from a lack of trying. He tried to put it together. It just didn't happen. Economics are tough [*laugh*].

And when you figure the budget is just a fraction of what a movie costs. We tried several different arenas. One was going to be that Broadway Alliance thing, which has 1200 seats. When that fell apart, we went to the Promenade and when that fell apart, it was Variety Arts, and the Public. It just never panned out. With that kind of a cast you'd think the thing would sail.

MG: What's the play about and when did you write it?

SS: I started it in September of '92 and it's the first full-length play I've finished since *A Lie of the Mind,* which is about seven years ago. So in that sense I was real eager to get started with it. It's always difficult to try to explain what it's about. It's rivalry between two close friends that have known each other their whole lives, and it involves women and horses and all kinds of stuff, gambling, deceit, envy, jealousy, rage . . . shit like that. [He orders the quesadillas and the special shrimp salad and another cappuccino.] It's the stuff you can't help writing about. I had a real difficult time after *A Lie of the Mind* trying to extend anything. I had several different efforts that kind of crapped out at 40, 50 pages, you know. I've got many, many unfinished plays. This is the first that evolved out and took hold and became a three-act play. . . . *A Lie of the Mind* marked the end of a kind of cycle of stuff that I've been workin' on. Not that it was intentional.

MG: A cycle of family plays?

SS: I suppose if you want to call them family plays, yeah. I didn't want to repeat that. I kept looking for other avenues to explore. And the only one that finished itself out was *States of Shock,* which was a short play. It was a difficult time. And this is the first one that extended itself and became a whole play.

MG: Any clue why you were able to sit down and write it?

SS: Other than the fact that I had exhausted a certain element of myself and was trying to find other areas.

MG: What other areas had you tried, things that didn't work out?

SS: Characters that weren't related by blood [*laugh*]. Characters of non lineage. I wanted to try and get out of that cycle of lineage.

MG: In this case you have two friends, not brothers . . .

SS: Although they behave very much like brothers.

MG: Is it at all like *True West?*

SS: Yeah. Somewhat but it's not as simplistic, maybe. It's a little more elliptical. It goes around. There's more of a history in it, which is what's really different about it. There's a kind of elaborate history involved. A mysterious history. I'm still working on it. The guts are there . . . I never think in terms of Broadway or Off-Broadway. Just that it's a play. The only reason we were persuaded toward this Broadway Alliance thing was that somehow they could get ticket prices down within reasonable territory where people didn't have to spend 50 bucks a night. I'd just as soon be Off-Broadway. I don't see any reason to beat your head against the wall. It's not that I would prevent it from happening. It's just that the opportunity has never presented itself.

MG: I suppose *A Lie of the Mind* might have moved.

SS: That never happened. It just got to the end of itself.

MG: I thought you might have had a run on Broadway with *True West* or *A Lie of the Mind*.

SS: The deep pockets didn't present themselves [*laugh*]. Whoever they are.

MG: If you did *True West* now with Malkovich and Sinise . . .

SS: He kind of cut his teeth on that play.

MG: Were you happy with *States of Shock*?

SS: I'm not sure it came off exactly the way I intended it to. It was kind of an odd reception, that play. I sort of envisioned it as this monster play. A play about a monster . . . the central character is an avaricious character. Somehow it succeeded in offending people. But it didn't work on the level I thought it was going to work on, which was on a kind of *Ubu Roi* Alfred Jarry type of level. Or maybe it did work on that level [*laugh*]. It offended people in the wrong way, as though it was an adolescent backwards turn I was making towards the '60s. It was very odd. That wasn't the intention, back to peace and flowers and love fest.

MG: Malkovich was very funny in it.

SS: Oh, he was outrageous, which is what I wanted. Just incredible. I thought it was an amazing performance. Tremendous energy!

MG: That must have been discouraging: the only play during the seven-year period.

SS: It was a little bit. Of course it was completely different with *A Lie of the Mind*. Maybe a lot of people had come expecting an extension of *A Lie of the Mind*. They come seeing the last one and think this is going to be another family saga. . . . I have this habit of finishing something and then immediately wanting to go into production. I sort of put Wynn Handman in a corner and said I really want to get this thing on, and he manipulated his season to accommodate us. I had[n't] finished it; I was still writing the end of it.

MG: Small point: do you work on a typewriter or computer?

SS: Notebooks. Then typing.

MG: That was hot off the notebook.

SS: Literally.

MG: I was under the impression that in contrast to your plays in the '60s you worked and worked over your plays.

SS: I do much more rewriting now than I used to. Most of that is in production. That comes from seeing that the actors are really what shape the production. Most of the rewrites have to do with moving it towards the actors rather than off somewhere else.

MG: Is that harder or easier when you're directing it yourself?

SS: It's the only way to do it. Then you're right in contact with the actors. I like doing the first productions myself, then letting go.

MG: That's a lesson learned from bad first productions?

SS: It's the frustration of having to relate always indirectly to the actors.

MG: I thought you would never be back at the Public again after the *True West* experience.

SS: Well, I had a falling out with Mr. Papp, you know, God rest his soul. Now it seems like it's a new regime in there. I just want a situation where I don't have to worry about the money. Simple as that.

MG: What is the piece you're doing with Chaikin now?

SS: We're experimenting on a two-character thing. It has a kind of folktale legend aspect to it. Having to do with revenge. We have Murray Abraham and an actress going to read it tomorrow. [Joe] will direct it.

MG: Chaikin and the Open Theater are a through line in your work.

SS: He's a tremendous influence on me, not so much writing, but theater itself. In the '60s in particular, there was a lot of experimentation going on with actors. But his laboratory that he had with those actors seemed to be extremely focused toward certain ideas, certain avenues. That was not the case in other situations that I encountered. There was a lot of experiment but the focus was vague, or wandering, or hit and miss kind of stuff. Joe's focus was very clear all the time. No matter what the idea was, it had a direction and an aim. That interested me more than anything, seeing actors working in a certain channel. Also he was coming at acting from all different angles. It was not simply Stanislavski method or Grotowski, but coming at acting from many different directions—at once—which was very very interesting particularly for a writer because you began to see the possibilities. Character could be understood in many different ways rather than just the ones we had . . . character took on a different aspect. It was also the nature of the time with Beckett and others, with character having a different meaning.

MG: Would you have been the playwright you are without Chaikin?

SS: I don't know. That's hard to say. A writer always goes off and does his work alone no matter what but to have an access to a laboratory like that where people were constantly working, trying to develop new ideas—it was quite great. You don't find that nowadays. It may be going on but . . .

MG: In contrast to the Open Theater work, which was very collaborative, the pieces you've done with Chaikin have been intense monologues.

SS: That's because the first pieces were structured with him in mind as the performer. This is the first real dialogue piece we've written.

MG: I've always wondered how you could write in collaboration.

SS: Difficult. The first time we got together I didn't see how it was going to happen. Very early on, before his aphasia, before his stroke, when we started to work on *Tongues*, he simply said in the first meeting it doesn't have to be a play. It can be anything. Just that notion shifted everything into new territory and made it somehow possible. Not [to] think of it as a play but as some other kind of presentation. A monologue of voices. It's presented in front of an audience. It shifts and goes through these changes and it has music, without having to encumber it with the idea of being a play. Somehow that idea was liberating.

MG: The last one, *The War in Heaven*, was very moving.

SS: We began that in Boston before his stroke, and kind of abandoned it. Afterwards when he first discovered the aphasia, we began to work on it again, and in a funny way the broken language that he was experiencing found its way into the piece. Became inherent to the piece.

MG: In the other plays, do you ever write with specific actors in mind?

SS: Not necessarily. I mean I have. *Fool for Love* I wrote for Ed Harris.

MG: And *States of Shock* for Malkovich?

SS: Not really, though he was ideal for it.

MG: And *Simpatico*?

SS: I wrote that with Fred [Forrest] and Ed [Harris] in mind. In the background. That's why it was incredibly lucky to get both of them, and bad luck to lose them.

MG: During those seven years, you had the movies to fall back on. Acting and directing. You have that one with River Phoenix coming up.

SS: It should be out in January. It's so anticlimactic. I wrote the thing five, six years ago.

MG: Plays are quicker . . . except for this one.

SS: This is the first experience I've had where a play flat fell through. I've been pretty lucky in the past . . . I'd have to think twice where I'd enter into another situation with private funding. Don't trust them. I had the actors coming out here renting apartments, shipping their stuff from California and waiting around on the fence. Jennifer Jason Leigh turned down a role in the David Rabe play. Ed turned down a movie to do this play. Now they're all out . . . I mean, they'll all find work. It was just bad feeling, and all of them were great. They hung right in there to the bitter end.

MG: Did backers simply back out?

SS: One of them died. So he was out. The other one apparently had a conflict of interest. They were going to go on the road with a show, and didn't feel they could afford to spread the money. Then there were several others that came in and fell out.

MG: What was the cost of the production?

SS: Here at the Public it was going to be $300,000; $800,000 on Broadway; and other little Off-Broadway theaters around 4-450, which is gas money on a movie.

MG: How do you like the movie world?

SS: The movie world? Well, I don't have much to do with it, except sitting in trailers and getting dressed up in costumes.

MG: You spend a lot of time there.

SS: Not in L.A., unless it's a studio situation. It's a good opportunity for writing, locked up in a trailer.

MG: When you were writing *Simpatico*, what movie were you shooting? *Pelican Brief*?

SS: I was finishing the sound on the film I directed, doing the sound mix on *Silent Tongue*.

MG: You wrote *States of Shock* and *A Lie of the Mind* while shooting something?

SS: I think I was between things on both of those, but I've written a lot of prose, short stories, on film locations.

MG: Do you find movie acting easier as you go on?

SS: Not easier, but it becomes more interesting. The more you find a way to relax in front of a camera, the more interesting it becomes. When you start, there's an incredible extra tension that you find you simply don't need. When that tension falls away, it's more possible to focus on something else.

MG: You felt that tension earlier? During *The Right Stuff*?

SS: Oh yeah. *Days of Heaven*. This great big bug eye watching me all the time. At first, the main thing I was worrying about was just getting away with it. Then it became more and more possible to get into notions about acting itself, how to play characters.

MG: Is there a parallel with your playwriting, looking way back to your Village Gate days, of writing plays and getting away with it—people would think you were a playwright? And learning while you were doing it?

SS: No. Initially, I never really took myself too seriously as a playwright. I was trying to do something that wasn't quite theater, although it was on stage. It wasn't performance art, either. I was trying to do something with language, which I thought was different.

MG: Early on, you said you wanted to be a rock and roll star.

SS: Everybody did, in the '60s.

MG: You never became a rock and roll star, but you became a movie star.

SS: Something happened. Well, I never really intended to be a movie star. That's the outcome of something else. I thought it might be interesting to try to act. I think acting is more interesting than starring.

MG: And writing is more interesting than getting a play on Broadway?

SS: Yeah. Ultimately.

MG: Do you feel you're bringing more a sense of character to your roles?

SS: I think it becomes more and more possible to get inside the character. You can follow some emotional life, some intellectual life in a way that makes sense. The surprising thing about acting to me—and I don't know if other actors find it so—[is] that oftentimes the thing that you most want to accomplish in a scene isn't accomplished directly. It's indirect. It happens as a result of some other strange process. There's no way you can force emotion. There's no way you can force the truth of the scene. You can't force these things; you can't objectively cause them to happen. They have to happen through some indirect means. That process, how that occurs, is something that happens to me through relaxation.

MG: How do you relax?

SS: [*Laughs*] I think by getting rid of all the external concerns, about whether the makeup's on straight, the hair's straight, the outfit's in the correct position, your elbow's supposed to be here, or your eyes . . . you get rid of all the external. Those aren't the focus at all; even though everybody is conspiring to make you feel that is the most important thing on the film, everybody from the cameraman to the light designer to the director. Because that's what's being photographed.

MG: Have you ever had any acting lessons?

SS: No. I've been around a lot of actors.

MG: You haven't had playwriting lessons, and I would never ask that question.

SS: Didn't have those either. I was around a lot of people like Grotowski and Peter Brook and Joe and observed a lot of stuff.

MG: But the only acting I ever saw you do on stage was playing in the band.

SS: I did that one thing with Patti Smith uptown. *Cowboy Mouth.*

MG: No desire to act on stage?

SS: Too frightening. That's scary.

MG: When we talked more than 20 years ago when *Operation Side-winder* was opening, you were still relatively anonymous. You said you liked that, that you believed in the primitive feeling that if they photograph you, your spirit gets stolen.

SS: [*Hearty laugh*] Well, he certainly contradicted himself, didn't he? You know contradiction is the stuff of life [*said assertively*].

MG: You don't like that your anonymity has been stolen?

SS: It hasn't entirely. It's still possible . . .

MG: . . . to come to New York quietly, and people don't bother you.

SS: Yeah. It's not like Michael Jackson, or somebody. He can't go anywhere.

MG: But if you were in town with Jessica Lange, that would add another dimension.

SS: Yeah. [*Silence*]

MG: It's a long way from 1969.

SS: I'm still the same person.

MG: You are?

SS: [*Laugh*] Essentially.

MG: Bit more successful.

SS: Well, yeah.

MG: Where do you live today? Are you still in Santa Fe?

SS: Just as soon not talk about that.

MG: Somewhere out of town.

SS: Out of town [*and clams up*].

MG: You have no place in New York?

SS: No. New York is still a great kind of place though, for energy and people. I don't think I could live here. I prefer the country.

MG: You grew up in the country. That stays with you.

SS: Yeah.

MG: Do you have a ranch?

SS: Yeah. [*Silence*]

MG: You said your kids were coming up for the weekend. How many do you have?

SS: I'd soon not talk about all my private life.

MG: I thought we might get over it quickly.

SS: No, no, no, no. It's not necessary. If you don't mind.

MG: Couldn't we just sketch it in?

SS: I have four kids.

MG: You take them Christmas shopping when they come up?

SS: Oh, yeah.

MG: You try hard to keep your private life private.

SS: Yeah.

MG: Can you do it?

SS: To a large extent [*laugh*].

MG: People see you on the big screen and think they know you.

SS: Curious about the big screen.

MG: You watched a lot of movies when you were a kid. Gary Cooper and all the rest?

SS: Audie Murphy, Roy Rogers, Hopalong Cassidy, Tex Ritter, Godzilla. He did his own stunts.

MG: In those days, you never thought about making movies, did you?

SS: No, never occurred to me.

MG: Is there any way for you to talk about the shape of your career?

SS: The essence of the whole thing is writing.

MG: Could you give up the acting?

SS: I could if I could pay my rent.

MG: Some playwrights teach, some playwrights make movies, some write movies. Very few can just write plays.

SS: Obviously there's not a lot of money in playwriting. If you can't even get a play on.

MG: You should have stayed with something more remunerative.

SS: I didn't initially start out to make money. Writing is something I just found myself doing. Of course it cost a little less to live—in the '60s—when you're single on Avenue C and 10th Street.

MG: Why did you write your first plays, *Cowboys* and *Rock Garden*?

SS: I was working at the Village Gate as a busboy and Ralph Cook was the headwaiter. Kevin O'Connor was one of the waiters. A whole bunch of actors. Ralph was starting this Theater Genesis. And I was living on Avenue C and writing some stuff. He said he wanted to see some of it, and I showed him these two little one-act plays. He said let's do 'em, and the next week we were in production. That's the way it was back then. You could write a play overnight and get it done the next day, or get it started. Everything was accessible. That was the cause of Off-Off-Broadway, getting it done, because you couldn't get it done anywhere else.

MG: At one point did you realize you were a playwright?

SS: I found that was the thing that fascinated me more than anything else, the thing I found I was able to do. Kept doing it. The light didn't go on and I said, I'm a playwright. I just kept doing it; it kept fascinating me.

MG: It helped seeing it on stage.

SS: It was a revelation. At first it was a shock, then [I] slowly began to figure out how to deal with it. What you learn more than anything is the limitations of the stage—what is possible—and how to work within those limitations.

MG: One of your contributions is that you changed some of those limitations.

SS: Yeah. But you understand that an actor can't do a 20-page monologue without catching his breath. Simple things like that.

MG: Speaking of people who were important to you: Peter Brook was one.

SS: Yeah. Very much. Again, just from the standpoint of thinking of theater, rather than writing per se. His ideas about what is theater, opening up, the question of what is character, what is story, what are these elements we're dealing with. The people who presented questions about it were the most important ones, about the essence of theater, like Grotowski, opening up for questions rather than defining it. They were bringing these incredible questions: Is this possible? What's possible with the actor's voice? Grotowski spent years on that, where up to then everyone sort of assumed the actor's voice was in his head. Maybe the actor's voice is in his spine. Maybe it's in his foot.

MG: And Brecht was important to you.

SS: Oh, yeah. I think Brecht just for his sheer guts. I'm not a big fan of his dogma but he's a very gutsy writer. There's a sinewness, a muscularity about his work, and a kind of poetry. And again exploding ideas about form and character and story and all the rest of it. Experimenting.

MG: Your work would not be related to him—and others—in terms of subject matter.

SS: It's funny how many subjects are related, conflict within the family structure, for instance, or aloneness.

MG: And revenge.

SS: Revenge, and all that kind of stuff.

MG: And the earlier plays dealing with folklore and myths and country music and rock and roll. They were not the subjects of Brook, Brecht, and Grotowski.

SS: No.

MG: That was your turf. And that traces back to your childhood?

SS: Yes, I suppose. Peter used to say we all work with the soil that we're born into. We're given a certain kind of soil. We got rocky soil; the soil that you got, that's what you work with. That's where you plant your seeds. A little idea like that can liberate you, toward your own thing. Rather than say, gee I wish I had loamy soil, you go ahead and work with what you got.

MG: In your case, it's literally soil.

SS: But in a rather odd way, I find that many of those things have a kind of superficiality to them that doesn't penetrate to the real ruptures that are going on, for instance, now. They act as masks for deeper arteries. A lot of that mythology isn't true mythology. It's disguises, or fantasies, imaginary beings. Although it might lead you to something, those things in themselves aren't the essence of it.

MG: Do you think your plays are political?

SS: In certain ways, they can't help but be, just from the cultural references that you have. They can't help but be political. They're not overtly political.

MG: Looking back at the plays, I realized that when *Geography of a Horse Dreamer* was first done in London, you had Stephen Rea and Bob Hoskins in the cast.

SS: That was the first play I ever directed. I had this astounding cast, which is great. For a first-time directing job, you couldn't ask for better. I just kind of sat back and marveled at it. Didn't say a whole lot. Just saw Stephen here when he was doing that Irish play [Frank McGuinness's *Someone Who'll Watch Over Me*].

MG: How did you like that play?

SS: I liked it okay. Literary, very Irish. Stephen's great. I love watching him.

MG: Did you see *The Crying Game*?

SS: Yeah. He was great in it. And he'd done a lot of work in London before that.

MG: Can you say what effect that English stay had on your work?

SS: I sort of exhausted a period of time in New York, where I felt I had to get out. And I arrived in London when the fringe theater was still pretty active, and ran into the same kind of situation that was here, with availability of actors and theaters. The access to the place to do the plays was no big problem. And tremendous actors over there, really great actors from the provinces, Ireland, Scotland. The Royal Court opened its doors for me, and I got to use the upstairs. And the other theater that Nancy Meckler had, the Hampstead Theatre Club. It was a tremendous experience over there. I didn't do a whole lot of writing. Well, I wrote *Tooth of Crime*.

MG: You just turned 50, in the month of the Hawk Moon?

SS: Yeah. I did.

MG: How do you feel about that?

SS: It's not as bad as 40. 40 was tough. 50 you're already cruisin' [*laugh*]. You better be. There ain't no way to stop it.

MG: What is the month of the Hawk Moon?

SS: It's part of an Indian mythology I picked up somewhere along the line. November.

MG: Tell me about your role in *The Pelican Brief.*

SS: It's not much. I play a constitutional lawyer having an affair with what's her name. Julia [Roberts]. . . . It's a pretty extensive character in the book. In the film he just sort of kicks the film off in terms of setting her up as the probe into the investigation. Gets bumped off early. Blown up. Shot in New Orleans which is a good town to be stuck in, if you have to get stuck.

MG: Any guidelines how you choose your roles? Has to interest you.

SS: Hopefully. Some more than others. Sometimes it has to do with the people you're working with. You work with a good director, good cinematographer, good actors. I've never been entirely happy with the role. I've always resculpted it a little bit. It has more to do with the director and the overall script, and the personality of the people you're working with, whether or not you want to spend time working with those people. I've worked with a lot of good people. [Alan] Pakula's no slouch. He's done a lot of good movies.

MG: *Country* was a good movie.

SS: Yeah. Jessie worked really hard on that one, getting it produced.

MG: She's a very good actress. Hard to think the first time I saw her was in *King Kong.*

SS: Yeah.

MG: The fact she can start projects. Very admirable.

SS: Oh yeah. [*Pause*] Well . . . [*seems ready to finish up*].

MG: Very early on, you said, the "similarity between the actor's art and the playwright's art is a lot closer than most people suspect. The playwright is only the actor who gets to play all the parts." This is before you were acting a lot.

SS: To a certain extent I think that's true.

MG: Do you play all the parts in your head as you're writing?

SS: In a kind of way. Obviously, not in the way an actor does. He embodies it. But the best writing is when you feel yourself to be inside the characters, rather than outside looking in. A sense of being moment to moment with the characters.

MG: And you can do this even writing opposing characters, rivals?

SS: Yeah, because in one way or another I feel like all characters are related. They're not entirely broken. There's always some connecting thread. Maybe not in life, but in a play it feels like they are. Maybe not. I don't know. The fact that we are all human [*nervous laugh*].

MG: Where do your characters come from? From your life?

SS: To a certain extent, but then sometimes they're just aspects. They're not intended to be derivative or imitations of people in real life. They're not intended to be imitations or replicas of people I have known.

MG: People would say about the family plays that so and so was like your father.

SS: Yeah. *Like* my father. They're not intended to be representations at all. There's nothing interesting about that. That's like taking a photograph. I'm not a photographer. I'm not interested in duplicating life situations. Just doesn't appeal to me at all. To me a play is an exploration of something. It's not an imitation.

MG: Will you always draw on your father?

SS: No. He happened to have been a very rich, salty character. But even when I draw that stuff, there are variations off of him that spin forever, into other men I've known, my uncles, friends. There's a certain kind of *maleness* that I'm very familiar with. That has to do not only with my family but characterizes many men that I know.

MG: The American family has changed since you began writing plays. It's more . . .

SS: You mean, collapsed!

MG: When you first began writing about families, the word dysfunctional wasn't used.

SS: I had never heard of dysfunctional.

MG: Are all dysfunctional families alike?

SS: I don't know the answer to that. I don't think there's a formula. But I do know that we're suffering a tremendous grief from the loss of the father, in this culture. I think the father being absent in American families is a cause for a great deal of tragedy. There is no father anymore. The father's disappeared, except as a kind of memory. Nobody knows what the father means.

MG: What does it mean today?

SS: What *does* it mean? [*laugh*]. Good question. I'm searching for it as much as anybody else. I don't have the answers to it. All I know is that there's a great absence of the father.

MG: You're a better father to your children than your father was to you, aren't you?

SS: I would hope so, but that's no salvation. It's not stretching it too much to be better than my old man [*ripple of laughter*]. At least I'm *around*. I really do think it's a disastrous development.

MG: There's all this violence too in families.

SS: It's all been just layin' in wait. Just layin' around. Just been waitin' to happen. An accident waiting to happen. The funny thing is, it all existed in the '50s. It's just now surfacing, and being in the public's eyes, and becoming media fodder.

MG: Was it as widespread?

SS: I think it was. But it was more under the table.

MG: The cliché would be that violence began with the Kennedy assassination.

SS: Violence began with the Virginia colonies.

MG: Violence began with Cain and Abel. But one is more and more conscious of it, and it's not the media as such playing it up more.

SS: Oh, I think the media has a great deal to do with it. It's a circus. It feeds itself; it's self-perpetuating.

MG: How do you bring up a child today?

SS: I don't have any answers. I'm searchin' for that every day. Certainly not with violence.

MG: I remember, in '69, going to your first wedding. If there ever was an artifact of the 1960s. It was the most peaceful time. When the minister said, who gives this bride, everyone said, "We do!" [*He laughs in memory.*] Everything must have been more . . . peaceful. No? Underneath it was the same?

SS: I think so. How do you gauge that stuff?

MG: Do you go to theater much?

SS: No. I don't live here.

MG: You've been here for a week. Did you see *Angels in America*?

SS: No. I saw *Remains of the Day*. Anthony Hopkins is remarkable! He's just an extraordinary actor. Absolutely amazing, and the writing is quite beautiful. I had read the book. His performance—it's hard to believe an actor can do that.

MG: Do you feel that way about American actors?

SS: Well, obviously, we have some great actors. Pacino and De Niro and all those guys. What I feel with the English actors is more than anything they bring a certain kind of intelligence. Not to say that American actors are *dumb*. They're not. But their intelligence is directed in a different way. The English actor directs his intelligence in an entirely different aspect of character. And that always distinguishes them in a certain kind of way. What the English actor does [*watching his words*] is never forget the character in relation to the whole, to the whole script. He's always relating the character to the story, to the whole spectrum and never losing himself entirely in the character at the expense of the story, which I feel American actors tend to fall victim to. Movie actors in particular. And often with extraordinary results, but robbing this relationship to the script.

MG: Some of the English actors I know are great admirers of American actors. Michael Gambon's favorite actor isn't Olivier or Hopkins, but De Niro.

SS: You can't take anything away from any of them.

MG: He would feel that a De Niro would get a lot closer to the essence, the guts of a character.

SS: But I feel often that it turns into—and it may be the nature of American films—that films are surrounded around a star vehicle and therefore the star has every excuse to indulge himself entirely . . . where you don't find that so much in European films.

MG: What's the best of American film acting?

SS: Obviously Pacino, De Niro, Ed Harris, Harvey Keitel, Tommy Lee Jones. Great actors.

MG: Are they as great as Gary Cooper and Spencer Tracy?

SS: They're great in a different aspect. Those guys were personalities. I don't think they were great actors. Tracy's a different ballpark. I think Tracy was a great actor. Cooper just put on his suit all the time.

MG: You should work with Hopkins.

SS: I'd love to. . . . It's difficult to cast English as Americans.

MG: But your plays have been done over there.

SS: It's often Irish or Canadians.

MG: What about your career as a movie director?

SS: I think it's finished [*laugh*]. I think it's in the pits!

MG: One thing you did that I liked less was *Far North*.

SS: Well, wait and see the new one. First time out, I didn't have any footage. . . . I got to run.

We share a cab uptown. He says, it took a year to write the play [*Simpatico*], from September to September. In early days he would write a play a week.

Simpatico has innuendo in Spanish; "it means camaraderie of the heart, *corazon*, empathy of the heart. Just like *todo el mundo* is not just the whole world, but more than that—everyone."

He drove a truck to New York and put [it] in a garage. Where does he drive from? Santa Fe? Virginia? He's not saying.

Asked if he has been seeing old friends, he says he has few old friends. He hasn't seen Lance [Lanford Wilson] in 20 years.

His plan was to work with Chaikin in the morning and rehearse the play in the afternoon. Now the actors, having turned down offers, are going elsewhere, and he has afternoons free—to see a movie, to shop for his kids for Christmas.

Slay 'em Again, Sam

Brian Case / 1996

From *Time Out* [London], July 3–10, 1996, pp. 24–26. Text owned and provided courtesy of Time Out London Limited.

Pulitzer Prize–winning playwright, actor and all-American cowboy around town, Sam Shepard is a living legend. As a season of his plays comes to the BAC [Battersea Arts Centre], Shepard looks back to his formative days on the '70s London Fringe.

"I came to London because I just bottomed out here in various dimensions," says Sam Shepard, sitting in a coffee shop off Union Square, New York. "Artistically, I felt I was drying out, then there was some trouble with drugs, women. I just wanted an alternative and I was somewhat lazy because I chose somewhere they spoke English." He had said that he first discovered what it meant to be American while living in London. "Yeah. Americans get so absorbed inside it, there's a blindness. I realized its isolation, I guess. Its cut-offness. The sense of it being an entity unto itself, not related to the rest of the world. A lot of the inventiveness about America comes from that sense that we're the only beings on the planet."

When Sam Shepard settled in London a quarter of a century ago, the West End theater fielded David Mercer's *After Haggerty*, Pinter's *Old Times*, John Mortimer's *A Voyage Round My Father* and—the hot ticket—Peter Brook's RSC production of *A Midsummer Night's Dream*. He didn't see any of them. "I don't go to the theater," he chuckles richly. "I went to dog racing."

There was a London rash of Fringe theater in 1971, with nudity everywhere on stage, but, unlike Shepard's work, few of the plays proved revivable (to prove the point, a hefty chunk of Shepard's output goes on show at BAC this week). The economy was strong enough to support alternative companies like The Welfare State and the Pip Simmons Theatre Group which, with *Do It!*, based on a Jerry Rubin text, tilted at a rock 'n' roll theater.

A few names, however, were made on the Fringe. David Hare, Howard Brenton and Trevor Griffiths. Mike Figgis, a prime mover with the People Show, is now a hot film director, and recently offered Shepard a starring role provided he got his crooked, discolored teeth fixed. "I said, '*Whaaat?* I don't know if I can do that.' The deal fell through."

The playwright is currently in New York with Gary Sinese's Steppenwolf production of his *Buried Child*, the first performance ever of Shepard on Broadway. He won the Pulitzer for it in 1978. "I never figured anything I wrote would be legitimate," he laughs. He has rewritten half of the text. "I was never really happy with the play. It was somewhat raggedy, areas of it were sloppy. When the Steppenwolf production started, a whole territory of the play became clear to me. I started tailor-making it for this production." It has received critical raves.

"Gimme hard-ass shit-kickin' music," wrote Shepard in the memoir *Motel Chronicles*, in which he dreams of Keith Richards. "Keith standing alone, outside in the California night. Standing in his Python boots staring at a kidney-shaped pool, the kind Brian [Jones] died in. Staring at the water. The air blowing his crow feather hair." "Keith? I knew him. He reminded me of those old blues guys, just sit down and play. There was something other-worldly about him. This guy's from Mars, and at the same time he's a very down-home musician. A good man. A straight shooter. There's a kinda benevolent demon about him, I guess."

Like Hendrix, Shepard settled in London to advance his rock career, but it wasn't until his return that he got to accompany Bob Dylan on his 1975 Rolling Thunder tour. "I was just a backbeat drummer. It just didn't happen. The English musicians were so technically astounding, and drummers like Ginger Baker were brilliant. They drummed circles around me."

He lived in Hampstead and Shepherd's Bush and he wrote. He had three Obies for his Off-Off-Broadway plays at Café La MaMa already, and his first play, *Rock Garden*, written at 19, had been bought up by Ken Tynan and inserted into *Oh! Calcutta!* He lived with Patti Smith at the Chelsea, and worked on the screenplay of Antonioni's *Zabriskie Point* and Robert Frank's *Me and My Brother*. His early work simply poured out uncorrected as if dictated by his characters. Like Saul Bellow, who said of discovering the voice of Augie March, "All I had to do was to be there with buckets to catch it."

"That's true in some cases, yes. *Curse of the Starving Class* more or less wrote itself, but *Tooth of Crime* I struggled with. It has to do with the material. Gabriel García Márquez said *One Hundred Years of Solitude* was writing itself in his head on a trip from L. A. to Mexico, just exploding, and when he got to Mexico he locked himself in a room and wrote it very fast. Some things are like that."

London he credits with teaching him plotting, paring, piecing together. "The beginnings of discipline at any rate. I don't think I've ever quite learned that. That's a hard one. I began to sense that craftsmanship was significant. You had to practice, you had to work at this thing. With English actors and directors, even in the alternative theater, there's a craftsman thing at work. In London I ran into a ton of people who were passionate and at the same time workmanlike. In America you threw a lot of shit on the wall and hoped some of it stuck."

"I just tried things that were musically oriented and that didn't fit the stage a lot of the time," he told *T*[*ime*] *O*[*ut*] in 1972 on the eve of the world premiere of *The Tooth of Crime*, directed by Charles Marowitz at the Open Space. Like free form jazz musicians, he was blowing off the horn and outside the chord changes. His selection of music for Battersea's imminent Sam Shepard Festival is as hip as it gets: Charles Mingus, Dolphy, Meade Lux Lewis, Bechet, Skip James, Lightnin' Hopkins, Clifton Chenier. "I was inspired by Mingus. I lived with his drummer, Dannie Richmond, and a whole bunch of jazz musicians on Avenue C. Mingus's whole sense of percussion was just astounding. He was the first guy I heard to use that contrapuntal thing where you get a melody going and cut against it with a demonic rhythm. He was doing a collage thing, juxtaposing stuff in the same way that Rauschenberg and a lotta those painters were doing. It was a great inspiration to me, but writing's such a different bag. It can never be music, although you would like it to be." His play *Suicide in B Flat*, deals with, among much else, the clashes within jazz.

He'd had some unhappy experiences with American directors. "Because the plays had this improvisational attitude, they thought they could throw things in. Lotta off-the-wall productions. In England, they looked at the work itself. They were real generous to me at the Royal Court. They literally handed over the theater to me. It was the first directing I'd ever done." *Geography of a Horse Dreamer* played at the Theatre Upstairs at the Court in 1974, with Stephen Rea and Bob Hoskins. "Problems? Mainly my own fear. Terror at confronting these actors because they were so great. It was a cast made in heaven and it sorta directed itself."

He played poker with the cast, and took them to watch his greyhound, Keywall Spectre, race at White City and Hackney Wick. The play is about a man who dreams winners, gets kidnapped by gangsters and forced to predict first horses and then dogs, before turning into one. It could be an allegory about the pressures of being an artist in this hard commercial world. "The space inside where the dream comes. It's gotta be created . . . everything forces itself on the space I need." Whatever, there's lots of inside information about the sport. Don't be fooled by fast-improving pups, advises forecaster Cody, plunge on bitches a week before their season.

"The Irish greyhound I think is the epitome of the greyhound. The great thing about them is they're cat-like. You can put them in the house and they'll lay down and sleep for hours. Take them out, and they'll just go! The Irish are great animal people. They're great horsemen and they know dogs, too. Like Mexicans, I think they're part horse. I was walking the dog with these Irish guys on Hampstead Heath, and one looked at the greyhound taking a leak against a tree and he says, 'See dat, boys! It's gotta be just like champagne. Clear, bright, it's gotta have a little glisten to it.' He's talking about the dog's piss! The condition of the dog's piss was indicative of its fitness to run."

Shepard's *Icarus's Mother* played at the Roxy, *Cowboy Mouth* at the Basement Theatre, King's Head, and *The Unseen Hand* put a 1956 Chevy into the Theatre Upstairs, capacity 75 souls. *The Tooth of Crime* and *Geography of a Horse Dreamer* were written entirely here. The playwright knew nobody when he first arrived with his wife and son, but was soon taken up. "Peter Brook undeniably is one of the great minds in the theater. I had a conversation with him once about character, and he simply posed the question, what is the nature of character? For a long time it caused me to investigate that. Peter had so many probing ideas and new questions."

Selfhood is apparitional in much of Shepard's work. It's an old American theme. Gatsby invented himself. Life is random, disjointed, and his characters are driven to create a role for themselves to make any sense of it at all. Rootless, with little sense of identity, they're desperate to register, whether with a nickname or a rambling monologue that suggests deranged solipsism. It is not the traditional theater of Arthur Miller.

"It wasn't a reaction against anything. It was simply that I couldn't understand why, when you go into a bookstore and they have a section called Modern Drama, you'd find Chekhov, Ibsen, Tennessee Williams and Eugene O'Neill, but that was it. Okay—they're great, but there wasn't anything that seemed to relate to now. There's a huge hole there. You have classic drama then you fall off this precipice into a yawning gap. I was interested in this hole. Why don't I write something in that hole? Of course, Vietnam had a big influence on it too, the whole atmosphere of the time. What in the fuck is going on here? We've fallen off the edge of something and there's no response. None. Theater wasn't looked on as the arena for that kinda thing. There weren't any scripts. How do you relate O'Neill to the psychological atmosphere around Vietnam? It was very palpable, the psychological fire going on. Panic, terror, paranoia, all that shit that was happening—and there wasn't anything that responded to that climate."

He isn't a political playwright, but his recent *States of Shock* caused a furor. "It came out of this reaction to the Gulf War. What shocked me was that the war was so popular. The brainwashing of the American public was just complete, and it was very much in response to Vietnam. Let's not bring our soldiers back to animosity this time. Let's bring them back to flag-waving. Quite insane. I prefer to stay out of politics. It's a quicksand. It's only opinions and, like my old father-in-law used to say, 'Opinions are just like assholes—everybody's got one.'"

Shepard was raised on USAF bases, his father a flyer and later an alcoholic. They fought. His father moved to the desert to live alone. Much of Shepard's best work is about the contagion of families, bad blood, hostile siblings, the inescapable trap of heritage. It's a microcosm of America through a funhouse mirror. *Time* dubbed Shepard "the icon of the id."

The playwright shares a taste for aphasia with Mamet. "Nobody can disappear," says a brother in *True West*. "The old man tried that. Look where it got him. He lost his teeth." Shepard isn't that comfortable with the comparison. "It's an aspect. It's not a thematic issue. Maybe other people have done it better than either of us. Americans do have more and more trouble articulating their dilemma, and technology is replacing the basic need for language as communication." Also like Mamet, he has spread his work into the movies.

Phil Kaufman cast him as Chuck Yeager in *The Right Stuff* for "his intense dedication to the manly life, rejecting New York, the taste for cowboys and rodeos—and all with the look of a man in a leather jacket on a horse meeting a jet plane in the desert." The part won him an Oscar nomination and made him a star, not that he had sought stardom. "I turned it down because I was so intimidated by the Yeager mythology. How in the world can you play somebody who's this legendary? It scared the shit outta me. Finally, Phil talked me into it. What I portrayed has nothing to do with the man himself. I did my version, but Chuck is a different kinda man. Ed Harris would have been a more realistic Yeager." The only other film since that reflected that harsh, unforgiving presence was Volker Schlondorff's *Voyager*—a part originally meant for Bruno Ganz, but unthinkable without Shepard. And he's done some crap for money. "I don't deny that was part of it," he laughs.

"Trying to pay the rent. Playwrights don't make a lotta money. I'm interested in surviving at acting. I've never had any big interest in becoming a movie star. I think that's absolutely deadly, once that marketing thing grabs ahold of you. You're gone. You're dead meat."

His screenplay for Wim Wenders's 1984 *Paris, Texas* is the closest cinema has come to the essential Shepard. The films he directed himself, *Far North* and *Silent Tongue*, flopped. "I'm a slow learner and I saw them as experiments, but there's very little room for that in American filmmaking. I'd love to direct again, but the whole arena of two-thumbs-up, two-thumbs-down, this Roman gladiator shit, this off with their heads, isn't conducive to creativity. Guys like Jarmusch have the ability to hustle their work. I just have no interest in that." Married to Jessica Lange, he is no fan of Hollywood. "L. A. is not my favorite town. If you look at its history, there was a power that laid over that whole town way back when the Spaniards got there. They talked about this yellow glow which hovered in this valley."

He has a mystical take on the land. "In North America there's always been this conflict between the intellectual, which is the European point of view, and this primitive thing which was here for thousands of years before the Europeans came. Those two worlds will never be resolved, yet they're at the heart of so much of our conflict and torment and suffering and despair and confusion. These two things are in a hammerlock. So, I prefer Mexico. My old man spoke fluent Spanish and kept escaping to Mexico and dragging me down there. Every time I go I feel I've rejoined the human race. Go to Mexico and it's very simple. We're born and we're gonna die. Death is very much present. Death is alive, we reckon with it every day, and its presence makes life astounding! Real! The Indian thing, not the Spanish, is the powerful thing in Mexico." His intensity locks on to your eyes. "And the True West? The mythology about the West is quite different from the West itself. It's probably the most mysterious territory in the country, and I think that has to do with Indian culture."

Jackson Pollock, the pioneering cowboy painter who listened to Charlie Parker as he attacked his canvases, continues to fascinate him. "He came from Cody, Wyoming, one of my favorite places. I rodeoed up in there. He was influenced by Indian sand paintings, and that was where the notion of drip paintings came from. What really intrigued me was the evolution from those early figurative drawings into this other world. I could see how something moved from one territory into another. He discovered this explosion inside himself."

"Ridin' back and forth on the freeway just dreamin' my fool head off," says a character in *True West*, and you picture Shepard, driving his truck across vast lonely western landscapes, writing as he drives. "I've tried tape recording but it's not writing. I've got a notebook by the wheel and I can do that. Particularly out west where it's very open." He laughs. "And you can wander across the line without it being deadly."

Sam Shepard

Mona Simpson, Jeanne McCulloch, and Benjamin Howe / 1997

From *The Paris Review: Playwrights at Work*, edited by George Plimpton (New York: Modern Library, 2000), 329–45. Originally published as "Art of Theater XII: Sam Shepard" in *The Paris Review* 39 (Spring 1997): 204–25. Copyright © 1997 by The Paris Review Foundation, Inc., used by permission of The Wylie Agency LLC. Mona Simpson is the author of six novels. Jeanne McCulloch is the author of *All Happy Families: A Memoir* (2017). Benjamin Howe is the author of *My Korean Deli: Risking It All for a Convenience Store* (2011).

"The poet laureate of America's emotional Badlands" (*Newsweek*), Sam Shepard was born Samuel Shepard Rogers VII, November 5, 1943, on a southern Illinois army base where his father was stationed. After a period of frequent moving from base to base, the Rogers family settled on a ranch in California, where they raised sheep and grew avocados. Shepard spent a few years in a local junior college studying agricultural science, but his father's descent into alcoholism and the accompanying deterioration of the family scene caused him to flee. He joined a touring theatrical group and, despite having only a few months' acting to his credit, headed to New York to embark on a career in theater. Once there, in the emerging world of avant-garde theater on the Lower East Side, he quickly found an interest in writing.

His reputation was built with a series of short plays for Off- and Off-Off-Broadway theater, including *Chicago* (1965), *Icarus's Mother* (1965), *Red Cross* (1966), *La Turista* (1967), and *Forensic & the Navigators* (1967), all of which won Obie Awards. Their characteristic, somewhat jarring combination of visual and verbal imagery was due in part to the young Shepard's having written hastily, and to his early suspicion that revision violated a work's integrity. Around that time Shepard met the writer-director Joseph Chaikin, with whom he would collaborate during the seventies and eighties.

In 1971 Shepard moved with his wife of two years, O-Lan Johnson Dark, and their infant son to England, where he composed a number of well-received medium-length plays, including *The Tooth of Crime* (1972) and *Geography of a Horse Dreamer* (1974). In 1974 he returned to California and began writing the plays that have secured his reputation—*Curse of the Starving Class* (1978), *Fool for Love* (1983), and the Pulitzer Prize–winning *Buried Child* (1978). In 1983 Shepard divorced his wife and began a relationship with the actress-producer Jessica Lange.

Shepard made his feature-film debut as an actor in 1978, playing an affluent farmer in *Days of Heaven*. In 1984 he received an Academy Award nomination for his portrayal of Chuck Yeager in *The Right Stuff*. Although he has continued to receive numerous invitations to act, Shepard has limited himself to only a few roles, claiming, "The work just isn't that much fun."

He received the Golden Palm Award at the 1984 Cannes Film Festival for his screenplay of Wim Wenders's *Paris, Texas*. In 1986 he directed the original production of his play *A Lie of the Mind*, which won the New York Drama Critics' Circle Award.

The interview was conducted over several days in the living room of a Manhattan apartment by the East River. For the last meeting Sam Shepard arrived at the end of a late-afternoon snowstorm, his leather jacket unbuttoned in spite of the bad weather. He immediately became distracted by an out-of-tune Steinway in the corner, then returned to the couch for a discussion of his recently completed year-long retrospective at New York's Signature Theatre. He said he had been exhausted by the theater's rehearsals, by a trip to London the previous week, and by a hectic schedule of public readings. Nevertheless, at the end of the meeting he declined to be driven back to his midtown hotel, saying he would rather walk back through Central Park instead.

Like many writers, Shepard is easy to imagine as one of the characters of his own work. In person, he is closer to the laconic and inarticulate men of his plays than to his movie roles. Self-contained, with none of the bearing of an actor, he retains a desert California accent and somehow seems smaller than one expects.

INTERVIEWER: The West figures predominantly as a mythology in many of your plays. You grew up there, didn't you?

SHEPARD: All over the Southwest, really—Cucamonga, Duarte, California, Texas, New Mexico. My dad was a pilot in the Air Force. After the war he got a Fulbright fellowship, spent a little time in Colombia, then taught high school Spanish. He kind of moved us from place to place.

INTERVIEWER: Do you think you'll ever live in the West again?

SHEPARD: No, I don't think so. The California I knew, old rancho California, is gone. It just doesn't exist, except maybe in little pockets. I lived on the edge of the Mojave Desert, an area that used to be farm country. There were all these fresh-produce stands with avocados and date palms. You could get a dozen artichokes for a buck or something. Totally wiped out now.

INTERVIEWER: *True West, Buried Child, Curse of the Starving Class,* and *Lie of the Mind* are all family dramas, albeit absurdist ones. Have you drawn a lot from your own family?

SHEPARD: Yes, though less now than I used to. Most of it comes, I guess, from my dad's side of the family. They're a real bizarre bunch, going back to the original colonies. That side's got a real tough strain of alcoholism. It goes back generations and generations, so that you can't remember when there was a sober grandfather.

INTERVIEWER: Have you struggled with drinking?

SHEPARD: My history with booze goes back to high school. Back then there was a lot of Benzedrine around, and since we lived near the Mexican border I'd just run over, get a bag of bennies, and drink Ripple wine. Speed and booze together make you quite . . . omnipotent. You don't feel any pain. I was actually in several car wrecks that I don't understand how I survived.

At any rate, for a long time I didn't think I had a problem. Alcoholism is an insidious disease; until I confronted it I wasn't aware that it was creeping up on me. I finally did AA in the hard core down on Pico Boulevard. I said, "Don't put me in with Elton John or anything, just throw me to the lions."

INTERVIEWER: Do you feel like the drinking might have aided your writing?

SHEPARD: I don't feel like one inspired the other, or vice versa. I certainly never saw booze or drugs as a partner to writing. That was just the way my life was tending, you know, and the writing was something I did when I was relatively straight. I never wrote on drugs, or the bourbon.

INTERVIEWER: You said the men on your dad's side of the family were hard drinkers. Is this why the mothers in your plays always seem to be caught in the middle of so much havoc?

SHEPARD: Those midwestern women from the forties suffered an incredible psychological assault, mainly by men who were disappointed in a way that they didn't understand. While growing up I saw that assault over and over again, and not only in my own family. These were men who came back from the war, had to settle down, raise a family, and send the kids to school— and they just couldn't handle it. There was something outrageous about it. I

still don't know what it was—maybe living through those adventures in the war and then having to come back to suburbia. Anyway, the women took it on the nose, and it wasn't like they said, "Hey Jack, you know, down the road, I'm leaving." They sat there and took it. I think there was a kind of heroism in those women. They were tough and selfless in a way. What they sacrificed at the hands of those maniacs . . .

INTERVIEWER: What was your dad like?

SHEPARD: He was also a maniac, but in a very quiet way. I had a falling out with him at a relatively young age by the standards of that era. We were always butting up against each other, never seeing eye to eye on anything, and as I got older it escalated into a really bad, violent situation. Eventually I just decided to get out.

INTERVIEWER: Is he alive?

SHEPARD: No, a couple of years ago he was killed coming out of a bar in New Mexico. I saw him the year before he died. Our last meeting slipped into this gear where I knew it was going to turn really nasty. I remember forcing myself, for some reason, not to flip out. I don't know why I made that decision, but I ended up leaving without coming back at him. He was boozed up, very violent and crazy. After that I didn't see him for a long time. I did try to track him down; a friend of his told me he got a haircut, a fishing license, and a bottle, and then took off for the Pecos River. That was the last I heard of him before he died. He turned up a year later in New Mexico, with some woman I guess he was running with. They had a big blowout in a bar, and he went out in the street and got run over.

INTERVIEWER: Did he ever see one of your plays?

SHEPARD: Yes. There's a really bizarre story about that. He found out about a production of *Buried Child* that was going on at the Greer Garson Theater in New Mexico. He went to the show smashed, just pickled, and in the middle of the play he began to identify with some character, though I'm not sure which one, since all those characters are kind of loosely structured around his family. In the second act he stood up and started to carry on with the actors, and then yelled, "What a bunch of shit this is!" The ushers tried to throw him out. He resisted, and in the end they allowed him to stay because he was the father of the playwright.

INTERVIEWER: Were you there?

SHEPARD: No, I just heard about it. I think that's the only time he ever saw a production.

You know, all that stuff about my father and my childhood is interesting up to a certain point, but I kind of capsized with the family drama a long time ago. Now I want to get away from that. Not that I won't return to it, but a certain element has been exhausted, and it feels like: why regurgitate all this stuff?

INTERVIEWER: I read somewhere that you started writing because you wanted to be a musician.

SHEPARD: Well, I got to New York when I was eighteen. I was knocking around, trying to be an actor, writer, musician, whatever happened.

INTERVIEWER: What sort of musician were you trying to be?

SHEPARD: A drummer. I was in a band called the Holy Modal Rounders.

INTERVIEWER: How did you end up in New York?

SHEPARD: After the falling-out with my father I worked on a couple of ranches—thoroughbred layup farms, actually—out toward Chino, California. That was fine for a little while, but I wanted to get out completely, and twenty miles away wasn't far enough. So I got a job delivering papers in Pasadena, and pretty soon, by reading the ad sections, I found out about an opening with a traveling ensemble called the Bishop's Company. I decided to give it a shot, thinking that this might be a way to really get out. At the audition they gave me a little Shakespeare thing to read—I was so scared I read the stage directions—and then they hired me. I think they hired everybody.

We traveled all over the country—New England, the South, the Midwest. I think the longest we stayed in one place was two days. It was actually a great little fold-up theater. We were totally self-sufficient: we put up the lights, made the costumes, performed the play, and shut down. Anyway, one day we got to New York to do a production at a church in Brooklyn and I said, "I'm getting off the bus."

INTERVIEWER: Did you start right in?

SHEPARD: Not immediately. My first job was with the Burns Detective Agency. They sent me over to the East River to guard coal barges during these god-awful hours like three to six in the morning. It wasn't a very difficult job—all I had to do was make a round every 15 minutes—but it turned out to be a great environment for writing. I was completely alone in a little outhouse with an electric heater and a little desk.

INTERVIEWER: Did you already think of yourself as a writer?

SHEPARD: I'd been messing around with it for a while, but nothing serious. That was the first time I felt writing could actually be useful.

INTERVIEWER: How did you hook up with the theaters?

SHEPARD: Well, I was staying on Avenue C and Tenth Street with a bunch of jazz musicians, one of whom happened to be Charlie Mingus's son. We knew each other from high school, and he got me a job as a busboy at the Village Gate. The head waiter at the Gate was a guy named Ralph Cook. Ralph was just starting his theater at St. Mark's in the Bowery, and he said he'd heard that I'd been writing some stuff, and he wanted to see it. So, I showed him a few plays I'd written, and he said, "Well, let's do it." Things kind of took off from there. New York was like that in the sixties. You could write a one-act play and start doing it the next day. You could go to one of those theaters—Genesis, La MaMa, Judson Poets'—and find a way to get it done. Nothing like that exists now.

INTERVIEWER: Did Off-Off-Broadway plays get reviewed back then?

SHEPARD: For a while the big papers wouldn't touch them, but then they started to smell something, so they came down and wrote these snide reviews. They weren't being unfair. A lot of that stuff really was shitty and deserved to get bombed. But there was one guy who was sort of on our side. His name was Michael Smith; he worked for the *Village Voice*, and he gave a glowing review to these little one-act plays, *Cowboys* and *The Rock Garden*. I remember that distinctly, not because of the praise but because it felt like somebody finally understood what we were trying to do. He was actually hooking up with us, seeing the work for what it was.

INTERVIEWER: What were the audiences like?

SHEPARD: They were incredibly different. You really felt that the community came to see the plays. They weren't people coming from New Jersey to have a dinner party. And they weren't going to sit around if they got bored. The most hostile audience I faced was up at the American Place Theatre when we were putting on *La Turista*. They invited all these Puerto Rican kids, street kids, and they were firing at the actors with peashooters.

INTERVIEWER: Did it take a long time to find your particular voice as a writer?

SHEPARD: I was amazed, actually. I've heard writers talk about "discovering a voice," but for me that wasn't a problem. There were so many voices that I didn't know where to start. It was splendid, really; I felt kind of like a weird stenographer. I don't mean to make it sound like hallucination, but there were definitely things there, and I was just putting them down. I was fascinated by how they structured themselves, and it seemed like the natural place to do it was on a stage. A lot of the time when writers talk about their voice they're talking about a narrative voice. For some reason my attempts at narrative turned out really weird. I didn't have that kind of voice, but I had a lot of other ones, so I thought, well, I'll follow those.

INTERVIEWER: Do you feel like you're in control of those voices now?

SHEPARD: I don't feel insane, if that's what you're asking.

INTERVIEWER: What is your schedule like?

SHEPARD: I have to begin early because I take the kids to school, so usually I'm awake by six. I come back to the house afterwards and work till lunch.

INTERVIEWER: Do you have any rituals or devices to help you get started?

SHEPARD: No, not really. I mean there's the coffee and that bullshit, but as for rituals, no.

INTERVIEWER: What sort of writing situation do you have at home? Do you have an office?

SHEPARD: I've got a room out by the barn with a typewriter, a piano, some photographs and old drawings. Lots of junk and old books. I can't seem to get rid of my books.

INTERVIEWER: So, you're not a word-processor person.

SHEPARD: No, I hate green screens. The paper is important to me.

INTERVIEWER: What sort of country is it where you live?

SHEPARD: Farm country—you know, hay, horses, cattle. It's the ideal situation for me. I like the physical endeavors that go with the farm—cutting hay, cleaning out stalls, or building a barn. You go do that and then come back to the writing.

INTERVIEWER: Do you write every day?

SHEPARD: When something kicks in, I devote everything to it and write constantly until it's finished. But to sit down every day and say, "I'm going to write, come hell or high water"—no, I could never do that.

INTERVIEWER: Can you write when you're acting in a film?

SHEPARD: There are certain attitudes that shut everything down. It's very easy, for example, to get a bad attitude from a movie. I mean you're trapped in a trailer, people are pounding on the door, asking if you're ready, and at the same time you're trying to write.

INTERVIEWER: Do you actually write on the set?

SHEPARD: Film locations are a great opportunity to write. I don't work on plays while I'm shooting a movie, but I've done short stories and a couple of novels.

INTERVIEWER: What was it like the first time you saw your work being performed by actors?

SHEPARD: To a certain extent it was frustrating, because the actors were in control of the material and I wasn't used to actors. I didn't know how to talk to them and I didn't want to learn, so I hid behind the director.

But slowly I started to realize that they were going through an interpretive process, just like anyone else. They don't just go in there and read the script.

INTERVIEWER: Did becoming an actor help you as a writer?

SHEPARD: It did, because it helped me to understand what kinds of dilemmas an actor faces.

INTERVIEWER: Were you impressed by any particular school, like Method acting?

SHEPARD: I am not a Strasberg fanatic. In fact, I find it incredibly self-indulgent. I've seen actors come through it because they're strong people themselves, because they're able to use it and go on, but I've also seen actors absolutely destroyed by it, which is painful to see. It has to do with this voo-doo that's all about the verification of behavior, so that *I become the character.* It's not true Stanislavski. He was on a different mission, and I think Strasberg bastardized him in a way that verges on psychosis. You forget about the material, you forget that this is a play, you forget that it's for the audience. *Hey, man, I'm in my private little world. What you talkin' about? I'm over here, I'm involved with the lemons.* On film, of course, it works because of its obsessiveness; but in theater it's a complete block and a hindrance. There's no room for self-indulgence in theater; you have to be thinking about the audience. Joe Chaikin helped me understand this. He used to have this rehearsal exercise in which the actors were supposed to play a scene for some imaginary figure in the audience. He would say, "Tonight Prince Charles is in the audience. Play the scene for him," or, "Tonight a bag lady is in the audience."

INTERVIEWER: Is it true that you wrote *Simpatico* in a truck?

SHEPARD: Well, I started it in a truck. I don't like flying very much, so I tend to drive a lot, and I've always wanted to find a way to write while I'm on the open road. I wrote on the steering wheel.

INTERVIEWER: Really? What highway were you on?

SHEPARD: Forty West, the straightest one. I was going to Los Angeles. I think I wrote twenty-five pages by the time I got there, which was about five hundred miles of driving. There were these two characters I'd been thinking about for quite a while, and when I got to L.A. it seemed like I had a one-act play. Then another character popped up; suddenly there were two acts. And out of that second act, a third. It took me a year to finish it.

INTERVIEWER: How do you decide that a play is finished?

SHEPARD: The only way to test it is with actors, because that's who you're writing for. When I have a piece of writing that I think might be ready, I test it with actors, and then I see if it's what I imagined it to be. The best actors show you the flaws in the writing. They come to a certain place and there's nothing there, or they read a line and say, "Okay, now what?" That kind of questioning is more valuable than anything. They don't have to *say* anything. With the very best actors I can see it in the way they're proceeding. Sometimes I instinctively know that this little part at the end of scene two, act one, is not quite there, but I say to myself, "Maybe we'll get away with it." A good actor won't let me. Not that he says, "Hey, I can't do this"; I just see that he's stumbling. And then I have to face up to the problem.

INTERVIEWER: So, as you write, your thoughts are with the actors, not the audience.

SHEPARD: Well, no. I don't think you can write a play without thinking of the audience, but it's a funny deal, because I never know who the audience is. It's like a ghost. With movies you have a better notion of who's watching; there it's the whole population.

INTERVIEWER: Do you do a lot of revisions?

SHEPARD: More now than I used to. I used to be just dead set against revisions because I couldn't stand rewriting. That changed when I started working with Chaikin. Joe was so persistent about finding the essence of something. He'd say, "Does this mean what we're trying to make it mean? Can it be constructed some other way?" That fascinated me, because my tendency was to jam, like it was jazz or something. Thelonious Monk style.

INTERVIEWER: How do your plays start? Do you hear the voice of a character?

SHEPARD: It's more of an attitude than a voice. With *Simpatico*, for instance, it was these two guys in completely different predicaments who began to talk to each other, one in one attitude and the other in another.

INTERVIEWER: Do your characters always tell you where to go?

SHEPARD: The characters are definitely informing you, telling you where *they* want to go. Each time you get to a crossroads you know there are possibilities. That itself can be a dilemma, though. Several times I've written a play that seemed absolutely on the money up to a certain point, and then all of a sudden it went way left field. When that happens you really have to bring it back to the point where it diverged and try something else.

INTERVIEWER: On the subject of control, Nabokov, for one, spoke of controlling his characters with a very tight rein.

SHEPARD: Yeah, but I think the whole notion of control is very nebulous. I mean, what kind of control do you have, Vladimir? Don't get me wrong, I think he's a magnificent writer. I just question the whole notion of control.

INTERVIEWER: The monologue has become something of a Shepard trademark. You are famous for your breathtaking ones, which you've referred to as arias.

SHEPARD: Originally the monologues were mixed up with the idea of an aria. But then I realized that what I'd written was extremely difficult for actors. I mean, I was writing monologues that were three or four pages long. Now it's more about elimination, but the characters still sometimes move into other states of mind, you know, without any excuses. Something lights up and the expression expands.

INTERVIEWER: What was the genesis of *Fool for Love*? Your plays don't often have a male and a female character in conflict like that.

SHEPARD: The play came out of falling in love. It's such a dumbfounding experience. In one way you wouldn't trade it for the world. In another way it's absolute hell. More than anything, falling in love causes a certain female thing in a man to manifest, oddly enough.

INTERVIEWER: Did you know when you started *Fool for Love* that the father would play such an important role?

SHEPARD: No. I was desperately looking for an ending when he came into the story. That play baffles me. I love the opening, in the sense that I couldn't get enough of this thing between Eddie and May, I just wanted that to go on and on and on. But I knew that was impossible. One way out was to bring the father in.

I had mixed feelings about it when I finished. Part of me looks at *Fool for Love* and says, "This is great," and part of me says, "This is really corny. This is a quasi-realistic melodrama." It's still not satisfying; I don't think the play really found itself.

INTERVIEWER: Do you have any idea what the end of a play is going to be when you begin?

SHEPARD: I hate endings. Just detest them. Beginnings are definitely the most exciting, middles are perplexing, and endings are a disaster.

INTERVIEWER: Why?

SHEPARD: The temptation towards resolution, towards wrapping up the package, seems to me a terrible trap. Why not be more honest with the moment? The most authentic endings are the ones which are already revolving towards another beginning. That's genius. Somebody told me once that *fugue* means to flee, so that Bach's melody lines are like he's running away.

INTERVIEWER: Maybe that's why jazz appeals to you, because it doesn't have any endings, the music just trails away.

SHEPARD: Possibly. It's hard, you know, because of the nature of a play.

INTERVIEWER: Have you ever tried to back up from a good ending? Start with one in mind and work backwards?

SHEPARD: Evidently that's what Raymond Chandler did, but he was a mystery writer. He said he always started out knowing who did the murder. To me there's something false about an ending. I mean, because of the nature of a play, you have to end it. People have to go home.

INTERVIEWER: The endings of *True West* and *Buried Child*, for example, seem more resolved than, say, *Angel City*.

SHEPARD: Really? I can't even remember how *Angel City* ends.

INTERVIEWER: The green slime comes through the window.

SHEPARD: Ah, yes. When in doubt, bring on the goo and slime.

INTERVIEWER: What is it you have in mind when you think of the audience?

SHEPARD: You don't want to create boredom, and it becomes an easy trap for a writer to fall into. You have to keep the audience awake in very simple terms. It's easy in the theater to create boredom—easier than it is in the movies. You put something in motion and it has to have momentum. If you don't do that right away, there isn't any attention.

INTERVIEWER: Do you have a secret for doing that?

SHEPARD: You begin to learn an underlying rhythmic sense in which things are shifting all the time. These shifts create the possibility for the audience to attach their attention. That sounds like a mechanical process, but in a way it's inherent in dialogue. There's a kind of dialogue that's continually shifting and moving, and each time it moves it creates something new. There's also a kind of dialogue that puts you to sleep. One is alive and the other's deadly. It could be just the shifts of attitudes, the shifts of ideas, where one line is sent out and another one comes back. Shifts are something Joe Chaikin taught me. He had a knack for marking the spot where something shifted. An actor would be going along, full of focus and concern, and then Joe would say, "No! Shift! Different! Not the same. Sun, Moon—different!" And the actors would say to themselves, "Of course it's different. Why didn't I see that before?"

INTERVIEWER: Is an ear for dialogue important?

SHEPARD: I think an ear for stage dialogue is different from an ear for language that's heard in life. You can hear things in life that don't work at all when you try to reproduce them on stage. It's not the same; something changes.

INTERVIEWER: What changes?

SHEPARD: It's being listened to in a direct way, like something overheard. It's not voyeuristic, not like I'm in the other room. I'm confronted by it, and the confrontational part of theater is the dialogue. We hear all kinds of fascinating things every day, but dialogue has to create a life. It has to be self-sustaining. Conversation is definitely not dialogue.

INTERVIEWER: Do you acknowledge the influence of playwrights like Pinter and Beckett on your work?

SHEPARD: The stuff that had the biggest influence on me was European drama in the sixties. That period brought theater into completely new territory—Beckett especially, who made American theater look like it was on crutches. I don't think Beckett gets enough credit for revolutionizing theater, for turning it upside down.

INTERVIEWER: How were you affected by winning the Pulitzer Prize?

SHEPARD: You know, in a lot of ways I feel like it was given to the wrong play. *Buried Child* is a clumsy, cumbersome play. I think *A Lie of the Mind* is a much better piece of work. It's denser, more intricate, better constructed.

INTERVIEWER: Do you have a favorite among your plays?

SHEPARD: I'll tell you, I'm not attached to any of it. I don't regret them, but for me it's much more thrilling to move on to the next thing.

Shepard on Shepard: An Interview

Matthew Roudané / 2000

From *The Cambridge Companion to Sam Shepard*, edited by Matthew Roudané (Cambridge, UK: Cambridge University Press, 2002), 64–80. Reproduced with the permission of the Licensor through PLSclear. Matthew Roudané is Regents' Professor of English at Georgia State University and the author of *Understanding Edward Albee* (1987), *"Whose Afraid of Virginia Woolf?": Necessary Fictions, Terrifying Realities* (1990), *American Drama Since 1960: A Critical History* (1996), and *Edward Albee: A Critical Introduction* (2017).

Our conversation took place on 5 May 2000, in St. Paul, Minnesota, a city not far from where Shepard lives on a horse farm with Jessica Lange and their children. Exactly on time, casually dressed, and eager to get to business, Shepard exuded a quiet and slightly restless presence. He was ready, so we sat down and immediately launched into an afternoon's talk. Unpretentious and charismatic, clearly aware of and yet slightly uncomfortable with his celebrity status, Shepard enjoyed discussing some of the key issues that have long engaged his imagination. Like so many of his own characters, Shepard is a storyteller. What is probably not so apparent in reading this interview, though, is the energy, the voice, the animated quality of Shepard's talk. He would sometimes stare right in my eyes, big hands moving, while commenting on his plays and American culture. His humor seemed genuine, self-effacing, or ironic, depending on the point he was emphasizing. Shepard, who granted the interview exclusively for this *Companion*, was enormously helpful. Afterwards he even sent me a working copy of his latest play, though it was still several months before its premiere. Throughout he was thoughtful and carefully selected his words, often laughing at himself when recounting the private or professional situations he has found himself in over a four-decade career in the theater, and implicitly acknowledging that his life as a playwright, film star, director, and musician has been a chaotically amazing journey.

Roudané: Let's start with a few questions about the beginning of your career. You've mentioned that Theater Genesis was a kind of artistic home for you. What was it like to be a teenager arriving from California and finding himself caught up in the burgeoning Off-Off-Broadway theater scene?

Shepard: It was just amazing. Theater Genesis always felt like home base, really, because that's where I started, and it had a very different feel from all the other theaters. Each one of those theaters back then was very individual, although it was all called Off-Off-Broadway. They each had their own particular identity, and it depended directly on who was running it and who were the body of people involved. Looking back on it, it was quite an extraordinary tapestry of atmospheres. La MaMa was very different from the Judson Poets' Theater and from Caffe Cino. But I guess the church—St. Mark's—really felt like home base, but it was a center for many different things besides theater: there was poetry, there was jazz, there was dance, there was painting, sculpture, so it was kind of a magnet for the East Side. And also because it was on the East Side, this made it really very different from way over in the West Village by Caffe Cino, which was a little tiny cave. It was a really amazing time to be a kid there. It was the most fortunate thing for somebody who wanted to write plays. I just dropped down out of nowhere. It was absolute luck but I happened to be there when the whole Off-Off-Broadway movement was starting. I arrived there in '63 and by '64 Off-Off-Broadway was kicking out. It was just a great time for a writer.

Roudané: I've always wondered what you meant in the "Introduction" to *The Unseen Hand and Other Plays* when you suggest that the plays in that volume (i.e., many of your 1960s works) can't be fully appreciated unless contextualized within the time and place they were written. I ask, in part, because a lot of those plays still stand up so well.

Shepard: Well, hopefully they do, but I don't know. It's hard to say. They were very much of the time, they were very much written out of that chaotic atmosphere that was happening, and for that reason I guess I've always associated *The Unseen Hand* and those earlier plays with the sixties. There are still quite a few of the early plays being done now.

Roudané: Do you have ambivalent feelings about the sixties?

Shepard: You know, man, I'll tell you what: I feel like it's been romanticized, of course, like every era that goes by that tends to get romanticized, except that I've never heard anybody say anything good about the seventies! But the sixties, to me, felt extremely chaotic. It did *not* feel like some heroic effort toward a new world, like many people make it out to be. There was an idealism on the one hand that was so out to lunch in the face of the realities. Vietnam of course shaped everything. Vietnam was the fulcrum behind it all, and there couldn't have been a more serious, a more deadly serious anger. And I suppose you could say that it was morally correct to be against the war. But people got swept up in idealisms—the Jane Fonda thing of going with the North and getting buddy-buddy with Ho Chi Minh—and it was very confusing, and at the same time full of a kind of despair *and* hope. And then when the whole Civil Rights Movement kicked in, everything just doubled and doubled and doubled, until all the barrels were wide open and everybody was shooting and it felt very awesomely chaotic to me. Still, even after the Kennedy and King assassinations and all the killing in the war, it was the idealism that continued to astound, and it just seemed so naïve. The reality of it to me was chaos, and the idealism didn't mean anything. I was up against the war in Vietnam myself and was very much against it. But I wasn't ready to become a Marxist; I didn't think Marx was the answer to Vietnam any more than "flower power." There was a crazy kind of ethos—and the Berkeley thing turned me off completely. I never went to college. You know that great Creedence Clearwater song, "I Ain't No Fortunate Son"? I always identified exactly with that tune: I mean this was my anthem. "It ain't me!" And that's the way I kind of felt throughout the sixties: I was on the tail of this tiger that was wagging itself all over the place and was spitting blood in all directions. It was weird, very weird. And then to make it even more weird was acid. When acid hit the streets, then it became a circus. Then it became totally unfathomable because nobody had a *clue*. And there were all these Gurus coming along—Timothy Leary—and then you had the Black Panthers and then you had . . . it was really beyond belief. It was like somebody threw a lighted stick in an ammunition camp. Unbelievable.

Roudané: And this prompted you to go to London in 1971?

Shepard: Oh yeah, very much. I mean I wanted out. I wanted to get out of the insanity. Of course I was also running away from myself! But I figured you can't do that. London was a good respite because there was a really fantastic fringe theater scene going on there with a lot of good actors. I worked with people like Bobby Hoskins, Stephen Rea, and all those guys before they were known and they were just doing theater for nothing. London was the first place where I ever directed my own work—at the Royal Court—*Geography of a Horse Dreamer*, with Stephen Rea and Bobby Hoskins and Ken Cranham in 1974.

Roudané: Music has played an important role in many of your plays, and I understand you're a fairly accomplished drummer yourself.

Shepard: Naw, I wouldn't go that far. I can drum a little bit, yeah. I still play music a little bit.

Roudané: But hasn't that sense of music, from rock-and-roll to jazz and to country, that you've enjoyed, helped you as a playwright?

Shepard: Yeah. My dad was a drummer—he was a New Orleans jazz fanatic—and so I grew up listening to that music and he was always playing the drums in the house and stuff. So I've always felt that music is very important. Writing is very rhythmic, there's a rhythmical flow to it—if it's working. I've always been fascinated by the rhythm of language, and language is musical, there's no way of getting around it, particularly written language when it's spoken. The language becomes musical, or at least it should in one way or another. I still play music a little bit. In fact, we've got a band now with a friend of mine, T-Bone Burnett, called Void, and we're trying to put something together. But I haven't played for a long time. I used to play with a band called the Holy Modal Rounders in the sixties, which was fun and chaotic because everybody was on dope, everybody was pretty nuts, but it was fun! Music gives you a great insight into the world. When you go to places like Ireland or Mexico, where music is a deep part of the culture, you can get together and sing. Everybody knows the music. People come from very different villages but they know the same songs and sit down and sing them. And it's really great, and primitive. It used to be that way in this country, the Mountain music and all the fiddle players from Kentucky and Tennessee. That's why in part I like the Red Clay Ramblers, another band I worked with out of North Carolina. So, yeah, music is an important part of some of my plays. I use music a lot in *A Lie of the Mind*. They are a great band, the Red Clay Ramblers, who played in *A Lie of the Mind*. They did a great thing on Broadway called *Fool Moon*. That was a good show.

Roudané: Of the many compelling aspects of your theater that spark public interest and a private nerve, it's your exploration of the American family that, for many, stands out. Especially in such plays as *The Rock Garden*, *Curse of the Starving Class*, *Buried Child*, *True West*, *Fool for Love*, and *A Lie of the Mind*, strange or absent fathers, distant mothers, wayward sons, and confused daughters animate the stage. Many of us feel the way Shelly must have when she first enters the normal-seeming home in the second act of *Buried Child* only to find a rather bizarre family. Could you comment on your life-long interest in exploring the American family?

Shepard: One thing that keeps drawing me back to it is this thing that there is no escape from the family. And it almost seems like the whole willfulness of the sixties was to break away from the family: the family was no longer viable, no longer valid somehow in everybody's mind. The "nuclear family" and all these coined phrases suddenly became meaningless. We were all independent, we were all free of that, we were somehow spinning out there in the world without any connection whatsoever, you know. Which is *ridiculous*. It's absolutely ridiculous to intellectually think that you can sever yourself, I mean even if you didn't know who your mother and father were, if you never met them, you are still intimately, inevitably, and entirely connected to who brought you into the world—through a long, long chain, regardless of whether you knew them face to face or not. You could be the most outcast orphan and yet you are still inevitably connected to this chain. I'm interested in the family's biological connections and how those patterns of behavior are passed on. In a way it's endless, there's no real bottom to it. It started with a little tiny one-act play I wrote way back when called *Rock Garden* [1964], where there was, for the first time in my work, a father, a mother, and a son. It is a very simple one-act little play, but it keyed off into *Curse of the Starving Class* [1977], and that keyed off into *Buried Child* [1979], and that keyed off into *True West* [1980], *Fool for Love* [1983], and all of that. I mean, I look back on all of that now as being sort of seminal. It initiated something that I didn't even see, I didn't even recognize that this was going to be the impulse toward other things, and I certainly didn't see myself spending my whole life on it. I've got this new production of *True West* on Broadway now—and the play's twenty years old—and the amazing thing to me is that, now, in this time, for some reason or another, the disaster inherent in this thing called the American Family is very very resonant now with audiences. I mean it's much more so now than it was back when the play first started in 1980. When *True West* first came out, it just didn't seem to have the punch that it has now, you know what I mean? I mean it attracts an amazingly young audience; it's like the average age is something like 30 years old going to a Broadway play, and I just can't believe the reaction to it—the standing ovations every night. And, granted these are remarkable actors, they are extraordinary actors doing amazing things, but, still, there is a resonance in the material that somehow catches like wildfire, and then you start to recognize the disaster.

Roudané: And there is a new generation seeing *True West* for the first time now. How do you feel about this younger generation of audiences seeing your plays?

Shepard: Oh, it's unbelievable! I mean there are kids going to see it who weren't even born when the play was written, and then I was standing in front of the theater one night and there were two or three guys standing over to the side and one of their buddies comes up to meet them to go into the theater and he's just yelling the lines of the play to these other guys. And they're not more than 25 years old—they couldn't be—and he's yelling these lines, you know, about "there aren't any mountains in the Panhandle," "It's flat" and all, and it was astounding. Really amazing to me that young people are directly relating to it. You mentioned you took your teenage son to see one of my plays. One of the great things about kids coming to the theater is that they are directly involved with the question of identity, of who they are. They are actively involved in that. Now we could still be actively involved with that when we're sixty or seventy or eighty years old, but for kids it's monumental because their lives are just becoming and I think that anything that speaks to that question of identity calls the kids' attention. I think we get fooled into this notion of maturity just because we are getting old. I mean there's maturity and there's maturity. A man could be intellectually extremely mature and emotionally a six-year-old. You see that all the time. No wonder people freak out. Our own culture is absolutely full of this, and there are no channels, there are no openings for discovering where to go. I mean there are these bullshit encounter groups but, that, well, you know.

Roudané: How do you feel about the current [2000] Broadway run of *True West*?

Shepard: Oh, I think it's wonderful. Matthew Warchus had done it like that in England. I don't know if the actors were English or expatriate Americans, but they did it in London, so he already had the experience of having handled the actors that way—with Austin and Lee switching roles. I thought it was a great notion because of the nature, the interchangeability of the characters. And you get two dynamite actors like John Reilly and Philip Hoffman and the play takes on an added resonance. The two actors switching roles on various nights is not an easy trick. It's a huge load, but they did it. I think they went a little nuts doing it, but they got it now.

Roudané: A number of playwrights address in various ways the whole notion of the "myth of the American Dream," however one chooses to define such a term. Many writers have said that the American Dream myth permeates all of American literature, forming an ironical cultural backdrop to the writer's story. Do you think such a myth informs your theater?

Shepard: Nobody has actually ever succinctly defined "the myth of the American Dream." What is the American Dream? Is it what Thomas Jefferson proposed? Was that the American Dream? Was it what George Washington proposed? Was it what Lincoln proposed? Was it what Martin Luther King proposed? I don't know what the American Dream is. I do know that it doesn't work. Not only doesn't it work, the myth of the American Dream has created extraordinary havoc, and it's going to be our demise. I mean if you want to—and I'm not an historian—but it's very interesting to trace back this European imperialism, this notion that not only were we given this land by God, somehow, but that we're also entitled to do whatever we wanted to with it, regardless of the consequences, and reap all of the fortunes out of the land, much to the detriment of everybody "below" this rampant, puritanical class of European colonialism. If you read in the journals of Lewis and Clark, it's just amazing how these guys approached the Plains Indians, particularly the Sioux, who were not very welcoming to them, as opposed to some of the other tribes to the North who got along with them better. But the Sioux couldn't care less about these jokers. They'd mess with them, they'd fool with them, they shot arrows at 'em, and Lewis and Clark hated the idea of going back through Lakota country because they knew they'd get the shit kicked out of them by these "crazy" people who they considered many notches below the European standard. Now if *that's* the American Dream, then we were in trouble from the get go; if that's the way the myth of the American dream was established, we were in deep shit. Granted, Lewis and Clark and these other guys were somewhat heroic, they were vigorous, they had all of this vitality and they had all of this adventure of going into strange territory and all of that stuff, but behind the whole thing is land-hungry Europeans wanting to dominate. That's behind the whole deal. So, again, there are so many definitions of the myth of the American Dream. I mean, now you could actually say the American Dream is the computer. It's presented like that: the computer is the American Dream, the computer is the Answer. The Internet is the Answer. Okay? Where does that leave you? I think we've always fallen victim to advertising from the get go. From advertising campaigns. The move westward was promoted by advertising. You know, "Come West!" "Free land!" "Manifest Destiny." So we've always been seduced by advertising, and now we're even more seduced by the computer and the Internet. We've fallen into that thing, you know. So the American Dream is always this fantasy that's promoted through advertising. We always prefer the fantasy over the reality.

  Roudané: That's very interesting in that some of our nation's first literature was, in part, a kind of promotional literature: John Smith's *New England Trials* [1620], *The General History of Virginia* [1624], and—listen to the title—*Advertisements for the Unexperienced Planters of New England* [1631]. Does this have something to do, in your plays, with the split within the individual's psyche to which you sometimes alluded?

Shepard: Right. I find it to be a huge dilemma. The friction between who we instinctively feel ourselves to be and anything that's influencing us to become something quite different. The friction there, the tensions there, particularly in this country, are huge. You see, there's always this battle going on between what I am inclined to believe through the influences coming from outside, and what I sort of instinctively feel myself to be, which is quite a different creature. So you can't help but get nuts in that predicament. You can't help it. It's almost like *Doctor Faustus*. It's the same predicament, this temptation for what I am not. I am sorry I am not more eloquent about explaining this. But it seems to be that this "split," which I worked with in *Simpatico*, creates a deep problem that we have very little understanding of. It can be divided in all different kinds of ways: male and female, violent and not so. And I think this "split" is where a lot of the violence comes from in the United States. This frustration between imagery and reality. I guess that's why professional wrestling is popular.

Roudané: Would this in part explain why so many of your plays have key male figures who have trouble functioning outside of the Mojave Desert?

Shepard: Yeah, *well*, I grew up in a condition where the male influences around me were primarily alcoholics and extremely violent and, at the same time, like lost children, not knowing how to deal with it. Instead, they were plunked down on the desert not knowing how they got there. And slowly they began receding further and further and further away—receding from the family, receding from society. You see it with some Vietnam vets. It was the same thing, except these guys—my father's generation—were coming out of World War II. I can't help but think that these wars had something to do with the psychological state that they came back in. I mean imagine coming back into the Eisenhower fifties. It must not have been easy. At all. Where everything was wonderful, the front lawns were all being taken care of, there was a refrigerator in everybody's house. Everybody had a Chevy, and these guys had just been bombing the *shit* out of Germany and Italy and the South Pacific and then they came back; I mean it just must have been unbelievable. I mean nobody ever really talks about that. Back then it was taboo to talk about it. "Nobody's crazy; everybody's in good shape." I mean can you believe it? And this happened across the country of course, but my dad came from an extremely rural farm community—wheat farmers—in Illinois, and next thing he knows he's flying B-24s over the South Pacific, over Rumania, dropping bombs and killing people he couldn't even see. And then from that into trying to raise a family and growing up in white America, you know. I mean it's extraordinary. It's amazing the way all that flip flops, from the fifties to the sixties. This monster appears. The monster everybody was trying to keep at bay suddenly turns over.

Roudané: Perhaps this is why you have so many baffled father figures in your plays, fathers who in part stand as an emblem for a wayward America.

Shepard: Yeah, but I don't think you ever begin a piece of writing with that intention; it comes out, you know what I mean? You begin from "character" and as it moves maybe it takes on some of those kinds of resonances. I don't think you begin from saying, "Okay, I'm going to make this father figure an emblem for America," you know what I mean? If it comes out through its own force, then it's fine. That's something I never really realized as a writer until I got into *Curse of the Starving Class*, and with *Curse* I began to realize that these characters were not only who they were in this predicament in this little subculture but they begin to have a bigger implication—there are ripples around them, particularly in the father.

Roudané: Your remarks remind me of what in part makes your plays so intensely personal and yet at the same time they transcend themselves, and touch a collective nerve the way, say, a Willy Loman in *Death of a Salesman* reaches audiences.

Shepard: Is it true that Miller wrote that in three days or something? It was very fast, right?

Roudané: He took about six weeks to finish *Salesman*, but he wrote the first act in one day.

Shepard: Yeah, that's happened to me before, too, and it surprised me when I read that because it is almost as if some plays write themselves, they just appear, and you're obliged to take things down. I mean that's almost the feeling. *True West* and actually *Buried Child* were like that. *Buried Child* wrote itself pretty fast. One of the amazing things about playwriting is that it really is a probe, it is a discovery, and there are many things about a play that you may not understand right in the moment of writing, and you may not really understand it actually until years later. *Buried Child* was like that. You know that Steppenwolf production they took to Broadway in 1996? Gary Sinise directed it. When I saw it, suddenly I understood aspects about the play I hadn't seen before—because of this production.

Roudané: Much has been said about your portraits of female characters, including that many of the women in your theater have been marginalized or exploited by the (often demented) male figures. Might you comment on the evolution of your female characters in your plays?

Shepard: Yeah, I've been thinking a lot about that. In fact, I've been working on a new play that has two female characters in it, mainly because I just came out of one that was almost all male. So I just wanted to shift a little bit. I'm not sure about the question of maturity or the evolution of my female characters, but I guess they have become more substantive characters rather than being emblems. I think in my earlier plays they were more emblematic, like Miss Scoons in *Angel City*, and stuff like that. I think that the shift in the development of my female characters began with *Curse of the Starving Class*, you know, with the mother and the daughter. And then the mom in *Buried Child*. Maybe some of the women in *A Lie of the Mind*, but the focus there is really on the men. That is one problem you have in the craft of playwriting: when you zero in, when you target two characters, and then you're obliged to have other characters, it's almost as though they're an intrusion, they're there as trappings around the others, which is kind of a fault in one way. But in another way it's probably better if you just write a two-character male play and forget about the others, and not even indicate them. Beckett had a great thing about why he put Nell and Nagg, the parents in *Endgame*, in trash cans. He said he did it so they wouldn't move around! It wouldn't be messy. But sometimes, unfortunately, you target on your central characters and then these other ones kind of pop up who you don't really have any vested interest in. They're trappings. They're almost like furniture, unfortunately, but that's the way it happens.

Roudané: When Tennessee Williams once was asked which of his female characters he was most fond of, he said Blanche from *A Streetcar Named Desire*. Looking back over all of your plays, which female characters stand out in your mind?

Shepard: Yeah, well Williams invested his entire being in Blanche. Blanche and Williams were inseparable. But I think Mae is a pretty solid character in *Fool for Love*. She's probably the most solid female character I've written. She really holds her own. And the mom in *Curse of the Starving Class*, but I think overall Mae is the strongest, not strong just in the sense of her own willfulness, but as a whole character.

Roudané: Could you discuss your long and rich collaborative association with Joseph Chaikin?

Shepard: We didn't really work together until *Tongues*, that was the first thing, at the Magic Theatre, and that was in the seventies. I had known him since the mid-sixties and he had, of course, the Open Theater, which was down on Spring Street, and I was going with a girl, Joyce Aaron, who was an actress in the company. And I used to go to rehearsals just to sit there and listen to Joe and watch him. He was so eloquent about what he was looking for in the actor. And what he was looking for was completely different from what was going on at the time, which was naturalistic, Stanislavski, Method School of Acting. Suddenly Joe opened up this whole new territory, and I think he was about the only guy in New York who was working in that way. There were some other splinter groups going on, but he was very specific about where he wanted to go with the actor. He was very inspiring, particularly to actors, because he presented opportunities that really you hadn't encountered before. I think the Method style of acting is very limited, to tell you the truth. It is one means of an actor approaching a character, but it certainly is not the final one. It wasn't just that Joe encouraged the actor to let go, but he asked the actor to consider many other possibilities, that the actor isn't only there to cause the audience to believe in his behavior as being real, as being like real life. That's not the only purpose of the actor. The actor can do many, many things. He can shift, go in many different directions: he can become an animal, he can go into all these different transformations, he can borrow from Japanese theater. The actor can borrow from all these different avenues. He can "declare" himself, he doesn't have to be just *On the Waterfront*. *On the Waterfront* is great, but there can be many other possibilities.

Roudané: When I met with Joe Chaikin recently he mentioned that when you two collaborated, what was most important was music and humor.

Shepard: One of the beauties of working with Joe early on was I was essentially working with him as an actor. He was *the* actor in the piece. He was an amazing actor, I mean this guy—oh my God!—he could do stuff with his voice and the face and body and nobody else was doing that. So I had the incredible luxury of having him, not only as an actor, but as a collaborator in the writing. As we worked, he performed or experimented. So I was directly working with an actor who was also a writer and a director. You can't get any closer to the source. He had a tremendous impact on my work, and it was a kind of writing that I probably would have never approached on my own as a playwright because it was truly a collaborative thing. Joe very much fed into that. Many, many times when we would work, I've used his language directly, particularly in things like *The War in Heaven*, which is almost all Joe's language that I just shaped. In *When the World Was Green: A Chef's Fable*, there's an emphasis on food at the end. That was Joe. The chef. Joe was obsessed with cooking and food, and he just insisted on this food thing. Every time we'd get together it was always about the food, and I just went along with it. I kind of liked this character, this Chef, this Chef who was a murderer. It was great working on *When the World Was Green*. We started off working on the Devil as a subject, and it moved into this other territory somehow.

Roudané: Do you think that it in some of your more recent plays, especially *When the World Was Green*, that you might be bestowing upon your characters a slight sense of hope, or that there may be some hint of a reconnection?

Shepard: I don't know, but I don't think you can make it general like that. Each play is so different that you try to be obliged to the material, what's there in the play, and not put anything on it. I think hope and hopelessness are intimately connected, and I don't believe in one or the other. In a way I prefer hopelessness to hope. I think there's more hope in hopelessness.

Roudané: A number of American playwrights see themselves, despite the carnage on their stages, as moral optimists. That it's too late for a John Proctor in *The Crucible* or Jesse Cates in *'night, Mother* doesn't mean the audience can't be shocked into some form of better awareness about the self and the other, and the culture at large. Do you ever consider yourself to be a moral optimist?

Shepard: I don't see myself in any particular light with that; I don't take any sides in that issue. Look at the violence in Shakespeare and, to me, Shakespeare is beyond morality, if you know what I mean. He's not taking sides, he's not interested in morality. What he is interested in is something eternal. He's interested in the gods. He's interested in the forces, the powers at work that cause all of this stuff, and how it flows through human beings, and how human beings behave in ways that they are not even conscious of, or if they become conscious of them, it's still beyond their control. Look at *King Lear*: "Let it not be madness." It *is* madness! There's no way you're going to get out of it. You can't get out of it. You're going to go *crazy*. And that to me is much much closer to the honesty of it than pretending to be on one side or the other of a morality that you don't even really believe in. As much as you can talk yourself into doing "the right thing" as opposed to "the wrong thing," it doesn't make any difference, because it's going to *happen, it's going to go down*, you know? These forces are going to go down, and for us to believe that we're somehow in the position that we individually can manipulate the forces is insanity. At the very best, I think that all we can hope for is to see that these forces are in action, and that we're being pushed and pulled and turned in one way or another and how we ride these waves. The great thing about the Greeks is that they had a god for everything. If the wind shifted, there was a god; if thunder struck, there was a god. Everything could be explained and annotated in certain kinds of ways. It must have been a fabulous culture. I mean, you could say the gods did this, and Zeus is over here causing this thing, and Athena is pissed off over here and, of course, you never know; right now, whether or not in our own contemporary notions of morality, we look at the Greek gods as being silly and illusionary. We have no idea what the Greeks' relationship was to these different cosmic powers. We as contemporary American human beings have no notion whatsoever what their real relationship was to the forces and the powers that were going on. Simply because they named them for this, that, and the other is not, to the Greeks, superstitious so much, as really having an understanding of the forces of nature, the forces that are driving us. I think they were much better off! That cosmology came in handy. It was a great culture. But all these myths about a yearning to reconnect to some higher ritual where there was some "meaning" never really existed in American culture, except in the American Indian culture, which definitely had something akin to that. But the European culture didn't. Manifest Destiny? Manifest Destiny didn't come close to Athena or Odysseus. As Lee says in *True West,* "Built up? Wiped out is more like it. I don't even hardly recognize it." Maybe this is why I've always had a great interest in Indian culture. From what I understand of it, and I've gotten this from some of the Indians I've gotten to know, there was a real relationship between the forces of nature and the human condition. The Indians didn't see human beings as being separate from these various natural forces. They were also big believers in signs, like if the hawk flew on the left side and crossed that way it's going to be a bad day. Which way is the wind turning and stuff like that was very important. The Indians were listeners and in sympathetic relationship with their rituals, and all of their stories and mythology, like the Hopi mythologies, are extraordinary. But they were put in that place because of a disaster and their purpose for living was intimately connected to the place where they were to step down at the end of that flood. It's biblical stuff and you begin to wonder how this all relates to us.

Roudané: You've long been involved with the cinema in various capacities, from *Zabriskie Point* [1970] to *Hamlet* [2000]—over thirty films and counting. Could you comment on your work in film? Has your work in Hollywood and in film helped you at all as a playwright?

Shepard: I'll tell you what it did do: it gave me a kind of perspective that was kind of surprising when I first started to do film because I didn't realize—and I don't know how anybody could foresee that before they stepped into doing movies—what a contrived situation it is. Everything's contrived: you're in this trailer out in the middle of a prairie getting make-up on and costumes, and people are running around with walkie-talkies and putting lights up. It's a kind of controlled chaos, and everything seems conjured out of somewhere, and really intruding into the atmosphere that's there. It's really this strange kind of little circus world that goes on out in the middle of nowhere. And that part of it fascinates me because it's this contest between total fantasy and very much real life. For instance, with hiring extras from the village who come in; I mean some of them have never even seen a movie, and you're hiring them with Hollywood casting agents. "Warren, sit over there!" That part of it really fascinates me—these extreme contrasts between the contrivance and the actual. And I think that actually plays an influence in some of my short stories, plays, and stuff like that, because you can't help but be shocked by it. We did this film in Mexico and shooting this film in Mexico reminded me of all this again.

Roudané: Mexico as place, as metaphor for the mind seems to play an important role in your dramas—I think of *La Turista*, *Seduced*, or *Eyes for Consuela*, for instance. What is it about Mexico—the air, the colors, the land, the culture, the history—that engages you?

Shepard: Mexico is what America should have been. Mexico still has heart, it still has extraordinary passion, it still has a sense of family and culture, of deep, deep roots. Some of it is awful—the poverty level, the oppression's awful, and stuff like that—but there are places you go in Mexico that just make you feel like a human being. The Indian culture is what I think does it for me. We just got back from Tulum. It really is paradise.

Roudané: Speaking of paradise, I recently read *Cruising Paradise*. I've read your earlier prose in *Motel Chronicles* and *Hawk Moon*, which I enjoyed, but I was in no way prepared for the imaginative leap you made in *Cruising Paradise*. Your prose was surprisingly textured in a way you don't always see in the stage language and, in a sense, it was as strong a writing as I've seen from you. How was it for you to write fiction as opposed to writing for the stage?

Shepard: Oh, thanks. I enjoyed writing that book. The strange thing about playwriting is that you reach certain points where you need to take a rest, and yet you can't completely rest. But the short story is a wonderful little side trip. You can go into a short story in such a way that it's not like writing a play but you can invest the same kind of force in them. I've always loved the form of the short story. It's very firm. It's such a wonderful form, and I like to keep working at it because I feel like I got such a long way to go. You read Chekhov's stuff and you go, "Goddamn, this guy's got volumes and volumes," and they're all amazing.

Roudané: This story "A Man's Man" in *Cruising Paradise* about the young man—you—unloading the stacks of hay was not only imagistically so vital, but it resonated for me because it brought me back to the time when I was a teenager unloading semis filled with heavy boxes in the warehouses in Chicago during the summer, and you never forget that heavy load.

Shepard: That kind of work never leaves you, does it? I don't do that kind of work anymore because, physically, you have to be fairly young. Those three-wire bales, I mean I'll never forget those suckers. They weighed like 150 pounds apiece, and you miss one of those things and you think, how am I going to do this all day long? Your whole body's scratched, your eyes are swollen, it's about 110 degrees! Yeah, that's in *Cruising Paradise*. Have you ever heard of Juan Rulfo, the Mexican novelist? He wrote a bunch of short stories called *The Burning Plain* that are some of the most extraordinary stories I have ever read. Oh, they're beyond belief. And he wrote a novel called *Pedro Páramo*, and he had a second novel that he didn't finish—he killed himself—that's just incredible. He has influenced me a lot.

Roudané: Do you see your work in prose helping you when you return to writing for the stage?

Shepard: It doesn't help with the language so much but with the material itself, the character's place, and the substance of that place, and what Frank O'Connor—one of my all-time favorite short story writers—called the "glowing center of action." He said that the short story must have that "burning center or burning core of interest." Particularly in the short story, that "burning" or "glowing" has to be apparent right away, and it has to be substantial, and it has to emanate from this "core." It's a tremendous thing to try to go into that and do something with it. I have written a whole bunch of short stories that haven't gone anywhere, that don't have a "glowing center." But it takes you a while to realize it. In fact, I have another book that's due, and I only have a third of it finished. I kicked out a whole lot of stories that didn't belong.

Roudané: Do you ever work on more than one play at a time?

Shepard: I have, but now I've just got one. I finished that one I worked on for so long, *The Late Henry Moss*, and I do have another one that's now about forty-five pages, but I think it's one of those I'm going to set aside and come back to. One interesting thing with *Henry Moss*, having left it for so long, and then come back to it, it was like a new play. I remember Mark Twain saying that he did that intentionally; he'd write something and then set it aside and wouldn't look at it for a year or more, and then would come back. It is another approach to writing. When you're younger you're too ambitious to do that.

Roudané: You've mentioned before that you've had difficulties with ending your plays. After nearly four decades of writing, do you feel that you've finally gotten a handle on closing your dramas?

Shepard: I still hate endings. Beginnings are great because there's so much tension, mystery, anticipation, and build-up, and you can reveal so much material to draw an audience in. But endings are so weird because suddenly you're forced to cut things off. I mean why end all this great action? Because people in the theater have to go home? So after all this tremendous emotional build-up, just to cut the action off seems crazy. All the action after all keeps going on.

Roudané: Speaking of endings, perhaps we could wrap up with a question about your latest work. Joseph Chaikin tells me that you've finished *Henry Moss*, which will open at the Magic Theatre in San Francisco in the fall.

Shepard: Yeah, right now it's titled *The Late Henry Moss*, which is actually a take-off of an Irish short story called "The Late Henry Conran" by Frank O'Connor. I've been working on it for the last ten years, off and on. I actually abandoned it at one point and then picked it back up again, a lot due to Joe, who read it again and thought that it would be worthwhile, and Joe actually did a workshop production of it. The play concerns another predicament between brothers and fathers and it's mainly the same material I've been working over for thirty years or something but for me it never gets old, although it may for some audiences. This one in particular deals with the father, who is dead in the play and comes back, who's revisiting the past. He's a ghost—which has always fascinated me. Do you know the work of [John Millington] Synge, the Irish playwright? He uses corpses a lot in his plays. And the corpse is present in the play and the corpse comes alive. I don't know, I find that fascinating, and this features in *The Late Henry Moss*. We start rehearsals October 3 and probably won't get it running to mid to late November, and then we can only run it up to Christmas, so it's a short run. We may subsequently do it in New York, I don't know.

Sam Shepard

Mel Gussow / 2002

Transcript of interview conducted on September 27, 2002. Container 139.3, Mel Gussow Collection, Harry Ransom Center, University of Texas. Reprinted by permission of Harry Ransom Center, The University of Texas at Austin.

Sam Shepard, in town to read from his new book of stories, *Great Dream of Heaven*, is staying with Jessica Lange at the Mercer Hotel. We plan to meet at Tribeca Grill at noon. I arrive early and he is sitting on the step outside of the restaurant having his picture taken. He has taken off his jacket, and looks, as usual, like a cowboy in the city. He smiles and greets me warmly. Inside, he joins me at a corner table in the rear and orders an iced tea, and later a cappuccino (and has a few cookies). He relaxes and seems to be in a friendly mood. He is still terse and laconic, but occasionally becomes almost expansive.

Mel Gussow: You don't like having your picture taken.

Sam Shepard: It's always felt uncomfortable. It hasn't gotten much easier. Still photography is quite different from a movie camera. I don't know why.

MG: I read the stories. Several of them, dialogues and monologues, could also be regarded as plays.

SS: Sometimes one crosses over into the other.

MG: What is the crossover? What makes a play, what makes a story?

SS: I love this thing of suddenly being able to discover raw dialogue without any stage directions or any indication where the characters are or who they are, which is one of the things I've always felt uncomfortable with in plays. You have to stop and describe stuff. I much prefer going with the dialogue. So in this situation you can virtually just write dialogue and have it exist on its own, have it live on its own.

MG: With several of the stories, you read them and wonder at first, who is speaking, which is a man, which is a woman.

SS: Then it settles in after a while. You understand. It's kind of a luxury to be able to do that kind of dialogue. You don't have to laboriously put in all the stage directions.

MG: They could be one-act sketches.

SS: They could. I wouldn't even mind if somebody decided to do them like that. I think somebody has from *Cruising Paradise*. *Cruising Paradise* had more of those straight dialogue things. There's only one in this one that's pure dialogue.

MG: There are others that are close to it, and several that could serve as monologues.

SS: Yeah. "Foreigners."

MG: I've always felt that with Beckett, his plays and his fiction are all of a piece, although he could be rigid about not wanting people to stage his prose. I felt that reading your stories, that the plays and stories are also all of a piece.

SS: They're all connected.

MG: The characters, the themes . . .

SS: Yeah.

MG: Did you write many of them while acting in movies?

SS: I did with *Cruising Paradise*, but this one was mostly written on its own. With *Cruising Paradise*, there were a lot of movie locations, especially down in Texas. Sittin' in a trailer [*laugh*].

MG: You could also write a play while sitting in a trailer.

SS: Story's very different. It's such a relief to be writing stories after so many years of plays. A brand-new form, and exciting to enter into.

MG: What else does it allow you to do?

SS: The great excitement with plays when I first started was the one-act form because I felt like there was an immediate attraction to that form because it was so quick, in a way, and accessible. And the same thing with the short story. There is an accessibility to it and a suddenness and a presence. I know I could never write a novel.

MG: I was going to ask that next.

SS: I'm unable to sustain interest for months or years or whatever it takes to do that. But the shorter form, it seems to me you can explode into it and exist with it for its duration and when it's finished go on to the next one.

MG: With plays, you started with one-acts, and they led to full-length plays. *A Lie of the Mind* was close to four hours.

SS: [*Laughs*] I think originally it was six.

MG: It was the equivalent of a novel.

SS: Horrendous length.

MG: Short things appeal to you more.

SS: They do, yes. They're less laborious. There's less of a feeling of trying to create some Work of Art.

MG: What are you trying to create? Is it still telling a story?

SS: I'm really looking for this experience, I guess, for lack of a better word, of the material suddenly speaking for itself. I think even in plays my best stuff has been when I've had that experience—of the material just speaking without me manipulating it so much. That's what I think these short stories—hopefully that's what I'm trying to get to.

MG: What plays are you thinking about when you say that?

SS: Well, there were some plays that came very quickly. They kind of exploded. Like *True West*. Not for *Fool for Love*—I struggled over that one. But *Curse of the Starving Class*. Things like that, that more or less told themselves. And told them in a relatively short period of time. And there are other plays that I labored over extensively.

MG: And once you wrote them, you didn't change them much.

SS: No. That's true. They pretty much stayed what they came out. Like *Tooth of Crime* I've rewritten countless times. It still doesn't work [*hearty laugh*]. Major rewrites.

MG: Tennessee Williams kept rewriting his plays.

SS: Did he? I didn't know that. I used to hate it but now I can see the point of it. I don't mind rewriting so much. I think it's a brand-new effort in itself. It's like another kind of writing. Where before I just thought it was labor.

MG: Some of those stories are absolutely complete—like short novels. For example, the title story, "Great Dream of Heaven." You get a full picture of those two men.

SS: Hopefully.

MG: Could you trace the genesis of that story?

SS: I actually started it in London, which is weird. I don't know why. I don't know why it started there. Then I set it aside for quite a while. Jessica was doing *Streetcar* over there and I was there with her. It was very dreary, rainy London weather as usual. I sat down and started writing this thing. I set it aside and left it and came back to it more than a year later, and picked it up, and started working with it.

MG: Do you often find you write about something in a setting totally alien to the piece?

SS: Yeah, yeah. Almost as though you're yearning for the place. Right. London is a great place to write because it makes you want to be out of there [*big smile*]. I wrote *Tooth of Crime* there, in London.

MG: And also *Geography of a Horse Dreamer* and *Suicide in B Flat*.

SS: Uh-huh.

MG: Good place to write.

SS: That's what I'm saying. The climate inspires you to transport yourself.

MG: When I read that story "Great Dream of Heaven," I imagined you sitting there in that diner. You stopped your car on the road and you sat there and you heard someone say something, and you saw a waitress.

SS: I had those two characters kicking around. I had at one time spent quite a while on the desert in a little place out by Indio that their house is sort of modeled after. It was quite remote. It was out in the middle of the desert. The great thing about it was that it was surrounded by quail, so every morning you get up and there'd be this covey of quail. It was quite fantastic—middle of the desert. So the place came back to me that way, but I wasn't in the place when I was writing it.

MG: As I see it, the principal theme of that story is betrayal.

SS: I don't know if it's actually betrayal, or if it's the perception of betrayal. Paranoid betrayal. Yeah. And also a kind of honor.

MG: Is honor the opposite of betrayal?

SS: Yeah, yeah. There seems to be an honor that exists unspoken between the two of them, and then it's broken by this very dubious—whether he actually crosses the line or not, I don't know. The thing that's always amazed me in deep relationships, especially long-term relationships, is how suddenly something will be interpreted in a very subtle way and it causes the upheaval of everything. Some very small, tiny thing that is construed as being huge and it causes the downfall of everything, without either party understanding exactly what took place.

MG: One of the memorable images of that story was of the two Stetsons being put down upside down. That's the ritual of both men.

SS: That actually was a thing. A long time ago, there were men who believed it would cause bad luck to turn your hat over. You didn't do it. You took your hat off and had to set it right. It's like the horseshoe. You place the horseshoe and the horseshoe has to be upright in order to catch luck. Turn the horseshoe over like that and it dumps it out. Little things like that.

MG: Do you believe in that?

SS: I'd like to say no, but there are superstitions that I still hold to. For instance, hawks, the flight of hawks. Hawks passing from right to left in front of you are good luck, left to right in front of you are bad luck.

MG: Seen any hawks lately?

SS: Oh, I see hawks all the time.

MG: How are they passing these days?

SS: So far, they're pretty good. I don't know why that's always stuck with me. The passage of birds. In Greek lore, there was actually terminology for the patterns of bird flights, divining which ways birds flew, and migrating. Stuff like that. Whether the crops were going to die.

MG: What other superstitions do you hold to?

SS: It's not that I hold to them so much. Hawks' flights is the big one.

MG: The image of hawks appears frequently in your work.

SS: The hawk is the most extraordinary animal—amazing to watch. I've got a pair of them on my place that hunt together, and you rarely see hawks hunting together.

MG: There's that strange story in the book, "Blinking Eye," about the woman who finds a hawk on the road and wraps it up and it attacks her.

SS: Well, it's injured, and she tries to save it. Wild animals if they're injured and you attempt to do something about it, they'll usually explode with terror and cause some damage.

MG: The moral is: never help a wounded hawk?

SS: I don't know. It turns out that the hawk is okay anyway. He flies away.

MG: Lot of horses too in the stories and plays. You still ride?

SS: Horses? Yeah, every day. Most every day—except when I'm in New York [*laughs*].

MG: You didn't ride your horse to New York.

SS: I wish I had. I've got some cutting horses now.

MG: What are cutting horses?

SS: For cattle. Separate cows and calves from the rest of the herd. Amazing animals because they move laterally. Most horsemanship is forward. Most horses move like this [*he moves his hands straight ahead*]. Cows try to get away from them, and the horses prevent them from getting back into the herd. Amazing athletes.

MG: Dogs and sheep, horses and cattle?

SS: [*Laughs*] Sheep have fallen by the wayside.

MG: As you say that, I have an image of those cowboy movies—like *Red River*. Horses separating the cattle.

SS: Was that John Ford, or Howard Hawks?

MG: Howard Hawks.

SS: John Wayne and . . .

MG: Montgomery Clift.

SS: And Richard Farnsworth. He was John Wayne's double on that movie. Isn't that amazing? He's the guy who took all the falls in the river. He was the stuntman.

MG: He killed himself.

SS: Yes. He was a great guy. I knew him for years. A really true horseman. This guy was an actual horseman. He grew up with them. Were you working at the [*Village*] *Voice* when I first met you?

MG: I was at *Newsweek*. Back in the '60s. I wrote a piece about Lanford [Wilson] the other day.

SS: How is Lanford?

MG: He's okay. He's having a season at the Signature. I knew he had some phobias, starting with fear of flying, but he listed them. There are so many, from fear of crossing the street, and of heights.

SS: Well, he's an Ozark boy living in New York. He's from the Ozarks. Probably needs to go back to Missouri.

MG: You don't like to fly either.

SS: I hate flying. I drove out.

MG: Why?

SS: I don't know. I never got along with it. I do fly occasionally—go down to Mexico. I get Xanax, that pill, makes you totally numb.

MG: There are stories in your book about driving to Mexico and the difficulty of going across the border.

SS: I love Mexico. We swam some horses across the river down there. That was amazing.

MG: Is that legal?

SS: No! Completely illegal. And we got a white mule once. The great thing about the border country down there is that it still feels as though it was 150 years ago. Still wild like that. Not just California, Tijuana and things— the whole stretch. Particularly down through Texas.

MG: Could you live down there? Or is it too wild?

SS: You could. I suppose you could. It would be kinda hard to make a living. I suppose as a writer you could live down there. I love Lajitas in the Big Bend country, great little town. There's no border guard at all. Mexicans still come across with horses and sit in the bars and watch TV and then have a few drinks and then ride back across and nobody says anything about it. Great. That's the way it should be. Just open the damn border.

MG: Last time when I was in Europe, I drove from France into Spain and there was no border guard.

SS: And they've changed the money too. That's too bad. The other money was more colorful.

MG: But borders should be open.

SS: Particularly the Mexican border. It's like Berlin. What the hell's going on? There's no way they can stop it anyway.

MG: Some of your stories are about that, about crossing the border.

SS: There's a great story about Wim Wenders, my friend, the filmmaker. He went down there—I forget for what reason—and he came back and they wouldn't let him back in the country, because his Green Card had expired. So he kept going back into the interior of Mexico and changing his appearance and trying to appear more American, and every time he would come to the border they would immediately spot him. He said it infuriated him more that he wasn't passing as an American than not being able to get back across. I think it was only after months of deliberation that he was able to pass back into America.

MG: The question arises: how do you pass as an American?

SS: Exactly! And he doesn't look that distinct. He's a tall, big man, but he doesn't look particularly European.

MG: Does he have a heavy German accent?

SS: He does, but I don't think he was even talking. He was wearing a baseball cap and pulling it down over his eyes. They picked him out.

MG: Your border stories come from your work with Wim Wenders?

SS: No. Different times I've been down there. The one film I was on wasn't a Wim Wenders thing. It was called *Voyager, Homo Faber* in Europe. Volker Schlondorff.

MG: How true to life are those stories?

SS: Some of them are very true, in the sense that events took place that it's mimicking. There is always some element of something that's occurred. Like fiction, you take off and either expand on it or go one way or another. It's hard for me to just completely invent something out of the blue, and start making it up—although people have done very well with that. In fact when I first showed those stories in *Cruising Paradise* to my friend Richard Ford, he said, "Is this fiction, or did this stuff happen?" It didn't occur to me to make that distinction but evidently with a lot of fiction writers, they just plunge into the deep blue and go from there.

MG: What did you say to Ford?

SS: I said it's all true—but it's fiction.

MG: From your plays and stories, my supposition is that your father has furnished you with lots of characters.

SS: Yes. He's since passed. In '94. I had never foreseen that, that he would be such a source of material. I never even looked at him as a source of material. And he had such a strong influence on me, I guess it was inevitable.

MG: Albee says that the character on stage in *Three Tall Women* is based on his mother, but that the character is far more interesting than his mother ever was. I would guess perhaps that's true of your father.

SS: I don't know. To me my father was deeply mysterious and I think in himself he was probably far more mysterious than I depict him on stage in any of the characters extrapolated from him. There is a mystery about him that still exasperates me, that still intrigues me. I don't know who he was, I never really knew who he was.

MG: He fought in the war, as a pilot?

SS: He was a pilot. He flew . . . 47 missions, I think.

MG: What do you mean when you say "mystery"?

SS: [*Thoughtfully*] I think he was a mystery to himself. He didn't understand this volatile nature that seemed to erupt. He was a very complicated man. He spoke fluent Spanish, he was a teacher, a Fulbright scholar. At the same time, he was extremely violent and could be quite mad and crazy and totally unpredictable and alcoholic and all this other stuff. There were many layers to him, which I didn't understand, and I'm not sure he did himself. What caused the sort of inconsistency in his behavior. He'd disappear and he'd go off and he'd be gone for periods of time. And then reappear somewhere. Strange man [*laughs*].

MG: And after he died, you found out that he had written things?

SS: Yeah, he had. He had lots of notes. He had written like little philosophical things. He'd spent a lot of time in New Mexico. He died in New Mexico, and a lot of it was descriptive stuff about nature, some sort of semi-political stuff. He had notebooks. I don't think he had ever aspired to be a writer. Earlier he had aspired to be a journalist. I think he worked for the *Chicago Daily News* for a while when he was much younger, in his thirties. I don't think he ever aspired to be a fiction writer.

MG: In one of the stories ["See You in My Dreams" in *Cruising Paradise*], the father says to his son, about the breakup of his marriage, "You may think this great calamity that happened way back when—might actually think that it had something to do with you, but you're dead wrong. Whatever took place between me and her was strictly personal. See you in my dreams." It's a very touching scene.

SS: That's something he actually said to me. There's a scene in *Fool for Love*, that's almost identical to a dialogue I had with him where he was showing me a picture of Barbara Mandrell on the wall. That's taken almost exactly from life. Just so incredible. At the time, I couldn't believe he was engaging me in a. . . . He says something to the effect, "You see that picture on the wall." [In the play The Old Man points at the wall. There is no picture but the character of Eddie stares at the wall.] And the other guy says, "Yeah," and he says, "Do you know who that is? Barbara Mandrell." He says, "Would you believe me if I told you I was married to her?" And the character says, "No." He says, "Well, see, that's the difference. . . ." He's trying to describe the difference between realism, his version of realism, and fantasy. He's using Barbara Mandrell as an instrument in this discussion. He says, "Actually I am married to Barbara Mandrell in my mind, and that's realism." That was his version of realism. So you see what I mean [he laughs]. He was a complicated man. He was married to Barbara Mandrell in his mind.

MG: He wasn't really married to Barbara Mandrell?

SS: God, no [he laughs heartily]. He was off in the middle of the desert living in a little house with a picture of Barbara Mandrell on the wall.

MG: The only play of yours that he saw was Buried Child?

SS: He was kicked out of the theater. I don't know exactly what happened. I wasn't there. Somebody had told him they were doing a production of Buried Child in Santa Fe. He lived on the outskirts of Santa Fe and he had come into town to see it, but he was stoned drunk, and he sat down in the theater and started yelling at the actors and telling them that what they were depicting was untrue. Things didn't actually happen like that. He knew because he was in it—and they kicked him out of the theater.

MG: They didn't know who it was?

SS: No. And then he explained that he was my father, and they let him back in. Well, he started back up again, talking to the actors [laughs].

MG: That's a complicated man.

SS: The only other time that happened to me: Bob Dylan came to see a play of mine called Geography of a Horse Dreamer. They were doing it, I think, at the American Place Theatre. I'm not sure. In the middle of the production, Bob stands up in the audience and starts yelling [laugh] at the characters, telling them that they can't treat the brother like that. And he stormed out of the theater. I'll never forget that one either. There's a scene toward the end of Geography of a Horse Dreamer, where the brothers come blasting back into the room with shotguns—and Dylan objected to this for some reason.

MG: I guess he was moved by it. In both cases!

SS: I don't know why I'm remembering these things. One other time, Gregory Corso, who was one of my favorite poets of all time, stood up in the middle of—I think it was *La Turista*, at the American Place Theatre, and yelled at the actor because he was pointing a gun into the audience. He started yelling, "Never, ever point a gun. I don't care if it's loaded or not. Never point a gun" [*helpless laughter*].

MG: The reason why your father was shouting back was because he recognized things in the play.

SS: Yes. He had a brother who had an amputated leg—from polio. Had a wooden leg. His mother is very clearly depicted, easily recognizable. All of the family members are pretty well depicted. Although they are overblown to a large extent—they're recognizable, certainly if you're part of that family.

MG: And you're the boy coming home?

SS: Yeah, I mean, that was the . . . fictional boy.

MG: The rest are real, you're fictional.

SS: Yeah, right.

MG: Have you ever wanted to go up on stage in one of your plays, because they were doing it badly?

SS: No. Never. I have wanted to yell at the audience a couple of times.

MG: For laughing too much?

SS: I forget why [*laughs*]. When I was first starting out, when I started doing those one-acts Off-Off-Broadway, my impression always was that the audience was an intrusion.

MG: What were they doing there?

SS: Right! Why is there suddenly an audience? I didn't quite get it.

MG: You soon learned why there was an audience. The audience paid the bill.

SS: Right. It was a wrongheaded thing.

MG: When you started out, you were pretty naïve about the theater, weren't you?

SS: I didn't have a clue.

MG: 1963 was the crucial year.

SS: That was the year I arrived in New York. In '65 I started to do the plays at Theater Genesis.

MG: This is from a piece you wrote for the *New York Times* about your arrival here in 1963: "I thought to myself the only thing to be in this life is an artist. That's the only thing that makes any sense."

SS: That was pretty much true. I didn't know what kind of an artist.

MG: You didn't sit down and say, "I'm going to be a playwright."

SS: No, no. I started thinkin', painting, acting, music, something like that. The plays really happened inadvertently because I started writing these dialogues.

MG: Inadvertently?

SS: Roundabout. I was living with musicians on the Lower East Side, surrounded by musicians, really, all jazz musicians.

MG: Could you have gone that way, been a musician? I remember I saw you play on stage in those early days.

SS: I learned drums through my father, and I played with the Holy Modal Rounders and some other bands. I like playing music. I don't know if I would have gone that way, as a way of life.

MG: Could you say what writing plays has done for you?

SS: I hadn't foreseen what it would open for me in terms of my own experience. I hadn't foreseen what simply exploring dialogue, exploring character, exploring place and time and situation and all that would offer in terms of discovering my own experience. It really in a way turned me toward my life in a way that was quite unexpected. Calling up all kinds of things.

MG: Have you learned more about yourself from writing?

SS: I'm not sure. It's given me an avenue to express certain areas that probably would have gone dormant if I hadn't found a form. Whether or not I've *learned* more about myself, I don't know.

MG: You learned more about your father.

SS: To some extent, yes. I think that there are certain things that always are going to remain inaccessible, to a large degree. I don't really look at it in a psychological way. I'm not interested in the analytical aspect of it at all. That never interested me. The whole psychoanalytic thing of trying to understand oneself through analyzing the details of one's behavior and what happened to you when you were three years old and all that shit doesn't appeal to me in the slightest.

MG: But in a strange way, as you write your stories and plays, you're working out a lot of those things, what it was like growing up. It leads the reader and the viewer to a greater understanding of what those people were like.

SS: Hopefully, the greater view has to do with something broader than a psychological understanding. A cultural thing, or something to do with the land, or history, or time, or the movement of cultures and America as a phenomenon, and things like that.

MG: Those are the overall themes you're dealing with.

SS: Yes. Because America is an extraordinary thing, and much much more interesting than we make it out to be, particularly in this time of patriotism and flagwaving, the chauvinistic appeal. It's much more complex and much more interesting—the fabric of America. It's extraordinary what's happened in such a brief period of time, within 150 years. The amazing weave of American culture, what's gone on, and now faced with this international dilemma that in a way is beyond us, I think. We're swimming in something that we don't have a good grasp on. Let's attack something! Let's attack something to give us purpose. What the hell. It's quite insane, I think, what's happening. Not only what's happening to us, but what we are perpetuating. Quite insane. This is not a rational time we're living in.

MG: People would not ordinarily think of you as a political playwright, but there is a great deal of politics in the plays.

SS: It's the politics of feeling, I guess, rather than the politics of what would you call it?

MG: The feelings between the characters: who's the more powerful, and who's the more betrayed. One thing I've always wondered: you've dealt with so many brothers in your work, but you don't have any brothers. You have sisters. Have you thought about that?

SS: Yeah. The dilemma of one's own knowledge about one's self is always split, I think, where you feel yourself to be in a dual identity—to me. Rather than making a psychological issue out of that, I've divided it into brothers, so that there are two aspects, there are always these two aspects.

MG: Of one person?

SS: Yes. To externalize it into brothers seems like a plausible way to do it, for fiction or theater, etc. You have these two arguments, two forces, two elements that are in fact a part of one identity. Not to make it too complicated, but that's basically what it is. Also, I think there are friendships that are akin to brotherly friendships that also should be included in that.

MG: Some of the relationships between brothers on stage come from your feelings about people who are close to you, with your friendships transformed into fraternal relationships.

SS: Yes. But I'm not interested whether or not the audience begins to analyze this thing as being two aspects of one. It affords the physical proposition of being able to have conflict on stage, in a bold way, not to say you couldn't do it with male-female. I've done that too.

MG: In *Fool for Love.* With *True West*, do you feel closer to either of those two characters? Or is it evenly split?

SS: I always identified with the rougher brother, the one from the desert, but it requires the other guy in order for him to have a life. I don't know whether you saw the most recent production where the actors swapped roles.

MG: I saw it here, and in London with Mark Rylance.

SS: I thought it was quite amazing the way they devoted themselves to each side of the issue, when they swapped. Not only is it a great actor's problem, but that they could enter into it, that they could do that, was quite incredible.

MG: For you as an actor, that would be a real challenge. Could you do that?

SS: I don't think so.

MG: Even though you created these guys?

SS: I don't think so. I could watch it, but I don't think I could do it—so convincingly. That's one of the best productions I've ever seen, simply that quality, that aspect of it.

MG: When Malkovich and Sinise did the play, I thought it would have been interesting if they had switched roles.

SS: They certainly could have handled it as actors. I don't think Steppenwolf could have survived. I think they were struggling on many levels. It was a dangerous idea. It could be dangerously kitschy to do that, but the actors were so good that they succeeded.

MG: When you wrote it, you didn't have that in mind.

SS: No, not at all. Never occurred to me. It would take a brilliant director to dream that up.

MG: What happened with that first production of *True West* at the Public Theater? It was such a mess.

SS: It was complicated because Joe Papp, bless his heart, tried to take over the production, in a sort of baldfaced way. I kind of rejected that, and it's too bad because Tommy Lee [Jones] is a wonderful actor, they're all wonderful actors. And Peter [Boyle], too. Tommy Lee was playing the wrong role. He was playing Austin. Maybe it should have been flipped around.

MG: It wasn't funny and it wasn't menacing.

SS: I never actually saw it. But then the play would have virtually disappeared if John and Gary hadn't done it at Steppenwolf and that was like two years later.

MG: Seeing them do it made me realize that this play I didn't like the first time around was actually one of your best.

SS: I was surprised that it didn't click [the first time]. I was down in Texas doing a film at the time. I wasn't able to be there.

MG: A play of yours that hasn't had a fair reading was *Lie of the Mind*. This year we've had *Frankie and Johnny in the Clair de Lune* and *Burn This* coming back, both plays of the '80s, as was *Lie of the Mind*.

SS: I loved the production we had uptown at the Promenade. Difficult play to do, very unwieldy play, still, I think, too long and verbose. I'd be glad to see it again. There were some extraordinary actors up there on stage. That theater was so great. It's an old Mormon tabernacle. Geraldine Page and Ann Wedgeworth, both married to Rip Torn, never spoke to each other through the whole production, never sat anywhere near each other in the dressing room, virtually never talked to each other on stage. They were on stage in parallel lives, never had anything to do with each other for the whole thing.

MG: If Rip Torn were in the play it might have made a difference.

SS: He was in a play of mine once, *Seduced*, at the American Place Theatre. He infuriated the other actor—I can't remember his name—because he refused to have the heat turned on. The heat had to be turned off for his character. It was the middle of winter. This guy came on at the top of the act with his prop gun and started firing at Rip, told him to turn the heat on.

MG: I thought the production was better at Trinity Square in Providence with George Martin. I reviewed it up there. It was really sharp.

SS: I didn't see that. I think that play is actually underwritten. I didn't work hard enough on that one. The opposite problem with that was *Lie of the Mind*. I would like to rewrite *Seduced*, because Hughes is such a remarkable character. There is boundless material. This guy was extraordinary. Evidently Warren Beatty has been planning for years to do something on Howard Hughes. I don't know why he never has. I think he owns the rights. What an incredible evolution.

MG: That was a rare case of your writing about a real—though fictionalized—person.

SS: Yes. I became really fascinated with him. I read several biographies of him. His latter days when he was transported into Las Vegas by Mormons, the Mormon secret service, and ordering ice cream in the middle of the night, and having to go out and get truckloads of ice cream and watching *Ice Station Zebra*, with all the curtains shut—and his nails grown out to here. Wow! The human psyche is just beyond belief. Beyond belief. And here's this guy who invented tits for Jane Russell, this broad, carried her in such a way that she became a sex symbol. The movies and the Spruce Goose. At one point he had a bungalow at the Beverly Hills Hotel, where he kept this woman, and he wouldn't let her out. Then he had two bungalows. She would stay in one, he would stay in the other. Wow!

MG: In one of your stories ["The Real Gabby Hayes"], the character talks about seeing Gabby Hayes in real life and you say, "That's what fame and fortune'll get you. Couple of blonde chippies and a shrimp cocktail."

SS: That's my old man talking. I did actually see Gabby Hayes when I was a kid.

MG: Was he with a couple of chippies?

SS: Yeah. And it was so amazing to me at the time. Course television was fairly young then. It was these old black and white westerns and stuff, in the '50s, so in some ways, those characters were even more mythologized by kids watching *Hopalong Cassidy*. Then when you saw them, I think that was the first incident where I actually saw an actor in real life that I had seen on television and I couldn't compute, I couldn't put the two together. It seemed impossible that this person could exist in life. Not only existed, but in an entirely different context than when he was on *Roy Rogers*. He was in a tuxedo and he had these prostitutes with him.

MG: I would suppose that people might feel something similar when they see you.

SS: I find that hard to believe. I suppose so. I remember seeing John Wayne once at a baseball game going into the men's room. Couldn't believe it. He was going in the men's room as I was coming out. The size of this guy! He was huge. He really was a big man. I think it was an L. A. Angels game.

[He gets up and goes to the restroom. He returns, laughing.]

I didn't know where it was, so I asked someone. It turned out to be De Niro. I thought he was the janitor. I said, "Where's the restroom?" He said, "Down there."

MG: You know he's one of the owners of the restaurant. It's his place. He's never been in one of your plays. There's someone that should be.

SS: He hasn't done much theater. I'd love to get him [in one of my plays]. My last experience with a cast chockful of movie stars was in San Francisco [with Sean Penn, Nick Nolte and Woody Harrelson in *The Late Henry Moss*]. They're all extraordinary actors, but it backfired on me in a way. The production became about this star-studded cast. It took on a very very weird flavor. The phenomenon of those name actors in a play in a way, I think, hurt the production. People came for the wrong reasons. I don't know if it's such a great idea. As uncanny as all those actors are—they did a fabulous job—I'm not sure the audience saw the play. Sean Penn, Nick Nolte, Woody Harrelson and Cheech [Marin]—just jampacked with monster actors.

MG: Are you satisfied with that play, or do you want to rewrite it, too?

SS: No, I'm satisfied with that. I'm not going to write another play until I can enter absolutely new territory.

MG: Trying to group your plays, I realized that your first plays were mystical and folkloric. Then there was a phase when you wrote about art and the artist, and then the five family plays, a full house. I thought what about the recent ones: *States of Shock, Simpatico* and *Henry Moss*? I couldn't categorize any of them. Whatever you felt like writing about at the time?

SS: Well, *States of Shock* came directly out of the Gulf War. *Henry Moss* I worked on for a long long time. I had actually packed it in. I started it in '95, or something, and set it aside and sent it to the archives down in Texas. Joe [Chaikin] and a couple of other people dug it up, and I started working on it again, and rewrote it. I've been working on that play a long long time.

MG: Your papers are in the archive at the University of Texas?

SS: Some of them, and some of them are in Virginia and some of them are in Boston. My friend Billy Wittliff has a library down there in San Marcos, Texas, at the university, Western writers library.

MG: Are there many false starts and unfinished plays?

SS: Yeah. And Boston University has some and the University of Virginia—when I was living there.

MG: Have you seen Chaikin since you've been in New York?

SS: No. I'm going to try and catch *Happy Days* [directed by Chaikin at the Cherry Lane Theatre] at a matinee tomorrow. *Happy Days* is one of my favorite plays anyway.

MG: You like Beckett?

SS: How could you not like Beckett? One of my favorite short stories, in fact, is one he wrote called "First Love." Amazing short story.

MG: Did you ever meet him?

SS: No. I should have gone out of my way but I didn't. You did.

MG: Yes, and he was well aware of your work.

SS: Was he? Huh. I'll be darned.

MG: He was also aware of your acting—tantalized by the idea of a playwright also being an actor. Something he would never do.

SS: I know. In fact, Peter Brook asked him to be in a movie years ago and he refused. Peter told me he had asked Beckett and he said no. Not surprising. Athol Fugard has acted quite a bit. He's a good actor.

MG: There are other playwrights who act. Wally Shawn.

SS: Shakespeare! Pinter.

MG: Have you learned more about acting by acting?

SS: Definitely. The extraordinary thing about acting is this business about vulnerability. The proposition of vulnerability. It's something you don't face so much as a writer because you aren't publicly witnessed as you're doing it. But the issue of vulnerability is huge in acting. How vulnerable you make yourself to material, and how protected you keep yourself is the difference between being able to accomplish something acting—and not.

MG: You've been able to make yourself more vulnerable?

SS: I've had to, because when I started out I was full of armor. I was trying not to be revealed. As I've gone on, I found the opposite is true. You have to become more and more vulnerable. It's an interesting process because you don't really face that the same way as a writer.

MG: [*I take out the list of his movie credits.*] I called your name up on the Internet and found one list that said you've made 35 films. Like a baseball player wanting to hit 40 home runs and steal 40 bases, you've made almost as many films as the plays you've written.

SS: Stayin' alive. I didn't know I made that many. Is this my list? [*He takes out his glasses to read it.*] I need my spectacles. I'm virtually blind. [*He reads down to the end of the list and* Bronco Bullfrog *(1969).*] *Bronco Bullfrog?* What's that? I don't remember that one. I don't think that's true. What was *Bronco Bullfrog?*

MG: Which ones do you remember?

SS: I remember all of them except *Bronco Bullfrog*. What's *Just to Be Together?* Oh, oh, oh. It could be an alternative title to this one I finished down in South Carolina. It was called "Leopold Bloom," but evidently they couldn't use that because of the character from *Ulysses*. I don't know what *Bronco Bullfrog* is and I don't know what *Just to Be Together* is.

MG: The other 33 you recognize? That's a body of work.

SS: Amazing.

MG: Which ones do you love and which ones do you hate? Which ones can't you watch?

SS: I don't know about "love." The ones that stand out for me of course are *Days of Heaven* and *The Right Stuff. Paris, Texas*. I wasn't in *Paris, Texas*. I wrote it. *Thunderheart* I really enjoyed doing. I loved being out there in South Dakota. *Hamlet* I loved doing.

MG: You played The Ghost. How did you do that?

SS: Well, you have to see it. And *Black Hawk Down* was an experience, too. *Bronco Bullfrog?*

MG: I remember *Dash and Lilly*. You played Dashiell Hammett.

SS: Years ago, Wim was trying to do, he did do a film on Hammett. It was called *Hammett*, and Francis Coppola was the producer, and Wim wanted me to play Hammett back then. And Francis wanted Fred Forrest. Fred

Forrest ended up doing it, but then years later the opportunity came to do this. He was an interesting character.

MG: Many years ago, Hammett lived in our apartment. It was during the period when he was not writing.

SS: I know the feeling.

MG: But you've written so much.

SS: You know, it's taken me six years to put this collection of stories together. It's only a 140-page book. There's 18 stories in it, but they're small. That's okay, but it's not exactly prolific.

MG: But put them next to your plays. How many do you have—about 60?

SS: I've slowed down quite a bit. I do have a new screenplay coming out with Wim Wenders. I better not say anything about it. I know he's protective to a certain extent. We've been working on it for about two years now. Next spring I think we get to start shooting.

MG: Are you working on a play too?

SS: No. I'm not even going to enter into a play until I find something that is territory I haven't entered before. The short story form satisfies me very well right now.

MG: You've worked a lot of philosophy into those stories. In "The Remedy Man," "Horse is just like a human being. He's gotta know his limits. Once he finds that out he's a happy camper." That's you talking?

SS: It's also horse trainer talk. I know a lot of old guys that speak like that.

MG: You've got to know your limits.

SS: Horse trainers, the old-timers especially, are full of homilies like that. They capsulize stuff, put it succinctly.

MG: August Wilson says that what he's trying to do in his work is test the limits of the instrument, which he takes from jazz. Have you found your limits yet?

SS: It's a strange thing about form, the form of the play, the form of the short story, the form of a poem. When you go into it, particularly when you're younger, you tend to want to believe it doesn't exist, or that you can obliterate it in some way, or ignore it, or tear it apart and reinvent it. And slowly you begin to understand—in the same way that any craftsman does— if you're going to make a chair, somebody has to sit on it. It's got to have four legs, got to have a back, got to have a seat. There are certain essentials in order for it to work that have to be honored. And if you don't honor those, if you don't pay respect to that, you're not going to go anywhere with it, you're not really going to go anywhere meaningful with it. It takes a lot of time. That's maybe why I wrote so many one-act plays. I was testing the form out, the structure, and the more you find out about that the further you can go. Things aren't boundless. There are limits. But then you get to know them so intimately and so well that you can cause them to do things that you couldn't without knowing them. I think it's true of any art form. Horsemanship's the same way. You got to know the horse inside and out.

MG: You have to know the limits of that horse.

SS: Absolutely. You don't just jump on one, spur him and whip him and hope for the best.

MG: But looking back at your first plays, you might say, you just jumped on those plays.

SS: To a certain extent, I did, but I quickly found the limitations. I quickly found you can't write 15-page monologues and throw them at the actor and expect him to just come up with it.

MG: And you want the audience to listen.

SS: You want some kind of attention to be exchanged.

MG: You never taught playwriting?

SS: Not actually. I've had some workshop situations where we discussed stuff and question and answer, but I've never tried to critique plays or teach it. I don't really know if you can teach it. I think you can have open discussions about it, and you can certainly have workshops in which you try things with actors, which I think is the most practical way to do it, where a writer tries to write for an actor and then gets into a dialogue with the actor.

MG: "Life is what's happening to you while you're making plans for something else." You saw that sign somewhere.

SS: I saw that sign in exactly that context, dangling over a bunch of fried chicken wings in some little cafe. I wrote the story and then months later I heard that it's a quote from one of the Beatles. I don't know if that's true. Something smart that John Lennon said?

MG: Is it true? Life is what's happening to you while you're making plans for something else?

SS: I think it's very true to a large extent. We tend to become engaged in the future, particularly when you're young. You're always thinking about what's ahead and the real meat and potatoes of life is passing by. I think that's true. One of those homegrown things. The present doesn't count. Only the future, and the past.

MG: Last time we talked you said, "40 was tough. 50 you're already cruisin'. You better be. There ain't no way to stop it." You're turning 59 this year, approaching 60. Are you still cruisin'?

SS: [*Laughs*] In overdrive. It's true, age catches you completely unexpectedly. Nobody can tell you what it's going to be like, when it starts catching up with you. Very strange, what happens with the body. Not as easy to swing up on a horse anymore. I work with a guy who is 73 years old. Bob McCutcheon. Extraordinary guy. Both of his knees replaced. I think a hip, and he still manages to get himself on horses from the ground without any help. And he rides every single day. He rides about 10 colts a day.

MG: You have no trouble getting on a horse?

SS: Not so much. It certainly isn't as easy as it used to be.

MG: In one story, you say, "Unfair question: what were you very very unhappy about?" What were you very very unhappy about?

SS: [*Laugh*] That's an unfair question. I was going through a period of extreme isolation, let's put it that way, and heavy drinking.

MG: And you've ended both?

SS: Well, yeah. You go through sessions, unforeseeable.

MG: You seem in a good mood.

SS: I'm okay. For now [*laugh*]. Not complaining.

MG: In "Stout of Heart," the father is buried in catalogs and says about his wife, "She wants to know where I've gone away to. . . . What territory of the mind!" Isolation and loneliness.

SS: I think there's an obsessive . . . how would you call it? There's a way in which particularly men—not women so much—I think men tend to obsess in their heads about certain things and go off and become very isolated, very estranged to the people who are very close to them. I think that's a male characteristic more than a female. I don't know why. It seems to me it's male. I could be wrong.

MG: Early on you were writing about sons and fathers, and you were the son. Now you're writing pieces in which you're the father.

SS: Yeah. Well, that's the way it happens. The son becomes the father.

MG: Does that change your perspective—having children?

SS: Oh, absolutely. I think you become more aware of the whole cyclical evolution of it, the way everything spills over into the other, the way we're all interconnected. And you certainly become more aware of what kind of influence you're having on your child. How subtle those influences are and how you can't help but influence your child through everything you do. Whether you're aware of it or not, you're influencing your kid.

MG: In the story "Coalinga ½ Way," the father says he would never abandon his son.

SS: And yet he does. It's very interesting how you can have certain mental scruples or ethics, you can make statements to yourself and then do the exact opposite. The opposite occurs against one's better instincts. The force of life is so powerful that you can't resist. There's no way that you can go up against it. Although you would like to say you're this way, you find yourself being that way. Life knocks you around. We think we're heroes in life, but we're not.

MG: Or the children think the fathers are heroes. Are you thinking of something in your life when you say that?

SS: In every area of my life, I can say. You have an idea about the way you would like to approach something, and you find yourself maybe doing exactly the opposite, or being forced in another direction. Unforeseeable. And that's interesting, the contradiction, the way we're in conflict.

MG: Does being a father help you understand better the mysteries of your father?

SS: Sure. It gives you the possibility of approaching a different view. I wouldn't necessarily say I understand him better, particularly in terms of his isolation, how he was so isolated, unable to communicate what was happening to him.

MG: I know nothing about your mother. Was she an important influence on your life?

SS: Oh, a great influence. The opposite of him. [*And no further explanation*]

MG: You said that Peter Brook told you, "We all work with the soil that we're born into."

SS: He said some extraordinary things, things you don't forget. He was a tremendous influence on me in the physical aspect of theater, of understanding the physical presence of theater—the actors, the stage, the relationship of the audience. Him and Joe [Chaikin] also, and Grotowski to a certain extent, but Grotowski was far more complicated and more remote. I didn't have as much of a dialogue with him. But he was a tremendous influence in his rigor, Grotowski's extreme tactics, very rigorous. Extraordinary man. I remember working with some of his actors. I've never seen anything like it—spartan actors.

MG: Talk about "testing the limits of the instrument."

SS: That's what's amazing—why that occurred back there then, and it doesn't seem to be now. That raw, extreme testing. It doesn't seem to be around anymore.

MG: Albee looks back on the '50s as the great period in the American arts, with Abstract Expressionism, and composers experimenting with music, in theater with the first plays by Beckett, Genet and Ionesco. And into the '60s—the liveliest scene. Where has it gone?

SS: It doesn't feel to me—I'm not completely aware of all of it—but the intensity of it is different now. The feeling that it had to do with one's life, that your life was on the line in some kind of way doesn't seem to be part of the way things are going now. And yet the times we are living in may be more extreme than they were then—in terms of being in a very dire situation. There was Vietnam, always in the shadow of everything. But we may be entering a time now worse than that.

MG: Is it the artist's obligation to write about that?

SS: No, but I mean it's the artist's obligation to convert one's experience of the time that we're living into forms of expression that are related. That doesn't mean you have to go out and write about Iraq. But you are obliged to be somewhat honest about your experience of living in this time: Otherwise, what are you doing?

MG: Where were you when the World Trade Center was attacked?

SS: I was in Minnesota, which is even odder.

MG: Riding a horse?

SS: No, actually no. I wish I was riding. But everything about that day was so bizarre. The weather was extraordinarily beautiful, just gorgeous, one of those fall days, that midwestern sky. You remember things like that. In the middle of the morning—I never watch television in the middle of the morning—and there's the TV. It is a day you never forget. Just last night I walked down to Ground Zero. They've got it all lit with these huge stadium lights. That little chapel right across the street, the little St. Paul's Chapel, with the fence with all of the banners and everything around it. It's extraordinarily moving.

MG: Was that your first time down there?

SS: Yeah. That little chapel just standing there, unscathed, with all of the tokens hanging off the fence, and then these mammoth klieg lights, like baseball stadium lights on this hole. It is beyond belief, really beyond belief. Usually when you go looking for a landmark, you look for a thing. Here you're looking for the absence of something. This hole. But the little chapel there—I don't know when it was built, it's got to be the 1800s—old little brick chapel, facing directly, right across from the hole. Not a brick out of place. Wow!

MG: You're living in Minnesota now. That's where you started.

SS: I was born in Illinois. My family are all from Illinois.

MG: How is the Midwest different from the South?

SS: Oh! They're opposites. Everything is different. They're like two different countries. They're two different worlds. Climate-wise, the people. The North is frigid [*laugh*]—in every way.

MG: Do you have a studio where you write? Where do you work?

SS: I have a little cabin that I've done a lot of work out of, on my farm where I've got cattle and horses. A little tiny cabin that was originally an old German cabin, torn apart and built back up, made out of white oak, just one room. Kind of neat. It's got some floor heating, and I put a big fireplace in it. It took a while to chink it. You have to chink it completely inside and out, or that cold air just finds its way through. About seven years old now. It's nice—gets better as it goes along.

MG: When you're home, do you write every day?

SS: No. I wish I had that kind of discipline, but I don't. I've never been able to do that, unless I'm in the middle of working on, say, a play that has a momentum of its own, and carries me from day to day. I've tried that thing of sitting down and writing, regardless. It doesn't work. I work a lot from notebooks now, especially these short stories. I hadn't seen that being a method or an approach, but it's quite great the way it works. It frees you up from having to feel obliged to write a piece. You just fill notebooks and at the end of the year, you start going through the notebooks, and things progress from that.

MG: What do you put in the notebooks? Things that happened to you, or what you're thinking at the time?

SS: Both. Everything. But they can be small, concise, like images. Small.

MG: Some of those stories are a page and a half. One image.

SS: There's a writer named Peter Handke who also wrote plays, *Kaspar* and *Insulting the Audience* [also translated as *Offending the Audience*], *The Ride Across Lake Constance*. He wrote a kind of journal and in this journal there are sentences. It's like a 200-page book, but they're all brief sentences. A fantastic book. You can pick it up anywhere in the book and there's something extraordinary. It's called *The Weight of the World*.

MG: You're not going to publish your notebooks?

SS: No. No, no. But I do think they have value now. Mark Twain said write something and then set it aside like wine and let it season. I always thought that was bullshit, but there's some sense to it.

MG: *The Weight of the World* reminds me of your story "The Hero Is in the Kitchen": "Don't buckle under the weight of a heavy beat." Why did the *New Yorker* publish only one of your stories ["An Unfair Question"]?

SS: The *New Yorker* is very selective. I was glad they published that one. That was an odd story because it was one of those notebook type of stories that I had started and got about halfway, stopped, then wrote the middle pieces as another thing, and then finally the end occurred to me. It was weird the way it happened. It happened in three sections.

MG: It's like a play in three scenes.

SS: It kind of fit together like that. I didn't realize at the time how it was going to evolve, because when it started out it was just about just going up to get basil.

MG: Now it's about guns and other things.

SS: It evolved into that. That's one of the wonderful things about fiction. You don't see it coming. You don't anticipate, and then it presents itself.

MG: You hadn't planned that scene in the basement with the guns?

SS: No, not at all. One thing led to another. That's what I love about Raymond Carver's stuff, although Richard [Ford], who was a good friend of his, told me that he was a meticulously hard worker. He was always rewriting. He rewrote and rewrote and rewrote. The impression you get from his stories is this spontaneous opening of the material that's going in directions that you don't know as a reader and you also have the impression that the writer is intuitively following something. I love that about his stories.

MG: [*I take out a copy of his book and point to the photograph on the jacket of a man and a boy sitting at the end of a pier, clearly Sam and one of his sons.*] I like that picture.

SS: Jessica [Lange] took that. That's me and one of my sons in Mexico. This is an old Mayan lake, ancient Mayan lake. It's quite an extraordinary lake, goes for miles and miles and miles, and there's all kinds of wildlife. My oldest boy also has a book of stories coming out, published by Bloomsbury. Jesse Shepard. His book should be out in the spring. He was a wrangler for years and worked a lot with horses. A lot of the stories have to do with his experiences as a wrangler, some very funny stuff.

MG: Like father, like son?

SS: He's really good and he's worked very hard at it. I like his stuff. He's thrilled to death to have a book coming out. It's called *Jubilee King*.

MG: [*I give him a copy of* Conversations with Pinter.] One of these days I'm going to look back on our conversations and see if there's enough to put together into a book.

SS: Oh, sure, yeah. Well, it was great to see you again.

Rock-and-Roll Jesus with a Cowboy Mouth (Revisited)

Don Shewey / 2004

From *American Theatre* 21 (April 2004): 20–25, 82–84. Used with permission from Theatre Communications Group. Don Shewey is the author of *Sam Shepard* (1985) and *Caught in the Act: New York Actors Face to Face* (1986).

"So, what are we up to here?"

It doesn't take long for Sam Shepard to get to the heart of the matter—casually, directly, existentially. Here we are, in a restaurant in downtown St. Paul, Minn., on a cold and gray November afternoon. What we're up to is an interview, obviously, though the occasion is a little murkier than usual. A playwright of Shepard's stature ordinarily sits down for a major interview only when there's a new project to promote. As it happens, Shepard does have a new play, but he's not quite finished writing it, and it won't be produced until the fall of 2004 at the earliest. The occasion for our meeting has more to do with the history of this magazine. Shepard appeared on the cover of the very first issue, and going back to him seemed like a felicitous way to mark the 20th anniversary of *American Theatre*.

What is Shepard up to these days? Plenty. The guy who first made his mark on American drama in the late 1960s with a torrent of wildly poetic one-acts bursting with rock-and-roll energy turned 60 in November. He remains steadily productive as an artist, just not necessarily in the theater. Since New York's Signature Theatre Company devoted its entire 1996–97 season to his work (on the heels of Steppenwolf Theatre Company's acclaimed Broadway revival of his Pulitzer-winning *Buried Child*), Shepard has produced only two new plays—*Eyes for Consuela* (adapted from an Octavio Paz story) at Manhattan Theatre Club, and *The Late Henry Moss*, staged at San Francisco's Magic Theatre in 2000 and the following year at Signature in New York.

Still, revivals of older works keep him in the public eye. The Broadway production of *True West* in 2000 starred the hot young film actors Philip Seymour Hoffman and John C. Reilly, who alternated in the leading roles. That show was directed by Matthew Warchus, who made a film of Shepard's *Simpatico* (released in 2000 and now available on DVD) and who will most likely direct his new play, a farce entitled *The God of Hell*, next season on Broadway. In addition, the Roundabout Theatre Company is considering a revival of *Fool for Love*, possibly directed by Sam Mendes.

While his theatrical writing has slowed down substantially, Shepard has also published two well-received volumes of prose, *Cruising Paradise* (1996) and *Great Dream of Heaven* (2002), both of which shuffle chunks of short fiction together with memoirs, dialogue and journal entries. And, of course, he has taken what seemed at first to be a fluky sideline into movie acting and turned it into an active and lucrative career. In the last five years alone, Shepard has acted in 16 features. They have ranged from Ridley Scott's Oscar-nominated action flick *Black Hawk Down* to run-of-the-mill TV movies such as *Dash and Lilly*, in which he played Dashiell Hammett to Judy Davis's Lillian Hellman. For theater aficionados, by far the most interesting Shepard-related film available is *This So-Called Disaster*, a documentary directed by Michael Almereyda, whose modern-dress movie version of *Hamlet* featured Ethan Hawke in the title role and Shepard as the ghost of Hamlet's father. The documentary has its theatrical premiere this month at the Film Forum in New York City.

This So-Called Disaster focuses on the Magic Theatre production of *The Late Henry Moss*, which Shepard directed himself with an eye-popping cast of movie stars, including Nick Nolte, Sean Penn, Woody Harrelson and Cheech Marin, along with longtime Shepard stalwarts Sheila Tousey and, in the title role, James Gammon. Halfway through the rehearsal period, Shepard saw that something extraordinary was happening and invited Almereyda in to witness the process. The result fascinates on two fronts. It's an unusually intimate portrait of high-powered actors at work. With this bunch, the testosterone level is extremely high, and yet their struggles are both touching (see Sean Penn wrestle with his own perfectionistic standards) and amusing (see Shepard attempt to explain Brechtian theory to Woody Harrelson—and succeed!).

The film also reveals Shepard himself to an unprecedented degree. Among the series of family plays Shepard has written since *Curse of the Starving Class* (1976), *The Late Henry Moss* is probably the most autobiographical, dealing directly with the death of his father and their complicated, ambivalent relationship. In the film, Shepard speaks about his father with a detachment born of deep grief and mourning, and we see how the events of the artist's life get transformed into theatrical poetry, especially through glimpses of Gammon's and Nolte's fierce performances.

I myself have an unusually keen interest in the dance between Shepard's life and his work, since the first book I published was a biography of him. That's another big reason why we're sitting down for this interview: I wrote a book about this guy, yet I've never actually met him before. Shepard has always been exceptionally protective of his privacy—"I prefer a life that's not being eaten off of," he once said. When I began researching my biography in 1984 (the book was published the following year, and a revised edition came out in 1997), publicity was the last thing he needed or wanted. He was right in the middle of leaving his wife O-Lan and their son Jesse to move in with Jessica Lange, and my attempts to contact him were met with a self-explanatory silence. After the book came out, we had a couple of close encounters—I saw him once in Central Park, looking grim and unapproachable, and at a press preview of *True West* on Broadway he passed by near enough for me to see that, like most actors his age, he dyes his hair—but neither seemed like the most auspicious occasion to introduce myself.

When I wrote to him proposing a 20th-anniversary *American Theatre* interview, he responded favorably, and we agreed to meet in Minnesota, where he and Lange live with their high-school-aged children. Shepard sounded friendly on the phone. He mentioned that his daughter had a concert coming up (she plays cello with the school orchestra) and that he'd recently taken his son fishing in Montana. As we sit down together, he says he's looking forward to moving back to Kentucky when his kids finish school; he prefers a warmer climate, where he has more room to raise horses, which is clearly his passion. At the moment he's only got five horses, but on his ranch he raises 300 head of cattle. He and Lange also bought some land in Mexico six years ago, and since they started spending time there Shepard has bitten the bullet and gotten over his famous aversion to flying, thanks to the miracle of Xanax.

Since I'd made it clear that I wasn't doing a *People*-magazine profile and that our interview would range over his body of work, I'm surprised and intrigued to know that personal details were not 100-percent off-limits. I soon discover, though, that interviewing Shepard is a little like walking a maze—what seems like an open channel can abruptly turn into a dead end. I've come prepared with pages of questions, many of which represent my interest in venturing below the naturalistic/autobiographical surface of Shepard's plays into the theatrical, poetic and spiritual layers that coexist in his work. I find that certain inquiries go nowhere—sometimes out of lack of interest (he doesn't think about his work theoretically or intellectually at all), sometimes out of ignorance (culturally he's admittedly out of the loop—he'd never heard of Suzan-Lori Parks, for example, and political theater for him means *Waiting for Lefty*), sometimes out of reticence (shielding his family but also his instinctive, emotional life, from which he prefers to draw without analyzing). Often I wish I was writing for an equestrian journal, because whenever we touch on the subject of horses his demeanor and his vocabulary become noticeably more energized.

Two things about Shepard I wouldn't have known without meeting him: he loves to laugh, and he has a whole arsenal of different ones (a chuckle, a giggle, a percussive *heh-heh-heh*) in different flavors (nervous, self-deprecating, jovial, male-bonding). And just as his plays are full of characters whose identities slip and slide around, he doesn't seem attached to any definitive self-image. Whatever energy he spends building up the persona of "cowboy" or "movie star," he spends just as much sidling away from it. He's a living example of the attitude espoused by Wyndham Lewis in his essay "The Code of the Herdsmen": "Cherish and develop side by side your six most constant indications of different personalities. You will acquire the potentiality of six men. A variety of clothes, hats especially, are of help in this wider dramatization of yourself. Never fall into the vulgarity of being or assuming yourself to be one ego."

The relationship between journalist and subject is a tricky one; that between biographer and living legend is even more so. Whether out of shyness or cowardice, I skip over the opportunity to acknowledge aloud that I'd written a book about him, and he doesn't bring it up, so the fact sort of slithers around our feet under the table like some harmless but slightly creepy snake.

DON SHEWEY: A lot of playwrights live and breathe theater, and you obviously don't. [*Giggles*] What keeps you writing plays?

SAM SHEPARD: I love the form. You have the actor, dialogue, lights, audience, sets. I can't think of another art form that combines so many elements and has so many possibilities. I've always had an affinity for it. I don't know why. It's like when a musician picks up a saxophone, he doesn't even look at a guitar or fiddle, it's all sax.

DS: You used to say you hate theater and you never go. What is the theater you write for if not theater that you go to see?

SS: It's a little brash to say I hate theater. I don't make a regular habit of going to the theater. There are some pieces of theater that are fantastic. Recently we went to the Guthrie [Theater of Minneapolis] and saw the Globe's all-male production of *Twelfth Night*. It was absolutely extraordinary. Every once in a while you come across things like that that wake you up. *The Beauty Queen of Leenane* . . . I loved that play! It's one of the few plays I went back and saw two or three times.

DS: Have you seen any other plays of Martin McDonagh?

SS: I haven't, actually. I've read some of them. I think he's very talented.

DS: Are there other writers you follow on a regular basis?

SS: Not playwrights, no. There are definitely other fiction writers I'm very interested in, such as Peter Handke. For a long time I've read just about everything of his. Another one is [Semezdin] Mehmedinović, he's Serbian. He accomplished the kind of book I've always tried to do and haven't totally succeeded at, which is a combination of poetry, prose, short stories, diary, all thrown into one thing. I love that form. He actually managed to do it with *Sarajevo Blues*. During that horrible conflict, he chose to stay there in the city. He had a wife and kids and decided to stick it out. It's an amazing account of a writer under fire.

DS: Are there writers or theater artists you've heard about that you're curious about, whether you've seen them or not?

SS: I'm sure there are, but I don't stay in the loop that much. I'm pretty much in the country.

DS: I wonder what people in the horse world or the movie world think about your theater life.

SS: They find it curious. I kind of apprentice with some of these older guys in horse things. One guy in particular I hang out with is 75 years old, Bob McCutcheon. He's very well known in the cutting-horse world. I travel with him a lot, going to horse shows. We're barrelin' down the road 80 miles an hour, talkin' about movies, and out of the blue he says, "Sam, whur is Hollywood anyway?" [*laughs*]. I just about fell on the floor. He didn't have a clue. Those are the kind of people I really enjoy being around [*laughs*].

DS: Do you have a sense of your place in the American theater?

SS: I don't, really. Every once in a while it's startling to come across other writers who have looked at my stuff and said that it inspired them to do their thing. If anything, I'd like to think that my work might inspire people not to imitate me but to find their own approach and go from there.

DS: When you think about your plays, do you break them down into categories or periods, either chronologically or thematically or geographically?

SS: [*Shakes his head*] I can't . . . it doesn't do me any good. I'm really not attached to them. I have been very fond of certain productions, like the one Matthew Warchus did of *True West* in New York. One of the beauties of the play is that it's like a piece of music. It can be played so many different ways. It was played by those guys in a way it had never been played.

DS: You liked that they switched roles?

SS: Not only that, but they actually conjured up their own characters in each case. You would never believe that these guys could reverse roles from one night to the next. What they came up with! It was just astounding. The first Steppenwolf production was interesting, but Malkovich was so overwhelming that Gary Sinise kinda got the floor wiped with him. You never saw the other side of the play. In Matthew's production they were two entities.

DS: I think other writers connect to either the early one-acts for their wild poetry, or the rock-and-roll energy of plays like *The Tooth of Crime*, and then there are the family plays. Are those categories you relate to?

SS: I didn't set out to write them like that. I suppose you can divide them like that. But if you go back and look at an early play like *The Rock Garden*, you can see the seeds of *Curse of the Starving Class*. I just went to a show the other day of Jasper Johns, not a retrospective but stuff from the '80s to the present. It's so radically different from his early stuff. But the way he repeats thematic stuff, repeating and repeating and duplicating and going over and running these things, is very much the way it feels to me a lot of times.

DS: He's a perfect example of someone who's stuck with certain images and worked all the variations you can on it. I'm curious how that is for you. You have this iconography of images that show up again and again, starting with the old man in the rocking chair in *Rock Garden* that shows up in these other plays. *The Late Henry Moss* is an evolutionary product of eight or nine of your plays, so halfway into the first act, you've got all these recurring or recycled images set up.

SS: A lot of people knocked it because it was interpreted to be a rehash of *True West*, which it wasn't. It was just that there were brothers again. There's no law against bringing brothers into the plays several times [*chuckles*]. I like this predicament, one brother sitting with the corpse, and the other one coming from a long distance and meeting around the death of the father. I thought it was an important predicament.

DS: What do you mean when you say it's an important predicament?

SS: There are predicaments and there are predicaments. There's *King Lear*, and there's Mickey Mouse and Donald Duck. You know what I mean? There's predicaments that resonate and there are predicaments that don't mean anything. They're not even predicaments, they're just excuses to write a play [*chuckles*].

DS: Your plays excite me most when they go from something naturalistic to something poetic. One version of that is this notion of mutually exclusive realities that exist on stage at the same time. The idea of someone being alive and dead at the same time. Which is in *Henry Moss* and in some other plays.

SS: The essence of that for me has always been this acknowledgment, which Brecht and Joe Chaikin introduced me to, of the actor being the actor first and the character second. It's not about dissolving into the character, which we do in movies, where it's no longer Clint Eastwood, it's the Pale Rider. In theater, the most interesting thing is to sustain the actor, not get rid of them. Keep the actor moving in and out of character, or being able to separate the two. This is one of the most interesting things in theater.

DS: Because it's so mysterious.

SS: Because it's so true to the performance aspect of theater, and we can't get away from that.

DS: It shows up in a lot of your plays. In the last image of *Buried Child*, there's a sense that Vince and the dead baby that Tilden brings in from the garden are the same character.

SS: Mmm-hmm.

DS: There's this overlapping reality in a spooky, metaphysical way. I'm curious to know how you explain that to yourself.

SS: I'm not interested in the explanation. I'm interested in the provocation. Explanations are a dime a dozen.

DS: *Suicide in B-Flat* is another example where there are these two mutually exclusive realms existing on stage at the same time, in different dimensions.

SS: Yeah. I'm not sure that play ever really succeeded. I was so absorbed in trying to find a parallel to jazz that I think I got lost in that and forgot about the craftsmanship of the play. I was very interested at the time in jazz musicians like Thelonious Monk or Mingus. There's something about them that's . . . "holy man" isn't the right word, but they have a spiritual charisma. In the mid-'60s there were musicians who carried a certain kind of wisdom and power with them—like a shaman. When they played, you had the feeling that they were enacting something far beyond jazz music. It was particularly true of the new wave of black musicians.

DS: Did you ever see Monk play in person?

SS: Yeah, I worked at the Village Gate and he played there quite a bit. He'd get up and dance around the piano in his top hat. He was one of the first real artists I ever saw. When you saw him you knew you were in the company of something from another world.

DS: When you re-use an image in that Jasper Johns way, is it almost like you've let go of previous versions of it, as if you haven't used it before?

SS: No. It's more like this thing that keeps coming back to haunt you.

DS: I'm thinking of simple images like the bathtub.

SS: I love the bathtub. There's something religious about the bathtub.

DS: Really?

SS: Yeah, it's like cleansing, and there's something about death in it. It's like a casket. It's like birth and like death. Certain objects have that power to me. A refrigerator on stage is a very powerful image [*laughs*].

DS: Those are almost icons in your plays.

SS: The kitchen has always been my favorite room in the house. The kitchen is where serious conversations happen, where genuine gathering together with family happens, where devastating things happen. Eating.

DS: So what's the refrigerator?

SS: I just love finding an object that's so domestic, so common in life, in an uncommon situation, on stage, as a character. It's another thing altogether.

DS: What is it on stage?

SS: Well, in the case of *Curse of the Starving Class*, it's this place where dreams and hopes were contained. Every time the thing's opened, there's some hoping, some hopeless hoping that goes on. Every time the light comes on, the yearning. We know it's empty. Why keep opening the door? Nobody's put anything in there! [*laughs*].

DS: Then there's a refrigerator in *Henry Moss* that only has jalapeño peppers in it.

SS: Right. Yeah. These things bring us back to—for lack of a better word—reality. My dad's place had nothing but a rocking chair and a refrigerator in it, and the refrigerator was full of jalapeño peppers or, when he had some money, booze, and that was it. It was not the place for food.

DS: I wonder if you ever find yourself writing a play and saying, Damn, there I go again, another play about two guys exchanging or merging identities?

SS: No, I don't care. As long as I have the feeling that I'm investigating something for real, I don't really give a shit how it comes off [*chuckles*].

DS: So *Henry Moss* has to do with death and having the corpse on stage, which doesn't have anything to do with *True West*. *Simpatico* is somewhere in between.

SS: Yeah. Yeah [*pause*]. Yeah [*chuckles*].

DS: But it doesn't feel like a repetition of *True West*?

SS: [*Cagey*] Well, do they feel like the same play to you?

DS: In some ways they do. Two guys who are in very different places swap identities. Underneath the surface *Simpatico* seems to be groping toward something about friendship between two men.

SS: Yeah. I'm very interested in that. I don't know what to say about it, exactly, but a real friendship feels easier between two men. And that friendship covers a huge amount of ground. The one between men and women can, too, but not without a sense of conflict.

DS: There's another recurring image that shows up in *Simpatico*—all these guys lying on the floor paralyzed and can't get up. Is there a meaning beyond the narrative level to that paralysis?

SS: No. I'm interested in characters who have a certain profound sense of helplessness. I think it's a lot closer to the truth than the illusion that people are on top of things, which is the impression you get every day from television, that we're all on top of it, we're exquisite performers in our life. Get the SUV and we're goin' to town. The whole nation's on a winning streak. Which couldn't be further from the truth. We're on the biggest losing streak we've ever had. How many people a month come home from Iraq with limbs missing? Yet we're supposed to be victorious in this thing. It's a fucking nightmare. Every day it's brainwashing, that this is a heroic thing we're involved in. It's unbelievable bullshit.

DS: So this is some of the stuff that you're talking about in these plays.

SS: Well, yeah. I've always found plays that are overtly political to be extremely boring. *Waiting for Lefty*. Incredibly boring. And yet at the same time, you have to deal with what's going on in the world. It's difficult now to find material that you feel is pertinent to a whole bunch of people. I'm not quite sure who goes to the theater anymore.

DS: In the '60s you were living in New York in the middle of a hotbed of theater that interested you. Then when you were in London you were exposed to a big theater scene there. In California you were part of the Bay Area/Magic Theatre community. Now you're . . .

SS: In Minnesota [*laughs disparagingly*].

DS: So do you have a sense of community?

SS: Not beyond family, no. A little bit with the horse thing, but there's not much of one.

DS: Do you miss being attached to an artistic community?

SS: You know, I never did really feel attached. There were certain people like Joe Chaikin that I was attached to, but I didn't feel like I was a member of the Open Theater. At the Magic Theatre, there were certain actors I enjoyed working with. But I didn't feel like there was that much of a community.

DS: I'm surprised to hear you say that, because I thought a lot of the work you did in California came from an ongoing connection. But you didn't feel any of that?

SS: No. 'Cause I've never felt like a member of anything [*laughs*].

DS: For the Signature season, you produced a new version of *The Tooth of Crime*, subtitled *(Second Dance)*. How was it for you to go back and re-write that play?

SS: I was very excited about it, because I was never satisfied at all with the second act. I tried to get away from the sentimentality and the self-pity of the hero. The demonic aspect of the older character became more interesting to me than the failing hero.

DS: You mean like Faust and Mephistopheles?

SS: Exactly. I felt like there was something inherent in that language I hadn't taken far enough. So I tried to carry it further. I didn't totally succeed. But it was much better than the first version; it was more venomous. One of the inspirations for *Tooth of Crime (Second Dance)* was working with my old friend T-Bone Burnett, who's now become quite famous for his persistence in finding essential music. [*Note: Burnett's soundtrack for Joel and Ethan Coen's film* O Brother, Where Art Thou? *sparked a revival of interest in Appalachian music.*] He wrote some amazing music for the show. Unfortunately, the production got lost in a whole lot of snarls and animosity between producers. I don't know exactly what happened to it. I had a good friend of mine direct it, Bill Hart. Maybe it's better if the director isn't a friend [*laughs*]. Maybe the play's snakebit.

DS: What does that mean?

SS: Bad luck (*heh heh heh heh*). T-Bone called me a month or so ago and said the Coen brothers have an interest in making a movie of it. I've always thought *Tooth of Crime* won't be finished until the right kind of actors get hold of it. I've always thought Tim Roth would be the ultimate Crow. He would push it to the edge.

DS: Who would be an ideal Hoss for you?

SS: I dunno. Malkovich? Can you imagine Malkovich and Tim Roth? [*laughs*].

DS: Speaking of how actors can finish roles, I want to ask you about the San Francisco production of *Henry Moss* and that once-in-a-lifetime cast.

SS: The odd thing was, having that many extraordinary actors on stage, this sort of social phenomenon happened. It became this social event in San Francisco that had nothing whatsoever to do with the play.

DS: Did you realize later you were a little naïve about what would happen if you got those guys together in one place?

SS: Totally naïve! It never even crossed my mind that this would be a circus for San Francisco socialites. They were very generous, they attended and dressed up and there were cocktail parties and all. But nobody saw the play. They saw Nick, they saw Sean, they saw Woody, they saw Cheech.

DS: Do you think it harmed the life of the play, that theaters thought, "Oh, we can't do that play unless we have superstars"?

SS: I guess it did. It was a kind of lesson for me. Maybe I shouldn't have directed it. I don't know if it would have been different.

DS: Your prose writing has developed in a way that's parallel to your plays. Your later fiction pieces have been more honed, more refined, just as your plays have gotten more attentive to form and structure. Is that right?

SS: Absolutely. It sounds ridiculous, but I'm self-taught. I learn everything by doing it. I wasn't born knowing how to write a play. You do it, and hopefully you keep evolving. One really great thing that happened was that I discovered Chekhov's short stories. I'm embarrassed to say I didn't really start reading them 'til about five or six years ago. I'd always kind of dismissed Chekhov and didn't really know why. When I came upon the stories, and started really reading and studying them, I couldn't believe it. I read every single one.

DS: What did you get out of them?

SS: How as a craftsman he could apply himself with this dogged attention to detail and come up with these amazing things.

DS: You have a new play. How many acts?

SS: One act in three scenes, about an hour and a half. So it's like a miniature three-act play.

DS: How many people?

SS: Four characters: three men, one woman. I've just finished the second draft. It's still not where it's supposed to be. I've got the tail end of it, but I'm having trouble with the way I get to the ending. It's a lot better than the first draft.

DS: What will you do with it when you're done?

SS: Matthew Warchus is my favorite director of the moment, and he'll probably be able to do it in the fall of 2004. In New York—I don't want to do the provinces anymore (*heh heh*).

DS: How much do your plays change from draft to draft?

SS: For each draft, I sit down and type through the whole thing, and as I retype I rewrite. It really works, because it causes you to go through it moment by moment like an actor. It's strange the way it happens. Little scenes open up. You discover new dialogue. You go off on little tangents and come back. I much prefer to do that than put Band-Aids on it or cut it open. I've never had good luck with that.

DS: Okay, last question: What do you know about playwriting now that you wish you'd known when you were starting out?

SS: Like I said, I'm a slow learner. It's taken all of this time to get to where I feel like I can now say I know how to write a play. It's such a strange, strange form. Because it's so dependent on these fragile ingredients. Not the least of which is this thing of the predicament. If you don't have this essential predicament, if it doesn't have real weight, real value, you can write 24 hours a day and it won't amount to anything.

DS: I love the word you use, predicament. It's very American.

SS: Another way of saying it is "stakes." What are the real stakes involved? You can play penny poker or play for the ranch.

DS: What are the stakes in the new play?

SS: They're pretty high. They're pretty damn high. I'm hoping that they'll have repercussions. This is the best play I've written since, maybe . . . uh, the best play I've written in a long time.

DS: Come on, go out on a limb—since when?

SS: *True West.* I knew when I wrote *True West* it was going to work.

On Shepard and Film

When Sam Shepard appeared as an early 20th-century Texas farmer in his first Hollywood feature, Terrence Malick's 1978 *Days of Heaven*, the movie world immediately took notice of him as an actor. Pauline Kael, the doyenne of film critics, wrote in the *New Yorker*, "Though the irregularly handsome, slightly snaggletoothed Shepard has almost no lines, he makes a strong impression; he seems authentically an American of an earlier era." Yet even when he won an Academy Award nomination for his performance as test pilot Chuck Yeager in Philip Kaufman's 1983 *The Right Stuff*, there was still the sense that Shepard the actor was moonlighting from his "real" job as a prolific, Pulitzer-blessed playwright. Who knew that 20 years later Shepard would be steadily employed as an actor, making one or two films almost every year? He can currently be seen in *Blind Horizon*, a thriller starring Val Kilmer and Neve Campbell. He just returned from Australia where he worked on a film called *Stealth*, directed by Rob Cohen, maker of big-box-office B-movies like *The Fast and the Furious*. And he will shortly begin work on a low-budget independent film called *The King*.

Shepard has written and directed two movies of his own (*Far North* and *Silent Tongue*), but they didn't create enough of a stir to ensure his future as a filmmaker. Although the search for financing has caused a series of delays, he and German director Wim Wenders (they collaborated on 1984's *Paris, Texas*) are ready to go with a new film called *Don't Come Knocking*, which Shepard wrote and is supposed to star in with Jessica Lange.

Appearing in films alongside a multitude of big names has given Shepard an opportunity to develop his own perspective on the differences between acting in film and acting on stage. *This So-Called Disaster*, Michael Almereyda's documentary film about the San Francisco production of *The Late Henry Moss*, lets us be the proverbial fly on the wall as Shepard works day-by-day directing actors like Sean Penn, Nick Nolte and Woody Harrelson in what is, for them, a rare stage appearance. I asked him about that.

DS: I'm guessing that the real experience for you was being in the rehearsal room with those guys.

SS: Yeah. Which is why I had the impulse to make a documentary. I knew this was sort of a chance of a lifetime, with this many great actors. The thing is that, as is true of any production, you don't see the work the actor does. You don't see the sweat, the real grit, the energy that goes into making the character. These guys were absolutely dedicated. For movie stars, this was something that a lot of them hadn't really encountered. The daily grind of showing up and the obligation to it. They were incredibly loyal.

With Sean and Nick, I could palpably feel that these guys had their ears up. They felt like they were being paid attention to as actors, and not just: What are you gonna look like with the furniture? How do you fit into the plot? Are you gonna speak loud or speak soft or be brutal here? You know what I mean? One thing about a play is that it requires teamwork. And that's not true of film. The grips, the lighting guy, all those guys have to work as a team. The actors don't. They can go solo the whole way. Half the time they're there by themselves anyway. Not to say there's not some craft in that. There's some brilliant film acting. But it's very different from going to the theater every day and working together in this team situation.

DS: Sean Penn is a really interesting actor, and he's done some stage acting. How was it to watch him work?

SS: I felt like Sean wanted to go much, much further than he allowed himself to go. Out of all the actors, I felt like he was the most vulnerable. He's a very sensitive, smart actor but scared a little bit by the possibility of laying it out there with the other actors. Nick—not a fear in the world. He's gonna crash and burn the whole way. He'll jump over the cliff for you. Sean is a lot more tentative, but a lot of yearning. I regret now that we didn't experiment more.

See, a film actor doesn't even get that opportunity to mess around. You come the day of work, you've got your lines, you put the costume on, you go to work and you do it. Here we were, day after day after day, in the lap of this luxury, being able to experiment, go places, move here, move there, for weeks.

DS: Tell me about being in *Hamlet* yourself.

SS: I loved doing that. The weird thing is, when I first ran away from home and decided I would go audition for this one-night-stand company called the Bishop's Company, they gave me a piece of Shakespeare. I don't even remember what play it was. I was so nervous, and I read the whole page. Only later I realized that I'd read Shakespeare and then the footnotes, scrambling it all together. The next day they hired me! Anyway, that was my first experience with Shakespeare. I thought never in a million years am I ever going to do Shakespeare. Then Michael, bless his heart, asked me to do this thing. I spent, I guess, a month and a half memorizing that thing. I was in Montana at the time, driving around in the truck, doing the lines. I thought, "This is the most spectacular writing I've come across in my life." By the time we went to film it, the language had found its way into me somehow.

DS: In a way that other movies hadn't.

SS: Never. I'm always rewriting my shit in films. I look at it and say, "I can't say this."

Sam Shepard's Master Class in Playwriting

Brian Bartels / 2006

From *The Missouri Review* 30 (Spring 2007): 72–88. Reprinted with the permission of Brian Bartels.

Cherry Lane Theatre, in Manhattan's West Village, is not located on Cherry Lane at all, but on Commerce Lane (nowhere near the Financial District in Lower Manhattan). It's a venerable theater company that has been around for years, not very big, nowhere near Broadway, tucked in a corner in one of the most beautiful neighborhoods in New York: an urban paradise. It would seem wrong if anything other than a theater company were in this location. After everything is gone, this place feels like it will still be here, waiting for an audience.

Monday, November 6, 2006, 7:46 p.m. Excitement hovers. The crowd is your standard theater audience: median age late forties, and I am, as always, one of the youngest people in the room. Women dominate the group: sweet, good-natured ladies who all seemed to know one another.

People meander inside Cherry Lane's second-stage space, which seats about fifty or sixty; every seat is taken. Some people are dressed like characters in one of Sam Shepard's plays. The event is being videotaped: a surprise, given Shepard's record of determined privacy. He doesn't do press junkets or interviews for the films he acts in. This is written into his contracts. Nor does he really like flying all that much. He has, however, in recent years, opened up somewhat, offering glimpses into his artistic and personal life such as he's generally shied away from. Perhaps that is why the Master Class you are about to read is a one-night-only window of opportunity; the experience is another taste of what continues to simmer on the stove before the lid goes back on and we keep cooking.

The stage is set. Orange stage lights illuminate the foreground, with a simple black chair and a small table nearby holding a bottle of water. A backdrop of white fabric outlines leafless branches. From a distance, the white fabric looks like embroidered music notes—fitting for a musician turned member of the American Academy of Arts and Letters.

Moments later Shepard is introduced, taking a purposeful stride toward the stage. This is the man responsible for *Chicago*, *Tooth of Crime*, *Geography of a Horse Dreamer*, *True West*, *Curse of the Starving Class*, *Simpatico*, *A Lie of the Mind*, the Pulitzer Prize–winning *Buried Child*, *The Late Henry Moss*, *The God of Hell*, and *Kicking a Dead Horse*. He drafted a book while traveling with Bob Dylan's 1975 Rolling Thunder tour, as well as cowriting "Brownsville Girl," one of Dylan's most treasured songs. His fiction includes *Motel Chronicles*, *Hawk Moon*, *Cruising Paradise*, and *Great Dream of Heaven*, as well as a new collection to be published in 2008. When he's not writing, he finds opportunities to act on stage and in feature films.

When he sits down on Cherry Lane's minimally decorated stage, his first goal as director of this one-night production is lighting. "Can we find a way to get these lights down here?" he says, his hand over his eyes as he squints into the crowd. "I could be getting a sunburn up here and not notice it until it's too late."

The Master Class will consist of a question-and-answer session, and the action gets going, as in any of Shepard's forty-five plays. A man in his mid-forties with endless notes is the first one called upon, and we dive into substance:

CROWD MEMBER: You're an alum of the Cherry Lane, and you were here in . . . ? Way back in 1968?

SHEPARD: Oh, way before then. I did a one-act here in 1964 or '65 that was called *Up to Thursday*, and then, of course, later came *True West*.

CROWD MEMBER: As an actor, what do you expect from your writers, and as a writer what do you expect from your actors?

SHEPARD: I don't compartmentalize things like that. I'm not interested in borders so much as I like putting things together. I don't ever look at things so black and white like that.

CROWD MEMBER: You had a play called *Angel City*, and you gave instructions to the director of that play. You said to anyone who directs this play—and one of the characters turns into a lizard—that what you'd rather have are characters that are fractured whole, with bits and pieces of the characterizations flying off the central theme of the play.

SHEPARD: I really think that we are not just one person. We are a multiplicity of beings, if you want to call it that. Not to get too philosophical about it, but it's very easy for me to see character in the shifting, myriad, ever-changing tableau rather than one part. We're used to looking at character in a traditional sense, of being something we can define by behavior or background. You know what I'm saying?

But it may not be like that; it may be much more interesting. For me, anyway. It may not be so interesting to lock down the character with specifics. What I'm interested in is this shifting of the character, you know, not the exactness of definition.

CROWD MEMBER: Have you been generally happy as a director, or as a playwright watching a director?

SHEPARD: No.

CROWD MEMBER: Are there any Brechtian influences in your work?

SHEPARD: Brecht influences everything. Absolutely. There's a play he wrote called *In the Jungle of Cities*, in which he pits a librarian against a gangster. An extraordinary play. A simple man, leading a simple life, and this demonic character comes in and says, "I am going to kill you," to this humble librarian. "Maybe not today, maybe not tomorrow, but someday, I will." And that's very upsetting, and that play influenced the writing of *Tooth of Crime*. This thing of total surprise. I think writing is like that. It's a total surprise. There's no way you can predict it. No way. As much as you think you know, and as old as we get, it can continually surprise.

CROWD MEMBER: I'm curious about why you rewrote *Tooth of Crime* so many years later.

SHEPARD: I felt the play was outdated, and I don't think a piece of writing should be forged in iron, and necessarily, and the great thing about a play is that it moves and shifts, from production to production, and we see that shift. I mean, I've never written a play that I couldn't rewrite.

CROWD MEMBER: In interviews from the '80s you said that a play isn't really thought up; rather, it's something that you catch that sort of exists. How does that work with craft?

SHEPARD: Interesting question. Songwriters that I admire the most—Willie Nelson and Dylan—both feel that way about songwriting. The song exists; it's there, and being out there you need to get ahold of it somehow. Willie wrote "On the Road Again" on the back of a napkin in about five minutes. Like the Beatles song "Blackbird," it's so simple that it could've been there the whole time. However, it doesn't mean that you don't have to struggle or practice craft. You don't know when it's going to land. Is that clear?

CROWD MEMBER: Is there too much craft in that process?

SHEPARD: I don't think you can have too much craft. Maybe you can't have enough. It's a funny balance between what we like to call inspiration and what we like to call work. And you can't do without either one. If you hang around and wait for something to hit you in the head, you're not going to write anything. You've got to work. You want to work *for* something. And these experiences, or accidents, can happen anytime. Through the back door. For instance, I've been working on these stories, fiction, for some time, journals and whatnot, and I'll be writing a while and take a look at something, and BOOM! there's a play that's developing while I'm working on short fiction, and I can't not write it in that moment. I'll think about all this time I've been spending working on this goddamn book, and then, what's justified?

CROWD MEMBER: Does that change the way you tell stories? Has our cultural evolution—the way technology continues to curb our attention spans—does that affect your cultural outlook?

SHEPARD: Well, culture itself is always gonna be poverty-stricken. We don't live in ancient Egypt, Mesopotamia or Greece. We live in a destroyed culture. There is no culture here. It's shreds of stuff. We're amongst shrapnel. So if you're looking for culture to support your attention, then you're out of luck. The question to ask is "What is attention? Do we even understand the first thing about what attention is?" I mean, they're these definitions that don't define anything. We don't understand what attention is because we've been hammered by nonattention. The thing to do is to try and discover what attention is, what is the substance of it. It's a tool that's also true of actors. We work with material that is constantly moving.

CROWD MEMBER: Sometimes you direct your own work. What motivates you to direct your own plays and work on your own material?

SHEPARD: What motivates it is not being able to find a director.

It's been a great thing in a way, because I've learned much more about production. As a director, you start to understand what it means to talk to actors, what it means to talk to a lighting designer, to work with space. You get to understand what theater's about, and it is about far more than what you as a writer think. For me, it's been a blessing not to have found the right director.

CROWD MEMBER: You've also been an actor. How does that correlate with the approach you take in working with a director?

SHEPARD: Are you talking about film or theater?

CROWD MEMBER: Film.

SHEPARD: Film is a different matter. Oddly enough, there are many film directors who don't understand what acting is even about. I'm telling you the truth. Very few understand, or even care. For the most part, acting in film means trying to stay above water. They are far more interested in other matters relating to the production, so as an actor you're expected to show up carrying the goods. In theater, you get six to eight weeks rehearsal time, whereas in film you show up ready to go. So the rehearsal time in theater is devoted to the actors, which it should be.

CROWD MEMBER: Do you think that will ever change?

SHEPARD: It'll never change. There's too much money in film. That's the attitude. You're talking about a machine that operates distinctly over money. There's no room to mess about with the actors. Film's . . . terrible.

CROWD MEMBER: A lot of your writing and directing is very musical.

SHEPARD: I am a musician. I'm not a studied musician. I've always found that music and writing are entangled.

CROWD MEMBER: How do you prepare for acting in film?

SHEPARD: It depends on the role, you know. But I'd rather talk about theater.

CROWD MEMBER: What do you consider your best play?

SHEPARD: I don't hang on to them like that. In the second week of the production, I've had it. I'm ready to move on to the next thing. Productions can be grueling. But *True West* a couple years ago, with Philip Seymour Hoffman and John C. Reilly, was an incredible production because they switched roles every third performance. And the reproduction of *Buried Child* that Steppenwolf did was a great thing to be part of. For the most part, I don't follow them like that and try to nurse them.

CROWD MEMBER: Could you tell us about the last days of Joe Chaikin? You had quite a moving experience with this longtime friend and collaborator.

SHEPARD: It was strange because I had experienced this earlier with a mother-in-law. He came out of unconsciousness, and you never think of language as being . . . he virtually lost the meaning of words, and it was so weird, because he was so eloquent. I would go out of my way to listen to him. We had exercises to get him out of this locked-down vocabulary, and as we were doing that, he had this idea of an angel—you know, Joe would have extraordinary ideas that came out of nowhere—and I couldn't tell if it was this mythological idea of a certain character, and we originally wrote it as a radio play, and then it became a piece in which we designed it so he could perform it himself. It was about an angel who crashes to Earth and doesn't know how he gets there, so everything is seen through that perspective, which is a shattered reality, and all of the language comes out of that experience. Sometimes the light goes out completely, and sometimes it comes back, and with Joe it went out completely. That piece was about trying to get him back.

CROWD MEMBER: How much does the environment in which you're writing affect you?

SHEPARD: I think the best writing, for me, happens on the move. When I'm riding in a train or a car. When you don't have a home. There's that feeling that when I'm traveling, I'm on fire, so I never figure out why this need to move all the time creates writing. It just goes.

CROWD MEMBER: Have you ever noticed any specific schools or traditions of acting that seem to get your work?

SHEPARD: The actors with the most chops are the ones who gather from all kinds of styles, not just the Method, not just Chinese theater, not just mimes. They have a taste of many different things and are open to many different things. They're fascinated by everything around them, and—

(A crowd member near the back takes a photograph.)

SHEPARD: Don't take any pictures, okay?

CROWD MEMBER: It's for the theater.

SHEPARD: Okay. Um, it's an interesting thing. Many actors who absorb in an internal way can't do the physical thing. And I always wonder why these things exclude each other. Peter Brook has experimented with this in the past. Actors should have a wide scope. They must have that, in order to bring something new to the theater.

CROWD MEMBER: I did a reading last week where I was praised for my dialogue, but got knocked down for my monologues. When monologues are lyrical and poetic and stand out . . . as someone so familiar with that element, do you ever feel that monologues that inhabit such poetic spins, like *Tooth of Crime* . . . is there a certain point where you need to cut it off or "dumb it down," so to speak?

SHEPARD: It's interesting. I'm writing a monologue now, and I just decided, within the last few days, to let it rip, let it go and not worry about whether it's lyrical or whatnot, and let it spin. And, on the other hand, I've done stuff where I've let it be very compound, very precise. I guess it depends on where you want to go with it. If you're gonna do this and it's gonna be on stage, why not let it go?

Though you look at somebody like Beckett, who is the master of conciseness. Look at *Krapp's Last Tape*. It's like acid rain, every word is. You couldn't replace a word in that piece. When he rolls, he rolls in a way in which he couldn't be more precise. But I don't think there are any rules. It's an interesting problem. And it's interesting for the actor, too. I've been guilty of writing way too much and then realizing, *Hell, an actor can't do this. He'll run out of gas. It doesn't make sense.*

CROWD MEMBER: Do you write every single day?

SHEPARD: I don't have a process. You have to take the plunge. It's easy to talk about the process, but it's a confrontation. You're confronting a blank page. It's like drawing. You stare at a blank canvas and it goes from itself. You can call it a process, but you're studying where this inspiration comes from. I don't even have a specific time I write.

CROWD MEMBER: Does your writing have a destination?

SHEPARD: Sometimes, but often I've found when you know where you're going, it deadens something. If I have some sort of a vague idea—or specific idea—you're already there, and you're not allowing yourself to travel to the end. It's like you're driving cross-country to Omaha, you know; if you're dreaming about Omaha the whole time, you're going to miss the trip. And it's not a bad idea to know where you're going, but you can't have that thing determine conclusions for you. What's in front of you is a big part of evolution. I'm not against having a destination, but that point can sometimes blind you from your trip.

CROWD MEMBER: Do you have . . . ?

SHEPARD: I have a hard time finishing anything I write.

CROWD MEMBER: Could you expand on the comment you had in a previous collection stating, "I don't want to be a playwright. I want to be a rock star."

SHEPARD: I think I was nineteen when I said that [*laughs*]. I discovered that I never really had a career. I'm just doing what I do. Back in the '60s, everyone wanted to be a rock star.

CROWD MEMBER: Do you ever think of audiences when you write?

SHEPARD: Yeah. Going back to Joe Chaikin, he developed the Open Theater, which was a very powerful, experimental practice in which many actors were challenged in their involvement. He'd do a Brecht play, a very simple, one-act Brecht play, like a clown piece; then he'd say, "Do it as though the Queen of England was watching your show," so it changed. "Now do it as though Muhammad Ali is sitting there. Now do it as though the fascists are about to take over." And it was amazing to see that and how it took over the actors. It led me in a lot of different directions in terms of thinking about the audience. Now, in monologue that's interesting because you have to consider the language and characters, whether you're addressing the audience or ignoring them.

CROWD MEMBER: There's a scene in *True West* in which the character Lee is remembering a scene from a film called *Lonely Are the Brave*, which is a Kirk Douglas film, and he talks about his horse dying. And no one else on stage has ever heard of that film. Can you talk a little bit about how that informs the audience?

SHEPARD: He's the kind of character who would like that movie. It's as simple as that. Why did he like that movie? Because he saw himself as that guy. He's the kind of character who would like that movie, regardless of whether or not anyone else liked it. It's part of his persona, his bravado, his deal. I can say that film made an impression on me. It was one of what they called "modern Westerns," and Walter Matthau played the sheriff. It was a nitty-gritty black-and-white film, almost symbolic, but at the same time the kind of film that never could be made now. It's a part of America that's gone now. It's a part of reality that's gone. Which is sad. We've lost touch with a real character.

CROWD MEMBER: Chemistry on stage. How do you develop it?

SHEPARD: I don't think in terms of chemistry. I know that term's used a lot, but I don't get it. What works well is excellent actors, and when you get those kind of actors together, great stuff happens. Actors who have the chops are like jazz musicians. You don't bring in people who can't play with the band. So if everybody plays well, you can make some pretty great sound. Great actors challenge each other, and before you know it, something happens. I don't get in their way. I think directors get in actors' way too much and prevent something worthwhile. There aren't enough directors who trust actors and who nurture. Somehow, in one way or another, I feel the English actors have a better way of creating that spark. They know how to allow characters to arrive.

CROWD MEMBER: How much do you prepare characters for your plays?

SHEPARD: I don't do a lot of character development. I think they . . . come. Pinter is interesting for that. Pinter, from what I understand, starts with almost nothing, and he writes these incredible characters. From a word, from something so tiny, and I've always admired that. It's like painting, again. You set up something and BAM! It becomes something else. Not to say that there aren't writers who consider tapestry. You'd be hard-pressed to say Shakespeare didn't think about his characters. But that's never been my fascination as much as the plunge of it all.

CROWD MEMBER: How did *True West* come about?

SHEPARD: My mother had gone to Alaska, and I was housesitting for her in California, and I was completely alone, with crickets, and I started to dream this thing up. It just started to come. I wrote it in its entirety in that house.

CROWD MEMBER: When you were beginning as a playwright, did you have another playwright you looked at for guidance?

SHEPARD: Beckett. He's the only guy. He could be the only playwright on earth. That's all we need is Beckett. I idolize Beckett from every aspect. He represented the epitome of the modern playwright. Nobody was doing that stuff. You gotta understand—I mean, you probably do understand—that nobody was doing what he started. He totally reinvented it. He absolutely stood it on its head. There had been nobody like him.

CROWD MEMBER: What do you think about the current state of American theater, and where do you think it's going in the future?

SHEPARD: I don't care. I'm only concerned with writing plays. I start worrying about the state of American theater, and I'm not going to get anything done. I'm sorry, but I'm not interested.

CROWD MEMBER: Did you love theater and decide you wanted to get into writing, or did you first love writing and see theater as a perfect conduit?

SHEPARD: Actually, I was interested in music and acting, but I didn't want to do the audition thing. I hated the audition thing. I wanted to be autonomous, and writing offered me a part of myself, to take a notebook and go to a coffee shop and write. I didn't have to depend on anyone, and I didn't need the money that a filmmaker needs. I love that immediacy, and also that thing about dialogue: it's a kind of way about doing music. That's a comparative form of literature for me. Written literature just stays in a book, and with theater you can go and do things in space and time. So playwriting, where you can build from nothing, you can incorporate just about anything into. Theater will swallow whatever you feed it, you know. You can put painting or sculpture into the acting; you can film or have film on stage; it's the whole thing. It has so much potential. And yet we think of it as this primitive form, but maybe that's why people keep coming back to it, for its rawness. And I also love that it's language spoken. It's language that hits a room.

CROWD MEMBER: Do you go to the theater?

SHEPARD: Sometimes. I'm not a big fan of stuff. Every once in a while, you get surprised. I know there's some good stuff out there.

CROWD MEMBER: Did you see *Pillowman*?

SHEPARD: Yeah.

CROWD MEMBER: What did you think?

SHEPARD: Well, he's a wonderful writer, Martin McDonagh. He is one of the guys. But that's not my favorite play of his. I love *The Beauty Queen of Leenane.*

CROWD MEMBER: I don't want to put a negative spin on it, but there's a lot of physical violence in your plays. Why do you include that?

SHEPARD: Because life is violent. Violence rules the world. So why not embrace it? We live in extremely violent times, in this world. I'm not all for heads rolling, but this is a violent country, is it not?

CROWD MEMBER: Are you drawn to country music or singer-song-writers in general, or something similar?

SHEPARD: I'm not particularly interested in forms. There's wonderful stuff coming out of country music. There's a whole thing going on right now with old-time music, and this thing with traditional instruments being played in new ways that pushes the envelope. When you're seeing someone playing the banjo like a saxophone, it's a push. I love the idea of breaking new barriers. It's gotta be like that. I don't think it's good to sit with one method and say that's the end-all.

CROWD MEMBER: You've mentioned painting repeatedly tonight. Is that another hobby?

SHEPARD: No. I draw a little bit, but painting is not something I do. I wish I could, but there's two things I can't do: painting and novels. Scratch those off the list.

CROWD MEMBER: Would you share with us what a beginning is for you?

SHEPARD: I think beginnings are by far the most exciting. That's where the fire starts. I have no problem with beginnings. But then you have to go on your nerve, and you have to follow your nerve, and that's why beginnings are also very important. It's just like music: you have to start with just the right note, or else the song can go bad fast. It's a question of paying attention to the potential. Not to say that you want to get tight and constricted with what that start is, but it's paying attention to where that start should be. Take *Krapp's Last Tape*, with the banana in the drawer. It's total surprise. Comes from nowhere. This guy's listening to tapes; then he pulls a banana out of the drawer and puts it in his mouth. All of a sudden, it's a comedy. He eats the banana, puts it on the floor, and slips on it later. It's absolutely brilliant. It's like a physical sight gag.

But the writing can't be vague. It has to be specific. Peter Brook wrote a fabulous book called *The Empty Space*, and what he's saying is, at the end, theater is this blank canvas, which is probably the most exciting thing in the world, and yet frightening. That, to me, is the essence of how you follow. What do you see happen? Say you're sitting in the audience, and you're the only one there. What do you see happen? What would you like to see happen? What completely surprises you? It's as wide-open as that, and not getting too concerned with the process and big ideas and politics. What physically happens between the audience and the play? Have you seen *Slava's Snowshow*? Clowns are boarding trains in which they become the train. It's an extraordinary piece in which they stare at the audience. Just by that, the audience goes nuts. It's technique, and yet, at the same time, it's doing its own thing. Great theater.

CROWD MEMBER: How do you make yourself finish things, if it's such trouble?

SHEPARD: I'm actually working on something that I started many years ago, and seeing its core value. Lot of times, you start something brand new and let it flutter away before you know it. You have to agree to work on the piece.

CROWD MEMBER: Could you give us an example of writing something like *Buried Child*?

SHEPARD: I dipped into this family thing for a little while, and I didn't really want to write family plays. It is that American tradition, those family plays, so I thought of writing something that hadn't been exposed or touched on. Then I started working on it, and it turned out to be pretty dark, and I wanted it to be a comedy, so that was the first time I started drawing up characters from my past and messing around in that territory: family-gone-wrong.

CROWD MEMBER: Can we go back to Beckett for a second? (*Shepard nods.*) Did you get into his work as a distant admirer or did you actually know him?

SHEPARD: No. It's one of my biggest regrets. I wish I had met him.

CROWD MEMBER: Did you ever act in any of his works?

(*Shepard shakes head no.*)

CROWD MEMBER: Would you like to?

SHEPARD: Maybe.

CROWD MEMBER: Do you find there are enough places to put on your plays?

SHEPARD: There's never been a political involvement. I was lucky enough to come from the '60s, where Off-Off-Broadway was the only alternative. Broadway was locked up, Off-Broadway was as locked up as

Broadway, all commercial theater. The doors were closed to experimental theater. And we invented it. And we said, "Okay, let's go do it in that space, that café or that church." The fire department was trying to close us down all the time because we didn't have exit signs over the doors, and we just did it. We made it happen. I'm not sure if that vitality still exists now, but I can tell you, Off-Off-Broadway existed because we said, "To hell with Broadway, and to hell with commercial theater. We're going to do it our way in the spaces available because we believe in it enough."

I find it hard to believe that the city has changed that much, that people who want to get stuff done can't get those things done. Somewhere. Take Ellen Stewart [*from La MaMa*]. This was a bulldog of a woman. She put plays on regardless. Get it done. I don't know if there are people like that around anymore. I find it hard to believe it's a political element or economic element. I mean, goddang, if people want to get stuff done, they'll find a way to get it done. Don't you think? What do you think? I don't know.

CROWD MEMBER: How do you know when a play's done?

SHEPARD: You write things in different states of mind. After a long day of writing, once you sleep on a story, that next morning isn't the same as when you were engaged the previous night. You look at it later and realize it isn't at all how you imagined it to be. So when you write a play ten years ago, and then come back to it, you're a different person. So I think, why not rewrite it in that new light?

CROWD MEMBER: How do you know when to do that?

SHEPARD: The play has a rhythm. You gotta listen to it. You'll know. I hate endings. I can tell you that. Always. Trying to force something. Not fun. Beginnings are extremely fun, middles are . . . [*grumbles*] and endings suck.

CROWD MEMBER: Do you do a lot of rewrites based on rehearsals with actors?

SHEPARD: Around actors, yeah. Oftentimes, good actors are great at finding bad writing. If you're watching your actors and listening to actors, they'll find a problem. A lot of times I've rewritten almost entirely around an actor. They find that communication with character. Ed Harris is like that. He'll just say, "What is that?" and he just knows what is and isn't working.

CROWD MEMBER: Do you write a lot of stage directions?

SHEPARD: I don't like stage directions that much. I like them abbreviated and concise. The problem with stage directions is that you're trying to locate the space, and the point of view is always shifting. So you have to work in the blueprint. So the best way to create direction is probably the traditional method, which is from the proscenium. You have to sort of designate where it's happening. Look at Beckett's stage direction. It's very specific and precise.

CROWD MEMBER: Is there any advice you can give us?

SHEPARD: Plunge in.

A Nod from One Sam to Another

Fintan O'Toole / 2007

From *The Irish Times*, February 24, 2007: The Arts, p. 1. Reprinted courtesy of *The Irish Times*. Fintan O'Toole was the drama critic of the *New York Daily News* from 1997 to 2001, and he has been the literary editor of *The Irish Times* since 2011. He is the author of numerous books, primarily on Irish history and culture and on modern politics.

At 63, Sam Shepard is still lithe, rangy and almost boyish. He still has the chiseled, angular features of a movie star and the easy self-possession of a rock star, reminding you that he is a great literary dramatist with more than a foot in popular culture. But he is warm and unfussy, speaks in a deep, drawling western accent and laughs a lot with a gleeful cackle that betrays no hint of cynicism or world-weariness. He has spent much of his time in the worlds of movies and music without apparently falling prey to their occupational hazards of egotism and incestuousness. He is full of enthusiasm about Dublin, the Abbey, and his old friend Stephen Rea ("He's so malleable, he can move in so many directions"), whom he is directing in the world premiere of his new play, *Kicking a Dead Horse*. He is as happy to talk about his admiration for other writers as about himself. You sense in him the curiosity and openness that fuel a writer who already has more than 50 plays, as well as dozens of screenplays, prose works, poems and songs, to his name.

He is full, for example, of two Irish writers whose work he has recently encountered. Seeing Fiona Shaw in the current London production of Samuel Beckett's *Happy Days* reminded him, he says, that "you don't realize how much you've been influenced." He encountered Beckett when he was a teenager trying to get away from the avocado farm in California where he grew up to be an actor in New York.

"Beckett is what caused me to start writing. I was messing around with acting and writing some fiction, back in 1961 I think, when somebody gave me *Waiting for Godot* and then *Endgame*. I'd never heard of Beckett. I remember very distinctly the confrontation with the script was something that overwhelmed me, I'd never seen anything like this. I hadn't realized you could do that sort of thing. That's the thing about Beckett that's so extraordinary. Not that you want to write like him (because nobody can) but that what he does is to offer up an entirely new perspective: You can do anything.

"To tell you the truth, I remember walking into bookstores back then and trying to find contemporary theater, and contemporary theater was O'Neill, Miller, Albee, Chekhov, Tennessee Williams—there's gotta be something more modern than that. Not to take anything away from any one of them— they were all particularly great in their time and still are—but it just struck me that nothing was being done in America comparable to what was being done in Europe, and particularly by Beckett. It wasn't naturalism and naturalism didn't seem to satisfy the impulses of the time, which were pretty chaotic, and the anger that was happening. So I thought, why not try to do that and at the same time stay with what you know, stay on an American terrain? It fired me up to take the American idiom and fool with it in a theatrical sense."

Forty-five years on, when his application of that European sensibility to a distinctively American terrain has produced some of the greatest plays in the language, Shepard is still capable of being struck by the same lightning. His newest discovery is another Irish dramatist, Tom Murphy. "I didn't come across *A Whistle in the Dark* until quite recently and I was just knocked out by it. I couldn't believe that I hadn't come across this thing before. And I started studying it, to re-read it and re-read it and see what it was exactly that made it work so well. And I discovered, after studying it methodically, that it has to do with movement. It's that the play never stops moving, it's in motion the whole time, it's beautiful, it's like a tapestry. That in itself was an inspiration. It's like if you're a musician and you hear somebody playing and you go 'What is that? How did you do that?' Musicians are always borrowing from each other, it's very much an eclectic bag, and so it is with writing, people are constantly sniffing around, taking things. Not stealing, just sharing."

The influences go both ways, of course. Martin McDonagh's *The Lonesome West* bears the marks of Shepard's *True West*, and Shepard is happy to have helped. "He wrote me a kind of apologetic letter once. It was very funny, something about referencing *True West*. I haven't seen *The Lonesome West* but I love his work. He's an absolutely extraordinary playwright. And these things are bound to pop up more than once. The idea of conflicts between brothers goes back to Cain and Abel."

Conversely, Shepard is happy to acknowledge the influence of two Irish writers on his own play *The Late Henry Moss*. The title, and a crucial part of

254 CONVERSATIONS WITH SAM SHEPARD

the plot, comes from Frank O'Connor's short story "The Late Henry Conran." "I lifted that thing out of there, where the man is in jail and is publicized as being dead by his wife. It's a fabulous story. I just lifted that notion—I hadn't ever done that before but it's directly out of it." He also drew for the play from *The Playboy of the Western World*: "the idea of the corpse. The dead one coming alive."

These literary connections are part of the reason Shepard feels so comfortable about his new—again utterly American—play having its premiere in Ireland. The single protagonist of *Kicking a Dead Horse* is, like so many of Shepard's characters, obsessed by the search for an elusive authenticity. Shepard himself admits to feeling something of the same tug in relation to Ireland.

"The thing with Ireland is of course the language, and the ancient aspect of it. It's not like America, where we go back to the 1600s and then get lost in the mist, here 1600 is nothing. There's the *Golden Bough* sense—the thing of the druids, the Celts, the mystery of the language and how powerful that is, and how it's had an effect on America. Still does—the Scotch-Irish in Appalachia and all the rest of it. It still plays a very strong part in the backbone of that part of the world. That's where my affinity with it is: because in the States we've lost so much contact with our own past. You talk to kids about the Civil War, they don't know what you're talking about. This notion, this implication, that we're connected to something ancient—it's good for a writer to feel that there's some connection to something very, very old. And that there's a continuation. It's a tribal thing."

In the U.S., as in *Kicking a Dead Horse*, the search for authenticity often centers on the image of the cowboy. Hobart Struther, the play's sixty-something protagonist, made his fortune collecting western art and now wants to live out that cowboy mythology for himself. I reminded Shepard of a line in an old poem by his one-time lover Patti Smith, called "Sam Shepard: 9 Random Years": "he was a man playing cowboys." Is the play in this sense autobiographical? "Oh sure," he laughs. "It's all autobiographical. Just there's a lot of masking going on."

Does he feel that cowboy impulse himself on the ranch in Kentucky where he does much of his writing? "Oh, of course. Everybody in America wants to be a cowboy and very few know what it's like to be one. It's not romantic, when you're out there castrating cattle and getting blood all over your hands, mending barbed wire and doctoring cows. It's hard, hard work and the guys who still are ranch hands in Montana or west Texas, they're a rare breed now. You would never see 'em in front of a TV camera. But it is quite shocking, you're in a place outside Tucson or somewhere and these guys walk in for a cup of coffee, with the high-heeled boots and the big rowel spurs and the chink chaps and blood all over 'em, sit down, never take their hat off. These guys are from out there. Then they get back in the truck and they just vanish, you know? I doubt any of the guys who dream about it would imagine that's what it's like. I grew up in it and was around it. I grew up with these guys. I rodeoed a little bit and played around with it, but never to the point where I had to survive by it."

There is, of course, a political dimension to this fantasy, and George Bush tapped into it. Shepard is wary of anyone seeing the new play as a political treatise and his stage directions have a wonderfully deadpan warning against overly metaphorical readings of its would-be cowboy and his eponymous expired equine: "The dead horse should be as realistic as possible. . . . In fact, it should actually be a dead horse." But the play's frantic comedy is undoubtedly informed by Bush and the Iraq war.

"His actions certainly bear on the play, this notion that the West wasn't enough to conquer, now we have to conquer the rest of the world, and we're going to continue this Manifest Destiny—what, in Iraq? That certainly is part of what feeds it, but I'm not trying to make a tract about it. There is this strange deal—from Lewis and Clark to Iraq. It's very weird that we're continually trying to devour territory. It was about territory and it still is about territory, and ownership, and imperialism and conquering—taking it and doing something with it that we consider to be more useful than what's being done with it now. And consequently creating havoc and devastation. It's frightening, absolutely frightening."

In a sense, almost all of Shepard's work is about this restlessness and the psychic vacuums it creates. "I'm interested in the impulses behind it. I do think that they're connected, that there's a history of this devouring, this possessive attitude. Thomas Jefferson and those guys were southern planters. Planters were guys who needed land and the quest to get to the West was really to get more land—let's get it before the Russians and the English and the French. It looks very innocent—what a glorious thing to make the continent one country. But it also has to do with this taking over, grabbing, getting hold of it. You have to go through several Indian tribes, you have to kill quite a few people. From those impulses, this whole thing was born. Bush didn't happen out of thin air."

If these historical and political resonances are never far away from Shepard's work, though, it endures because they are always rooted in the family. He remains mistrustful of theorizing and convinced that in the theater, everything stems from experience. "There's a dangerous thing where you uncover something and then it becomes a theme and it loses its sting, its power. What makes something like *A Whistle in the Dark* so wonderful is that these characters feel like they're coming from life. You can't write something like that without having it come from your connections to family. Father, mother, brothers, sisters—you can't really cut yourself off from that. Why would you want to? Because family is the real heart and soul of what you're about as a writer. What it becomes, how it unravels, is part of your craftsmanship, but if you cut yourself off from it, all that's dead.

"Even in Beckett, even though these characters seem to be existing in a kind of timeless netherworld, the mother's there, the father's there, the lovers are there, all of the relationships are very much coming from someone's direct experience. It's not about philosophy, it's not about esoteric existential shit. *Happy Days* is about Willie and Winnie and the dilapidation of their relationship. That human aspect is what makes the play work. There's nothing abstract about it." Shepard's gift is that nothing in his work, even a dead horse, is ever abstract either.

Sam Shepard

Michael Almereyda / 2011

From *Interview* 41 (October 2011): 42–45, 132–33. Michael Almereyda is an American film director, screenwriter, and film producer. Among his many films are *A Hero of Our Time* (1985), *Hamlet* (2000), and *Marjorie Prime* (2017).

One of the few truisms about Sam Shepard is that he has always been more difficult to know as a person, in the public sense, than he has been as a dramatist, as a writer, or as a performer. There has always been something vaguely punk rock about Shepard's work—a visceral directness coupled with the sense of never quite knowing what to expect or what he'll do next—that has made it feel as instantly powerful and iconic as he himself has seemed eternally elusive. It's a mix of qualities that has helped transform Shepard into a kind of mystical cult figure for teenagers who happen upon plays like *Cowboy Mouth* (which he co-wrote with Patti Smith in 1971) or *Buried Child* (1977) or *Fool for Love* (1983), only to later discover that the Pulitzer Prize–winning playwright who emerged from the experimental theater milieu of New York City in the 1970s is also an actor—and a revelatory one at that, who has brought a striking physical presence and contemplative air to a swath of films as diverse as Terrence Malick's *Days of Heaven* (1978), Philip Kaufman's *The Right Stuff* (1983), and Sean Penn's *The Pledge* (2001)—or vice versa.

Over the course of the last four-plus decades, Shepard has been astoundingly prolific, having written more than 40 plays, published six books of prose and poetry, acted in more than 40 films, and lent his hand to a range of screenplays, including the scripts for Michelangelo Antonioni's *Zabriskie Point* (1970) and Wim Wenders's *Paris, Texas* (1984). This month, though, he steps into his first starring role in more than six years in Mateo Gil's elegantly restrained new Western, *Blackthorn*, in which Shepard plays perhaps the most punk-rock cowboy of them all, Butch Cassidy, in an evocative re-imagining of what happened after the Wild West's most notorious outlaw set off for Bolivia on the run from the American authorities in the early 1900s.

Filmmaker Michael Almereyda, who collaborated with Shepard on two projects—an adaptation of *Hamlet* (2000), in which Shepard played the Ghost, and the documentary *This So-Called Disaster* (2003), which provided a behind-the-scenes look at Shepard's work process—caught up with him recently by phone from Los Feliz, California. Shepard, who next month will turn 68, was in Boise, Idaho, for a reading of *Ages of the Moon* that he was scheduled to do that evening with his *Right Stuff* co-star Scott Glenn, and had stationed himself at a local bed and breakfast.

MICHAEL ALMEREYDA: I once asked you when it first occurred to you to become an actor, and you mentioned seeing Burt Lancaster in *Vera Cruz* [1954]. Was there ever an equivalent experience that sparked the idea of becoming a writer?

SAM SHEPARD: Oddly enough, it was reading Eugene O'Neill. I'd read *Long Day's Journey Into Night* [1956], and I remember seeing Sidney Lumet's black-and-white film adaptation [released in 1962], which I still think is one of the best adaptations of anything—of a book, of a play—ever done.

ALMEREYDA: Lumet said it was his favorite movie he'd done.

SHEPARD: It's a beautiful little thing. But I remember being struck by the idea that it was a play, so I read the play and I read about O'Neill, and in an odd way, there was something that I connected with there. . . . There was something wrong with the family. There was a demonic thing going on that nobody could put their finger on, but everybody knew the ship was sinking. Everybody was going down, and nobody knew why or how, and they were all taking desperate measures to stay afloat. So I thought there was something about that that felt similar to my own background, and I felt I could maybe write some version of that.

ALMEREYDA: But it took a while before your plays reflected that kind of model. Had you been writing plays before you saw *Long Day's Journey Into Night*?

SHEPARD: No. When I first started, I didn't really know how to structure a play. I could write dialogue, but I just sort of failed beyond that, and kind of went wherever I wanted to go, which is how I ended up with these shorter pieces. I didn't venture into two-acts or three-acts until, I think, *La Turista* [1967]. So these things I was writing were all experiments of just tiptoeing into the waters of what it's like to write a play.

ALMEREYDA: It's funny that you say "tiptoe" because to me, those early plays are like explosions.

SHEPARD: Well, they are, but there was also this other thing—and it kind of shocked me—which was that theater seemed so far behind the other art forms, like jazz or Abstract Expressionism in painting or what they called "happenings" and the other kinds of experimentations that were taking place at that time. Theater still seemed to have this stilted, old-fashioned quality about it. So I couldn't quite understand why theater, as a form, was spinning its wheels and not really going anywhere. Writers like LeRoi Jones . . . what's his name now? Amiri Baraka . . . but back then he was LeRoi Jones, and he wrote some brilliant plays like *The Toilet* [1964] and *Slave Ship* [1969]. I think he was the most brilliant playwright of his era. And yet he was being overlooked as well. I don't know what it was . . . it's hard to say that it was because of the racial stuff. . . . I thought his plays were far and away above anything else that was going on, even though there were other people struggling to do that sort of experimental work.

ALMEREYDA: His famous one is *Dutchman* [1964].

SHEPARD: I got to know LeRoi Jones, or Amiri Baraka, a little bit, and he was always sort of wary of me . . . but I thought he was a brilliant fucking writer—in prose and poetry as well. He's overlooked in the scheme of things. He was angry . . . he was pissed. When I first met him, he was running around with an attaché case and a raincoat and was sort of neatly coifed and stuff. Then all of the sudden, he transformed into this revolutionary.

ALMEREYDA: Well, it was a revolutionary time. I did a little bit of homework, and I read a review that Edward Albee wrote in 1965 of one of your plays where he praised your "unencumbered spontaneity." I guess that became an early trademark—this feeling that you just kind of dashed off these plays and they were produced almost as quickly as you wrote them. But then you started to shift gears and think about bigger structures.

SHEPARD: Yeah. I don't know why that happened exactly except that the stuff just started to demand a bigger format. I guess the first real encounter I had with stretching it out was *Curse of the Starving Class* [1976]. In a way, it was the first sort of venture into writing about family, and it seemed to have more longevity. Then that morphed into *Buried Child* and some other stuff.

ALMEREYDA: When you first started up in New York, was there anyone who was a particular accomplice or guide or a friend who helped shape the work you would make?

SHEPARD: Well, Charles Mingus Jr. was a great friend of mine. I went to high school with him, and he was always close to me, but then our friendship got distorted and warped because of his . . . hell, I hate to say *paranoia*, but I started to feel as if the influence I was getting from him was more and more negative. I didn't quite know how to handle it, so I broke off the friendship. But he definitely had an influence on me, and so did his father and all of the jazz musicians around that scene, because I felt like jazz was really the art form of that decade. I don't know what it was about that music, but when you saw it live, there was something deeply glowing about it. The way those musicians presented themselves on stage, like [John] Coltrane and Eric Dolphy and Charles Mingus and Roland Kirk. . . . They were the heroes of that era. I still find it hard to believe that the whole era of jazz is over. It seemed like such an active force in the 1960s, a real expression of the times—and, of course, it was essentially black and angry [*laughs*]. I mean, when you saw Nina Simone singing at the piano, she was like a warrior—and a tyrant. When she sang the "Pirate Jenny" song, the hair on your neck stood up.

ALMEREYDA: You had something of a front-row seat to all that because you were working at the Village Gate.

SHEPARD: Yeah. I was a busboy.

ALMEREYDA: Did you go to other clubs, too?

SHEPARD: I also worked uptown, at the Oak Room. One of the great piano players, Mary Lou Williams, played at the horseshoe bar. It was Duke Ellington's favorite place for dinner. He'd come in every night with his entourage and his family and sit down in this huge booth. I remember busing his table many nights. Sir Duke [*laughs*]. It was kind of awesome.

ALMEREYDA: What was your sense of identity as an artist at that point? Were you just biding your time?

SHEPARD: No, I mean, I was writing all the time, so I wasn't waiting for anything. I think a part of the reason that those early plays were short was that I just kept having these ideas and I'd just go off and write them. I wasn't trying to write one-act plays—it's just how the ideas would be expressed. Every condition I was in seemed like it could be a play. Everything seemed like a possible play.

ALMEREYDA: It seemed like it was a time when the whole culture was kind of shaking itself awake.

SHEPARD: It was also a bit scary. I mean, people talk about the 1960s in a nostalgic way, but to me it was terrifying. People were getting assassinated. There was Vietnam. There were race riots. It felt like everything was going to get blown up sky-high. It didn't feel like flower power. It felt like Armageddon.

ALMEREYDA: But at that point, your work was getting out in the open, too. Albee had singled you out. Your plays were winning Obies. You must have had a sense of vocation by then.

SHEPARD: Well, I never . . . it's not like I have a *career*. I feel very lucky and privileged to be a writer. I feel lucky in the sense that I can branch out into prose and tell different kinds of stories and stuff. But being a writer is so great because you're literally not dependent on anybody. Whereas, as an actor, you have to audition or wait for somebody else to make a decision about how to use you; with writing, you can do it anywhere, anytime you want. You don't have to ask permission.

ALMEREYDA: Freedom is a big deal. I can't help but mention Roberto Bolaño, because the last time I saw you, you had a book of his interviews in your bag. I saw your new film, *Blackthorn*, last week after I'd just finished Bolaño's *The Savage Detectives*, so I think I had a filter or frame for everything I was taking in, and it seemed like Bolaño's themes of friendship and escape and adventure came galloping into the movie. You play Butch Cassidy, a survivor holed up in Bolivia, calling himself James Blackthorn. The movie seems in part about how to sustain a myth, but it also has a nice political undercurrent that ripples along. How did you get involved in the project?

SHEPARD: It actually came through the agency. They offered it to me, and right away I could recognize that it was a really great script.

ALMEREYDA: You're really at the heart and center of the movie. It's great to see you that way, and not just playing someone's father. [*Shepard laughs.*] I was surprised that your character is so affable. He seems more at peace than a lot of lone-rider Western characters, and has a sense of humor about his role in the world.

SHEPARD: Well, I did some research on Butch Cassidy. I didn't want to do an imitation of Paul Newman in *Butch Cassidy and the Sundance Kid* [1969], so I thought I would just start from scratch. I found out that he was actually raised Mormon in Utah, and he was pretty handy with horses and cattle at an early age. He went off with a man whose name was Butch, which is where he got his name, and as the guy told him more and more about horses, he became a better horseman. It turned out, though, that the guy was actually a rustler and was stealing horses and cattle, and Butch decided that was a good idea, so this was his first sojourn into the criminal life. It was an easier, more lucrative way to make a living than working in a saddle shop or making spurs or something like that. But, you know, I didn't have anything hard and fast in my head about who this guy was. I just kind of let it unfold.

ALMEREYDA: Where did the singing come from? Was that in the script?

SHEPARD: It was the director Mateo's idea. I had done a little singing with Mateo. You know the little gray instrument that I play on the horse? It's a beautiful little instrument—it's actually a traditional South American instrument. So we thought, well, that would be good to do in the film. Then later we decided that maybe I could sing some songs in the studio for the soundtrack. So I did those songs, too. I actually did them in Dublin.

ALMEREYDA: There are some great shots of you riding horses. There's a kind of thrilling galloping shot where you think, "Boy, they got a great stunt double." But then the camera reveals that it's actually you.

SHEPARD: [*Laughs*] One of the appeals of the part was that I got to ride. This guy, Jordi, a Spanish guy—he was the head wrangler. They brought the horses in from Argentina because there are hardly any horses in Bolivia due to the altitude. The horses have a difficult time in high altitudes if they're not acclimatized. Many times we were at 15,000 feet, which is really tough on both animals and people. So this guy brought those horses in early and got them used to breathing. A lot of them were ex-polo horses out of Buenos Aires, I think. Man, those horses could ride.

ALMEREYDA: Have you read *The Savage Detectives*?

SHEPARD: To tell you the truth, I've read part of it. Some of Bolaño's stuff is a little dense for me. It's hard to penetrate. Even *2666*—I cut right away to the murders [*laughs*]. That said, there's that extraordinary collection of his stories that they put out, *Last Evenings On Earth*. . . . There's also this other little story called "Beach" where this guy is trying to kick heroin. He buys a black Speedo and goes down to the beach and covers himself in oil and lays in the sun and observes beach life every day while he's trying to kick. He's taking methadone and stuff. It's the most unbelievable story. It's only about four or five pages long. Do you know that story?

ALMEREYDA: I've read about it. It's probably something from his life. It seems like he was very good at flashing a mirror in front of him and getting it all down.

SHEPARD: You get that feeling and then, at the same time, you wonder if he's making it all up. It's so plausible and believable as real-life documentary, and then all of a sudden you get the feeling that he's just conjured this thing. It's very weird and odd. What I like most about Bolaño is his courage.

ALMEREYDA: Courage in what sense?

SHEPARD: In terms of what he's writing about, how he's doing it, and then, of course, the background of it all is that, at a certain point, he realized that he was terminally ill. He had this liver disease and, evidently, he was waiting for a transplant that came too late. [Bolaño died in 2003.] But he never indulged in self-pity. I think there's only one piece I've ever read about his illness directly. But it's always in the background and, posthumously, we now understand that he was writing all this stuff while he was dying without indulging in that as a subject.

ALMEREYDA: One thing that was really moving for me about *The Savage Detectives* was that he was celebrating the life of writing, but he was also celebrating living itself, so there's this expansive feeling for all sorts of voices and people.

SHEPARD: I think Bolaño had a generosity about him that was unique. He seemed to include so many people in the circle of his adventures, whereas I felt like I was pretty selfish. When you get right down to it, I was only interested in these plays. And, of course, I did have some friends, but I don't think I was as generous as Bolaño in his depiction of the people who influenced him and who he hung out with. I was never a part of any kind of literary club. I didn't belong to any sort of brotherhood of writing, which Bolaño was always referring to.

ALMEREYDA: You were part of Theater Genesis [the experimental Off-Off-Broadway theater company]. You were kind of planted in that group, weren't you?

SHEPARD: That was when I was working at the Village Gate. The head-waiter there was Ralph Cook, who had started Theater Genesis at St. Mark's Church[-in-the-Bowery]. A lot of the waiters there—Kevin O'Connor, Robbie Lyons, and a bunch of guys that I worked with at that time—were actors, and all of those guys became involved in my plays after Ralph discovered that I was writing some dialogues. In fact, Genesis was the first place to ever put on one of my plays. Simultaneously, The Poetry Project with Anne Waldman was happening downstairs—William Burroughs was reading down there—and we were doing plays upstairs. St. Mark's was a happening spot.

ALMEREYDA: How many plays a year were you doing at the time?

SHEPARD: Oh, many. I started out with *Cowboys* and [*The*] *Rock Garden* [both 1964] at St. Mark's, and I did probably a half-dozen plays that first year. But then I started moving around. I did stuff at the Off-Off-Broadway places like La MaMa and Caffe Cino, which belonged to Joe Cino, who killed himself over on Carmine Street.

ALMEREYDA: What happened?

SHEPARD: I think he was a speed freak. He was a big Italian guy, great cook. Anyway, one night, Joe Cino hacked himself to death with a butcher knife in the kitchen and that was the end of him.

ALMEREYDA: You never hear of anyone doing that to themselves.

SHEPARD: Yeah, but it was drug-assisted, you know? There were a lot of very strange suicides at that time. There was a famous one where a guy danced out the window. This guy, this director, put some aria on and danced right out an open window and killed himself. Lots of kids died back then.

ALMEREYDA: How did you meet Patti Smith?

SHEPARD: I got together with Patti in 1969 or 1970, I guess. She was basically a writer at that point. She was a journalist doing interviews for different music magazines, and that's how I met her. She did an interview with me because she'd seen me play drums at the Village Gate with the Holy Modal Rounders. So we did an interview, and then I ran off and started living with her at the Chelsea Hotel.

ALMEREYDA: That was pretty spontaneous.

SHEPARD: It was pretty typically '60s.

ALMEREYDA: When your books came out at about the same time—your collection *Day Out of Days* and her *Just Kids*—you did a reading together, and she got a lot of mileage out of the passages featuring you. How did you feel about seeing yourself in that book?

SHEPARD: She's such an old friend of mine. . . . We have a kind of tacit understanding of that time. A lot of people found it very funny. . . . When you read it, it is kind of humorous.

ALMEREYDA: Your book, of course, is made up of stories, tales, myths, and hers is a memoir, but I think there's a kind of mythology to her book as well.

SHEPARD: Well, she's a good writer—a really good writer. So I think because of her inherent—I hate to use the word *talent*, but her ability to put words together, it's a little bit more than a memoir. It's probably laced with some imagination. And why not? It's essentially true.

ALMEREYDA: But the way she puts it in the book, when you guys first got together, she didn't know that Slim Shadow, the musician, was actually Sam Shepard, the playwright.

SHEPARD: Well, I think she was exaggerating a little.

ALMEREYDA: Seeing you two on stage together was wildly entertaining. I thought that you could just take the show on the road and be busy for the rest of your lives.

SHEPARD: It's always great to perform with her because she has absolutely no fear of the audience. I've never seen anybody so self-contained on stage. She's courageous, and it kind of rubs off on you in a way. .

ALMEREYDA: By a pure fluke, I ran into an engineer-slash-producer last night who works with Patti, and he mentioned that, a couple years ago, as a birthday present to you, she arranged a recording session where you sat down with an acoustic guitar and sang 12 songs. He said that it was an incredible session, and they made a CD of it that they handed off to you. What are you going to do with that stuff? Is there any chance it'll ever see the light of day?

SHEPARD: We did a bunch of old tunes. There was one gospel tune and another one by Richard "Rabbit" Brown called "James Alley Blues." It's actually on the Harry Smith folk anthology [*Anthology of American Folk Music* (1952)]. It's just the tip of the iceberg of all that string-band music from pre-bluegrass. Bluegrass music is sort of show-off music—you know, "Look how well I can play the banjo. . . ." Whereas the string band music is more ensemble stuff. My son, Walker, has a band called The Dust Busters. You know, he plays banjo, fiddle, guitar, and mandolin, so a lot of my interest in that kind of music comes from him constantly listening to this stuff. He's taught me the history of it. It's remarkable how these young kids are now turned on to more traditional old-time music.

ALMEREYDA: Well, I hope you follow through with Patti and that comes out at some point.

SHEPARD: Yeah, I like singing, and I'm getting more and more comfortable with it, so I think I'll do more of it down the road. Patti was actually going back into the studio in August to do a record, and she invited me to come in and do some tunes, but I didn't want to be in New York in August [*laughs*].

ALMEREYDA: I read on Wikipedia that you did a recording of Spalding Gray's last monologue.

SHEPARD: I did something for a documentary on Spalding that his wife was involved in, but I'm not sure what happened with it.

ALMEREYDA: I didn't know that you had that close of a bond with him. You're in one of his monologues, where he gamely recounts playing pool with you, and you wipe up the floor with him.

SHEPARD: Well, you know, Spalding was with Richard Schechner's Performance Group, and was in one of Schechner's early productions of *The Tooth of Crime* [1972], where they felt at liberty to take people's work and just throw it up all over the wall and make a mess of it. Schechner did several productions that had absolutely nothing to do with the play—you know, it was just trapeze shit, and fucking around for the sake of it. He was one of those intellectuals who—

ALMEREYDA: Override the text. Not your favorite.

SHEPARD: He was very influenced by [Jerzy] Grotowski [the Polish theater director], but he didn't have the guts of Grotowski. He didn't have the brains of Grotowski either.

ALMEREYDA: Samuel Beckett is kind of a touchstone for you. What has he meant to you over the years?

SHEPARD: He's meant everything to me. He's the first playwright—or the first writer, really—who just shocked me. It was like I didn't know that kind of writing was possible. Similar to the experience of reading [Arthur] Rimbaud, it was like, "Where the fuck did he come up with this?" Of course, with Beckett, you can say it was [James] Joyce, because he'd worked for Joyce, but it was more than that. His trilogy of novels *Molloy* [1951], *Malone Dies* [1951], and *The Unnamable* [1953] are essentially monologues, and to see how he moved from those to plays . . . it was an absolutely seamless evolution. To me, with *Waiting for Godot* [1953], *Endgame* [1957], *Krapp's Last Tape* [1958], and *Happy Days* [1961], he just gets better and better until he has just honed this thing. . . .

ALMEREYDA: It sounds like Beckett hit you harder than O'Neill.

SHEPARD: Well, I definitely read *Long Day's Journey* before I read *Waiting for Godot*, but it was all the same era. I suppose it was the form more than anything else that I was obsessed with, because I felt like the form of theater at the time was so retrograde. That's what Joe Chaikin [the theater director] was after—this theme of naturalism that was so present was so old-fashioned and backward and unexpressive of the times. Theater needed a brave new kind of expression, and Beckett had invented a brand-new form. Joe was about that with the Open Theater, too—about finding new forms of acting. And Grotowski was moving away from naturalism into something that was more intrinsically dramatic.

ALMEREYDA: It's slippery in your work, though, because, in some ways, you've gotten more naturalistic as you've gone on, but then you've veered off into other things that are more abstract or surreal. Did you ever meet Beckett?

SHEPARD: No, and that's one of my great regrets. I could have, because I'd worked with Joe for years, and Joe was friends with Beckett. In fact, Beckett wrote a couple of things *for* Joe. But I was remiss in not meeting him. I wish that I had.

ALMEREYDA: Both your papers and Beckett's papers are archived around Austin, Texas. What was it like looking through his papers?

SHEPARD: It was shocking. I was looking at *Malone*, which is one of his earliest novels, and every page was just peppered with these handwritten sketches. In the borders of every page there are these tiny abstract drawings. Some of them are demons or figures with big heads. Some of them are bicycles. Every once in a while, there is a totally abstract one that looks like a geometric figure. But all of them were drawn over and over again. It wasn't just doodling—he was doing something with these drawings. Some of the writing was in green pen—I don't know why—but it was all on this lined notebook paper. And then I looked at [Jorge Luis] Borges's stuff, too, which was equally remarkable. He got quite blind after a while, so his writing just starts to bloom out across the page. It gets bigger and bigger as he expresses the sentence or the paragraph. It's just amazing stuff. I mean, to see the handwriting of these people is very close to meeting them.

ALMEREYDA: You're right, in a way. You don't really know someone until you've either been over to their house or seen their handwriting.

SHEPARD: And in some odd way, because you're sort of alone with their aloneness with the paper, it's just haunting. They've got Walt Whitman there, too.

ALMEREYDA: What's his handwriting like?

SHEPARD: Small and tidy.

ALMEREYDA: I can't think of another writer in the Western hemisphere besides you who has been able to pull off this trick of writing and also acting in movies. Do you see any connection between the two activities?

SHEPARD: I think they're very connected. It's hard to explain why exactly, but I think that when I began writing plays, it was from an actor's point of view more than anything. I had the feeling that if you put yourself in the position of the actor on stage and write from that perspective, it would give you a certain advantage in terms of being inside of the play. Don't forget: Shakespeare played The Ghost.

ALMEREYDA: It's not good to compare yourself to Shakespeare. You walked into that one.

SHEPARD: It's true. You shouldn't compare yourself to Shakespeare!

ALMEREYDA: That's my advice for today. Anyhow, Shakespeare didn't get into movies [*both laugh*]. But as an actor, you are interested in a kind of naturalism.

SHEPARD: I'm not sure that you'd characterize it as naturalism. For me, it has more to do with the relationship with the camera. When I first started doing movies, I was terrified of the camera, so I felt I had to protect myself. But now, I'm beginning to lose that fear, and a whole new thing is opening up for me.

ALMEREYDA: Was that a big transition for you?

SHEPARD: I think it just evolved out of being in front of a camera many times. It used to bother me that so much of filmmaking was centered around the camera. Very little attention was paid to the actor, which is now fine by me. I don't care if the director is always looking through the lens. I'd rather have him paying attention to the camera, to tell you the truth.

ALMEREYDA: Because you can fend for yourself.

SHEPARD: Yeah. I don't think most filmmakers understand the first thing about acting. They're good at casting, and many of them know who to put in what role and have a kind of magic in that way. But as far as really talking to an actor in terms of what he or she is doing? They're not so hot at it—or so interested in it.

ALMEREYDA: Over the years, your work has existed, in some ways, outside of politics, and reflects the times in a more internalized way. But occasionally you've written a couple of things that seemed to explicitly re-act to political circumstances, almost like political cartoons. *States of Shock* [1991] was written around the first Gulf War and *The God of Hell* [2004] was written in the aftermath of the September 11 attacks and the second Gulf War. Are you conscious of writing those kinds of plays as a different kind of enterprise?

SHEPARD: With *The God of Hell*, I was kind of surprised by the play because it developed into something that I wasn't really expecting. It had a pretty good effect. I think *States of Shock* we never resolved, although I loved working with John Malkovich.

ALMEREYDA: He was amazing.

SHEPARD: He was totally crazy. He's one of my favorite actors on stage because he is so outrageous. I mean, he just doesn't give a shit, like Ed Harris.

ALMEREYDA: But would you say that those plays are fueled by anger?

SHEPARD: Yeah, in a sense, but they're not plays I enjoy as much as the plays where you don't really know where it's going.

ALMEREYDA: So you're working on a new play right now?

SHEPARD: Yeah. I've got an act finished, and I'm starting on the second one. I think I'm gonna do it next fall at the Signature Theatre with Jim Houghton. He's got a really beautiful set of new theaters—like, four or five of them in a complex. I don't know how he miraculously came up with money in the middle of an economic crunch, but he's got it going. I like him very much as an artistic director. He leaves you alone.

ALMEREYDA: Is there anything you haven't done that you'd still like to do?

SHEPARD: No. I'm pretty much doing everything that I want to do. . . . I would like to do some more music, so hopefully something will come of this thing with Patti.

ALMEREYDA: You're also kind of entering a new chapter in your life.

SHEPARD: Well, I'm working with the Santa Fe Institute. They're on the mountain with Cormac McCarthy. It's probably 95 percent scientists— you know, Nobel Prize winners like Murray Gell-Mann, who invented quark theory, and Geoffrey West. I had a fellowship there last year for six months, and I sort of fulfilled that, and now I just have an ongoing relationship with them where I've got an office in the library where I can work on the play, and then we have lunch and sit around and talk.

ALMEREYDA: So you're entering the scientific period of your life?

SHEPARD: If you will [*laughs*]. I'm much more productive in that kind of environment because it's almost a kind of workaday thing. Get the type-writer, go in there, work until noon, and then work in the afternoon. I've produced a lot more stuff. Whether it's any good remains to be seen. I'm trying to buy a house near there, but I'm not sure if it's going to happen.

ALMEREYDA: I'm sure they've got some houses around there.

SHEPARD: They've got plenty of houses—and it's a buyer's market, they say.

Sam Shepard: "America Is on Its Way Out as a Culture"

Laura Barton / 2014

From *The Guardian* (UK), September 7, 2014, https://www.theguardian.com/stage/2014
/sep/07/sam-shepard-true-west-philip-seymour-hoffman-robin-williams-observer-interview.
Copyright Guardian News & Media Ltd. 2019. Reprinted by permission. Laura Barton is a
journalist and the author of the novel *Twenty-One Locks* (2010).

Sunday evening in Santa Fe and Sam Shepard and I are sitting at a downtown bar, drinking tequila and eating tacos. The light is low, the night warm and the conversation darts and dives while the bartender rattles the cocktail shaker and behind us the tables begin to fill. Already we have covered several pressing matters, including the merits of Chekhov ("I'm not crazy about him as a playwright . . . why are you going to bring a dead bird on stage?"), the qualities of greyhound piss ("like champagne" apparently), and the ancient Egyptian goddess Isis: "The way she turns into a bird! Unbelievable. You can't make that shit up."

But now our conversation has turned to the subject of *True West*, the play Shepard wrote in 1980, now revived at the Tricycle Theatre in London. Directed by Phillip Breen and starring Eugene O'Hare and Alex Ferns, the production first appeared at the Glasgow Citizens Theatre last year, earning much acclaim, not least from Shepard himself, who was instrumental in ensuring its London transfer.

"I think Phillip's production is great," he says this evening. "And the actors are terrific. . . . You rely on great actors." He recalls one of the play's most notable stagings, in New York at the turn of the century, the two leads played by the late Philip Seymour Hoffman and John C. Reilly, who alternated parts every so often to keep things lively.

Shepard saw Seymour Hoffman a week before he died of a heroin overdose in February and says he had no inkling anything was awry. "He was overweight, but he was overweight a lot," he says quietly. "And he was pretty tired. He said he was going to go back and take a nap. . . . See, I don't think he meant to kill himself, I think he had some bad heroin. Though I didn't realize he was that much of a junkie."

He pauses. "I knew Robin [Williams] pretty well and Robin knew he wanted out—he had Parkinson's. The two guys were very similar in that they were both overwhelmed by their own thing. I know a lot of people who've died . . . who've taken their own lives," he continues after a moment of quiet. "But you know Patti [Smith], who's an old, old friend of mine, she wrote a review of the new Murakami book that appeared in the New York Times, and at the end of it she said, 'I don't want to kill myself, I want to see what happens.' And what a statement. I believe her."

For more than five decades, Shepard has been one of the most prominent and respected figures of American stage and screen. For some, he has been principally an actor—the star of *Days of Heaven, The Right Stuff, Frances,* where he first met Jessica Lange, who would be his wife for nearly 30 years, and more recently *Brothers,* opposite Jake Gyllenhaal, and *The Assassination of Jesse James [by the Coward Robert Ford]* with Brad Pitt.

But for others, certainly himself, he is first and foremost a writer. He began writing for the stage in New York in the early 1960s, having dropped out of an agriculture degree, spurred on by reading the work of Samuel Beckett and by the desire for contemporary America to have a theatrical voice. "Back then, there was a dearth of American theater," he explains. "There was nothing going on. American art was starving."

He wrote *La Turista, Angel City, Cowboy Mouth,* a collaboration with his one-time partner Patti Smith, among many others, before *True West, Fool for Love,* various short stories, sketches, essays and a screenplay for Wim Wenders's *Paris, Texas.* In 1979, he won the Pulitzer Prize for his three-act play *Buried Child.*

Today, he divides his time between his farm in Kentucky and his home in New Mexico, where he holds a post at the Santa Fe Institute—one of several "highly accomplished, creative thinkers [appointed] to catalyze transdisciplinary collaboration, synthesize ideas and methods from many disciplines, and enhance, or even define, new fields of inquiry," according to the institute's literature.

"I go there every day," is how Shepard puts it, his tone hovering lightly. "It's kind of interesting—it's a thinktank situation, 95% of it is scientists. Me and Cormac [McCarthy] are the only two writers. Everybody else is a nuclear physicist. Which is cool, you know. But it leads to a lot of conversational dead ends." He laughs wheezily—many of his sentences end this way, in a warm, chest-deep rasp.

At the moment, he is writing his first novel. "After six book collections, basically I thought, 'God, wouldn't it be so great to be able to sustain something?'" But he is hesitant to expand on plot or themes. "Errrhhh," he says, stickily. "I don't know how to explain it. I really don't. Hopefully it's a novel, but I have the hardest time sustaining prose. I feel like I'm a natural-born playwright but the prose thing has always mystified me. How to keep it going?" Another long chuckle. "How do people do it, for years and years? I've been working on this for 10 years!"

The Institute has helped. In Kentucky, he would be tempted away from work, by his horses and his cattle, by the easy pleasure of riding a tractor around the farm. Here, he has a desk and the air of academic rigor radiated by an institution. "It's a great discipline," he says. "So I'm very content for that reason. I mean I produce . . . pages. Pages!" He looks faintly amazed. "Whether they're any good or not. . . ."

The trick to balancing the demands of writing, acting, theater, film and novels is simply "that I don't do them all at once. Not like Peter Ackroyd, he works on a history, a biography and a novel all at the same time, he just goes away for a day and does that," he says, astonished. "I read a long interview in the *New York Times*; they asked him, 'What do you do when you're not writing?' He said, 'Drink.'" Shepard laughs, and raises a toast. "Sláinte," he says. "Cheers."

Born in Illinois (though probably conceived, he points out, in Texas, where his father, an air force pilot, was stationed and where "my mother tracked him down and jumped the fence. . . ."), Shepard was raised in California and lived variously in New York, California and London before New Mexico and Kentucky. Even now, at 70, his life is often led by the roaming nature of film-sets, most recently shooting in New Orleans and Florida.

Not surprisingly, an itinerant quality has imbued much of his work, a feeling that, as he says this evening, "I don't belong much anywhere." It has been writing, he says, that has been his mainstay, his home, and by way of illustration he tells me about traveling with Bob Dylan's Rolling Thunder Revue in 1975: "It was pretty insane. Now that I look at it, it wasn't really, but I wasn't accustomed to transience, every second was all about movement. And I was glad to get back to a kind of constancy. Writing was the constancy."

He is inspired "not so much by landscape but by its connections to the past," and talks of the pueblos that once covered New Mexico, the

2,000-year-old pottery you can kick up with your feet in the desert. His own connection to this area goes back a long way too: "I can remember going through this town when I was eight," he recalls. "On my way to Chicago. I remember being very alone. Very, very alone. Being stranded on the train in the middle of Indian country."

It's the kind of recollection that makes you consider the extent to which Shepard is, like Clint Eastwood, Aaron Copland or Frederic Remington, bound up in the mythology and narrative of the American West, his life plaited into his writing and his roles, and how much this has been part of his appeal.

He set *True West* in the suburban California made familiar to him by his mother's home in Pasadena. It focuses on a fierce sibling rivalry between Austin, an Ivy League-educated screenwriter, and his wayward brother, Lee, who claims to spend much of his time in the Mojave Desert, making dubious ends meet. As the pair house-sit for their mother, they come into increasing conflict over the sale of a screenplay, and their contrasting lifestyles, their tussle set against the sound of crickets and coyotes, the death of house plants, the stealing of toasters.

In essence, the play explores the ideas of the insider and the outsider, identity, family and America's idea of itself, examining the point at which the new West of civilized, suburban America meets the wild and uncontained old West. And so it seems fitting to be sitting in a desert city with Shepard this evening, to listen to him take stock of American culture 34 years after *True West* was written.

Shepard's first example of an outsider was his father. He laughs with a frustration that has faded to fondness. "He thought it was all ridiculous, this idea of being a solid citizen. And he went further and further off in the direction of being an outsider, mainly, in simple terms, of alcoholism. My mother was the opposite. Very together, figuring out how to get along."

I wonder how Shepard has for so long negotiated a career that has required careful calibration of his own outsider and insider inclinations, the placating of studio executives, producers, publishers, theaters, who see films, plays and books principally in commercial terms. "I don't get along," Shepard says gruffly. "It's difficult. I know as an actor you have to negotiate but I can't handle the whole idea that art and commerce are synonymous. It drives me nuts. And then you get the reputation of being difficult to work with." There are, he adds, producers who "seem to really care" but he's skeptical of "the big studio guys" and Netflix, and those people who "don't think what the actor's going through, what the writer's going through, what the artistic essence is."

Still, he enjoys acting, "now that I've figured out how to do it. I didn't like it at first. I didn't know where to look because this thing—the camera—was looking at me the whole time."

A theater audience has always felt different, he says. And it is still theater that lights him up. When he talks about it today—the physical space, the actors, the language—there is a reverence for it, a wonder. "You know, writing for the theater is so different to writing for anything else. Because what you write is eventually going to be spoken. That's why I think so many really powerful novelists can't write a play—because they don't understand that it's spoken, that it hits the air. They don't get that."

He pauses, returns to thinking about his novel. "But of course I have the opposite problem," he concedes. "I can hear language, I can hear it spoken out loud. But when it comes into the head I have a much harder time."

Prose demands a carefulness he finds troublesome. "You need to be a lot more pedantic," he says. "I think. I don't know. The language of dreams is so different to the language of academics. It's beyond me. But the difference of spoken language and the language of the head is vast. Huge. It used to be all spoken. All out front and in the air."

These days, he reads a lot of Irish writers. "They are head and shoulders above," he says. "It's the ability to take language and spin it." And a lot of South Americans, too, "because they seem to have a handle on the ability to cross time and depth." He struggles to think of contemporary American writers he rates, beyond Denis Johnson. "The thing about American writers is that as a group they get stuck in the same idea: that we're a continent and the world falls away after us. And it's just nonsense."

Did he ever get stuck in that idea? "I couldn't see beyond the motel room and the desert and highway," he says slowly, and turns his glass a little. "I couldn't see that there was another world. To me, the whole world was encompassed in that. I thought that was the only world that mattered.

"And it's still there," he adds, "but now it's redundant because everything's replaced by strip malls."

The situation, he believes, is irredeemable. "We're on our way out," he says of America. "Anybody that doesn't realize that is looking like it's Christmas or something. We're on our way out, as a culture. America doesn't make anything anymore! The Chinese make it! Detroit's a great example. All of those cities that used to be something. If you go to a truck stop in Sallisaw,

Oklahoma, you'll probably see the face of America. How desperate we are. Really desperate. Just raw."

But why, I ask, is the world still so infatuated with American culture? Why, even, do we remain gripped by a play such as *True West*? "Oh, because they all believe the American fable," he says. "That you can make it here. But you don't make it."

You've made it pretty well, I say.

"Yeah but I've also . . . I've . . . yeah," he hesitates, laughs, a long, rich wheeze. "But you know, oddly, I wasn't even fucking trying."

An Urban Cowboy Returns to Broadway

Alexis Soloski / 2016

From *New York Times*, January 31, 2016, p. AR5. © 2016 The New York Times Company. All rights reserved. Used under license. Alexis Soloski was the theater critic for *The Village Voice* and is now a theater critic for the *New York Times*.

"You change," the playwright and actor Sam Shepard said. "You go through all kinds of contortions. But the play is the same."

Mr. Shepard, 72, dressed in jeans, work boots, a ribbed sweater and a down vest, was sitting on an upper floor of a Midtown rehearsal studio, its windows facing the synthetic glamour of 42nd Street. He looked as if he'd rather be somewhere else, a quieter place, a vaster one, with fewer flashing lights. He is still strikingly handsome, with his cowboy mouth and sidewinder gaze, though he describes himself as "craggy," and his hands, the left one bearing a tattoo of a quarter moon, are somewhat crabbed.

He has returned to New York for the New Group's production of *Buried Child*, a wrenching family drama—part comedy, part tragedy, part mystery, part horror show—that exerts an astonishing hold on the actors who have appeared in it. The play had its premiere at San Francisco's Magic Theatre in the summer of 1978 and moved to New York a few months later. It won the Pulitzer Prize for drama the next year and helped to transform Mr. Shepard from a fringe writer to a major playwright. That's a label he doesn't necessarily agree with.

"A lot of American playwrights seem to have a career as a playwright," he said. "I don't consider it a career at all."

And Mr. Shepard has never rested entirely easily with *Buried Child*. He rewrote it for its 1996 Broadway debut, and now, 20 years later, even though he says the play is unchanged, he is reworking and refining it—adding a joke here, altering a word there. The characters, however, are still the same: Dodge and Halie; their sons, Tilden and Bradley; and Tilden's son Vince, who suddenly arrives back at the Illinois homestead with his girlfriend, Shelly. Though Vince believes he's merely stopping in on his way across the country, the house and its secrets won't let him go so easily.

For the New Group revival, which begins performances on Tuesday, the director Scott Elliott has assembled a cast including the married actors and longtime Shepard collaborators Ed Harris and Amy Madigan as Dodge and Halie.

During his lunch break, Mr. Shepard spoke about theater, family and which of his plays could use some work. These are edited excerpts from the conversation.

Q: Do you remember what image or impulse got *Buried Child* started?

A: It came from a newspaper article, actually. It had to do with an accidental exhuming of a body, a child, in a backyard.

Q: I understand this was the first play you ever rewrote, in rehearsals at the Magic Theatre in 1978. Why?

A: I listened to it, I guess. When you listen intensely to anything you see how it can be improved. It's a rhythmic thing. Like music. You can feel the way that language lifts and turns around itself. The problematic character for me has always been Vince. Because he's closer to autobiography than anything else in the play—everyone else is pieces, figments, fragments. Vince is more the guy himself.

Q: Has it become a different play as you've aged?

A: Not really. It remains the same clunky play.

Q: One of the first plays to make a real impression on you was Eugene O'Neill's *Long Day's Journey Into Night*.

A: It's the greatest play ever written in America. But what I wanted to do was to destroy the idea of the American family drama. It's too psychological. Because this and that happened, you wet the bed? Who cares? Who cares when there's a dead baby in the backyard?

Q: Is the family still as central to your work? Your recent collaborations with the Abbey Theatre in Dublin—*Kicking a Dead Horse* and *Ages of the Moon*—seemed to be moving away from it.

A: Well, the last thing we did was a variation of *Oedipus*. You can't get any more familial than *Oedipus*.

Q: Do you think an outsider can ever really understand the dynamics of a family?

A: I remember as a kid, going into other people's houses. Everything was different. The smells in the kitchen were different; the clothing was different. That bothered me. There's something very mysterious about other families and the way they function.

Q: As a child, did you know that your family's behavior wasn't normative?

A: I thought this was all the way it was supposed to be. I remember a great friend of mine in high school, he took me aside and he said, "I know your father was a little off the deep end, but I didn't know he was crazy." And that sort of shocked me a little bit.

Q: You went on to have a volatile relationship with your father. When you had your own children, did you try not to become your father?

A: Yes. It doesn't help. You find these portions in you that are beyond the psychological, beyond what you think you can control. And then suddenly you are your father. You look at really old photographs, photographs that date back to the 1800s, the bone structure of the face is pretty much implanted. Where does it come from?

Q: You've worked with Ed Harris often. What makes him a good actor for your work?

A: He's just a good actor. He's handy, beyond handy. It's very rare to find an actor who's as good on stage as they are in the movies.

Q: Are you good on stage?

A: Not as good as I am in the movies. You don't have to do anything in the movies. You just sit there. Well, that's not entirely true. You do less. I find the whole situation of confronting an audience terrifying.

Q: Have you ever had any sense of what makes an actor good in your work?

A: Adventure. An actor who's willing to jump off the cliff, he's going to go anywhere.

Q: What makes someone a good director for your work?

A: Somebody who leaves actors alone, who doesn't interfere, who lets them play out all the things they need to play out before they hit pay dirt.

Q: What did you think of the recent Broadway revival of *Fool for Love*?

A: I thought the production was great. Good actors. The sound design was beautiful. I was quite impressed with it. Especially in that theater. I thought that theater would be too big for it. It wasn't.

Q: You still like that play?

A: Yeah.

Q: Do you like all your plays?

A: No. There's stuff you wish you'd spent more time on. Like *Curse of the Starving Class*. Kind of raggedy.

Q: Do you want to fix it?

A: Only in production. I wouldn't go back and just rewrite something to be rewriting it.

Q: Where do you need to be—mentally, physically—to write?

A: Right at the heart of it. You wait, but you don't wait too long, and then you pounce and sit right in the middle of it. I'm working on a monologue now. At the very beginning I thought, oh, if I wait a couple of days maybe more material will come. But I didn't, and I'm glad. More material would have come, but I wouldn't have written it down.

Q: Can you write pretty much anywhere?

A: I used to. I used to write in the kitchen mostly. I wrote *Buried Child* in a trailer at an old ranch house we had in California.

Q: Where do you work now?

A: More and more by myself. Absolutely by myself. If there's even a dog in the room, I get a little nervous.

Q: Can you write on a set anymore?

A: A little bit. Depending on the size of the role and how much distraction there is. I can't be changing costumes in the middle of writing. I do a lot of reading instead. César Aira, Roberto Bolaño. I think the South Americans are head and shoulders above North Americans in terms of fiction.

Q: You're so prolific—plays, fiction, film acting. Do you ever put aside work?

A: It's difficult but important to do nothing if you can. You have to school yourself.

Q: What's your version of doing nothing?

A: Sitting and watching the wall. Listening. Seeing light change.

Q: Do you take vacations?

A: I'm always on vacation. I know that I have to finish certain things. So I have obligations in a way. But not to a landlord, not to a boss.

Q: So you're your own boss. Are you too stern?

A: I demand too much.

Q: You're often spoken of as the greatest living American playwright. Do you feel you've achieved something substantial?

A: Yes and no. If you include the short stories and all the other books and you mash them up with some plays and stuff, then, yes, I've come at least close to what I'm shooting for. In one individual piece, I'd say no. There are certainly some plays I like better than others, but none that measure up.

Index

Aaron, Joyce, 194
Abbey Theatre (Dublin), 252, 277
Abbott and Costello, 56
Abraham, F. Murray, 153
Abstract Expressionism, 222, 259
Academy Award (Oscar), xiii, 97, 106,
    170, 174, 226, 236
Ackroyd, Peter, 272
Actors Studio, 133
Adams, Brooke, 96
Adderley Brothers, 91
*Advertisements for the Unexperienced
    Planters of New England* (John
    Smith), 191
After Haggerty (David Mercer), 166
Aira, César, 279
Albee, Edward, 92, 208, 222, 253, 259, 261
Allen, Lewis, 150
Allen, Rev. Michael, 4
Allen, Woody, 91
Almereyda, Michael, xviii, xix, 226, 238,
    258
Altman, Robert, 120, 147
American Academy of Arts and Letters,
    240
American Conservatory Theatre, 37
American Dream, 190–92, 274–75
American Indian, 73, 123, 134, 142, 161,
    171, 191, 197, 198, 255, 273
American Place Theatre, 40, 94, 132,
    178, 209, 210, 214

American Repertory Theater (ART), 68
American Theatre (journal), 227
American West, 73–74, 107, 109, 171,
    174–75, 191, 255, 273
Angels in America (Tony Kushner), 163
Ansen, David, 53
Anthology of American Folk Music
    (album), 265
Antonioni, Michelangelo, 3, 27, 40, 43,
    53, 83, 96, 167, 257
Appalachia, 234, 254
Arquette, Patricia, 108
Artaud, Antonin, 146
*Assassination of Jesse James by the
    Coward Robert Ford, The*, 271

BAC (Battersea Arts Centre) (London),
    166, 168
Baez, Joan, 96
Baker, Ginger, 167
Baker, Kathy, 100
Baraka, Amiri. *See* Jones, LeRoi
Bartels, Brian, xx
Baryshnikov, Aleksandra (Shura) Lange,
    107
Baryshnikov, Mikhail, 97, 107
Basement Theatre, King's Head
    (London), 169
"Beach" (Roberto Bolaño), 262
Beatles, The, 4, 219, 241
Beatty, Warren, 54, 214

Beauty Queen of Leenane, The (Martin McDonagh), 229, 248
Bechet, Sidney, 168
Beckett, Samuel, xviii, xix, xxv, 11, 17, 49, 55, 58, 105, 124, 136, 153, 184, 194, 202, 216, 222, 244, 247, 249, 251, 252–53, 256, 266–67
Beethoven, 41
Bellow, Saul, 167
Bishop's Company, xiv, xvi, 30, 35, 44, 90, 106, 177, 238
"Blackbird" (Lennon and McCartney), 241
Black Hawk Down, 217, 226
Black Panthers, 45, 187
Blackthorn, 257, 261–62
Blind Horizon, 237
Blunderpuss, 19
Bolaño, Roberto, 261, 262–63, 279
Borges, Jorge Luis, 267
Boyle, Peter, 213
Brando, Marlon, 58, 129
Brecht, Bertolt, xix, xx, 20, 21, 31, 65, 95, 124, 159, 226, 231, 241, 245
Breen, Phillip, 270
Brenton, Howard, 167
Bright Angel, 126
Brimley, Wilfred, xiii, 86
Broadway, 51, 92, 107, 151, 152, 156, 167, 188, 189, 190, 193, 225, 226, 249–50, 278
Broadway Alliance, 150, 151
Brook, Peter, xv, 56, 94–95, 128, 135, 156, 159, 166, 169, 216, 221, 244, 248
Brothers, 271
Brown, Richard "Rabbit," 265
"Brownsville Girl" (Bob Dylan and Shepard), 240
Buñuel, Luis, 112–13
Bunyun, Paul, 88
Burnett, T-Bone, 188, 234
Burning Plain, The (Juan Rulfo), 199

Burns Detective Agency, 177
Burn This (Lanford Wilson), 213
Burroughs, William, 263
Burstyn, Ellen, 40, 43, 50, 53
Bush, George W., 255
Butch Cassidy and the Sundance Kid, 261

Café La MaMa, 3, 92, 99, 167, 178, 186, 250, 263
Caffe Cino, 11, 92, 99, 186, 263
Campbell, Neve, 237
Captain America, 91
Carver, Raymond, 224
Case, Brian, xvi
Cassidy, Butch, 257–58, 261
Cassidy, Hopalong, 158, 215
Chaikin, Joseph, xix–xx, 38, 41, 48, 71, 82, 97, 107, 119, 128, 132, 137–38, 139, 150, 153–54, 156, 165, 173, 180, 181, 183, 194–95, 200, 216, 221, 231, 234, 243–44, 245–46, 266
Chandler, Raymond, 24, 183
Chaplin, Charlie, 128
Chekhov, Anton, 95, 169, 198, 235, 253, 270
Chenier, Clifton, 168
Cherry Lane Theatre, xx, 68, 216, 239, 240
Chicago Daily News, 208
Chino, California, 39, 90, 177
Chubb, Kenneth, xv, xvi, xvii, xviii, xix
Cino, Joe, 11, 263–64
Citizens Theatre (Glasgow), 270
City of Hope, 29
Civil Rights Movement, 14, 187
Civil War (American), xxi, 254
Clift, Montgomery, 205
"Code of the Herdsmen, The" (Wyndham Lewis), 228
Coen, Joel and Ethan, 234
Cohen, Rob, 237

Coltrane, John, 32, 118, 260
Combat Zone (Boston), 96
Come and Go (Samuel Beckett), 17
Conversations with Pinter (Mel
    Gussow), 224
Cook, Ralph, xiv, 10–11, 39, 91, 106–7,
    158, 178, 263
Cooper, Gary, 85, 105, 158, 164
Copland, Aaron, 273
Coppola, Francis Ford, 217
Corso, Gregory, 8, 90, 210
Country, 85–86, 97, 106, 161
Court Theatre. *See* Royal Court Theatre
Cranham, Kenneth, 187
Creedence Clearwater Revival, 187
Cristofer, Michael, 38
Crosby, Bing, 96
Crucible, The (Arthur Miller), 196
Crying Game, The, 160

D'Angelo, Beverly, 150
Dark, Johnny, 95
Dash and Lilly, 217, 226
Davis, Judy, 226
Day of the Locust (Nathanael West), 140
Days of Heaven, xvii, 40, 43, 50, 53, 68,
    96, 106, 107, 127, 155, 174, 217, 236,
    257, 271
Dean, James, 133
Deane, J. A. "Dino," 54, 121, 134
Death of a Salesman (Arthur Miller),
    193
Defenseless, 127
De Niro, Robert, 118, 163, 164, 215
Didion, Joan, xix, 58
D'Lugoff, Art, 91
Doctor Faustus (Christopher Marlowe),
    192
Dog of the South, The (Charles Portis),
    124
dog racing, xx, 5, 16, 24, 26, 94, 107, 166,
    168–69, 270

Do It! (Jerry Rubin), 166
Dolphy, Eric, 168, 260
Douglas, Kirk, 246
Dowling, Robert M., xxii
Drake, Sylvie, xiv, xv, xviii
Drama Desk Award, xiii
Duarte, California, 29, 38, 39, 44, 55, 89,
    90, 106, 174
Durning, Charles, 108, 121
Dust Busters, 265
Dutchman (LeRoi Jones), 92, 259
Dylan, Bob, 43, 48, 53, 55, 87, 95–96,
    136, 137, 167, 209, 240, 241, 272

Eastwood, Clint, 231, 273
Ellington, Duke, 260
Elliott, Scott, 277
Empty Space, The (Peter Brook), 135,
    248–49
Endgame (Samuel Beckett), 136, 194,
    252–53, 266
Esslin, Martin, 53
Eureka Theatre, 38

Farnsworth, Richard, 127, 206
Fast and the Furious, The, 237
Feiffer, Jules, 16
Ferlinghetti, Lawrence, 8, 90
Ferns, Alex, 270
Figgis, Mike, 167
"First Love" (Samuel Beckett), 216
Five Spot, 49
Fonda, Jane, 187
Fool for Love (film), 98, 120, 147
Fool Moon (Bill Irwin and David
    Shiner), 188
Ford, John, 205
Ford, Richard, xix, 124, 126, 207, 224
Foreman, Milos, 131
Forrest, Frederick, 83, 150, 154, 217–18
Frances, xvii, 68, 97, 106, 107, 271
Frank, Robert, 83, 96, 167

Frankie and Johnny in the Clair de Lune (Terrence McNally), 213
Frisch, Max, 126
Fugard, Athol, 216

Gambon, Michael, 164
Gammon, James, 226, 227
Ganz, Bruno, 170
Gelber, Jack, 141
Gel-Mann, Murray, 269
General History of Virginia, The (John Smith), 191
Genesis. *See* Theater Genesis
Genet, Jean, 222
Gere, Richard, 96
Ghana, 80
Gil, Mateo, 257, 262
Glenn, John, 86
Glenn, Scott, 258
Goldberg, Robert, xiv, xix, xx
Gordon, Edith, 91
Graham, Billy, 48
Gray, Spalding, 265
Greer Garson Theater (New Mexico), 176
Griffiths, Trevor, 167
Grotowski, Jerzy, 111, 153, 156, 159, 221, 266
Guare, John, 39
Gurdjieff, G. I., 106
Gussow, Mel, xiii, xiv, xv, xvi, xvii, xxi
Guthrie Theater, 229
Gyllenhaal, Jake, 271

Hadler, Walter, 4
Haggard, Merle, 93
Hamill, Pete, xiii, xiv, xv, xvii, xviii
Hamlet (film), 197, 217, 226, 238, 258
Hammett, 83, 217
Hammett, Dashiell, 24, 217, 218, 226
Hampstead Heath (London), 94, 167, 169
Hampstead Theatre Club (London), 160
Handke, Peter, xix, 49, 58, 95, 223, 229
Handman, Wynn, 132, 152

Happy Days (Samuel Beckett), 216, 252, 256, 266
Hardwick, Elizabeth, 3, 40
Hare, David, 167
Harper, Tess, 108
Harrelson, Woody, 215, 226, 235, 237
Harris, Ed, 100, 146, 150, 154, 164, 170, 250, 268, 277, 278
Hart, Bill, 234
Hawke, Ethan, 226
Hawks, Howard, 205
Hayes, Gabby, 214–15
Haynie, Jim, 63
Heath, Edward, 16
Hellman, Lillian, 226
Hendrix, Jimi, 167
Hoffman, Philip Seymour, 190, 226, 243, 270–71
Hollywood, 7, 27, 28–29, 32, 40, 52, 53, 83, 88, 96, 105, 140, 171, 198, 229, 236
Holy Modal Rounders, xvii, 4, 39, 55, 87, 93–94, 107, 177, 188, 211, 264
Homo Faber (Max Frisch), 126, 207
Hopkins, Anthony, 163, 164
Hopkins, Lightnin', 168
Hoskins, Bob, xv, 107, 160, 168, 187
Houghton, James, 268
Hughes, Howard, xiii, 87, 214

Ibsen, Henrik, 169
Indian, American. *See* American Indian
Insulting the Audience (Peter Handke), 223
In the Jungle of Cities (Bertolt Brecht), 20, 241
Ionesco, Eugène, 222

Jagger, Mick, 28, 53, 96
James, Jesse, 88
James, Skip, 168
"James Alley Blues" (Richard "Rabbit" Brown), 265

Jarmusch, Jim, 171
Jarry, Alfred, 152
jazz, xvii, xx, 8, 9, 10, 30, 32, 39, 40, 44,
    49, 53, 54, 55, 90, 91, 92–93, 106,
    115, 168, 177, 181, 182, 186, 188, 211,
    218, 231, 246, 259, 260
Jefferson, Thomas, 255
Johns, Jasper, 230, 232
Johnson, Denis, 274
Johnson, O-Lan. *See* Shepard, O-Lan
Jones, Brian, 167
Jones, George, 93
Jones, LeRoi, xix, 49, 92, 259
Jones, O-Lan. *See* Shepard, O-Lan
Jones, Tommy Lee, 164, 213
*Joseph Chaikin & Sam Shepard: Letters
    and Texts, 1972–1984*, xx
Joyce, James, 266
Jubilee King (Jesse Shepard), 224
Judson Poets' Theater, 11, 99, 178, 186
Just Kids (Patti Smith), 264

Kael, Pauline, 236
Kaspar (Peter Handke), 223
Kauffmann, Stanley, 87
Kaufman, Philip, 170, 236, 257
Kaye, Lenny, 47
Keaton, Buster, 128
Keitel, Harvey, 164
Kennedy, John F., 45, 163, 187
Kentucky, 142, 227, 254, 271, 272
Kerouac, Jack, 8, 44, 54, 90
Kidd, Captain, 88
Kilmer, Val, 127, 237
King, Martin Luther, 190
King, The, 237
King Lear (William Shakespeare), 196, 230
Kirk, Roland, 260
Koko, the gorilla, 56
Krapp's Last Tape (Samuel Beckett),
    244, 248, 266
Kurosawa, Akira, 112

La MaMa, 3, 92, 99, 167, 178, 186, 250,
    263
Lancaster, Burt, 85, 86, 258
Landis, John, 113
Lange, Jessica, xvii, 85–86, 87, 97, 107,
    108, 127, 147, 157, 161, 171, 174, 185,
    201, 203, 224, 227, 237, 271
"Late Henry Conran, The" (Frank
    O'Connor), 200, 254
Laurel and Hardy, 97
Leary, Timothy, 187
Leigh, Jennifer Jason, 150, 154
Lennon, John, 219
Lewis, Meade Lux, 168
Lewis, Wyndham, 228
Lewis and Clark, 191, 255
L'Image (Samuel Beckett), 105
Lincoln, Abraham, 190
Lincoln Center, 3, 4, 21, 51, 93
Lion, John, 28, 30, 31, 32, 34–35
Lippman, Amy, xvi, xvii, xviii, xix
London, England, xv, xvi, xvii, 5, 16, 17,
    18, 24, 30, 32, 34, 40, 44, 94, 95,
    107, 128, 160, 166, 167, 168, 174,
    187, 190, 203, 212, 233, 252, 270,
    272. *See also* Hampstead Heath;
    Shepherd's Bush
Lonely Are the Brave, 246
Lonesome West, The (Martin
    McDonagh), 253
Long Day's Journey Into Night (Eugene
    O'Neill), xviii, xix, 77, 258, 266, 277
Lorca, Federico García, 105, 115, 122
Los Angeles Actors' Theater, 37
Lowell, Robert, 40
Lumet, Sidney, xviii, 258
Lyons, Robbie, 263

Madigan, Amy, 277
Magic Theatre, 30, 34, 35, 37, 38, 52, 60,
    61, 68, 70, 95, 107, 121, 194, 200,
    225, 226, 233, 234, 276, 277

Mahagonny (Bertolt Brecht), 20
Malcolm X, 45
Malick, Terrence, 40, 50, 53, 96, 107,
    236, 257
Malkovich, John, 129, 132–33, 143, 146,
    152, 154, 213, 230, 234, 268
Mallarmé, Stéphane, 141
Malone Dies (Samuel Beckett), 266, 267
Mamet, David, 170
Mandrell, Barbara, 130, 209
Manhattan Theatre Club, 225
Manifest Destiny, 197, 255
Marin, Cheech, 215, 226, 235
Marin Community Playhouse, 54
Marines' Memorial Theatre, 61
Mark Taper Forum, 38
Marowitz, Charles, 94, 168
Márquez, Gabriel García, 167
Martin, George, 214
Marx, Karl, 187
McBride, Stewart, xiii, xiv, xv, xviii, xix
McCarthy, Cormac, 269, 271
McCutcheon, Bob, 220, 229
McDonagh, Martin, 229, 248, 253
McGuinn, Roger, 96
Meckler, Nancy, 160
Mehmedinović, Semezdin, 229
Melfi, Leonard, 39
Mendes, Sam, 226
Mercer, David, 166
method acting, 79, 103, 118, 153, 180, 195,
    244
Mexico, 40, 171, 188, 198, 206, 224, 227
Midsummer Night's Dream, A (William
    Shakespeare), 166
Miller, Arthur, 169, 193, 196, 253
Mingus, Charles (son of jazz musician),
    xvii, 39, 55, 90, 91, 92, 106, 177, 260
Mingus, Charles (jazz musician), 40, 49,
    91, 168, 231, 260
Minnesota, 108, 113, 114, 185, 222, 227,
    233

Mitchell, Joni, 96
Moffat, Donald, 108
Mojave Desert, 175, 192, 273
Molloy (Samuel Beckett), 266
Monk, Thelonious, xx, 91, 181, 231
Moon, Keith, 87
Mortimer, John, 166
Mount San Antonio College, 35
Mozart, Wolfgang Amadeus, 41
Mr. Hulot's Holiday, 112
Mulligan, Gerry, 93
Murakami, Haruki, 271
Murphy, Audie, 158
Murphy, Tom, 253
My Uncle, 112

Nabokov, Vladimir, 181
National Theatre (London), 30
Nelson, Willie, 241
Neruda, Pablo, 83
New England Trials (John Smith), 191
New Group, The, 276, 277
Newman, Paul, 261
Newsweek, xvi, 52, 53, 173, 206
New York Drama Critics' Circle Award,
    xiii
New Yorker, 44, 223–24, 236
New York Post, 11
New York Review of Books, 40
New York Times, 210, 271, 272
'night, Mother (Marsha Norman), 196
Nolte, Nick, 215, 226, 227, 237–38
Norwood (Charles Portis), 124

Obie Award, xiii, xv, 43, 53, 167, 173,
    261
O Brother Where Art Thou?, 234
O'Connor, Frank, 200, 254
O'Connor, Kevin, 158, 263
Oedipus Rex (Sophocles), 72, 277
Off-Broadway, 3, 5, 12, 18, 43, 53, 68, 87,
    92, 151, 155, 173, 249

Off-Off-Broadway, xiv, 4, 11, 12, 51, 53, 92, 158, 167, 173, 178, 186, 210, 249, 250, 263

O'Hare, Eugene, 270

Oh! Calcutta!, 4, 12, 107, 167

Old Times (Harold Pinter), 166

Olivier, Lawrence, 164

One Hundred Years of Solitude (Gabriel García Márquez), 167

O'Neill, Eugene, xviii–xix, 17, 33, 35, 49, 76, 105, 124, 138, 169, 170, 253, 258, 266, 277

"On the Road Again" (Willie Nelson), 241

On the Waterfront, 195

Open Space Theatre (London), 19, 168

Open Theater, xix, 71, 107, 137, 153, 194, 234, 245, 266

Oscar. *See* Academy Award

O'Toole, Fintan, xxi

Outer Critics Circle Award, xiii

Overtones Theater, 54

Pacino, Al, 163, 164

Page, Geraldine, 214

Pakula, Alan J., 161

Papp, Joe, 33, 41, 60, 153, 213

Paris, Texas, 83, 87, 136, 137, 140, 171, 174, 217, 237, 257, 271

Paris Review, xv, xvi, xviii, xx, 144

Parker, Charlie, 118, 171

Parks, Suzan-Lori, 228

Parton, Dolly, 106

Patrick, Robert, 39

Paz, Octavio, 225

Pearce, Richard, 85, 86

Pedro Páramo (Juan Rulfo), 199

Pelican Brief, 155, 161

Penn, Sean, 215, 226, 237, 238, 257

People Show (London), 167

Phillips, Georgia Lee, 4

Phoenix, River, 154

Pillowman (Martin McDonagh), 247–48

Pinter, Harold, 166, 184, 216, 224, 246

Pip Simmons Theatre Group (London), 166

Pitt, Brad, 271

Playboy of the Western World, The (J. M. Synge), 254

Pledge, The, 257

Poetry Project, 263

Pollock, Jackson, 36, 171

Ponti, Carlo, 27

Portis, Charles, 124

Promenade Theatre, 98, 150, 213–14

Public Theater, 53, 150, 151, 153, 155

Pulitzer Prize, xix, 37, 60, 76, 184, 276

Pynchon, Thomas, xiii, 87

Rabe, David, 154

Raggedy Man, 53, 63, 68, 86, 106

Raitt, Bonnie, 127

Rauschenberg, Robert, 168

Rea, Stephen, xv, 160, 168, 187, 252

Red Clay Ramblers, 98, 109, 188

Redford, Robert, 86

Red River, 205

Reed, Lou, 43, 47

Reilly, John C., 190, 226, 243, 270

Remains of the Day, 163

Remington, Frederic, 273

Renaldo and Clara, 96

Resurrection, 40, 43, 50, 53, 68, 106

Richards, Keith, 167

Richardson, Tony, 96

Richmond, Dannie (Charles Daniel), 8, 91, 168

Ride Across Lake Constance, The (Peter Handke), 223

Right Stuff, The, xiii, 68, 86, 88, 97, 106, 127, 155, 170, 174, 217, 236, 257, 258, 271

Rimbaud, Arthur, 266

Ritter, Tex, 158

rock 'n' roll, xvii, 18, 20, 43, 47, 53, 55,
    87, 93, 107, 108, 156, 159, 166, 188,
    225, 230
Rock Springs (Richard Ford), 126
rodeo, 54, 76, 77, 126, 146, 170, 171, 255
Rodgers, Jimmie, 84
Rogers, Jane Elaine Schook (mother),
    6, 12, 38, 41, 56, 89, 122, 221, 247,
    272, 273
Rogers, Roy, 91, 106, 158, 215
Rogers, Samuel Shepard (father), xiv, xvii,
    5, 6, 12, 38, 39, 41, 43, 55, 89, 97, 106,
    115–16, 122, 162, 170, 171, 173, 174,
    175–77, 188, 192, 207–9, 210, 211,
    215, 221, 226–27, 232, 272, 273, 278
Rogers, "Steve" (childhood name), 89,
    91, 106
Rolling Stones, 4, 28, 87, 94
Rolling Thunder Revue, 43, 48, 55, 95,
    167, 240, 272
Romeo and Juliet (William
    Shakespeare), 72
Rosen, Carol, xvii, xviii, xx, xxi
Roth, Tim, 234
Roudané, Matthew, xiv, xv, xviii, xxi
Roundabout Theatre Company, 226
Royal Court Theatre (London), 5, 19, 22,
    40, 94, 107, 160, 168, 187
Rubin, Jerry, 166
Rulfo, Juan, 199
Rylance, Mark, 212

Sabella, Joseph, 135
Salinger, J. D., xiii, 54, 87
San Francisco, California, 37, 38, 41, 45,
    52, 54, 60, 68, 70, 95, 107, 121, 135,
    200, 215, 225, 234, 235, 237, 276
Santa Fe, New Mexico, 87, 97, 109, 157,
    164, 209, 269, 270, 271
Santa Fe Institute, 269, 271, 272
Sarajevo Blues (Semezdin
    Mehmedinović), 229

Savage Detectives, The (Roberto Bolaño),
    261, 262, 263
Schechner, Richard, 21, 265–66
Schlondorff, Volker, 126, 170, 207
Sessums, Kevin, xvi, xix, xx
Shakespeare, William, 177, 196, 216, 238,
    246, 267
Shaw, Fiona, 252
Shawn, Wallace, 216
Shepard, Hannah Jane, 107
Shepard, Jesse Mojo, xv, 38, 44, 54, 91,
    93, 94, 107, 224, 227
Shepard, O-Lan (née O-Lan Johnson;
    later O-Lan Jones), xv, 4, 38, 44,
    54, 93–94, 107, 173, 227
Shepard, Sam: on acting, 22, 23, 50,
    56–57, 62–64, 66, 79, 100–101,
    102–3, 118, 128–29, 133, 147, 153,
    155, 156, 163–64, 179, 180–81,
    194–95, 216–17, 242–43, 244, 246,
    250, 267–68, 278; on audience,
    13, 20, 57, 60, 64, 75, 81–82, 112,
    137, 145, 180, 181, 183, 195, 228,
    245–46, 249; on childhood, 5–8,
    16, 29, 38, 44, 55, 89–90, 106,
    122, 159, 174–75, 278; on direct-
    ing, 22–23, 25–26, 57, 68–69, 79,
    99–103, 111, 120, 128, 242–43,
    246, 278; on musicality in plays,
    xvii–xviii, 19–20, 30, 32, 40–41,
    48, 49, 51, 54–55, 69, 74–75,
    79–80, 92–93, 109, 134–35, 154,
    168, 188, 230, 243, 277; on myth,
    72–73, 133–34, 160, 171, 196–97,
    215 (*see also* American Dream);
    on New York City, early years,
    8–13, 45–46, 91–94, 158–59,
    177–78, 210–11, 259–61, 263–64
    Works: *Action*, xv, 30, 32, 36, 148;
    Ages of the Moon, 258, 277; *Angel
    City*, 27, 28–29, 30, 36, 40, 48,
    88, 96, 106, 135, 138, 140, 183, 194,

240, 271; *Back Bog Beast Bait*, 3;
"Blinking Eye," 205; *Blue Bitch*,
xv; "The Bodyguard," 96; *Buried
Child*, xix, 37, 38, 41, 43, 46, 49–50,
53, 56, 60, 68, 71, 80, 82, 87, 88,
105, 110, 113, 134, 167, 174, 175,
176, 183, 184, 188, 189, 193, 194,
209, 225, 231, 240, 243, 249, 257,
259, 271, 276–77, 279; *Chicago*,
10, 17, 18, 173, 240; "Coalinga ½
Way," 220–21; *Cowboy Mouth*, xvi,
47–48, 93–94, 108–9, 147, 156, 169,
257, 271; *Cowboys*, xv, 9, 10–11, 39,
44, 45, 55, 91, 107, 148, 158, 178,
263; *Cowboys No. 2*, 9; *Cruising
Paradise*, 198–99, 202, 207, 208,
226, 240; *Curse of the Staving
Class*, xix, 33, 38, 41, 53, 63–64,
68, 71, 80–81, 88, 105, 110, 131–32,
134, 136, 167, 174, 175, 188–89, 193,
194, 203, 226, 230, 232, 240, 259,
279; *Day Out of Days*, 264; *Dog*,
13; *Don't Come Knocking*, 218,
237; *Eyes for Consuela*, 198, 225;
Far North, 108, 109–10, 112, 113,
121, 129, 134, 135, 136, 137, 164, 171,
237; *Fool for Love*, xix, 68, 71, 76,
78, 84, 87, 99, 100, 106, 127, 130,
136, 141, 146, 154, 174, 182, 188,
189, 194, 203, 208–9, 212, 226,
257, 271, 278; "Foreigners," 202;
Forensic & the Navigators, 3, 173;
Fourteen Hundred Thousand, 15;
Geography of a Horse Dreamer,
xv, 5, 13, 16, 17, 19, 23, 24, 40, 55,
94, 106, 140, 160, 169, 174, 204,
209; *The God of Hell*, 226, 235,
240, 268; *Great Dream of Heaven*,
201–2, 203–4, 205, 207, 218, 219,
220–21, 226, 240; "Great Dream of
Heaven," 203–4; *Hawk Moon*, 68,
87, 89, 198, 240; *Heartless*, 268–69;

"The Hero Is in the Kitchen," 223;
Icarus's Mother, 14, 15, 23, 105, 169,
173; *Inacoma*, 121; *Kicking a Dead
Horse*, 240, 252, 254–55, 277; *The
Late Henry Moss*, 199, 200, 215–16,
225, 226–27, 230, 231, 232, 234–35,
237–38, 240, 253–54; *La Turista*, 3,
40, 68, 104, 106, 150, 173, 178, 198,
210, 258, 271; *A Lie of the Mind*,
xix, 98, 99, 103, 109, 110, 129, 130–
31, 134, 135, 136, 140, 150, 151, 152,
155, 174, 175, 184, 188, 194, 202, 213,
240; *Little Ocean*, xv; *Mad Dog
Blues*, 19, 88; "A Man's Man," 198–
99; "Maxagasm," 4, 28, 96; *Me and
My Brother*, 96, 167; *Melodrama
Play*, 104; *Motel Chronicles*, 68,
83, 85, 87, 89, 124, 144, 167, 198,
240; *Operation Sidewinder*, 3, 4,
51, 93, 94, 157; *A Particle of Dread
(Oedipus Variations)*, 277; "The
Real Gabby Hayes," 214–15; *Red
Cross*, 104; "The Remedy Man,"
218; *Rock Garden*, 12, 107, 148,
158, 167, 178, 189, 230; *Rocking
Chair*, 13; *The Rolling Thunder
Logbook*, 55; *Savage/Love*, 41, 71,
82; *Seduced*, 87, 94, 198, 214; "See
You in My Dreams," 208; *Silent
Tongue*, 141, 145, 155, 171, 237;
Simpatico, 150–52, 154–55, 164,
180, 181, 192, 216, 232–33, 240;
States of Shock, 130, 132, 134, 137,
142–43, 145, 148, 151, 152, 154, 155,
170, 216, 268; "The Stout of Heart,"
220; *Suicide in B♭*, 106, 168, 204,
231; *Tongues*, xx, 41, 48, 71, 82, 132,
138, 154, 194; *The Tooth of Crime*,
xv, xviii, 8, 16, 17, 18, 19, 21, 24, 36,
38, 40, 47, 48, 55, 68, 94, 106, 116,
134, 141, 148, 160, 167, 168, 169,
174, 203, 230, 240, 241, 244, 265;

Tooth of Crime (Second Dance), 234; *True West*, xix, 41, 52, 53, 54, 55, 57, 59–67, 68, 71, 75, 79–80, 81, 87, 88, 105–6, 132–33, 135, 136, 151, 152, 153, 170, 172, 175, 183, 188, 189, 190, 193, 197, 203, 212–13, 226, 227, 230, 232–33, 236, 240, 243, 246, 247, 253, 270, 271, 273, 275; "An Unfair Question," 220, 223; *The Unseen Hand*, 3, 23, 24, 141, 169, 186; *Up to Thursday*, 12, 240; *The War in Heaven*, xx, 128, 140, 154, 195, 243–44; *When the World Was Green: A Chef's Fable*, 195–96; *Zabriskie Point*, 3, 27–28, 40, 43, 83, 96, 167, 197, 257

Shepard, Samuel Walker, 107, 116, 265

Shepherd's Bush (London), 5, 17, 18, 94, 167

Signature Theatre, 206, 225, 234, 268

Simone, Nina, 10, 45, 91, 106, 260

Simpatico (film), 226

Sinatra, Frank, 96

Sinise, Gary, 133, 152, 167, 193, 213, 230

Sixties, the, 44, 45, 47, 66, 96, 178, 184, 186–87, 188, 193, 260–61

Slava's Snowshow, 249

Slave, The (LeRoi Jones), 92

Slave Ship (LeRoi Jones), xix, 259

Sloman, Larry, 96

Smith, Harry, 265

Smith, John, 191

Smith, Michael, xv, 11, 45, 87, 92, 178

Smith, Patti, xvi, xix, 43, 47–48, 53, 91, 93–94, 107, 108, 147, 156, 167, 254, 257, 264–65, 269, 271

Soloski, Alexis, xiii, xix

Sophocles, 95

Spacek, Sissy, 53

Stanislavski, Konstantin, 103, 153, 180, 195

Stealth, 237

Steel Magnolias, 106

Steppenwolf Theatre, 133, 167, 193, 213, 225, 230, 243

Stewart, Ellen, 11, 250

St. Mark's Church-in-the-Bowery, 4, 9, 10–11, 47, 55, 91, 106, 178, 186, 263

St. Paul's Chapel (New York), 222

Strasberg, Lee, 103, 133, 180

Streetcar Named Desire, A (Tennessee Williams), 194, 203

Strindberg, August, 95

Synge, John Millington, 200

Talmer, Jerry, 11

Tati, Jacques, 112

Terry, Megan, 39

That Obscure Object of Desire, 113

Theater Genesis, xiv, xv, 4, 11, 12, 21, 55, 91, 92, 99, 106–7, 158, 178, 186, 210, 263

This So-Called Disaster, 226–27, 237–38, 258

Thoroughbred Times, The, 148

Thunderheart, 127, 142, 217

Time (magazine), 170

Toilet, The (LeRoi Jones), xix, 259

Tolstoy, Leo, 115

Tootsie, 97

Torn, Rip, 214

Tousey, Sheila, 226

Tracy, Spencer, 164

Traffic, 112

Traven, B., 88

Travolta, John, 54

Tricycle Company / Tricycle Theatre (London), 5, 270

Trinity Square Repertory Company, 214

True Grit (Charles Portis), 124

Tubes, The, 96

Turner, Ike and Tina, 43, 54

Twain, Mark, 199, 223

Twelfth Night (William Shakespeare), 229

Tynan, Kenneth, 167

Ubu Roi (Alfred Jarry), 152
Urban Cowboy, 54

Vallejo, César, xix, 83, 124
van Itallie, Jean-Claude, 39
Vanity Fair (magazine), 127
Variety Arts Theatre, 151
Velvet Underground, 43, 47
Vera Cruz, 85, 258
Vietnam War, 6, 116, 142, 169–70, 187,
    192, 222, 260
Village Gate, xiv, xvii, 4, 10, 11, 39, 45,
    90, 91, 93, 97, 106, 155, 158, 178,
    231, 260, 263, 264
Village Voice, xv, 11, 43, 45, 52, 55, 92,
    126, 128, 178, 206
Villon, François, 47
Voyager, 126, 170, 207
Voyage Round My Father, A (John
    Mortimer), 166

Waiting for Godot (Samuel Beckett),
    xviii, 9, 39, 44, 77, 90, 105, 252, 266
Waiting for Lefty (Clifford Odets), 228,
    233
Waldman, Anne, 263
Warchus, Matthew, 190, 226, 230, 235
Washington, George, 190
Washington Post, 105
Wayne, John, 89–90, 205–6, 215
Weber, Steve, 47
Wedgeworth, Ann, 108, 214

Weight of the World, The (Peter
    Handke), 223
Welfare State (London), 166
Wenders, Wim, 83, 87, 140, 171, 174, 207,
    217, 218, 237, 257, 271
West, American. *See* American West
West, Geoffrey, 269
West, Mae, 88
Western Horseman (magazine), 87
Wetzsteon, Ross, xiii, xvi, 87
Whistle in the Dark, A (Tom Murphy),
    253, 256
Whitman, Walt, 267
Who, The, 18, 94
Williams, Dean, 86
Williams, Hank, xx, 84, 93
Williams, Mary Lou, 260
Williams, Robin, 271
Williams, Tennessee, 9, 49, 53, 169, 194,
    203, 253
Wilson, August, 218
Wilson, Flip, 91
Wilson, Harold, 16
Wilson, Lanford, 39, 165, 206
Wittliff, William D., 86, 216
Woodruff, Robert, 37, 38, 41, 57, 66, 70
World War II, 122, 192

Yeager, Chuck, xiii, 86, 88, 106, 170, 174,
    236

Zoo Story (Edward Albee), 13, 92

About the Editors

Jackson R. Bryer is Professor Emeritus of English at the University of Maryland, College Park. He is the editor of *Conversations with Lillian Hellman* (1986) and *Conversations with Thornton Wilder* (1992), as well as the co-editor of *Conversations with August Wilson* (2006) and *Conversations with Neil Simon* (2019), in the University Press of Mississippi's Literary Conversations Series.

Robert M. Dowling is professor of English at Central Connecticut State University. His biography *Eugene O'Neill: A Life in Four Acts* was named a Los Angeles Times Book Prize finalist for biography in 2015. He is currently working on a biography of Sam Shepard.

Mary C. Hartig is coeditor of *Conversations with August Wilson* (2006) and *William Inge: Essays and Reminiscences on the Plays and the Man* (2014). She is also coauthor/coeditor of the *Facts on File Companion to American Drama* (2 editions, 2004 and 2010).

contradictions

yearning for the west
critical of it

horseman who rode in   unworde
critical of his father   alcoholism,
                              — an
   Martin McDonagh   alcoholic.
                                   himself

   out
story of politics — stories of
                              Ghost
making movies —   criticizing them
writing plays —   criticizing
                    theatre
                  · I never go to it
writing plays about — claiming its
        his   all about
          father,   a bland
   his 'muse'   of characters

clams of Western   lives in
                       kentucky

CPSIA information can be obtained
at www.ICGtesting.com
Printed in the USA
BVHW032311290821
615262BV00003B/9

9 781496 836618